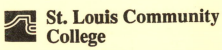

POLITICS OF
DISILLUSIONMENT

Studies on Contemporary China

**THE POLITICAL ECONOMY OF CHINA'S
SPECIAL ECONOMIC ZONES**
George T. Crane

WORLDS APART
RECENT CHINESE WRITING AND ITS AUDIENCES
Howard Goldblatt, editor

CHINESE URBAN REFORM
WHAT MODEL NOW?
*R. Yin-Wang Kwok, William L. Parish, and Anthony Gar-On Yeh
with Xu Xueqiang, editors*

REBELLION AND FACTIONALISM IN A CHINESE PROVINCE
ZHEJIANG, 1966–1976
Keith Forster

POLITICS AT MAO'S COURT
GAO GANG AND PARTY FACTIONALISM
IN THE EARLY 1950s
Frederick C. Teiwes

MOLDING THE MEDIUM
THE CHINESE COMMUNIST PARTY
AND THE LIBERATION DAILY
Patricia Stranahan

THE MAKING OF A SINO-MARXIST WORLD VIEW
PERCEPTIONS AND INTERPRETATIONS
OF WORLD HISTORY
IN THE PEOPLE'S REPUBLIC OF CHINA
Dorothea A. L. Martin

POLITICS OF DISILLUSIONMENT
THE CHINESE COMMUNIST PARTY
UNDER DENG XIAOPING, 1978–1989
Hsi-sheng Ch'i

Studies on Contemporary China

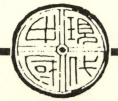

POLITICS OF DISILLUSIONMENT

THE CHINESE COMMUNIST PARTY UNDER DENG XIAOPING, 1978-1989

HSI-SHENG CH'I

An East Gate Book

M. E. Sharpe, Inc.
Armonk, New York
London, England

An East Gate Book

Copyright © 1991 by M. E. Sharpe, Inc.

Available in the United Kingdom and Europe from M. E. Sharpe, Publishers, 3 Henrietta Street, London WC2E 8LU.

Library of Congress Cataloging-in-Publication Data

Chi, Hsi-Sheng.
    Politics of disillusionment : the Chinese Communist Party under Deng Xiaoping, 1978–1989 / by Hsi-Sheng Ch'i.
       p.   cm. — (Studies on contemporary China)
    Includes bibliographical references and index.
    ISBN 0-87332-689-X (C). — ISBN 0-87332-690-3 (P)
      1. Chung-kuo kung ch'an tang. 2. Teng, Hsiao-p'ing, 1904–
3. China—Politics and government—1976– I. Title. I. Series.
JQ1519.A5C475356   1991
324.251′075′09048—dc20   90-20867
                                                                CIP

ED   10 9 8 7 6 5 4 3 2 1

To Bridie and Bernard

Contents

Tables

Preface

THE CHINESE Communist Party (CCP) has experienced phenomenal growth in the last forty years. When it first came to power in 1949, it had only about 4.5 million members. By early 1989, the party had 48.3 million members, and nearly 3 million basic-level organs.[1]

The party's presence in Chinese society has become more visible during the past forty years. In 1949, there was one party member for every one hundred Chinese. By late 1980s, there was one party member for about every twenty Chinese. If the ratio between party members and the adult population is measured, then the party's presence is even stronger.[2]

As is true with many things pertaining to China, scale is an important consideration. The CCP has the distinction of being not only the largest Communist Party in the world, but also the largest political party of any kind in the world. The Chinese party has more members than all other Communist parties combined, and its membership is larger than the population of more than three-fourths of the countries in the world. Such sheer magnitude commands attention in its own right.

But a far more important reason for studying the CCP is that it is indispensable to any understanding of politics in China. The Marxist-Leninist ideology bestows upon the party the special status as the "vanguard" of the revolution. As Chinese Communists are proud to claim, Communists are made of "special materials." They are supposed to be ideologically committed, politically active, and progressive. They are armed with scientific knowledge on how to build a good society, and their personal conduct is supposed to serve as the model for ordinary people. They are imbued with a strong dedication to serve the people, "to be the first ones to endure hardship but the last ones to enjoy life." It is these superior qualities that entitle members of the Communist Party to occupy a supreme position in all aspects of Chinese life.

Historically, Chinese Communists have always put strong emphasis on the party's own development. Even during the years of protracted armed struggle against the Japanese and the Nationalists, Mao Zedong insisted on the principle that the party must command the guns and not vice versa. The CCP's military successes became impressive only after enormous effort had been made to reorganize and unify the party (1942–45). After Liberation in 1949, the party's role was greatly expanded in its capacity as China's ruling party. As students of PRC politics know well, whereas the state has provided the muscle in the Chinese political system during the past forty years, the party has actually been its soul. Broadly speaking, the party has had to perform two major functions: to rule and control several hundred million people, ensuring the survival of the regime without heavy reliance on the secret police or the military; and to run the government, provide essential services, and carry out the task of socialist construction. To perform the former function, the party needs strong organizational sinews and good discipline among its members, whereas to perform the latter, it needs expertise in management and development.

During the past several decades, a generation of meticulous and insightful scholars has produced a rich body of literature in the English language concerning many critical aspects of the politics in the People's Republic. These scholars have taken different approaches to deciphering the secret of Chinese politics. Some have chosen political leaders (Mao Zedong, Zhou Enlai, Liu Shaoqi, Deng Xiaoping, etc.) as the subjects of their investigation.[3] Others have looked critically at the nuances in Chinese interpretations of the Marxist ideology or Mao Zedong's Thought. Still others have examined various branches of the bureaucracy (including the People's Liberation Army) or specific public policies. Political campaigns (such as the Great Leap Forward or the Cultural Revolution), factional activities (as within the Politburo), and purges (the Gao Gang–Rao Shushi affair, the dismissal of Peng Dehuai, the Lin Biao affair) have also received great attention. To the extent that these works deal with the party as such, however, most of them tend to focus attention on activities on the elite level.

Thus, although the party is offered as a critical explanatory variable for many important aspects of Chinese political life, relatively little effort has been made to date to delve beneath the leadership level and examine in detail the party's organizational and behavioral characteristics on the rank-and-file level. In short, the party as a political organization has remained largely a black box.

This gap in the existing literature is unfortunate, because the Chinese themselves have regarded the party rank and file as having the utmost importance. As party propaganda contends, whether the party's general line and specific programs can be implemented ultimately depends on the basic-level organs and individual members.

The need to fill this gap is particularly urgent at present as Chinese politics have clearly undergone a major transformation since Mao's death, which inevitably entails a fundamental redefinition of the party's functions of control over the state and society and its functions of managing the economy and developing socialism.

During Mao's lifetime, the control functions were exercised ruthlessly but the management and development functions were carried out inefficiently. Mao was obsessed with the need to "let politics take command" over everything. As a result, many of the PRC's development projects, such as the Great Leap Forward and collectivization programs, were subordinate to ideological considerations and led to disastrous economic consequences. Meanwhile, many more campaigns, such as the antirightist campaign, the four-cleans campaign, and the Cultural Revolution, were politically motivated but were conducted according to the "storming approach," with heavy emphasis on class struggle that seriously impeded the party's development objectives.

Chinese politics entered a new era after Deng Xiaoping's return to power in the late 1970s. Between then and early 1989, when Deng resigned from his last post as the chairman of the Military Affairs Committee, he exerted a dominant influence in shaping the party's own development. During this period, Deng either quietly discontinued or explicitly rejected many of the distinguishing features of the Maoist legacy as he tried to lead China onto a different path. Insofar as the party's control functions were concerned, Deng rejected the brutal Cultural Revolutionary tactics of "beating, smashing, and looting" and reemphasized the party's qualities of dedication, honesty, and responsibility, which entitled it to rule over China. With respect to the management and development functions, he totally rejected the Maoist approach of letting politics take command in all fields of work; instead, he adopted a more rational approach of building socialism through the introduction of many reforms inside China and the opening of the country to increased contact with the outside world. Deng's short-term development goal was the realization of the four modernizations (in industry, agriculture, science and technology, and national defense) by the end of this century. His ultimate development goal was the completion of the construction of both material and spiritual civilizations in order to create a socialist state with Chinese characteristics. While Mao liked to be called the "great helmsman" (*weidade duoshou*) for guiding China's revolution, Deng preferred the title of "chief architect" (*zong shejishi*) of China's reform and progress.

As with Communists in other countries, however, the Chinese also take seriously the task of characterizing the nature of a historical era and then of prescribing what the party must possess to fulfill its historical mission. Since the historical mission of the new era as defined in the early 1980s is to build new material and spiritual civilizations, the party must also transform itself to shed some of its Maoist attributes and acquire the ability to tackle the challenges of the future. The main purpose of this book is to investigate whether the CCP's development in the 1980s has made the party better qualified to perform its control and development functions as assigned by Deng under the new circumstances. But the party's ability to control and manage the society and economy is also closely related to its ability to maintain its own legitimacy and China's long-term political stability. In this connection, the massive demonstrations in Beijing and elsewhere during April–June 1989 require explanation. Should the Tiananmen Square incident be regarded as a chance happening that is unlikely to be repeated? Or should it be treated as a symptom of deep-rooted problems in Chinese politics that may pose recurrent challenges to the regime? To what extent did the CCP's own development under Deng contribute to the violent outbursts of public anger at Tiananmen Square? In what ways has the incident affected the party's future role in Chinese politics?

All these are questions of great importance and should be explored. More specifically, the materials in the present volume are organized in the following order:

Since Deng's return to power marked a new era in Chinese politics, it is important to know what strategies he employed to regain power. With whom did he ally? What obstacles did he have to overcome in his path back to power? These issues are analyzed in chapters 1 and 2.

For obvious reasons, Deng needed a leadership whose loyalty he could trust and whose expertise he could utilize to promote his socioeconomic programs. Here the concern is not with factional rivalry among the top leaders, but with the larger population of middle-level leaders. What measures did he take to get rid of unreliable and ineffective leaders? How were new leaders selected? What qualities were expected from these new leaders? Did the selection process produce the intended results? Chapters 3 and 4 address these problems.

It is, of course, not enough for the party to have a few tens of thousands of reliable and proficient middle-level leaders. To realize the enormously ambitious modernization objectives, the party must have a revitalized rank and file in the millions to serve as catalysts of development in all walks of life. In addition, the party must not merely think of its immediate tasks, but must look ahead to the next century as it endeavors to reach the forefront of the world's advanced countries. Given the predominantly rural nature of the CCP under Mao, it is imperative that the party under Deng try to intellectualize as rapidly as possible, to undergo a thorough renovation of its human composition and intellectual character. But has the party been able to attract educated people into its ranks? The party's recruitment policy is discussed in chapters 5 and 6.

The discipline of party members has two significant dimensions. One is the organizational control enjoyed by the party center over its branches and cells, allowing the party to operate as the "headquarters" or nerve center of all operations, backed up by the "fortress" functions performed by the basic-level organs. Is the party center able to control its rank and file through the many layers of organizations, ensuring that its directives are faithfully implemented and that the rank and file "maintains unity with the party center"? Are the basic-level organs capable of performing their "fortress" functions?

The other dimension is the style of work (*zuofeng*) of party members, which can affect the masses' respect for and confidence in them. Do the party members conduct themselves in a way that inspires awe and admiration from the masses? Do the masses have such high regard for the party members that they also want to join the party? Do the masses consider the party members as deserving the right to rule over China? These questions are examined in chapters 7 and 8.

One major distinguishing feature of the Chinese Communist Party, in contrast to its fraternal Eastern European parties, is its huge rural component. This rural component was laboriously cultivated during the Maoist era and constituted an important legacy of the Maoist era. In spite of the PRC's strategy of industrialization at a forced pace, the rural sector accounted for roughly half of the party's basic-level organizations and membership. A segment of such magnitude deserves attention. How can the rural sector of the party be characterized, and what special problems did it encounter? How did the rural party handle the major issues of the 1980s with respect to leadership, organization, recruitment, and discipline? Chapter 9 provides some answers to these questions.

Finally, for nearly fifty days in the spring of 1989, the world's attention was focused by the high drama unfolding at Beijing's Tiananmen Square. Did the demonstrations have any connection with the issues examined in this volume? What sense can one make out of this tragedy? Where does the party now stand, and what challenges is it likely to confront in the future? These questions are addressed in the concluding chapter.

China's top leadership is bound to undergo radical changes within the next five to ten years with the passing of Deng and his cohorts, but it may take much longer for the Chinese Communist Party to change its nature. Although scholarly investigations of the high-level elite should be encouraged, our understanding of Chinese politics will remain severely handicapped unless we also acquire a sound appreciation of the party's lower-level leadership and rank and file. The present volume is a modest effort to fill a glaring gap in the existing literature: it draws attention to the issues of organizational strength and leadership qualities, work style, and the capacity to improve the members' educational and professional qualifications. Regardless of changes among the top leadership, the question of whether the party can justify its vanguard role in Chinese politics and convincingly and effectively perform the functions of both control and development will ultimately depend on its ability to meet the challenges posed by these issues.

Acknowledgments

ALTHOUGH my interest in Chinese Communist politics first began during my days as a graduate student many years ago, it was not until 1976 that I was afforded the opportunity to observe the subject matter personally. That year I made my first trip to mainland China since 1949, and my talks with friends and relatives gave me a new appreciation of life under communism that was at considerable variance with the prevailing thinking in the Western academic world or mass media.

The return of Deng Xiaoping to power raised the expectations of many people, including myself. It also gave me a strong incentive to follow Chinese political development more critically. In the ensuing decade, my own education in Chinese politics was enriched by two main sources. First, the new leadership greatly liberalized its control over the press and allowed an unprecedented amount of information to be made publicly available that shed light on many more facets of Chinese politics than ever before. This was a bonanza for all China scholars. Second, during the last decade I made more than a dozen trips to mainland China to give lectures, conduct research, or simply observe. Both on these trips and in the United States, I was fortunate to have the opportunity to talk to a large number of Chinese citizens of different ages, sex, geographical origins, and educational background, ranging from high-ranking cadres to ordinary citizens in the streets. While I studiously avoided asking them to divulge confidential official information, I learned from them about how they perceive, interpret, and evaluate Chinese politics. Even though our ideological positions and moral convictions often differed, these conversations were still extremely revealing and instructive.

I am particular grateful to those who trusted me enough to share with me the most intimate details of their private lives and thoughts, and who were patient enough to teach me their esoteric knowledge on political life in China. Their tutorship helped me to acquire a greater sensitivity and ability to interpret the public information, and to bridge gaps in my formal training. Without their trust and friendship, I probably would have remained semiliterate in Chinese politics to this day. As these goodhearted people are too numerous to mention by name, I wish to use the opportunity here to thank them all. The judgments and interpretations contained in this volume are of course entirely my own, and I assume full responsibility for them.

POLITICS OF
DISILLUSIONMENT

1

Deng's Rise to Power and His Agenda

POLITICAL events in China unfolded in a dramatic manner after the death of Mao Zedong in September 1976. Hua Guofeng, a relatively junior member of the old hierarchy, quickly became the new leader. Within a month of Mao's death, the most powerful figures in Chinese politics during the Cultural Revolution years were deposed in a bloodless coup and branded as antiparty elements by a coalition of the party's old guard in collusion with key military leaders.

But the new leadership was immediately confronted with the problem of a breakdown of social order in many provinces. Widespread labor unrest, sabotage of production and transportation, and even open armed conflicts between rival factions may have led to the loss of as many as 45,000 to 50,000 lives throughout the country. These incidents certainly occupied much of the attention of the new leaders, and it was only in mid-1977, after harsh measures were adopted, that public order was restored.[1]

In spite of the overthrow of the Gang of Four, Hua Guofeng basically wanted to maintain the continuity of the Maoist legacy. Ideologically, Hua continued to uphold the validity of the Cultural Revolution, the authority of Mao Zedong's Thought, and the policies of the entire Maoist era. He not only endorsed the radical thoughts and practices of the Cultural Revolution, the thesis of continuous revolution under the dictatorship of the proletariat, and the insistence on class struggle as the party's basic principle, but introduced the even more extreme doctrine of total and blind acceptance of everything associated with Mao. On February 7, 1977, in a joint editorial carried by the *People's Daily*, *Hongqi*, and the *People's Liberation Army Daily*, Hua announced the doctrine of "two whatevers" (*liangge fanshi*), which asserted that "we will resolutely support whatever decisions Chairman Mao made; we will unflinchingly obey whatever instructions Chairman Mao issued." This famous slogan was Hua's direct answer to the popular demands to exonerate the participants in the Tiananmen incident of 1976, and to reassess the meaning of the Cultural Revolution.[2]

Hua's position on personnel questions was only slightly more flexible. He was willing to remove only those leaders who had very close personal or factional ties with the Gang of Four, and to rehabilitate a small number of disgraced leaders whom Mao had not personally denounced. Thus, for example, personnel changes involving the State Council and provincial party first secretaries between late 1976 and mid-1977 included only a modest number of rehabilitated leaders.[3]

But Hua Guofeng's total identification with Mao's ideology and policies not only posed serious obstacles to the correction of many of the excesses that had caused mass discontent in China, but also hampered the process of exonerating many important leaders accused as anti-Maoists, including Deng Xiaoping. By insisting that Mao had not made any mistakes during his last years of life, Hua was rejecting the popular demand for the return of Deng to the party's leadership. Consequently, serious ideological and political confusion continued in 1977 and 1978.

Return to Power

Amid this fluid situation, a coalition of Politburo members and provincial leaders began to exert pressure in the spring of 1977 for the rehabilitation of Deng Xiaoping. Hua finally gave in to their demands and sanctioned Deng's rehabilitation, which was officially announced by the Third Plenum of the Tenth Congress, convened during July 16–21, 1977.[4] In August the CCP's Eleventh Congress elected Hua Guofeng as the party's chairman and Wang Dongxing as its vice-chairman. In February 1978, the Fifth National People's Congress elected Hua premier.

Although at the time of his rehabilitation Deng promised never to "overthrow the political verdict," Hua's doctrine of "two whatevers" posed a serious problem for Deng's political career. Many party leaders still opposed Deng and accused him of "cutting down" Mao's Thought. Deng himself realized that if the "two whatevers" were rigidly applied, his own rehabilitation could not be justified.[5] Deng's defense was that his opponents were guilty of holding onto fossilized thoughts, and of rigidly and unquestioningly accepting everything Mao had said. In May 1978, Deng's supporters suggested that "practice should be the only criterion to validate truth," which was another way of saying that all acceptable ideological lines must correspond to social, economic, and political realities.[6] At the Military Political Work Conference held on June 2, 1978, Deng used the same argument to counter the criticism of his opponents and to argue that the basic tenet of Mao's Thought was respect for facts (*shishi qiushi*). Hua and his associates were increasingly criticized as the "whatever faction" (*fanshipai*).

Deng's strategy of regaining power was through a circuitous route: eschewing a frontal bid for power, he set out to use his supporters to whittle away the ideological foundation of the Hua regime and to create a political atmosphere that enhanced his own prestige.

During the next four months, the dispute over the norm of truth dominated Chinese politics. Deng's new position received strong support from the PLA through the *Jiefangjun bao* (PLA news) in an editorial on August 1, 1978, and through provincial papers throughout the whole country. By October, it was clear that Deng had been able to undermine Hua's leadership position by using Maoist doctrines as a weapon. Deng's approach was to suggest that not everything that Mao had said or done was necessarily always right. In this fashion, Deng was able to imply that in governing China, it was more important to apply ideologies flexibly than to adhere dogmatically to Maoism. Pragmatism became more significant than dogmatism in judging political issues. In early December 1978, Deng set the tone of the forthcoming Third Plenum of the Eleventh Party Congress by stating, "If a party, a country, a nation approaches everything dogmatically, applies rigid thought, and is superstitious, then its vitality will stop. The party and the state will collapse."[7]

At the Third Plenum, held from December 18 to 22, 1978, Deng scored a major victory on several fronts. First, he achieved success in personnel and organizational control by sending three more supporters to the Politburo (Deng Yingchao, Hu Yaobang, and Wang Zhen). Although Hua Guofeng was still the party's chairman, the vice-chairmen now included Ye Jianying, Deng Xiaoping, Li Xiannian, Chen Yun, and Wang Dongxing. Deng's supporters also gained control over the party's General Office, and over the departments of organization, propaganda, and united front work. The party created a Central Discipline Inspection Committee, with Chen Yun as first secretary.[8]

Second, Deng became increasingly effective in setting the party's agenda and the tone of discussion. He criticized the theme of the "two whatevers," affirmed the principle that practice was the only reliable criterion to evaluate truth, and asserted that it was also the only way to liberate thoughts and correct erroneous thinking. The plenum also set the precedent of rehabilitating leaders who had been personally vilified by Mao. Peng Dehuai and Tao Zhu were exonerated posthumously, and several other surviving leaders (including General Huang Kecheng and Chen Zaidao) were readmitted to the Central Committee as full members.[9]

The year 1979 saw even more dramatic gains for Deng. While constantly criticizing the leaders who had risen to power during the Cultural Revolution, Deng did not press for their immediate removal. In return, he was able to add his own supporters to the Politburo and the Central Committee. Deng also pushed through changes that facilitated the expansion of his power base. The party's Secretariat, Deng's old stronghold in the 1950s and 1960s, was revived, and Hu Yaobang was given control over the daily operation of the party. At the recommendation of Chen Yun, a Central Discipline Committee was created. With Chen as its first secretary, the committee was empowered not only to enforce discipline among party members but also to review cases of political oppression involving veteran cadres.[10] In September 1979, at the Fourth Plenum of the party's Eleventh Congress, Deng scored more victories in extending his power base. Twelve more recently rehabilitated leaders who had been disgraced during the Cultural Revolution were admitted as members of the Central Committee. Two important allies, Zhao Ziyang and Peng Zhen, were also elevated to the Politburo.[11]

Throughout 1979–80, Deng continued to wage an unrelenting ideological battle against Hua as he believed that it was extremely important to settle this theoretical point as a foundation for his policies.[12] By early 1980, Deng had gained enough organizational control to allow him to take on his opponents. At the Fifth Plenum, convened at the end of February 1980, Hu Yaobang and Zhao Ziyang were promoted to the Standing Committee of the Politburo. More important, Deng finally succeeded in removing from the Politburo the four major figures who had benefited in the Cultural Revolution—Wang Dongxing, Wu De, Ji Dengkui, and Chen Yonggui. With these moves, Deng had gained a clear majority in both the Politburo and its all-powerful Standing Committee, isolating Hua Guofeng in both organs.[13] In addition, Deng acquired extensive control over the party organization when the plenum appointed Hu Yaobang as the general secretary of the party, and Deng's men filled the ranks of the Secretariat.[14] Shortly afterward, Zhao Ziyang replaced Hua Guofeng as premier. With its power in the Politburo greatly strengthened, the Deng group was in a much better position to promote its reform package.

Meanwhile, the Deng group made great efforts to reorganize the leadership from the ministerial to local levels. In the early spring of 1980, the commanders of China's eleven military regions were either replaced or reassigned, an important move that disrupted the military's domination of regional politics and gave Deng's forces direct control over local leaders. Finally, in December 1980, Hua's loss of power became complete when he yielded his party chairmanship to Hu Yaobang, and his Military Affairs Committee chairmanship to Deng. The Politburo also adopted a resolution criticizing Hua's doctrine of the "two whatevers." Deng had basically fulfilled his plan to regain power on the national level.[15]

Immediate Challenges

Deng's journey back to power spanned about forty months, from July 1977 to December 1980. For the first fifteen months, Deng's strategy was to lie low, to make his return unobtrusive, to make himself useful, but to betray no political ambitions.[16] Meanwhile, he quietly regrouped his supporters and used proxies to create an ideological atmosphere unfavorable to Hua. He scored his first major organizational victory at the Third Plenum in December 1978 by putting his supporters into key party positions, which increased his strength in an incremental way. He scored his second victory at the Fifth Plenum of February 1980 by driving some major opponents (the radicals, beneficiaries of the Cultural Revolution) from office, which led to the increasing isolation of Hua, culminating in Hua's own removal from power in December 1980. In a sense, Deng's political power play bore a close resemblance to the CCP's military strategy of surrounding the cities from the countryside. It also conformed to the dialectical principle of achieving many small victories, thereby fundamentally changing the power equation and rendering the opponent impotent.

It should be remembered, however, that the path of Deng's return to power was not free of all obstacles. His attention and energy could not be directed entirely to top-level political maneuvers. His political astuteness was tested by major challenges along the way. Deng's ascension was facilitated by his demonstrated ability to fend off challenges from without, and to consolidate power from within. In those years, four major issues affected Deng's prospects of regaining power. These were the dissidents' protests, the trial of the Gang of Four, the rehabilitation of old cadres, and the proper evaluation of Mao and Maoism.

Defending the Party Against Outsiders: The Democracy Wall

During Deng's return to power, one threat to the party was the agitation by dissidents, primarily educated youths, from outside the party. Deng and other Communist leaders had always believed in the premise of one-party dictatorship. According to this premise, the ruling party had the obligation to impose stringent requirements upon its members to strengthen ideological training and organizational control and assure the fulfillment of its mission. The party would never allow its authority or the validity of its ideology to be questioned by anyone outside the party. Only the party had the capacity to rectify its own mistakes, and only the party had the authority to interpret the ideology.

This premise came under severe criticism as soon as Deng returned to power. The immediate cause for the outburst of dissension was the popular demand for the exoneration of participants in the Tiananmen incident of April 5, 1976, which the party had condemned as a counterrevolutionary activity. In early October 1978, Wu De was removed from the Beijing municipal party leadership. Then, on November 15, 1978, the Beijing Municipal Party Committee officially excused the incident and exonerated its participants.[17] Although the exonerations were originally intended to placate the abused cadres, they actually provoked more fundamental criticisms from educated youths outside the party in the form of big-character posters, which appeared in an area in Beijing that subsequently came to be called the "Democracy Wall." The posters and discussions along the Democracy Wall often drew daily crowds of several thousand people.

On December 5, 1978, Wei Jingsheng posted an article on the wall entitled "The Fifth Modernization." In it he argued that the party's four modernizations program was viable only when accompanied by a concomitant political modernization. His article triggered a torrent of criticisms against the party, its ideology, and its leadership. As the boldness of the attacks on fundamental and sensitive political issues increased, so did the number of publications and the size of the following among the youths.[18]

Confronted with such vehement criticism, Deng Xiaoping's initial reaction was to counsel calm by the party. In a speech of December 13, 1978, Deng argued that there was no need to be unduly alarmed by a few discontented people making trouble at "Democracy Wall." He expressed the confidence that approval of the Tiananmen incident could only increase the party's popularity among the people. He said that the masses should be allowed to express their opinions or criticisms without provoking overreaction from the government. He criticized those who were eager to conduct political investigations of the critics, asserting that this kind of suppression must cease. Finally, he said that the people's judgment must be trusted and their democratic rights protected through laws.[19]

Reflecting this attitude, the Chinese press also initially counseled forbearance by the masses. It urged them to appreciate the value of unity and stability, to direct their energy toward the modernization drive, and not to be consumed by bitterness about the past.[20]

But in the spring of 1979, demonstrations and even riots by young educated people broke out in Beijing, Shanghai, Yunnan, and other parts of the country. They attacked or occupied public offices of the party and government. They also conducted sit-ins and fasts, blocked traffic, encouraged people to participate in demonstrations, and caused serious disruptions of production and the social order.[21]

Within weeks, Deng's attitude toward the dissidents' movement changed drastically. To Deng, even though the dissidents constituted a minority, they now posed a mortal threat to party and state organs because they had attracted a large following. The dissidents had tried to exploit the many problems left by Lin Biao and the Gang of Four to stir up discontent among the masses. Deng was convinced that the dissidents' objective was to derail the party's four modernizations program. In addition, he suspected them of having secret organizations throughout the country and links with Taiwan and other foreign powers. As a result, Deng became even more determined to suppress them.[22]

The party quickly took action to crack down on the dissidents. In March 1979, the municipal party organs of Beijing and Shanghai introduced new regulations banning all antiparty and counterrevolutionary wall posters. Soon, other cities adopted similar regulations and forced the closing down of the democracy walls throughout the country. A wave of arrests of prominent leaders of the democratic movement occurred, and their publications either stopped circulation or went underground. The most celebrated case was the arrest of Wei Jingsheng in March and his trial in October 1979 in a Beijing municipal court, which sentenced him to fifteen years of imprisonment for treason and counterrevolutionary behavior. The party's suppression of the democratic movement was capped in January

1980 when Deng branded the young democrats as antisocialist and recommended the removal of the four guaranteed freedoms of speech from the Constitution of the PRC.[23] Deng's recommendation was promptly accepted and acted upon by the government.

These disturbances distracted party leaders from other party affairs. They also put Deng Xiaoping personally in an awkward position. In the early months after his rehabilitation, Deng had projected a liberal public image, and his statements were generally supportive of democracy, and of the need to liberate thoughts and to confront and correct all mistakes honestly. He also advocated a pragmatic attitude and the relaxation of control. But as the democratic movement spread, Deng increasingly emphasized party control and leadership, and opposed the liberalizing tendency. In the face of attacks from outside, he could not admit the validity of the dissidents' complaints about the party's shortcomings, even though Deng had previously criticized some of these same shortcomings himself. The assault by outsiders made it necessary for him to defend the party, if only to strengthen his own position within it and not give his opponents any excuse to depose him.

Paradoxically, however, it was Deng who ultimately benefited from this crisis. The democracy movement provided him with a great opportunity to enhance his stature within the party as a resolute leader. When other leaders were undecided on how to react, Deng resolutely advocated harsh, repressive measures. The greatest danger of the democracy movement, from the party's perspective, was its potential to attract industrial workers. This was a particularly worrisome prospect for China's leaders because they had already witnessed the disruptive impact of the Polish Solidarity Movement and were loathe to see a joining of forces between China's dissidents and its workers to create a Chinese Solidarity Movement. Although Deng's callous treatment of the dissidents might have caused him to lose prestige in the public eye, he definitely gained in stature within the party as he demonstrated his ability to lead the party through a major political storm.

Handling the Crimes of the Gang of Four

After 1976, the campaign against the Gang of Four was conducted on two different fronts: first, exposure of their conspiratorial activities and identification of the high-level people who had close connections with the Gang; second, definition of the nature of their political crimes and refutation of their ideological teachings.

Of these two tasks, the first was originally thought to be the easiest to accomplish. Immediately after the Gang's downfall, the party center proceeded to change the leadership in many provinces where the Gang's diehard followers were in power. It was thought at the time that the task of flushing out the remnants of Gang supporters could be accomplished by February 1978 when the

Fifth National People's Congress was scheduled to convene.[24] But this turned out to be an overly optimistic prognosis, and the investigation on the Gang remnants had to be continued in the provinces for all of 1978.

When the Third Plenum of the Eleventh Party Congress convened, the party leaders concluded that they had only completed the "first wave" of exposing those with blatant factional connections to the Gang of Four.[25] In the next year, Deng intensified his effort to cleanse the Gang's supporters from the provincial party organs. By the spring of 1980, all provincial party first secretaries who were in office at the time of Mao's death had been removed except one.

To complement the operation to weed out Gang supporters, Deng also introduced the idea of institutional reforms on a broad basis. He argued that the party should adopt a retirement system and should take the age factor into account when formulating its cadre policy.[26]

The second task, that of defining the nature of the Gang's crimes, was far more complicated, not only because many of the group's actions had a strong ideological basis, but also because they had shared a special relationship with Mao's own ideological positions. From 1976 to 1978, the leaders were uncertain whether to characterize the Gang's activities as being inspired by the enemies of the people (such as the Nationalists), or whether they were involved in rightist opportunism or ultra-leftist excesses.

The question of what to do with the Gang of Four also needed to be resolved. Should they be tried in an open court, or should they be disciplined by internal party mechanisms? Of what crimes should they be charged? Should they be held responsible for everything that occurred during the Cultural Revolution, or only for those deeds in which they directly participated? Were they to be tried separately from the Lin Biao group, or were they to be lumped together? Finally, and most important, what was to be the official version of the relationship between the Gang of Four and Chairman Mao?

Deng's return to power gave him more say in deciding these questions. The idea of holding an open trial for the Gang of Four drew much opposition within the party, primarily from those who still held powerful positions but who had participated in certain aspects of Cultural Revolution activities and did not wish to have their own activities dragged into the spotlight.[27] These differences of opinion within the party took a long time to resolve.

Once the decision was made to have an open trial, no detail was left open to chance. Deng and his associates were directly involved in planning the strategy of the trial, and in supervising its actual proceedings after it began in November 1980.[28]

The trial basically went as Deng had wished. He was able to protect himself and his associates, who emerged as loyal party members victimized by the devious and ambitious Gang members. The other leaders who had survived or even thrived during the Cultural Revolution were not openly implicated. But the trial certainly planted doubts in the public mind as to their worthiness as leaders.

Although the Chinese masses might have preferred harsher punishment for the Gang members and a broader review of the records of many more leaders, the trial was turned to Deng's advantage as he helped many party members to vent their grievances against the Gang, and to end the political careers of some of his worst rivals.

Rebuilding a Power Base through Rehabilitations

Returning to power in 1978 after a prolonged absence, Deng could not afford to be content with planting a few close associates in the top party and state positions. A large number of national posts, and the overwhelming majority of provincial and local positions, were still in the hands of people whom he could not trust for either ideological or factional reasons. If Deng was to impose his own political agenda on the nation, he needed to rebuild his coalition of supporters, and the only people he could trust were the old comrades he had worked with before the Cultural Revolution but who lost out in the ensuing power struggle. This group had to be rehabilitated from political disgrace to strengthen his power base.

Rehabilitation, or exoneration (*pingfan*), in the late 1970s had three components. First, the political stigma surrounding the victims was removed and their reputations restored. Second, the victims were given back their political and material prerogatives, including housing and salaries. Third, they were reinstated to their old jobs or assigned to comparable new positions.

The review of cases of miscarriage of justice was performed by the discipline committees on various levels.[29] The task of settling past mistakes was a stupendous one. Often hundreds of thousands of cadres and ordinary party members had been mistreated in a single province, with many being killed.[30] Although rehabilitation started shortly after the fall of the Gang of Four, progress was slow under Hua Guofeng. Between late 1977 and early 1979, only about 100,000 cadres had been rehabilitated.[31]

The implementation of the rehabilitation policy was plagued by many problems. Often leaders tried to shirk responsibility, delay decision, withhold judgment, and wait for other people to make the first move. Others remained adamantly opposed to the policy itself because they were still uncertain about the correctness of the programs, or because they believed that it was a bad practice to repudiate the party's past verdict.[32]

Even after Deng's return to power, the party rank and file were still worried about the possibility of radical reversal of the party line. They figured that the Politburo was still stacked with people who had ascended to power during the Cultural Revolution or who had embraced the doctrine of "two whatevers." If the reformers (Deng, Chen Yun, Ye Jianying, Li Xiannian, etc.) should die early, then the leftists might regain control.

The recently rehabilitated cadres were particularly worried that they might again become targets of denunciation if the leftists should return to power. If Liu Shaoqi was not officially exonerated, if Mao was not openly criticized, then the rehabilitated cadres could be criticized as anti-Maoists should the leftists revive themselves. Rehabilitated cadres were reluctant to carry out the reform programs lest they give the leftists more excuses to attack them later.[33]

These anxieties were by no means unfounded, for it was known that many sympathizers of the Gang of Four were waiting for a day of reckoning to come. Therefore, to reassure the rehabilitated cadres, Deng increased his rehabilitation efforts in 1980 and 1981. By the end of 1982, the party's Organization Department reported that some three million "cadres" had been rehabilitated throughout the nation. Party membership was restored to more than 470,000 party members who had been unjustly expelled during the Cultural Revolution. The erroneous punishments given to another 120,000 party members were annulled. "Tens of millions" of cadres and ordinary people who had been implicated in fabricated political crimes were cleared of their charges.[34]

The rehabilitation process for cadres was essentially completed in many provinces by early 1983.[35] Each case of rehabilitation created its own ripple effect: once a senior cadre was restored to power, the people affiliated with him factionally could also seek his support for their exoneration.

In time, the party also came under great pressure to expand the scope of its rehabilitation program beyond the victims of the Cultural Revolution. In June 1980, General Secretary Hu Yaobang revealed that rehabilitation would eventually affect about one hundred million people and would include the victims and their family members in all previous political campaigns.[36] Soon afterward, the rehabilitation program was extended to cover injustices inflicted upon other categories of cadres and common people, such as rightists, rich peasants, landlords, and small merchants. These cases created an enormous additional workload for the party organs on all levels.[37]

Clearly, Deng's decision to accelerate the pace and expand the scope of the rehabilitation program was to broaden his base of support. By giving all victims of previous political struggles a chance for a new life, he hoped that they would develop a stake in the viability of his leadership, thereby killing the chances of a political comeback by the leftists.

But even the party's redoubled efforts were not enough to satisfy the people's demands for justice. Starting in 1979, hundreds of thousands of average Chinese people decided to bypass the regular party and state channels for direct appeals to higher authorities. One way to do this was to write letters of complaint to provincial or national authorities. These pleas for justice reached such avalanche proportions that the party and the State Council had to set up special offices to handle them.[38]

An even more dramatic form of appeal was to journey to Beijing to seek meetings with central authorities in the hope of having a case resolved on the spot. Hundreds of people from the provinces poured into the city every day.

These ragged people frequently took their entire families along and camped out on the sidewalks, in parks, under highway bridges, or in train stations. Their prolonged stays in the capital in such huge numbers created not only serious traffic and sanitation problems, but a potentially explosive political situation as well.[39]

To meet the enormous popular pressure for justice, the party center had to form a special task force in September 1979 of over 1,000 cadres to receive the visitors. In addition, several hundred cadres were sent in small investigative teams down to the provinces where they were greeted by even more complaints. In the six months following September 1979, more than 200,000 cadres through-out the entire country were mobilized to process these complaints. They pro-cessed 1,050,000 cases and resolved 820,000 of them. Even so, the phenomenon did not sharply diminish until late 1982.[40]

There is no doubt that Deng gained much support both within the party and among the people because of his energetic implementation of the rehabilitation program. He succeeded in rebuilding a vast coalition of party cadres, bureau-crats, and military figures by rescuing them from political oblivion and returning them to power. These were the people who became Deng's political capital in his bid for power, and the supporters of his political-economic programs.

Criticism of the Maoist Legacy

The refutation of the ideology of the Cultural Revolution was an important component of Deng's strategy of winning political support both within the party and among the Chinese people. But it was almost impossible to refute the philos-ophy and policies of the Gang of Four without also casting doubt on the philoso-phy and policies of Mao.

While Deng's personal feelings against the Cultural Revolution were strong, he was initially reluctant to criticize either that event or Mao himself to avoid any unnecessary complications in his pursuit to gain power. Thus the communiqué of the Third Plenum of Eleventh Party Congress dwelt only on Mao's enormous contribution to revolution as "a great Marxist," and evaded the issue of whether Mao made any mistakes. With respect to the Cultural Revolu-tion, the communiqué indicated that it was necessary to adopt a historical, scien-tific, and pragmatic attitude to treat it. It pointed out that Mao had initiated the Cultural Revolution for an understandable reason—to prevent the recurrence of Soviet revisionism in China. Although mistakes might have been committed during the Cultural Revolution, it was still too early to make a judgment. The assessment must wait for a right time in the future. The communiqué, which did not mention a single mistake by Mao nor any specific mistakes of the Cultural Revolution, basically reflected Deng's personal views at this point.[41]

The pressure for a more honest and forthright assessment of Mao mounted, however, as Deng's program of rehabilitation of old cadres reached the point when all cadres persecuted exclusively by the Gang of Four, without Mao's direct involvement, had been exonerated. There remained a large number of cadres whose persecution had been sanctioned by Mao personally. Unless Mao's mistakes were acknowledged, there would be no grounds for rehabilitating these cadres. The silence on Mao's role became a cause for dissatisfaction among many cadres, particularly the surviving family members of former high-ranking leaders who had lost their lives (e.g., Liu Shaoqi and Tao Zhu).

The pressure began to build in the early spring of 1979 when some official publications now controlled by the sympathizers of unrehabilitated cadres raised the issue of injustices inflicted upon Wu Han and Peng Dehuai, depicted as loyal party members who had faithfully followed the party's line. Some publications went so far as to say that Mao personally made many mistakes. Thus, within the party, public opinion demanding a reassessment of Mao was being formed, and the leaders felt that they had to address the issue to mollify party members, particularly high-ranking cadres.[42]

In his speech commemorating the thirtieth anniversary of the PRC, Ye Jianying said on September 30, 1979, that the Thought of Mao Zedong was by no means the product of Mao alone, but the collective wisdom of numerous party leaders over the years. He also made the first official denunciation of the Cultural Revolution as a decade of "suppression, tyranny, and bloodshed."[43] Ye's statement indicated that the new leaders were now ready to make a distinction between Mao, the person, and Mao Zedong's Thought, the ideology. By collectivizing Mao Zedong's Thought, they sent a signal that it should be held above partisan struggle. But by denouncing the Cultural Revolution, which was clearly Mao's personal policy, they greatly relaxed the restrictions on criticism of Mao as a leader.

During much of 1980 and early 1981, the Deng leadership felt mounting pressure to confront the issue of the proper evaluation of Mao and his legacy. In February 1980, the CCP finally exonerated Liu Shaoqi.[44] Although the blame for Liu's persecution was still placed upon the Gang of Four, it was already quite clear that the party could not avoid the issue of Mao's role much longer, because it was Mao's decision that had brought about Liu's downfall.

On April 10, 1980, Huang Kecheng wrote an article for the *Jiefangjun bao* on the proper handling of Mao and his thoughts, which signaled the party's readiness to allow this topic to be discussed openly.[45] In the meantime, the party secretly had begun to draft and circulate a comprehensive evaluation of Mao's contributions and mistakes among selected cadres and party members for feedback.

As revealed later by Deng in an interview, the party took almost a year and half to refine the first draft into a resolution, which forced the postponement of the party's Sixth Plenum, originally scheduled for late 1980. Not surprisingly, the idea of criticizing Mao provoked considerable opposition from Mao's faithful followers. The trials of the Gang of Four further complicated the matter, because the Gang's strongest defense was that they did everything either at Mao's explicit behest or with his blessings.

The actual writing of the resolution not only was closely supervised by the top leaders, but involved endless consultation and mediation sessions among contending forces within the party. Intense debate occurred. The draft was circulated and revised many times before reaching its final version.[46]

This extreme care was necessary because Deng needed to strike a balance between placating the cadres seeking exoneration and offending the cadres whose careers and convictions were closely tied to Mao and his policies. The final product, in the form of a party resolution entitled "Resolution on Certain Historical Issues of the Party Since the Founding of the PRC" (Guanyu jianguo yilai dangde rogan lishi wenti de jueyi), was passed by the Sixth Plenum of the CCP Central Committee on June 27, 1981. It was a document of political compromise, both criticizing Mao's mistakes and affirming his contributions. Although it pleased nobody, it enabled the new leaders to have several more years of reprieve on the question of Mao, and to assert that since all past injustices had been corrected, the party should now look forward to leading the country into a new era.

A New Agenda: The Primacy of Economic Objectives

Even as Deng was busy building a coalition within the party, his overriding objective was always to achieve economic growth. This was a top priority in his political agenda for both intrinsic and utilitarian reasons. Intrinsically, Deng was totally disillusioned with the Maoist revolutionary strategy, which emphasized politics at the expense of economics. Deng was anxious to leave the destabilizing political campaigns behind so that he could get on with the task of economic construction. From a utilitarian point of view, he also realized that his popularity and support would be greatly increased if he could give the Chinese people a better living.

This agenda was adopted as the party's new line at the Third Plenum of the Eleventh Party Congress which came under the control of Deng and his supporters. The plenum's communiqué (December 24, 1978) became the most important statement of Deng's economic programs.

The plenum proclaimed the end of the era of political mass movements, including those aimed at criticizing Lin Biao and the Gang of Four, and conducting large-scale, stormy class struggle. It declared the year of 1979 to be a new beginning whereby the entire party's work was to be directed toward implementing the socialist modernization program. As the communiqué stated, "the major missions of the new historical era" were to accelerate socialist modernization, to increase production, and to improve people's livelihood.[47] The importance of this historical mission was given stronger emphasis by Ye Jianying shortly afterward when he declared that "the construction of the four modernizations constitutes the most important politics at the present. National security, social stability, and the improvement of people's livelihood all must ultimately depend on the success of the modernizations and the increase of production. All our effort must revolve around the construction of these modernizations."[48]

To give the economy a boost, the leaders vowed to reduce political interference in economic activities; to decentralize leadership to basic levels; to streamline economic administrative agencies on all levels; to adopt systems of individual responsibilities and differentiation of responsibilities; and to change management methods, activities, and thought patterns.[49]

Deng and his associates believed that the most effective way to develop the economy was to give people material incentives and to mobilize their enthusiasm.[50] As Deng pointed out, "at present, the most pressing issue is to expand the autonomy of economic enterprises and production teams, to make sure that every production unit will try its very best to be creative."[51] The communiqué of the plenum declared: "All the efforts made by the party are intended to provide favorable conditions for the transition of the party's main task to socialist modernization."[52]

These were monumental tasks indeed. Many of the plenum's proposed measures were radical or even heretical by Maoist standards. The leaders believed in 1978–79 that to implement these measures, the party itself must be unified and must exercise strong leadership.[53]

Deng argued that a favorable political environment could exist only if the four basic principles were upheld.[54] To Chen Yun, the most important factor affecting the success or failure of this task was that the party must achieve solidarity and stability internally. Chen placed particular emphasis on the unity of party leaders and argued that only when leadership unity was present could the party perform its functions efficiently.[55]

After the Third Plenum, Chen Yun was put in charge of economic work. The party moved to scale down drastically the ambitious but impractical objectives put forward in Hua Guofeng's version of the four modernizations of 1977–78. At this point, China's economy was still suffering from the aftereffects of the enormous dislocation of the Cultural Revolution. Serious imbalances existed between agriculture and industry, and among the different sectors within industry. The energy sector was far too backward to meet the needs of industry and transportation. The traditional strong emphasis on capital accumulation had resulted in serious depression of the people's living standards. Hundreds of thousands of youths each year could not find suitable employment. It was estimated that one out every three economic enterprises in China was poorly managed and had inadequate production.[56]

Confronted with these problems, Chen Yun recommended that the party devote the next three years to restoring order in the economy and increasing its vitality. His specific proposals were to readjust priorities, reform institutions, rectify management systems, and increase production.[57] Chen's recommendations were approved by the party's Central Work Conference in April 1979. Meanwhile, the party also drew up three different economic plans to cover short-, medium-, and long-range developments.[58]

On January 16, 1980, Deng proclaimed in an important speech entitled "On Current Conditions and Missions" (Muqian de xingshi he renwu) that China's three major missions for the 1980s were to oppose hegemonism in foreign policy, to reunify with Taiwan, and to launch the four modernizations. Deng pointed out that, of these three missions, the most important as well the most fundamental mission was economic development, because the pursuit of the two other missions could only proceed from a sound economic foundation. He further argued that the realization of the objectives of economic modernization must be predicated upon four preconditions: a clear and correct political line, a political environment of unity and stability, dedication to work hard, and a capable cadre corps to handle the challenges of socialist construction.[59] If these conditions could be set, Deng predicted that China's economy could quadruple between 1980 and 2000.

In late 1980, Deng reiterated his view that the single most critical variable affecting the viability of the new economic policies was whether there existed a stable and unified political situation, without which, he warned, economic development could not proceed.[60] Confronted with the enormity of these economic challenges, the leaders were understandably anxious to relegate other issues to the back burner and to produce quick economic results during 1979–1981 so that the medium- and long-term plans could be implemented on schedule.

Although the new concept of economic development was based on more realistic assumptions, it was not implemented effectively during 1979–1980 because many cadres did not appreciate its importance or take it seriously. In fact, government deficits increased, and prices continued to soar. In response, Deng had to instruct the government to cut its own spending, to reduce basic construction projects, and to overhaul or close inefficient factories.[61]

In fact, it was not until 1981 that the party finally was able to move ahead in the economic field. In early spring, a new agricultural policy was announced.[62] Later in the year, Zhao Ziyang unveiled to the Fourth Session of the Fifth National People's Congress a ten-point program of economic development, which was the most ambitious and comprehensive statement of what the party intended to accomplish. It signaled the leaders' readiness to experiment with even bolder alternatives. These new policies aimed to improve agriculture, increase the quality and volume of consumer goods, improve the efficiency of energy utilization, upgrade the country's technologies, overhaul industrial enterprises, and improve the country's scientific and educational infrastructures.[63]

China's economic relationships with the rest of the world were also significantly redefined. In early 1979, Deng said that while "self-support" would remain as the basic principle, it must be complemented by efforts to win foreign assistance and to introduce advanced technologies from the West.[64] In July 1979, the PRC promulgated its first set of regulations governing Sino-foreign joint economic investments as a measure to attract foreign capital into China. The new policy promised to foster an even closer economic relationship with the outside world. Controls over foreign loans and investments would be relaxed, and several Special Economic Zones would be created in the coastal provinces for the specific purpose of attracting foreign trade and investments.[65] In January 1982, the party and state also announced the plan to overhaul state-run enterprises.[66]

The CCP's Twelfth Congress

Between late 1978 and 1981, Deng was deeply concerned with personnel changes at the very top, as he attempted to stack his supporters in the Politburo and Central Committee. He also moved to secure control initially over several strategically located provincial leaderships, such as Guangdong and Sichuan, and to expand gradually his territorial control. He acted decisively to repudiate the Cultural Revolution in order to heal the wounds within the party and among the people, and to make sure that the leftists did not have a sound ideological basis to attempt a comeback.

The abbreviated chronological review also indicates that Deng and his associates had been eager to push forward their economic programs almost from the beginning of their return to power. They not only had a vision of turning China into a "modernized" country by the year 2000, but they had adopted a series of timetables as well as concrete economic plans to translate their vision into reality. In their view, a unified national leadership constituted the essential precondition for their economic program.

Deng's wish to have a unified national leadership was fulfilled by September 1982 when the party's Twelfth National Congress was convened. Deng Xiaoping called this congress the most important meeting of the party since the Seventh Party Congress of 1945; Hu Yaobang called it the summation of a great historical transition.

The congress passed a new Party Charter, which effectively removed many features associated with Mao and his policies, such as class struggle, continuous revolution, and recurrent cultural revolutions. It also abolished the position of party chairman. Hua Guofeng was driven out of the top echelon and allowed to keep only his place in the Central Committee. New party institutions were formalized. Hu Yaobang was made the general secretary. The leadership had finally achieved a complete independence from the shadow of Mao.[67]

The Central Committee of the Twelfth Party Congress in 1982 was also massively overhauled. Of its 210 full members, 97 (46 percent) were new to the committee. They were younger, more educated, and closer to the Deng group. When both full and alternate members were counted together (a total of 348 members), 62 percent (211 members) were in the Central Committee for the first time. They included the leading cadres of provinces and municipalities, national ministries, and other central offices. Even though military figures still constituted about 20 percent of this Central Committee, the percentage was much lower than in the previous Central Committee. In addition, there was considerable change in the composition of the military figures on the Central Committee. Fifty military figures of the Eleventh Central Committee were retired and replaced by forty new military faces. Only a handful of people (about 16) had gained advancement during the Cultural Revolution. A good number of retired members of the Central Committee were invited to join the Central Advisory Committee, but many more simply lost power and were forced into complete retirement.[68] Hua Guofeng was removed from the Politburo, the Standing Committee of which now consisted of Deng, Chen Yun, Zhao Ziyang, Hu Yaobang, Ye Jianying, and Li Xiannian. Deng had been successful in changing the power structure at the party's top levels. Presumably, the party was finally poised to carry out his agenda of achieving the four modernizations.

But during these years when Deng and his associates expended enormous energy on intense power struggles, restoration of economic order, and formulation of long-term development plans, they had almost given no consideration to the possibility that the party's organizational strength and style of work on the lower levels could pose major stumbling blocks to the fulfillment of their economic objectives. They had always assumed that the key issue was the top leadership. Once the top positions were occupied by Deng's supporters, the party's rank and file would carry out their instructions faithfully and efficiently. This assumption, as will be seen, turned out to be completely erroneous.

2

The Party's Emergent Crises

ALTHOUGH the party's discipline suffered a serious blow during the early years of the Cultural Revolution, it was basically re-tightened during the early 1970s. But the death of Mao and the overthrow of the Gang of Four quickly brought a marked deterioration of discipline among party members that persisted in spite of Deng Xiaoping's regaining of control over the central party apparatus. While this deterioration affected many aspects of party life, it was most forcefully manifested in three areas: the breakdown of organizational life, the corrupt lifestyles of the members, and the relationships among public agencies.

Breakdown of Organizational Life

Party Meetings

Probably the best indicator of the party's ability to enforce organizational discipline was the status of its internal "organizational life," which consisted primarily of two types of meetings: "internal party life" meetings (*dangnei shenghuo*), which were held by all party organs; and "democratic life" meetings (*minzhu shenghuohui*). Traditionally, both types of meetings were held at frequent and regular intervals by all basic-level organs.[1] The party's organizational theory had always asserted that to function as a unitary whole, party members must be totally integrated into the party, their lives must revolve around the party, and they must have the same heartbeat as the party.

At these meetings, the members not only discussed routine matters of party management and recruitment, but also offered self-criticism, engaged in "heart-to-heart talks" (*tanxin*), exposed their inner thoughts, and "surrendered their hearts" (*jiaoxin*) to their comrades.[2] Party rules further stipulated that both leading members and regular members were equally obligated to attend these meetings and to take them seriously.

Starting in the late 1970s, however, party organizational life became increasingly lax or even nonexistent in many areas. Leading cadres employed a variety of excuses to hold either fewer meetings or none at all. Some cadres regarded attendance at these meetings as an obligation only for ordinary members, claiming leading members should be exempted from attendance. Many also justified their nonattendance on the grounds of being too busy with their other official duties.[3]

When meetings were held at all, their quality also deteriorated. The attendees showed little enthusiasm, declined to engage in frank discussion, and avoided making criticism or self-criticism. Tough ideological or political issues were seldom raised. The meetings often degenerated into idle chitchat or squabbles over petty issues. This atmosphere of casualness and boredom was in sharp contrast to the attentiveness and tension that had marked such meetings in earlier eras. The purpose of the meetings had been defeated, and no one attempted to use them to improve themselves or their comrades.[4]

Closely related to the decline of the quality of meetings was the nonperformance of some of the party's most routine organizational responsibilities. Many party organs could not, or would not bother to, collect dues from members for months or years.[5] Political education programs also fell by the wayside, and some basic-level units suspended political study programs entirely.[6]

Job Assignments

During the Maoist era, the party commanded absolute obedience from its members in the area of job assignment and transfer. Individuals never questioned the wisdom of such personnel decisions, because a good Communist was supposed to carry out the party's instructions unflinchingly. By the late 1970s, the situation had changed substantially. Many party members or even leading cadres either openly haggled with their superiors about job assignments or transfers, or employed delaying tactics to show their displeasure. Now, party members often defied orders of job transfer on the grounds that their spouses and children objected to them. It became difficult to transfer party members from the cities to the countryside, or to jobs that entailed a heavy workload or difficult living conditions. It was not unusual for cadres to opt simply to stay home for long stretches of time rather than accept an undesirable job assignment.[7] Likewise, many party organs also disobeyed their superiors' orders to transfer members in or out of their units unless they could benefit from such transfers. Some units even demanded cash payments or other favors before allowing such transfers to take place.[8]

Party Secrets

The CCP had long insisted on maintaining a clear distinction between party and nonparty forums. While a party member presumably had the right to register his criticism or opposition to the particular directives, policies, or resolutions within the party's organizational confines so long as he or she observed the rules of "democratic centralism," members never aired their personal views about these matters to a nonparty audience. The CCP's legitimacy as the vanguard of revolution critically depended on its ability to maintain an aura of infallibility and an image of unity of purpose among its members. All party members had the obligation to serve as propagandists to win the masses' acceptance and support of the party's programs. It would be intolerable for party members to spread dissension among the masses, or to cast doubt on the wisdom of the party's programs.

Until the Cultural Revolution, the party always took pride in its members' ability to keep party secrets. The CCP had created a highly stratified, multitiered system of access to information in which the ordinary people were invariably the last ones to learn about any events or policies of importance. But even within the party, there was a rigid information distribution system with differentiated access granted according to rank and status.

In addition, the CCP's concept about "secrecy" was so broadly and loosely defined as to encompass nearly everything that had not been released through the mass media. Party members jealously guarded their privileged access to information, because such access confirmed their status as a political elite in the eyes of the masses. The party's guidelines to its members were "not to talk about matters you should not talk about, not to ask questions you should not ask, and not to read documents you should not read."[9]

The fastidious observance of this rule by party members cast a veil of mystery over the party's internal operations and made the party less vulnerable to popular criticism as long as the general public remained poorly informed. In the long years of waging internal and external struggles against a multitude of presumed and real enemies, the party's preoccupation with secrecy was a crucial factor in the party's survival and revolutionary success.

But in the late 1970s, this long tradition was violated on a massive scale. Not only did ordinary party members talk glibly about the proceedings of party meetings and reveal the contents of the latest party internal communication, but even leading cadres became careless with sensitive party documents and information, allowing them to fall into the hands of family members and friends who in turn circulated them among the general public. High-level cadres and their family circles became the major sources of the so-called side channel information (xiaodao xiaoxi), which floated rampantly in the society and became a constant source of embarrassment to the party.[10]

Several factors contributed to this laxity in keeping party secrets. One factor was the bad precedent set during the Cultural Revolution when factional leaders deliberately leaked sensitive information to their favorite Red Guard faction as ammunition to denounce their political rivals. Another factor was the superiority complex afflicting some leaders who wanted to show off their inside knowledge. A third factor was that many rehabilitated leaders who had become old and infirm had to conduct official business from their family residences, which enabled family members to gain illegal access to their official information. But the most important factor of all was that inside information about the party had gained a value that it never had before. Previously, timely inside information might give the possessors psychological gratification or some political advantage, but now it could give them enormous economic benefits and career opportunities. This explains why the family members and close friends of influential party leaders sought out party secrets so much more aggressively than before.[11] After 1979, party members no longer respected party secrets or the "distinction between party and nonparty."[12]

The wanton spread of party secrets inevitably damaged the party's public image. As the average Chinese citizens listened to the lurid details of party scandals and witnessed party members' brazen attacks against their leaders and policies, the awe with which the masses used to regard the party eventually gave way to contempt and cynicism. In time, the masses acquired the mentality of giving more credence to rumors generated by sources inside the party than the official media. Even the party press acknowledged that never before had the Chinese people been treated to such an intimate look into the party's plans, controversies, and programs on such a grand scale.[13]

Personal Lifestyles

A second area where the deterioration of party discipline was most visible was the abuse of privileges by party leaders and rank and file on a gigantic scale. The Communist Party had always been a "new class" of privileged people in China, but only a small number of high national and provincial leaders were afforded the opportunity to indulge in a materialistic high life prior to the Cultural Revolution. Living behind high walls in government compounds, totally segregated from the public, these civilian and military leaders were able to maintain a veil of mystery without offending the public's sensibilities. Middle- and lower-level party and government cadres, on the other hand, were afforded only a modest range of privileges, which, while publicly known, were quietly enjoyed so that they did not arouse the ire of the masses.

The exposés of the Cultural Revolution years shocked both the Chinese people and the party's rank and file when they learned about the magnitude of the abuse of privileges in high places. These revelations painted a picture of top leaders living a life of opulence, decadence, and frivolity. Even though some of these revelations were undoubtedly exaggerated to smear political opponents, there was enough truth in them to create widespread resentment and cynicism. After the downfall of the Gang of Four, a striking development was the naked pursuit of the good life by party cadres and members on nearly all levels. Starting in the late 1970s, there were ample signs to indicate that party cadres and members had become progressively more corrupt.

Private Residences

In spite of the popular Western belief during the Maoist era that life in China was egalitarian, it actually had always been highly stratified. Housing assignments were made on the basis of position and seniority. While ordinary citizens sometimes had to make do with one room for the entire family, high officials had independent residences, sometimes with courtyards, and auxiliary buildings for government-issued nurses, governesses, cooks, servants, and guards. Space and segregation from the masses were the major status symbols in the Maoist years.

In the late 1970s, many leaders were no longer content with space but pursued additional comfort and luxury. Rumors abounded in the capital that leaders tried to outdo each other by using public funds to renovate their houses, equipping them with expensive imported furniture and other modern amenities.[14] This style was soon imitated by lesser cadres and members throughout the whole country. Provincial- and local-level cadres began to seize farmland in choice locations to erect their own minimansions with public funds, construction materials, and work crews. Like their superiors, they too took pride in "home modernization," acquiring Western furniture and artsy decor.[15] This trend became widespread in the countryside and gravely interfered with the party's new economic policy, which was to encourage the peasants to maximize the utilization of land for productive purposes. The local potentates' seizure of land not only removed a considerable amount of land from production, but set examples of a lifestyle of conspicuous consumption that could not fail to have adverse impact on the villages.

Expensive Travel

In Maoist China, the major modes of transportation for most people were either bus or bicycle. But the late 1970s ushered in a mentality among influential people that these were undignified ways to get around. Many public agencies spent large sums to buy automobiles for leaders and their family members.[16] In the big cities, the number of imported motorcycles registered to private individuals increased noticeably. Since motorcycles were not available in the market, the owners could only have been influential people who used illegal means to obtain these vehicles.[17]

Leading cadres also developed a partiality for extensive travel. They seized the slightest excuse to get out of town to "investigate local conditions," to be "close to the masses," to "borrow the experience from other advanced models," or to attend meetings. When the leaders arrived, they would visit a few showcases, but they would spend most of their time for personal pleasure.[18]

Leaders typically traveled in style.[19] The lower-level cadres were notified in advance of the leading cadres' visit and were expected to make elaborate preparations to receive them. Many leaders took a large retinue in tow to show off their importance, sometimes even banning traffic from the streets as they passed through to give a regal aura to the visit. The local subordinate units were invariably saddled with the bill. Localities with attractive tourist spots were bombarded by these "visits" so frequently that they were forced to seek financial relief from above to pay for them.

As China broadened its contact with the outside world, the abuse of privileges by cadres extended beyond the national boundaries. Numerous delegations were sent abroad in the name of promoting friendship, learning Western technology, or making commercial contacts. Often, the majority of delegation members were not experts in related fields but high-ranking cadres and their relatives. Once they arrived in a foreign country, they showed little interest in performing their official mission, but rushed to sight-seeing tours or on shopping sprees, frequently making the foreign hosts pick up the tabs of their purchases.[20]

Excessive Feasting and Gifts

Party cadres and members acquired a new addiction for good foods and exotic gifts in the late 1970s as well,[21] generating social expectations that put tremendous pressures on the lower-level cadres to conform. Leading cadres on inspection tours had to be entertained lavishly. Feasting was considered the indispensable highlight of all official functions. Sometimes the excessive eating and drinking reached pathological proportions.[22]

No visit could be happily concluded without the obligatory presentation of "souvenirs," which were often not symbolic gifts of local craft, but articles of practical use and substantial monetary cost paid for with public funds.[23] Subordinates were expected to present gifts to their superior for the latter's birthday, wedding, funeral, childbirth, housewarming, and countless other occasions.

After a hiatus of nearly three decades, many social customs returned to China with a vengeance. The cost of social obligations became substantial, and disproportionate to people's income. To satisfy their own acquisitive instincts and to meet their social obligations, the lower-level cadres' only alternative was to engage in graft.[24] The upshot was that palm greasing became a standard practice in China whenever a citizen needed something from the bureaucracy. Services that used to be rendered by the government or the party free of charge now carried price tags. People in powerful positions peddled their official powers as special favors to those who could afford to pay. This new social trend greatly increased the value of "human connections" (*guanxi*) and "back door channels" (*houmen*) and changed the relations between the government/party and the people in an insidious way.[25]

Transactions between Public Agencies

It would be an error to think of *guanxi* as a necessary evil only when average citizens had to deal with the party or the bureaucracy. In fact, human connections were equally indispensable in transactions between public agencies. By the late 1970s, many cadres had totally erased the fundamental distinction between public and private property and showed no hesitation to exploit their public positions to advance their personal interest. Whereas a private citizen's means of fostering connections usually involved cash, cigarettes, liquor, and other gifts of modest value, when one public agency sought favors from another, the price tag could range from large sums of money, equipment, and machinery to highly imaginative forms of transfer of resources.[26] Thus, for example, leading cadres frequently extracted substantial tribute from production units under their jurisdiction, under the pretext of "testing samples." Many cadres would shower leaders of other units with lavish gifts and received gifts in return under the pretext of cultivating "professional ties" (guanxihu). Frequently, influential people could obtain commodities and services at prices far below the official price or for nothing at all.[27]

To carry out their normal operations, many public agencies were compelled to acquire and hoard commodities outside their own lines of production in order to satisfy the demands of other units on whose goodwill they must depend. If such demands were not promptly met, retaliation might swiftly follow.[28]

In conjunction with the decentralization of economic decision-making power, plant managers and salespersons also became vulnerable to the pressure from their guanxihu. They had to pay bribes not only to suppliers in the free market to obtain materials, but even to other state enterprises for supplies that had been earmarked to them under the state's central planning. Even small-scale county-level factories sometimes had to spend tens of thousands of dollars on gifts, banquets, and other forms of entertainment to keep their guanxihu happy.[29] Without these lubricants, it would be hard or even impossible to carry out official transactions between enterprises or governmental and party organs. Through tens of millions of such loopholes, big and small, huge sums of public funds were siphoned into the pockets of party and government cadres.

As time went on, misconduct by cadres and party members increased in magnitude and extended into new territories. The more adventurous cadres were no longer content with petty larceny, or eating and drinking, but went after much larger loot. Cases of illegal acts exceeding a million yuan became more common.[30] Many public agencies engaged in massive pilfering of public properties with the connivance of their leading cadres. Networks of economic criminals sprang into existence to engage in illegal activities in collusion with a substantial number of party members and cadres.[31]

An increasing number of party members regarded themselves as standing above the party's rules and regulations. There emerged a mentality among party members who had seniority, meritorious revolutionary records, or high positions, that they constituted a "special category of party members." This mentality led them to contend that the party's repeated injunctions against misconduct were intended merely for ordinary members, and definitely not for them.[32] By the early 1980s, the discipline of party members had reached a low point. This not only seriously undermined the efficiency of public institutions but eroded the people's trust in the integrity of the state and party. The damage to the political legitimacy of the CCP was enormous, and possibly irreparable.[33]

Public Discontent and the Crisis of Confidence

That the misconduct by party members would provoke public discontent was only to be expected. By the late 1970s, a crisis of confidence of major proportions had pervaded Chinese society. Of course, many other factors had contributed to the onset of the crisis. The painful memories of the Cultural Revolution and the history of oppression by the party had depleted the people's reservoir of goodwill and trust. The policy of opening up to the outside world brought the first shocking realization of how backward China was, not only in comparison with Western countries, but even with neighboring East Asian countries. Whereas previously many Chinese had genuinely believed in their nation's superiority and often used it to justify the human sacrifices that the system entailed, the incontrovertible evidence of China's backwardness brought a new dimension to their assessment, for they now concluded that the Communist system was highly incompetent as well.

But probably the most important reason that provoked people into profound doubts about the party, socialism, and Marxism was their daily witnessing of the worsening discipline displayed by party cadres and members. The latter's reckless materialistic acquisitiveness and abuse of privileges finally drove the people to despair, causing them to lose hope for the future under the present system.

Gauging public sentiments in a totalitarian society has always been a difficult task since the media are tightly controlled. It is even more difficult to obtain quantifiable data on public opinion in such a society, and China is no exception in this respect. The decline of the prestige of the Chinese Communist Party was an undeniable development, however, and could be corroborated by at least two other phenomena. One was the vehemence of the dissident movement; the other was the popularity of protest literature.

The Democratic Movement

The most forceful indication of the crisis of confidence was the attempt by the radical urban youths to make political statements through big-character posters and mimeographed journals. The political threat they posed to the Deng leadership has already been discussed; here the concern is with their ideological challenges. While the youths were by no means a homogeneous group, their political views raised several explosive issues.

First, their position on the Cultural Revolution and the Maoist legacy went far beyond the limits of tolerance set by the Deng leadership at that time. Some posters denounced Mao as a dictator and the Cultural Revolution as a fascist reign, and advocated an unequivocal repudiation of both the Cultural Revolution and Mao's Thought, as well as a wholesale rehabilitation of all victims of previous political struggles.[34]

Second, they made stinging criticisms against current leaders and their policies. Some writings challenged the legality of Hua Guofeng's position and condemned the terrible deeds committed by other incumbent leaders. Wei Jingsheng, the best known of this group, even rebuked Deng Xiaoping for having betrayed his democratic pledges and for having become a dictator. He called upon the people to protect their own political rights against the encroachment by the party and the state.[35] In Shanghai, the "Democratic Discussion Group" (Minzhu Taolunhui) vowed to "resolutely and thoroughly criticize the CCP" and said that they wanted to finish off the "capitalist roaders" that the Gang of Four had failed to eliminate.[36]

Third, their writings were a frontal attack against some of the most sacred doctrines of the party and the state. Many writings expressed doubts about the validity of Marxism, the superiority of socialism, or the trustworthiness of the Communist regime, and rejected the principle of leadership by the party. Even those who conceded the possible necessity of leadership by the CCP during the revolutionary era nonetheless asserted that the party had become quite dispensable during the era of socialist construction. Others were less generous and pointed to the numerous past mistakes made by the party, suggesting that it had forfeited its right to rule.[37] The "Thaw Society" (Jiedongshe) issued a declaration that openly opposed proletarian dictatorship on the grounds that it divided the human race. [38]

Fourth, some writings expressed unreserved admiration for the capitalist societies. Many were attracted to Western-style democracy and believed the multiparty system in the capitalist countries was a better system. They regarded capitalism as superior to socialism. Therefore, China's problem was not four modernizations but social reform, that is, to replace socialism with capitalism.[39]

Others demanded the guarantee of civil rights, a free press, freedom of assembly and association, and even free competition between Communists and Nationalists through a nationwide electoral process.[40] Many were particularly impressed by the human rights policy of the United States and drafted a "Human Rights Declaration" for China. Some even appealed to President Carter to monitor the abuse of human rights in China.[41]

In the spring of 1979, democracy became a hot topic in Beijing and other major cities and threatened to become a major national movement. The radical youths' antagonistic attitudes toward the entire socialist system were marked by a boldness unprecedented in the history of the PRC. Although the democratic movement was suppressed in 1979, its legacy was not easily eliminated. Starting in October 1980, students on many college campuses defied the wishes of their party secretaries and began their own campaigns for elections to student bodies or to the basic levels of the People's Congress. Student publications propagating democratic ideas also appeared in large numbers.[42] The magnitude of the movement revealed the number of discontented young urban educated people. Although the college students were not politicized soon enough to play an active role in the spring 1979 unrest, they were heavily influenced by the iconoclastic attitudes of their radical precursors toward their own society and system, and they became one of the most disaffected subgroups of the Chinese population.

Protest Literature

The year 1977 marked the debut of a new genre of literature that subsequently acquired the name of "scar-tissue literature," or "literature of the wounded" (*shangheng wenxue*). The writers adopted the safe strategy of recounting the pains and suffering endured by good and honest people or by loyal party members in previous years under Communist rule. The typical story line resembled a morality play in which the bad people were able to torment the good people for a while but eventually met their own demise, due, of course, to the correctness of the party's policy and the wisdom of its leaders. The difference between the writings of this genre and literary works of previous eras was that the bad people were not landlords, capitalists, or Nationalist spies, but party members or even leaders who had turned into political conspirators or followers of the Gang of Four. Scar-tissue literature marked the first time since Liberation that writers wrote about the dark side of life under socialism and showed that flesh-and-blood Communists actually committed hideous deeds.

By early 1979, many writers began to go beyond the blood-and-tears accounts of past political injustices to a more critical and penetrating examination of prevailing social and political ills. This approach led them to confront the most sensitive aspects of the socialist system, and the issue of the proper interpretation of the party's history. Not surprisingly, the major works of this time all accentuated the sharp contradictions between socialist ideals and rhetoric, on the one hand, and social realities, on the other.[43]

Many writers in this group, which was also called the school of "new socialist realism," were active in literary circles in the 1950s until they were branded as rightists in subsequent political campaigns. Their literary skills were much more sophisticated than those of the writers of the scar-tissue pieces.[44] The objects of their criticisms were no longer the alleged antiparty conspirators or opportunists of the Cultural Revolution variety, but the party's stalwarts.

A common feature of many works was their focus on the misconduct of cadres and leaders who were recently rehabilitated from disgrace and returned to power. The unsavory characters now included old revolutionaries, national and local leaders, senior cadres, and average party members. Several famous literary works even used military leaders of the PLA as their negative characters.[45] These were bold moves, because the PLA had never been depicted in Chinese literary works in anything but the most glowing and laudatory terms. But the stories of new realism dared to expose the leading figures of the PLA as self-serving, greedy, lustful, and downright criminal.

In the new realistic works, the party's negative sides were laid bare and old taboos about writing were discarded. The stories were unsparing in their treatment of certain inherent aspects of the socialist society and system itself. They focused their attention on the numerous manifestations of cadres' abuse of privileges and bureaucratism. They vividly depicted their corruption, incompetence, and decadence, especially when they occurred on the high levels. They highlighted the sharp contrast between two classes in the socialist society, a class of corrupt cadres and party members who shamelessly and ruthlessly exploited their power and positions for self-aggrandizement, and another class of common people (intellectuals, workers, and farmers) who led simple, honest, spartan, painful, and oppressed lives.

These works implied that the lifestyles and personal conduct of certain party figures were so repugnant that they probably deserved to be smashed during the Cultural Revolution and should never have been rehabilitated. These works broadly hinted that such behavior occurred not in isolated cases but was reflective of the behavior of a sizable number of people in the party. Unlike the scar-tissue variety, the works of the new socialist realism declined to go along with the party's attempt to place the blame for the deterioration of the members' discipline on the Cultural Revolution and the Gang of Four, or its attempt to perpetuate the myth that the party was in good shape with a great tradition.[46] By accentuating the social contradictions between the rulers and ruled, these works left no doubt in the readers' minds that the real cause of mass discontent was the conduct of those in power, mostly in the Communist Party.[47]

Although each of the above groups employed its own medium, they both reacted strongly against the misconduct of party members and raised doubts about the fitness of the party to rule. Each phenomenon attracted a different kind of follower. The Democracy Wall primarily attracted youths who had been educated during the Cultural Revolution and who had become totally disillusioned with the system. While many people were persuaded by the soundness of some of their viewpoints, their posture was so explicitly political and so openly antiparty that they had no time to grow into a genuine national force before they were suppressed.

On the other hand, the scar-tissue and new socialist realism writers became instantly popular precisely because their political commentaries were presented as artistic experiments. They were neither antiparty nor antiregime; many of them were actually party members who supported the current regime. But they wanted to use art to reflect reality, and their literary products (poems, plays, and short stories) succeeded in evoking resonance among the country's very large literate masses in all age groups. The popularity of these two groups served as good gauges of the public's mood. Each group in its own way helped to spread gloom and despair, and deepened the crisis of confidence.

In the face of the mounting crisis, the party's initial reaction was twofold. First, the party reaffirmed its right to rule, coupled with the intensification of ideological work. In March 1979, Deng enunciated his "four cardinal principles" (socialism, leadership by the CCP, Marxism, and proletariat dictatorship), and insisted that only "socialist democracy" was permissible. He left no doubt that he intended to uphold the ideological supremacy of Communism as well as the CCP's domination over the state and society.[48]

The party's stock answer to criticisms was that there would have been no "new China" had it not been for the leadership of the Chinese Communist Party. The party insisted that there was no ground for people to cast aspersions upon the party just because the party had committed mistakes, because it was always the party itself that admitted the mistakes, corrected them, and revitalized itself. What both party members and the general population needed was more ideological indoctrination so they could learn to behave well, to trust the party, and to restore their faith in socialism.

Second, the party also counterattacked its detractors in the hope of stamping out the heretic thoughts. The party press denounced human rights as a hypocritical bourgeois concept and accused the human rights advocates in China as traitors who had no self-respect when they pleaded to the imperialists for their attention.[49]

After suppressing the Democracy Wall in 1979, the party expended more energy in 1981 to suppress the new underground journals and illegal publishers that had come into existence on the college campuses. The party tried to intimidate the youthful activists by calling them "dissidents" (yiji fenzi), and threatened to use stern laws to deal with them.[50]

In early 1981, some PLA leaders had become extremely agitated by the tendency of artists and writers to focus their criticisms on the abuse of privileges in the military and decided to launch an attack against the cultural and ideological developments since 1978.[51] In April 1981, the military press began to denounce Bai Hua's "Kulian" (Bitter love) as the representative of an erroneous tendency that must be resolutely opposed. This was promptly echoed in the party press.

Meanwhile, the party also began a campaign to oppose "liberalization" in the literary world, which quickly led to the imposition of tighter censorship over publications and the banning of plays and motion pictures that contained politically harmful materials. The political atmosphere became tense again, and threats were made to clamp down on uncooperative intellectuals.

To counter these criticisms, to rebuild its legitimacy, and to win back the admiration of the people, the party also launched a succession of campaigns to rekindle "socialist morality."[52] But the crisis of confidence had already become a pervasive phenomenon whose existence even the official press could not deny.

At first, however, the party line still sought to blame the people's loss of confidence entirely on Lin Biao and the Gang of Four for having twisted the meaning of socialism, and asserted that there should be no further basis for a crisis of confidence after the downfall of the Gang.[53]

But by late 1980, *Hongqi* finally acknowledged that the party's reputation had suffered a continuing decline. While maintaining that the party's policies and leadership were both basically sound, it conceded that some problems of poor discipline existed, and it suggested that the party must first improve its own leadership style before it could effectively exercise leadership over the country.[54] The process whereby the party became aware of its problems of poor discipline, defined the nature of the problem, and attempted to solve them is the subject of the next section.

Attempts to Correct Poor Discipline before 1983

Initial Analysis of Poor Discipline, 1978–79

Disciplinary problems of party members began to emerge immediately after the death of Mao, and discipline continued to deteriorate as the top leaders were locked in an intense power struggle. Neither Hua Guofeng, Deng Xiaoping, nor their associates had the time or energy to grapple with the disciplinary problems. For instance, at a Central Work Conference (March 13, 1977), Chen Yun argued that the "two important issues confronting the party after smashing the Gang of Four" were to redefine the public demonstration at Tiananmen in April 1976 as a positive movement of the masses and to permit Deng Xiaoping to resume his political career at the party center. He took the optimistic position that the difficulties encountered by the party at this time were "temporary" in nature, and that the party would have a bright future and its problems overcome "if our entire party could unify around the party's center, engage in collective consultation, and achieve unity of will."[55] In other words, at this point, Chen did not view the party as in any kind of serious crisis, but thought that there were some internal divisions that could be overcome by resorting to old methods of reestablishing unity within the party under the national leadership. Even after Deng's rehabilitation in 1977, his group was preoccupied with the need to lay ideological and political foundations to justify their return to power, to build coalitions, to chip away at Hua's power base, and to prevent the resurgence of the supporters of the Gang of Four and their leftist lines.[56] The discipline of party members was a low priority item on their busy agenda.

The neglect of discipline can be seen in the absence of any criticism of poor discipline in the communiqué of the Third Plenum of the party's Eleventh Congress in late December 1978, the first major document drafted by the Deng forces upon their return to power.[57] Likewise, Deng's personal speeches of 1978 also hardly addressed the deterioration of party discipline.

Although the Third Plenum created a Central Discipline Inspection Committee (Chongyang Jili Jiancha Weiyuanhui) and appointed Chen Yun as its first secretary, its chief function was not to rectify the "personal misconduct" of the party members. Instead, the committee's basic mission was to restore the rules of good "organizational conduct" to strengthen the party, which meant the restoration of the party's rules of democratic centralism to make it impossible for future party leaders to impose personal dictatorships on their subordinates in the fashion of Mao or the Gang of Four.[58]

Chen Yun cited the history of the Bolshevik Party in the Soviet Union to show that the danger of usurpation of power by ambitious people like Khrushchev and Brehznev was greatest when the party's internal life became abnormal and its organizational discipline lax.[59] In contrast, he pointed to the CCP's success in the 1942–44 party rectification in Yan'an to illustrate that when the party's top leaders practiced democratic centralism and set a good example for the rest of the party, then party life would be healthy. In Chen Yun's view, good "organizational conduct" was the most effective way to achieve party solidarity, to prevent the mistakes of the Cultural Revolution, and to enable the party to accomplish socialist construction objectives. Therefore, he concluded, the ability to re-create the norms of democratic centralism within the party "was the most important issue of the entire party," and only the achievement of this goal could assure party stability and solidarity.[60]

This view was more frankly stated by Hu Yaobang when he said (in July 1979) that the foremost mission of the committee was to promote and protect the party's new line, programs, and policies.[61] General Huang Kecheng, a ranking member of the committee, also asserted that only when the party strengthened its organizational work could it guard itself against the attempt by the leftist remnants of the Cultural Revolution to seize power.[62]

These statements made it clear that when party leaders looked at the problems of party discipline at this time, they were thinking primarily in terms of how best to achieve unity and solidarity within the party. Their prescription was to admonish leaders to practice democratic centralism to set good examples for their subordinates. Once the whole party achieved unity, it would be capable of carrying out its political and economic missions.

But what were the causes of poor discipline? The leaders also subscribed to a simplistic explanation that placed the blame exclusively on Lin Biao and the Gang of Four. According to this analysis, it was Lin and the Gang who set the bad examples of abusing privileges and disregarding organizational norms. They poisoned people's minds with such erroneous notions as "when one has power, one has everything," or "use your power in hand to its fullest extent while it lasts or it may slip away."[63] They resorted to factional strife to split the party and seize power. Finally, they even totally suspended the party's disciplinary system for ten years and denounced disciplinary organs as "black outposts" and "trash-cans."[64]

Since the responsibility for the party's current poor discipline was all attributed to either Lin or the Gang of Four, it followed that, to restore discipline, it was only necessary to repudiate the culprits, denounce their erroneous ideas and practices, and revive the party's good tradition. There was no need to search for the causes of poor discipline elsewhere.

Consequently, after its creation, the Central Discipline Inspection Committee's primary functions were to guard the party against the leftists' attempt to seize power, to prevent conduct that might harm the party's organization (as the Gang of Four did), and to undo the harm to the party inflicted by the Gang and their followers. A centerpiece of the Committee's operation was the rehabilitation of people who had been unjustly hurt by the Gang, because these people would provide the best defense against the Gang's revival. In reality, the committee soon became preoccupied with processing the huge backlog of cases of political persecution by Gang members, handling visitors and letters of complaints against injustice, and establishing disciplinary committees on lower levels to carry out the same tasks. The committee optimistically stated that after these steps were taken, the party's discipline problems would virtually disappear.[65] The personal misconduct of the ordinary members in the current context was not treated as a serious problem.

But even in 1979, Deng did express appreciation of the utilitarian value of good discipline and regarded the latter to be a functional prerequisite for economic development. He believed that the task of socialist economic construction must depend on the participation of the general populace who must be inspired by the good conduct by party members, especially party leaders.[66] This view was faithfully echoed in the *People's Daily*, which contended that the problems of poor discipline by some party members must be solved because China had entered into a new historic era of concentrating the entire country's work on achieving modernization, and because "a good party style is the fundamental condition of the party's leadership of the people to achieve the four modernizations."[67] No leader at this early stage, however, showed any anxiety that discipline could also affect the party's survival or the people's continued trust in the party.

Combating Poor Discipline, 1980

What steps did the party take to improve discipline? Not surprisingly, the leaders believed that conventional means from the party's own repertoire would suffice to solve the problems. A substantial number of articles and speeches made by top leaders many years ago were reprinted in the press to suggest the close parallel between contemporary problems and those of the past, and by implication, the current validity of old solutions as well.[68]

Probably the most persistent effort to draw parallels was to cite the *zhengfeng* (rectification) campaign of 1942–44 as a model for inspiration and guidance.

According to the party's current interpretation, the successful *zhengfeng* in Yan'an was brought about by several key factors, including a correct theoretical guidance, a correct assessment of the nature and extent of deviations within the party, the identification of the major contradiction, and the proper methods of rectification. If these same factors could be employed, then the poor discipline in the late 1970s could also be corrected.

There was much appeal in this analysis because it greatly simplified the leaders' task in solving the problem. Since the correct theoretical line was already set by the Third Plenum, and since the main deviation in the party was already identified as "leftist thoughts" whose manifestations were bureaucratism, abuse of privilege, feudalism, and factionalism,[69] the party only needed to lay down a set of explicit guidelines on permissible and impermissible conduct for members and leading cadres.[70] Once the members understood the standards of good conduct, they would live up to them.

This reasoning led the leaders to take three steps. First, and most immediately, they revived a number of old party rules that were suspended during the Cultural Revolution. Among the major rules reactivated in 1979 were the "Provisional Regulations on Safeguarding National Secrets," "Standards of Leading Cadres' Living and Treatment," and "Regulations Concerning the Style of Living and Treatment of High-Level Cadres."[71]

Second, they drafted a few new rules to fill the gaps or to fit the new circumstances. The most comprehensive one was the "Guiding Principles for Inner-Party Political Life,"adopted in February 1980.[72] Third, they rebuilt the network of disciplinary organs on provincial and lower levels to wipe clean the slate of past injustices suffered by party members, and to enforce the new rules.[73]

But these measures soon proved ineffective in stemming the decline of party discipline. When confronted with mounting reports of embezzlement and extravagant lifestyles of the cadres, the Central Discipline Inspection Committee could do little more than issue and reissue "instructions" or "injunctions" against such conduct.[74] Even in egregious cases, the central party only dragged out a few local-level cadres to punish as "negative examples," while higher-level perpetrators were almost invariably shielded from criticism or punishment.[75]

Yet even such mild forms of criticism and punitive measures were vehemently opposed by many in the party at this time. They still found it difficult to accept the need for strong party actions against poor discipline. Some suggested that the party should not discuss its disciplinary matters in the public media lest the party's prestige be damaged by these revelations.[76] In spite of the fact that the top leadership had already specifically blamed the Gang of Four as the source of breakdown of discipline, many cadres and leaders still argued that even Gang remnants should be treated leniently. They invoked the party's tradition of regarding cadres as "the most valuable assets of the party" to argue that even Gang remnants should neither be expelled from the party nor brought to trial before the courts of law. Instead, all Gang members, even including the diehard followers, should be given a chance to repent and undergo reform.[77] In particular, these views were strongly held by important elements in the PLA who advised the party against being too aggressive in rectifying its members.

By early 1980, even Deng had gained a better appreciation of the complexity of the party's disciplinary problems as his effort to cleanse the party of the Gang's ideological and organizational influence and to implement his own policies had both run into much resistance from below. Deng now admitted that the party must manage its own affairs competently in order to restore its prestige. He also acknowledged that the cause of poor discipline was not just a few Gang remnants but the party's membership (then at thirty-five million), half of which had joined the party under the Gang's domination and were poorly qualified to be party members. While recommending both education and legislation as remedies, he also asserted the necessity of dealing sternly with misbehaving members in the future.[78]

In the spring of 1980, party leaders were jolted by the discovery that poor discipline existed not only on personal levels, but sometimes on organizational levels. The Ma Shukui incident, which received wide publicity in April 1980, clearly showed that many local party organs had become "little kingdoms" under the domination of local cadres who perpetrated their criminal deeds with the aid of bureaucratic power bases and resources. They had erected elaborate collective defense arrangements with other disgruntled remnants of the Gang and did not hesitate to defy the party whenever their selfish interests were threatened.[79]

Incidents of this kind were most disturbing because they showed that even though Deng Xiaoping and his supporters had wrested power from the people with known connections to the Gang at the top, they had by no means gained firm control over the party apparatus on all levels. The transition of power at the top did not stamp out the factions as such, but only forced the latter to assume lower profiles. These remnants of the Cultural Revolution era were still entrenched in numerous local "little kingdoms" but had switched their tactics from open defiance to subterranean activities and made it infinitely more difficult for the party center to expose and deal with them. The seizure of power by the Deng group only forced these remnants into tighter pacts to ensure their own survival. While they might not dare to espouse the Gang's ideology, they retained much latitude in deciding whether to enforce or disobey the party's policies to suit their own needs.[80]

Such manifestations of the "little kingdoms" and their factional activities sharply contradicted the benign view of the top leaders concerning the reliability and competence of the party to reform itself with existing organizational means or channels. Such cases changed the leaders' perspectives regarding poor discipline in two ways. First, their previous diagnosis that poor discipline was caused by the erroneous ideology and personal examples of the Gang of Four was obviously wrong, because the elimination of the Gang leaders did not bring about a return of good discipline. They now realized that in addition to the leftist ideology, the poor quality of the party members themselves and the weakness of the party organization also contributed to poor discipline. Therefore, solutions must aim at both changing individual attitudes and conduct and strengthening the party's organizational sinew.

Second, they previously wanted to eliminate poor discipline because it was dysfunctional to economic modernization. Now they realized poor discipline could pose a serious danger to the party's survival. In August 1980, Deng made the famous speech to the Politburo entitled "Institutional Reforms of Party and State Leadership" in which he emphasized the need to make major institutional reform of the party and state leadership to increase their ability to implement the modernization programs. He also reiterated his warning about the danger of the remnants of Lin Biao and the Gang.[81] In November 1980, Chen Yun went a step further and ominously declared that the "discipline problems of the ruling party (CCP) can affect the party's life and death."[82]

The Gradual Evolution of a Rectification Campaign, 1981–82

The new assessment of the gravity and complexity of the party's disciplinary problems gradually shook the leaders out of their complacency and convinced them that more drastic measures might be necessary.

In March 1981, in his talks with leaders of the Political Department of the PLA, Deng admitted that many erroneous ideological and political tendencies still existed in the party, the military, and society. Although he demanded that political and ideological work be intensified to cope with the problems, he indicated for the first time that "at an appropriate time in the future, we may have to conduct a zhengfeng. Without a zhengfeng, the problems probably won't be solved."[83] Although no timetable was given, Deng was already reconciled to the need for a campaign, albeit a limited one, to correct the party's style of work. Meanwhile, many other leaders echoed Chen Yun's dire warning about the party's survival being threatened by poor discipline.

1982: The Year of Action

At the beginning of 1982, the party announced that it would concentrate on two policies: smashing economic crimes and streamlining the bureaucracy. Although the specific purpose of the former was to increase economic efficiency and the latter to cut bureaucratic fat, both were closely related to the fundamental problem of discipline. If economic crimes were smashed, then other types of misconduct could be deterred more effectively. By the same token, if bureaucratic streamlining worked, then many bad cadres, Gang factionalists, and leftists could be eased out of their positions. If both tasks could be implemented successfully, there might not be any need for launching a formal rectification campaign. Of these two, undoubtedly the campaign to smash economic crimes would provide a direct indication of the effectiveness of the party's disciplinary measures.

By the beginning of 1982, the widening scope of economic crimes persuaded the leaders that the party's organizational framework was itself defective. As the misconduct no longer involved just individuals but often groups of individuals interconnected by common interests, it became extremely difficult to even find out the truth about the extent of criminal deeds. Cases of misconduct now implicated a large number of people who would form a tight pact to protect one another. Very often even the local leading cadres whom the party center had designated to investigate these cases were direct participants of such deeds, or were bribed to keep their silence. Many leading cadres were reluctant to offend anybody and chose to ignore the illegal activities of their subordinates. In some instances, the whole work units engaged in illegal activities from top to bottom and then tried to justify such activities as measures to promote the collective welfare of their units.[84]

The official press publicly acknowledged that the extent of corruption, smuggling, theft of public properties, and embezzlement had become far worse in both scope and severity than similar activities even at the height of the "Three-Anti" and "Five-Anti" campaigns of 1952. For example, in just one year (1981), there were over 30,000 cases of economic irregularities in the province of Fujian alone. In 250 of these cases, the sums of money involved were more than RMB $10,000 each. As Fujian's first provincial party secretary, Xiang Nan, candidly stated, many of these cases would not have been possible without the collusion of cadres from inside the party and government.[85]

The leaders' denunciation of economic crimes increased in fervor almost from the first day of the year. On January 5, 1982, Chen Yun stated, "I suggest that we deal sternly with those who have committed serious economic crimes. Impose prison terms on several of them or even execute them. We should carry out this policy sternly and stick to it, and publicize it in the newspapers. Otherwise, we will not be able to rectify party discipline."[86] In February 1982, the leaders decided to launch a campaign specifically aimed at smashing economic criminals. Amid much fanfare, the National People's Congress promulgated a new set of regulations to deal harshly with economic crimes.[87] This was promptly followed by the promulgation of a similar set of regulations jointly by the party and the State Council. Finally, the leaders decided to deal sternly with the issue of poor discipline when their economic projects had run into serious trouble.

In April 1982, Deng indicated that the policy to smash economic criminal activities was not an isolated one. He told the Politburo that the realization of socialism must be accompanied by four guarantees: institutional reform, socialist spiritual civilization, smashing of economic crimes, and rectification of the party's style and organization.[88] It is important to note here that, except for minor modifications, these four items eventually became the main objectives of the party rectification campaign of 1983.

To implement the campaign against economic crimes, the party now vowed to employ severe punishment, including the death sentence, of the perpetrators regardless of their rank or seniority in the party. But the party sought to give the perpetrators a last chance to confess their crimes before a deadline in exchange for reduced penalty. The party also required lower-level party organs that were plagued by serious ideological, political, or organizational shortcomings to undergo reorganization, and it threatened to disband totally those organs with excessive problems. Aided by an intense propaganda barrage, the party and government obviously expected this campaign to be sufficient to arrest the decline of the party's prestige.[89] Through these measures, the party finally elevated the task of combating poor discipline to the status of a "campaign," albeit a narrowly focused one.

Failure of the Campaign to Smash Economic Crimes

It soon became obvious that the misbehaving members were not intimidated by the party's dire warnings. Nobody stepped forward to admit guilt before the announced deadline to seek leniency, and the small number of economic criminals who were "smashed" were mostly minor figures. Meanwhile, cadre corruption and misconduct continued unabated.[90] The lower-level party organs that were charged to enforce the new regulations actually subverted them. Many lower-level organs pointed out that since the focus of the campaign was to prosecute the "major cases" (da'an), the minor cases of economic irregularities should therefore be glossed over. Others argued that since the campaign's focus was on economic crimes, other types of misconduct were excluded from scrutiny. Still others regarded the campaign as being directed only against high-ranking cadres, and therefore the average misbehaving cadres should not be prosecuted. Many also declined to take actions because they predicted (correctly) that the party could not afford to allow this campaign to turn into a frenzied mass movement or to disrupt normal economic activities.[91]

In fact, the "major cases" involving higher-ranking perpetrators were even more immune from prosecution. Leading cadres often came under tremendous social pressures or material inducements to cover up the crimes of their subordinates or prevent their prosecution. If they were unable to nip the prosecution in the bud, they resorted to delaying tactics and hoped that the superior organs would simply lose interest in pursuing the cases.

Even when the higher level persisted and succeeded in establishing evidence for criminal deeds, the lower-level leading cadres could still allow the criminal to go free. Taking advantage of the CCP's long-standing policy of "severely punishing those who resisted but showing leniency to those who confessed," the lower-level leading cadres could let criminals go free on the grounds that they had voluntarily cooperated with the authorities, offered thorough confessions, and made sincere gestures of contrition, and therefore the "educational purpose" had been served. When worse came to worst and some form of punishment seemed inescapable, the culprits were ordered to pay a fine to close the case. In other words, rarely were the culprits given a prison sentence or other forms of administrative punishment.

The net effect was that the new regulations produced little in the way of deterrence. Not only was the chance of getting caught very slim, but even when caught and proven guilty, the worst that could happen to the criminal was to be forced to return his loot. This situation prompted many people to reach the perfectly rational (and cynical) conclusion that crimes paid as long as the perpetrators could commit crimes more frequently than they were caught.[92]

The deliberate obstructionism of the leading cadres on the lower levels made it extremely difficult for central party authorities to rely on existing organizational channels to enforce party discipline. Many cases of successful exposure of criminal deeds during the campaign were the result of persistent and direct intervention from the party center. In many cases, the national party actually had to send its own work teams down to the local level to take direct charge over the investigation, prosecution, and judgment of these cases in the face of countless roadblocks thrown up by the local party leaders. Yet, in the public eye, most of these cases still only punished the so-called shallow water sharks or flies, leaving people to wonder where the deep water sharks or tigers were.[93]

The Central Discipline Inspection Committee admitted subsequently that during the eighteen months following the onset of the anti–economic crime campaign, a considerable number of higher-level organizations on the provincial and municipal level and many large and medium-sized enterprises never actually conducted this campaign. They only transmitted the directives and passed the buck to the lower-level organs. But the lower-level organs also took note of their superiors' lack of interest and did little to pursue the criminals. The committee admitted that even though many more major cases of economic crimes were committed by people on the higher levels than the lower levels, the higher-level organs' leading cadres simply ignored the whole campaign.[94]

The Impact of the Campaign's Failure

The failure to smash economic crimes was by no means the only disappointment to the leaders. As stated earlier, the party's other major program for 1982–83 was bureaucratic streamlining. While this policy was conceived for a number of reasons, it was closely connected to the issue of discipline. Since the party leaders viewed poor discipline as being partially inherent in the old institutional arrangements, they believed that institutional reforms could help the party and the state to eliminate these problems. In addition, reforms could also weed out unfit and misbehaving personnel and replace them with loyal and capable new blood.[95]

But as the implementation of institutional reform went into high gear in 1982, it actually created even more serious disciplinary problems. Upon being notified that they were slated to be abolished, many agencies actually hastily created new subsidiaries to survive in different guises. When the party decided to reduce personnel at a given level, the leaders of their work units would quickly promote them to the next higher level to escape the cut. As a result, the size of the bureaucracy actually increased in many places.[96]

When the institutional reform reached the provincial and local levels, even worse cases of disruption and insubordination surfaced. Leading cadres of work units targeted to undergo institutional reform sometimes actually seized the opportunity to distribute their units' public assets to their workers illegally. When a particular unit was abolished or merged with another one, its inventory of products and cash reserves were often divided up as bonuses, its furniture taken home by the employees, and even its work spaces converted into living quarters.[97]

Such shocking exhibitions of lawlessness left no doubt that the party's disciplinary problems had indeed become a "life and death" matter. Deng and his associates were quick to see the ghost of the Gang of Four behind every case of insubordination and misconduct, and they believed that the remnants of the Gang must be stamped out by even more decisive and thorough means. It had also become clear to them that a large portion of ordinary party members had indeed become demoralized and unscrupulous and placed their personal interests above those of the party and state. Unless the party acted expeditiously, their presence could only further corrode the quality of the party, cause the already serious and pervasive crisis of confidence among the masses to deepen, and render the party totally incapable of fulfilling its modernization missions. To forestall these possibilities, a full-scale party rectification finally emerged as the only effective solution.

To be sure, the idea of a full-scale party rectification campaign to improve discipline was by no means new to Deng. He first broached the issue in 1975 but did not follow through because he had neither the power nor the time to pursue it. In 1977, he again probed the idea as a way of dealing with the remnants of the Gang of Four, but he was soon preoccupied with other, more pressing issues.[98] In 1981, Deng again indicated the possible need to conduct a *zhengfeng* at an unspecified future date. The *zhengfeng* concept implied that the rectification campaign only needed to be of a modest scale to rectify a few specific errors, mostly concerning the party's "style of work."

Although it was not officially presented as such, the campaign to smash economic crimes certainly had the key features of a *zhengfeng*. As mentioned previously, the Deng leadership had since 1978 regarded economic development as the most important component of their general line. They also gave high priority to stamping out the influence of the Gang's followers from the party and the state to guarantee the universal acceptance of their general line. The rampant economic crimes directly threatened their economic programs, and the continued presence of suspected Gang followers was perceived as a time bomb within the party.

The dismal failure to reduce economic crimes, compounded by the exhibition of blatant insubordination by lower-level party organs during the implementation of the bureaucratic streamlining in 1982–83, finally compelled Deng and his associates to conclude that the limited *zhengfeng* approach was inadequate, and that nothing short of a comprehensive *zhengdang* could arrest the dangerous decline of the party.

Hindsight suggests that Deng and his associates had obviously paid a heavy price for achieving their success in seizing power. For, during the process, they had also allowed the party's organizational sinew and style of work to deteriorate significantly. The irony for Deng was that precisely at the time he had defeated most of his contenders for power at the top to gain command over the party's machinery, he also realized that this machinery had become unwieldy and was in need of an overhaul before it could implement his political programs.

In contrast to *zhengfeng*, the concept of *zhengdang* reflected the leaders' belief that the party's problems were diverse but interrelated and required a comprehensive, integrated solution. Hence, in the final analysis, the combination of the leaders' frustration with the party's ability to perform its economic tasks competently and their perceived threat to the party's own "life or death" pushed them to adopt the radical approach of "a general and comprehensive rectification campaign."

3

The Change of Leadership

LEADERSHIP plays an important part in any country's attempt to develop and modernize. It plays a critical part in a socialist country such as the People's Republic of China where the only legitimate authority to generate political actions lies with the Communist Party.

From the very beginning of Deng's return to power in 1978, he realized that he had to have a corps of solid supporters to ensure the survival of the new regime first and then to mount a program of economic construction. But the basis must be a unified party under a unified leadership.[1]

Initially, however, he probably thought that this unity could be achieved by two measures. One measure was to bar those with known deviant tendencies from entering into the leadership. While leaders who had previously made mistakes were allowed to repent and redeem themselves, certain types of people were disqualified to serve as leaders. They included party members who had engaged in destructive activities, had strong factional propensities, or had mistreated other comrades and betrayed the party's interest.[2] A second measure was to ensure that the people to be incorporated into the leadership were politically reliable and ideologically correct. This need was met by the rehabilitation of old cadres. It did not take long, however, for Deng and his associates to realize that these measures were not enough.

Even though known deviants were blocked from entering the leadership, many more deviants had already occupied leadership positions on all levels. Unless they were removed, party unity would be an illusive goal. On the other hand, although the rehabilitated old cadres met the requirement of political reliability, their competence was highly doubtful. Eventually, the party concluded that the best way to ensure the continuity of their reform programs was to reconstitute thoroughly the leadership on all levels. Only when the party's organization was placed under the firm control of a new generation of revolutionary successors could its reform programs have a fair chance of success.

Therefore, any understanding of the party's policy on leadership must address the party's three needs. First, the party must rid itself of people who actively pursued antiparty activities. Since these people were politically unreliable, a purge seemed the only appropriate method to deal with them. Second, the party must also remove the people who, although politically reliable, were incompetent to fulfill the party's programs. The retirement policy was adopted to accomplish this purpose. Finally, the party needed to install a new leadership that was both politically reliable and professionally competent to carry forward the four modernizations. The party's solution was to create the "third echelon" of revolutionary successors.

The "Three Types"

As early as 1975, Deng had already begun to worry about the possibility that the Gang of Four might attempt to seize complete control over the party after Mao's death. Deng was particularly alarmed by Wang Hongwen's threat that the Cultural Revolutionists could afford to wait for another decade to settle the scores with the party's old guard (i.e., after Mao's expected death and by about 1985). Deng, of course, was acutely aware of the Gang members' advantage in youth over the old guard in the forthcoming power struggle, and he believed that the old guard's only chance of winning was to invigorate their own ranks with younger blood.[3] But at that time Deng was impotent to put his ideas into operation, and he himself was soon swept out of office by the Tiananmen incident of early 1976.

No sooner had Deng returned to national politics than he began to advocate the necessity for a wholesale change of leadership at the top levels of the party, state, and military to get rid of all elements suspected of close ties with Lin Biao or the Gang of Four.[4] After a wave of exposures and dismissals of these elements, Deng felt confident enough to declare in March 1979 that the mass movement to criticize Lin Biao and the Gang of Four had been triumphantly concluded because the counterrevolutionary forces associated with these groups had been smashed, and because the leadership of the party, state, and military on all levels had been transferred into the hands of reliable cadres. With these accomplishments, he said, the task of the whole party should henceforth be directed toward the building of "socialist modernization."[5]

Deng soon discovered that his optimistic assessment had been unwarranted: the task of exposing the remnants of the Cultural Revolution had not been implemented thoroughly enough. The diehard followers of the Gang had indeed been removed from offices on the higher levels, but a substantial number of them still remained in key leadership positions at the middle and lower levels.[6] In July 1979, for instance, the first party secretaries of several key provinces (Wan Li in Anhui, Xi Zhongxun in Guangdong, and Chen Peixian in Hubei) all warned that the remnants of the Cultural Revolution were still actively spreading leftist thoughts in opposition to the party's new reforms, and using their leadership positions to create turmoil in the party.[7]

Deng himself changed his tone at the end of July 1979 and renewed his warning that there existed a substantial number of people who opposed the party's new leaders and policies. In addition, there was a different group of leaders who had embraced the leftist ideas of the Cultural Revolution but did not have close personal ties with either Lin Biao or the Gang of Four. The presence of both groups continued to pose serious threats to the stability of Deng's leadership and his reform programs.[8]

Throughout 1980, Deng repeatedly cautioned the party never to underestimate the destructive potential of these remnants of the Gang of Four. He vowed that not a single one of these elements "should ever be allowed to enter the leadership on any level, and those already in the leadership must be dismissed. If we do not increase our vigilance, and if we allow them to hold leadership positions, then they will renew their two-faced intrigues, plant their roots, and conceal their identities. Even though they may constitute a small minority, they are capable of bringing us inestimable harm."[9] Deng complained that some comrades had not treated these dangers seriously enough, pointing out that some work units had already been captured by these troublemakers.[10]

As time went by, the new leaders became increasingly convinced that the Cultural Revolution remnants were busy at work to obstruct every major policy or program they had introduced. Deng reported in late 1980 that remnants in many places openly called for the mounting of a second Cultural Revolution. They were accused of inciting riots, engaging in illegal or violent acts, spreading counterrevolutionary propaganda, and in general scheming to destabilize the current leadership.[11] Such fears were further reinforced by developments in subsequent years. Thus, when the party decided to revamp its leadership and streamline organization in 1982, the Cultural Revolution remnants were seen as deliberately ignoring the new criteria for choosing new leaders and trying to fill the leadership vacancies with their fellow factionalists. When the party mounted the campaign to smash economic crimes in 1982–83, the Cultural Revolution remnants were suspected of concealing crimes committed by their fellow factionalists and causing the campaign to fail. They were also suspected of attempting to seize the party's organization on all levels by nominating their fellow factionalists as candidates, rigging their elections, or even presenting them as candidates to be revolutionary successors.[12]

In addition, the new leaders blamed the remnants as the main culprits for the sharp decline of discipline among party members, because the remnants had set poor examples of conduct by openly challenging the current leaders' legitimacy to rule, and by opposing their policies and the party line since 1976 in the name of defending the Maoist legacy. When the party tried to enforce discipline among its members, the Cultural Revolution remnants were also seen as trying actively to frustrate its efforts. In short, these remnants were not merely an embarrassment to the new leaders, but a mortal danger to their reformist agenda. What worried the new leaders the most was the Cultural Revolution remnants' blind acceptance of the doctrine that "to rebel is justified," which could directly threaten the current leaders' desire to maintain order, stabilize expectations, and bring a more peaceful life to the people. Their great destructive potential was attributed to their close and elaborate factional ties as well as their ability to conceal their true identities.[13]

The age factor was a matter of added concern to the post-Mao leaders. On the whole, these remnants were young, better educated, and extremely ruthless and unscrupulous. Many of them had lamented openly that they should have treated the old guard without mercy and completely annihilated them during the Cultural Revolution. Since they believed that the rehabilitated cadres' days were numbered, they brazenly vowed to do their best to hold onto their party membership and wait until after the current leader's death to recapture power and settle their accounts.[14] These sentiments were known to be widely shared by the remnants, leading Deng to the belief that "we must never underestimate the capacity of these remnants. Otherwise, we will be making a big mistake."[15] Quite aptly, the new leaders regarded the remnants as "time-bombs."[16]

The intensity of the leaders' anxieties also convinced them that they should not give the remnants a chance at reeducation and repentance. They contended that many remnants never possessed the necessary qualifications to become party members in the first place. More important, they were convinced that the remnants would always hold fast to the ideas and practices of the Cultural Revolution and could never faithfully accept the party's new policies.[17] The new leaders also rejected the view that the remnants were themselves the victims of the Cultural Revolution who only played out their prescribed roles scripted by the Gang leaders. Instead, the party leaders regarded the remnants as the perpetrators of the Cultural Revolution and its main beneficiaries. To the new leaders, "the objective lesson of history" had made it amply plain that to allow such elements to stay in office would eventually bring grief to the party and the country. Hence, the only effective way to repudiate the Cultural Revolution was to resolutely cleanse the party of these elements.[18]

In 1983, the party finally decided that a rectification campaign was needed to deal with the multiple problems plaguing it. One major objective of this campaign was to achieve "purity of organization." The resolution to launch the campaign stated clearly that the party's organization could be purified only when three kinds of people were driven out of office.[19] First, there were those who gained power as a result of engaging in rebellious acts during the Cultural Revolution. They closely followed the Lin and Jiang Gangs, engaged in factional strife, and had since been promoted to become leading cadres. Second, there were those who had espoused the ideological line of the Lin and Jiang Gangs, and who continued to oppose the party's line after 1978. Third, there were those who had committed serious acts of "beating" (and torturing people to cause serious injury or death, or persecuting people on false charges), "smashing" (official organizations), and "looting" (government documents or properties), and who masterminded and led people to fight armed battles.[20] Together, these groups were labeled the "three types of people." Subsequently, the party also employed the term "five types of people" to include those who opposed the new party line since 1978, and those who committed serious economic and other kinds of crimes.[21] But the most important targets throughout the rectification campaign were the "three types," and their removal from power was the absolutely essential precondition to purifying the organization and reconstituting leadership on various levels. The party's goal was to enable more reliable cadres to be promoted into leadership positions. As Deng pointed out, these new cadres had to possess "revolutionary qualities," which meant that they must insist on the socialist road and leadership by the party. It was believed that only when such a leadership was installed could the party acquire an organizational guarantee for the continuity and stability of its reforms.[22]

Purging of the "Three Types"

That the offensive against the "three types" should encounter difficulties was not hard to imagine. By 1982–83, most of them had already taken steps to conceal their identities. Even the most devout Cultural Revolutionists either took a low profile or pretended to accept wholeheartedly the current party line. Exposing these well-camouflaged figures became a difficult task to perform. Many had already left the original localities where they had committed misconduct, which made it difficult for the party to track them down.[23]

When exposed and prosecuted as such, many "three types" refused to admit personal responsibilities for their conduct on the grounds that they had merely carried out orders from above during the Cultural Revolution as loyal party members should. This line of defense was often effective, because many people still had confused ideas about the Cultural Revolution even in the early 1980s and believed that they had acted correctly. Many argued that the Cultural Revolution was such a gigantic turmoil, in which violent acts were committed indiscriminately and on a massive scale, that it would be both futile and unfair to fix blame on a few individuals.[24]

Probably the greatest difficulty in flushing out the "three types" was factionalism. The responsibility for investigating and exposing the hidden elements within the party and preventing them from entering the new leadership was to be borne primarily by the party secretaries and party fractions, not by average party members.[25] Yet leaders in many party organs often applied factional standards to decide which "three types" to expose. They dragged out only those in the rival factions, protecting those within their own faction.[26] The investigation of the three types in some cases rekindled the old grudges dating back many years and as a result turned into a vicious factional warfare.[27]

One particular subgroup of the "three types" that posed especially difficult problems consisted of what Chen Yun called the "schemers" or "advisers" who masterminded many of the destructive activities during the Cultural Revolution. While the "three types" who had committed explicit acts of violence during the Cultural Revolution could be tracked down more easily, their instigators had stayed behind the scene at the time and remained well camouflaged. Under the conditions of the 1980s, such people not only pretended to be very docile, but also demonstrated considerable competence in their professional work. Consequently, they not only could escape punishment, but might even lull their superiors into picking them to become candidates for the third echelon.[28]

The party also realized that if the term "three types" was applied too literally, it could cause widespread panic in the ranks and make everyone feel threatened. To avoid this situation, the party announced that the rectification was directed primarily against the "ringleaders" who had planned, organized, and led criminal acts during the Cultural Revolution, and not against their followers, especially if the latter had not opposed the new leaders since 1978.[29] By virtue of this distinction, the party hoped to isolate the factional leaders from their followers. It was believed that once the former were neutralized, the capacity of the latter to do harm would be greatly reduced. Furthermore, the party also believed that to deal effectively with the "three types," it was necessary to repudiate the Cultural Revolution thoroughly and to provide people with clear standards of right and wrong.[30]

As a result, the party leaders pressed on with both an unrelenting propaganda offensive against the erroneous ideology of the Cultural Revolution and stern organizational measures to drive the "three types" out of their offices. They rejected repeated suggestions by some people that the operation against the "three types" had gone far enough, or that the "three types" had been rendered organizationally harmless, but instead remained determined to pursue the purge of the three types.[31]

In late 1983, when the leaders took stock of the national situation, they reported that the majority of the "three types" had been exposed and expelled from the leadership of the national- and provincial/municipal-level organizations, but that a substantial number of them were still well hidden and entrenched on the county and lower levels, in economic enterprises, and in auxiliary administrative organizations. They vowed that the party should not rest until the purge of the "three types" had been thoroughly carried out all the way down to the local level. Otherwise, such elements could resurface to cause problems even after a hibernation of ten to twenty years.[32]

In the following year, "massive and exhaustive work" against the "three types" was conducted by units that were undergoing party rectification at this time.[33] More "three types" were exposed and dismissed from office, together with a number of leading cadres who were not "three types" themselves but who had been ineffectual in exposing the "three types."[34] Special effort was made to screen out those "three types" who had snuck into leadership positions, or who had been designated as revolutionary successors. Such people were promptly removed from their positions. A number of organs were themselves disbanded or reconstituted if they were dominated by such people, and culprits were brought to trial in the courts.[35] By December 1984, Bo Yibo was able to report that some 50 percent of people identified as "three types" had been dealt with since the beginning of the rectification campaign.[36]

Thus, shortly after the Third Plenum of the Twelfth Party Congress, Deng showed his confidence by stating, "I believe we now have a mature party central leadership who can handle things with deliberateness." He mentioned not only Hu Yaobang and Zhao Ziyang among the second echelon, but also a number of younger people in the State Council and the party's Central Committee as very capable members of the third echelon whom he could trust to get things done right.[37]

In spite of these accomplishments, the leaders still refused to reduce their vigilance. Throughout 1985, official publications reiterated the party's concern with the "three types" and stressed the need for their total elimination. For example, in July 1985, Hu Qili, deputy director of the Central Rectification Guidance Committee, urged party members on all levels to carry on unrelentingly the task of screening out the "three types" and declared that the screening would not cease for as long as there were "three types" left.[38] As rectification entered its second phase, exhaustive screening of the "three types" was extended to the lower levels where special inspection teams were created specifically to screen out the "three types," and to investigate their crimes.[39] Party organs in many places declared a commitment to devote the year 1985 to conduct yet another thorough exposure and verification of the crimes of the "three types."[40] Official pronouncements suggested that impressive gains were achieved during 1985 in the purge of the "three types" in many provinces.[41] Bo Yibo also confirmed in late 1985 that good results were achieved during the first stage of party rectification.[42]

By this time, most "three types" had been effectively eliminated from the national and provincial/municipal leadership positions, and they probably constituted only a tiny minority in the leadership positions of party and state organizations or economic enterprises even on the local levels. Their old factional affiliations had lost much of their political relevance. Even for those who stayed in office, they were so dispersed that they no longer commanded enough resources to endanger the new leaders' positions or the party's new line. Therefore, when the party rectification was officially concluded in mid-1987, Bo Yibo could claim with genuine satisfaction that the task of purging the "three types" had achieved great results. In contrast to the leaders' paranoia about the danger of the "three types" in earlier years, Bo's summation report devoted only a short passage to this entire issue.[43]

In its actual implementation, the screening of the "three types" was the only aspect of the rectification that was conducted in the fashion of a conventional "purge." As will be discussed in the following chapters, the rectification campaign was a multidimensional undertaking, but the differences between the elimination of the "three types" and the other aspects of the rectification are quite apparent. The party normally drew from its repertoire of standard operating procedures (e.g., criticism and self-criticism) to resolve intraparty and nonantagonistic contradictions. It usually allowed party committees on the same level to pass verdicts on their own members' conduct. But the party showed little interest in using these procedures to reform the "three types." Instead, its objective was to remove them from power. To achieve this goal, the party employed special task forces to investigate the crimes of the "three types" and gave superior organs the right to pass verdicts on their conduct.

Furthermore, party leaders realized that the most effective way to destroy the factions of the "three types" was to break up their ringleaders' power base. Once such bases were demolished, the lower-level followers' ability to do harm would be drastically reduced. The latter might continue to commit misconduct, but they could no longer threaten the party's general line. Consequently, the party was decisive in exposing and smashing the "three types" on the top at the outset of the rectification campaign, which made it much easier to deal with the "three types" on the lower levels in the later stages of the campaign.

The task of exposing and removing the "three types" was pursued with a thoroughness that bordered on vengeance. Once people were categorized as the "three types," they were immediately dismissed from office or expelled from the party.[44] Mercy was rarely shown to these people. This was quite uncharacteristic of the tenor of rectification as a whole. Obviously, the leaders accepted very literally the old Chinese folk wisdom that "one must pull out the roots to kill the weeds."

This degree of thoroughness accounted for the campaign's success in this particular respect. The task was essentially accomplished even before the rectification campaign was concluded. The ideology of the "three types" was destroyed as well as their factional organization. By the mid-1980s, any realistic hope of their return to power had completely vanished.

Of course, the purging of the "three types" was not conducted in isolation, but was aided by other steps taken by the party to improve its overall leadership quality. Under the party's new retirement policy, many of the older "three types" who escaped the purge during the rectification process were retired when they reached the mandatory age. The party's succession policy also created a new generation of leaders who numerically overwhelmed the few surviving "three types." Meanwhile, the social and economic changes in China had created such a different environment that the political convictions of the Cultural Revolution era now seemed like anachronisms, and any intention of returning the party to its radical past was no longer a realistic option. The new leaders had indeed scored a major victory, because the possibility of the "three types" posing as a conspiratorial threat seemed to have vanished forever.

Retirement of Old Cadres

A serious problem common to nearly all totalitarian systems is the lack of rules governing the orderly circulation of the elite. Leaders either stay in power until death or are driven from office in disgrace. The heavy price that totalitarian systems pay for leadership stability usually includes rigidity, lack of innovativeness, and, above all, gerontocracy.

The Chinese Communist Party was a youthful party when it came to power in 1949. Since most first-generation revolutionary leaders were still in their late forties or early fifties, they hardly felt any need to address the question of retirement; nor did they have any precedent from other socialist countries to serve as guidance. The notion of a retirement system was briefly considered in the early 1960s but never implemented.[45]

During the Cultural Revolution, leaders' age became a relevant political factor when Mao used the Red Guards to overthrow the established leaders to regain personal control over the future course of the Chinese revolution. Mao proposed that the ideal formula of revolutionary power-sharing should be the combination of the old, middle-aged, and young leaders. Although this formula brought about a noticeable decrease in the age of leaders on many levels, it was not a retirement system, because the senior leaders were purged from power and did not retire with honor.

After Mao's death and the fall of the Gang of Four, the Chinese cadre corps was made up of several groups. One group consisted of those who joined the party during the early phase of revolution and started their career in the old liberated bases. By the late 1970s, they had risen to be leaders on the provincial and district levels and were already in their sixties or even seventies. A second group consisted of those who went underground during the Sino-Japanese War or joined the cadre ranks during the civil war. These were mostly local cadres. By the late 1970s, they had risen to become county-level leaders and were in their fifties.[46]

Although numerically these two groups constituted a tiny minority of the party's cadre corps in the late 1970s, together they constituted the overwhelming majority of leading cadres on the high and middle levels and were generally referred to as the "old cadres." The fact that the CCP's earlier armed revolutionary activities occurred primarily in rural areas meant that most of the old cadres were drawn from the ranks of peasants and PLA soldiers. Thus, one distinct feature of the leading cadres was their low cultural and educational qualifications and deficient professional knowledge. Yet the revolutionary values instilled in them made them proud not only of their humble social backgrounds, but also of their cultural and educational deficiencies. Vulgarity became a badge of honor and an indispensable mark of a true revolutionary in Maoist China. The radical position of dismissing the value of knowledge only further convinced them that their poor education was a revolutionary asset and not a liability.[47]

In contrast to the old cadres, the majority of cadres had entered the cadre corps since Liberation. These post-Liberation cadres were in general younger and better educated. But by the late 1970s, very few of them had been promoted into positions of leadership. A final group consisted of people who entered the cadre force during the Cultural Revolution. They were younger but not necessarily better educated; and their political orientations were potentially unreliable.

Shortly after Deng's return to power in 1978, the massive rehabilitation program brought back tens of thousands of previously disgraced and exiled leaders to reclaim their old positions from the Cultural Revolutionists. Although this policy almost immediately increased the age of the leadership corps by ten to fifteen years, it was widely assumed at this point that the traditional practices would be honored to allow rehabilitated cadres to stay in office until their deaths. Two factors lent further weight to this assumption. For one reason, the rehabilitated cadres were the most ardent supporters of Deng against his political rivals. For another reason, these old cadres had suffered years of hardship and were thought to deserve compensation in power, position, and social prestige.

The Need for a Cadre Retirement Policy

It soon became clear that the rehabilitated leaders actually constituted a serious liability for the Deng leadership under the new circumstances. One serious problem with the rehabilitated cadres was that age had finally caught up with them. By the early 1980s, the majority of leading cadres on the national and provincial levels consisted of those who had joined the party during the early phases of the revolutionary struggle. Most of them were in their sixties, with a substantial number in their seventies. In 1982, for example, the average ages of members of the four top party and state organs were, respectively, 64.4 years for full members of the Central Committee, 73.1 years for full members of the Politburo, 74.5 years for members of the Standing Committee of the Politburo, and 63.7 years for State Council ministers. In the provinces, the average age for provincial party secretaries was 68.5 years.[48] Even many leading cadres of municipal bureaus or county-level party secretaries were in their fifties and sixties.[49]

Frail physical condition became a widespread impediment, as many cadres were utterly incapable of following a full work schedule. For instance, when Deng talked to a high-level cadre conference on November 2, 1979, he said, "the old cadres are now mostly over sixty years of age. . . . Their energy level has declined. Otherwise, why are many cadres holding offices at home? Why can't they tough it out in the office for eight straight hours?" Deng estimated that less than half of his audience at this conference had the stamina to endure an eight-hour workday.[50]

Many cadres were hospitalized and had to carry out their official duties from their hospital beds. It was common for work units to be half-empty and their operations to be half-suspended during inclement weather because their leading cadres had to go to sanatoriums or resort hostels to rest and recuperate. Even though many national and provincial agencies nominally had a full complement of leaders (e.g., party secretary, many deputy secretaries, and numerous other assistants), usually no more than two or three persons had the physical strength for the normal workload.

Even as pivotal a figure as Chen Yun of the Politburo admitted in 1979 that he could function only two half-days (or one full day) per week; but, at age seventy-five, he was by no means the oldest nor the most fragile member of that august body.[51] The frail health of these rehabilitated cadres made them poor guarantors of the continuity of Deng's political power, since very few of them had the energy to fight protracted battles against the young radicals. The mortality rate had reached an alarming proportion among leading cadres, and attendance at funeral services of deceased comrades had become a nearly daily obligation for the surviving leaders.[52]

In addition, a large number of cadres were not exactly loyal followers of the Gang but had profited from the Cultural Revolution, and these people felt their personal interests threatened by the ascendance of Deng's group. They were the opportunists who temporarily made peace with Deng but who might side with the diehard radicals if the latter attempted a political comeback. Therefore, it was important to Deng that these fence-sitters be neutralized as well.

An equally serious weakness of the rehabilitated cadres was their inability to contribute to Deng's ambitious reforms. Most old cadres were at best experts at violence and political control but were woefully deficient in other professional fields. In this respect, the situation in the city of Beijing would provide a good illustration because it was one of the few places in China that had a high concentration of the most qualified leaders. Yet, in 1981, less than one-tenth of them had any professional training.[53]

After Deng's return to power, however, the party could no longer afford to depend merely on violence or political control but had to offer a meaningful program to shore up its sagging legitimacy. The result was the party's pledge to achieve the four modernizations by the year 2000. To fulfill this objective, the party urgently needed cadres who had modernist outlooks and possessed the requisite managerial and technical skills in the related scientific and economic fields. The old cadres were simply incapable of meeting these demands. Deng recognized this problem and said, even as early as 1979, that "at present our country is confronted with a serious problem. It is not that we do not have a correct policy and line with regard to the four modernizations. It is that we do not have a large number of talents who are capable of realizing this policy and line."[54]

Without a group of young and energetic cadres equipped with professional knowledge, the four modernizations would be simply empty talk. He warned, "We must recognize that it is an issue of strategic importance to pick our successors carefully. It is an issue that will affect the long-range interests of our party. If we do not resolve this issue in the next three or so years, we will not be able to predict what may happen ten years from now."[55]

Therefore, by requiring all aging cadres to retire, Deng could ease out the unreliable elements as well as the loyalists and replace both groups with a generation of young successors who would be better educated, more capable, and trustworthy. The merit of a retirement policy was that it would solve both the party's power concern and its concern for improved efficiency to achieve the modernization goals without precipitating a showdown within the party or re-opening factional wounds. Furthermore, this system would accelerate the speed at which younger, more qualified cadres entered leadership and allow time for the old and young cadres to work together to effectuate a smooth transition of power.[56] In this sense, the retirement policy became a critical component in Deng's long-term strategy to consolidate power and restore legitimacy.

Evolution of a Retirement Policy

The retirement issue was put on the political agenda shortly after Deng's political triumph at the Third Plenum. But in the spring of 1979 when Chen Yun began to talk about the need to introduce new blood into the leadership, he was not yet thinking in terms of large-scale replacement of existing leaders in the immediate future; he only contended that it was necessary to appoint a few (up to five) able-bodied young people to each agency as "back-benchers" to apprentice for leadership positions under the tutelage of the incumbents for an unspecified period of time. He did not give a clear indication, however, as to when the aging incumbent leaders should actually be replaced.[57]

Among the top leaders, Deng was probably the first to accept the necessity of a genuine retirement system. This was understandable, because his political conflict with the Cultural Revolutionists was the sharpest, and because the four modernizations had become the main focus of his personal political platform. By mid-1979, if not earlier, Deng realized that even though the party had adopted his political line, he still needed cadres to implement it faithfully and effectively. This became a question of organizational control for Deng, as he stated on July 27, 1979: "Now that the political line has been settled, we need people to implement it. What kinds of people are going to implement it? The consequence will be very different whether the party's political line is implemented by those who support it, or by those who oppose it, or by those who have a neutral attitude toward it. This then poses the question of who will become the successors."[58]

As the struggle for power on the national level turned decisively to Deng's favor in 1980 with the removal of Hua Guofeng and other cohorts from important offices, Deng and his associates decided that the time was ripe to encourage more of their own loyal supporters to relinquish their positions in favor of younger cadres. In February 1980, the Fifth Plenum of the Eleventh Party Congress formally abolished the practice of guaranteed lifetime tenure for regular party cadres. On April 28, 1980, this ban was extended to the leadership level when the party decided not to allow old leaders in poor health to become members of the Central Committee of the Twelfth Party Congress. In August, Deng recommended that rules governing the tenure and retirement of leading cadres be formulated.[59] In September 1980, several aging leaders resigned from their posts as vice-premiers to make room for younger people and set the precedent for voluntary retirement. At the Sixth Plenum in June 1981, Deng Xiaoping, who could have taken the top post of the CCP, declined to do so but instead persuaded his colleagues to accept Hu Yaobang, a younger person, as the CCP's topmost leader.[60]

By May 1981, Chen Yun's sense of urgency had obviously also increased considerably. He now believed that the CCP was confronted with a fundamental choice of either allowing the status quo to continue and facing a dangerous leadership crisis in the near future, or promoting qualified young and middle-aged cadres "by the thousands and tens of thousands" into leadership positions immediately and cultivating their leadership skills on the job.[61] Chen argued that an infusion of new blood of this magnitude was required to improve work efficiency on all levels and to guarantee a smooth transition of power. To promote only a small number of people might create political complications and would not contribute to institutionalization. Furthermore, only by promoting tens of thousands of reliable younger cadres to leadership positions could the party insure itself against the danger of an attempted comeback by the Cultural Revolutionists.[62]

On May 8, 1981, Chen Yun submitted his views to the Politburo and received the prompt support of Deng Xiaoping and Hu Yaobang (who was then the party's chairman as well as secretary general). Further consultations were held with leaders of the CCP's Organization Department and the PLA's General Political Department for more concrete recommendations.[63] Finally, in February 1982, the party formally adopted the resolution to introduce a "system of retirement for old cadres."[64]

But how did the old cadres respond to the new regulations? What strategies did the party use to enforce these regulations? And how successfully was the policy implemented?

Why Cadres Abhorred Retirement

Under normal conditions, the leadership of many countries has a fluid and diversified age structure. Old leaders are retired either by mandatory process or by the democratic process. Leaders can also become nonleaders when they change jobs or professions. The leadership consists of people in different age groups and stays in flux as people constantly enter and exit leadership positions. In Communist China, the situation was quite different. Once a person acquired the status of a leading cadre, he would keep that status for the rest of his life no matter where he went and what line of profession he was assigned to.

Traditionally, the Chinese cadre system put a premium on the cadres' political reliability with little emphasis on technical proficiency. Consequently, promotion to leadership was regarded as a confirmation of political reliability rather than competence. The only way a leading cadre could lose his status was by death or by political purge. Therefore, most leading cadres acquired the mentality that they were entitled to leadership positions as long as they made no serious political mistakes. Retirement was regarded as a way to drive them from the political arena, and therefore a form of personal disgrace that must be opposed at all costs.[65] While ordinary workers expected to retire at the mandatory age, retirement was a totally alien idea to party members and cadres.

Many cadres also believed in their own indispensability to the party and the state. Gerontocracy had long cultural and historical roots in China. In Chinese political culture, age was synonymous with wisdom and maturity and commanded respect automatically. Youth, on the other hand, was viewed as the equivalent of inexperience and immaturity. The Communist system seemed to have done little to change this mentality. Many cadres genuinely believed that only old cadres could steady the ship of the state.

Another factor that reinforced this mentality was the leaders' own disastrous political experience during the Cultural Revolution. Many cadres distrusted youths because they had suffered in the latter's hands and witnessed their arrogant and ruthless conduct during that era, which led them to perceive all young people as having "horns on their heads and thorns on their bodies."[66]

Finally, cadres resisted retirement for very practical reasons. First, in Communist China, cadres' lives were often totally immersed in the party. Their social activities revolved around other party members. Party members in distress always sought assistance from their party organs. For cadres, and particularly leading cadres who had spent a lifetime with a small circle of friends and comrades, the prospects of ceasing to be a cadre and severing their social and organizational ties were simply too painful to contemplate.[67]

Second, cadres were acutely aware of their special political status, which entitled them to participation in political activities that were denied to the general population. Of particular importance was their access to information that was distributed according to the recipient's official rank (e.g., province-army, district-division, or county-regiment levels). Only leading cadres had the privilege to read certain types of internal documents and "reference materials," to listen to tape recordings of secret speeches by important national leaders, and in general to stay informed about major policies and events in the country. Information gave them both psychological gratification and political power.

Third, cadres were provided with substantial materialistic benefits that covered nearly every aspect of life, from where they lived, what schools their children attended, the quality of medical service they received, to what restaurants they dined in, what entertainment they enjoyed, and what class of train they traveled in. The majority of old cadres were accustomed to expect the party to take care of every aspect of their livelihood. They had been separated from the rest of society for such a long time that they had genuinely lost the ability to lead an ordinary citizen's life in the Communist society. There was a popular saying in China that "the Nationalists craved money, but the Communists craved power." Under Communist rule, so many things in life depended on power that many cadres firmly and correctly believed that "benefits come with staying in office, disadvantages come with retirement."[68] Retirement was abhorred because it might deprive the cadres of all the privileges and reduce them to the same level as the ordinary masses. Retirement meant that they had been discarded by the party, and that their lives would rot away.[69] It was not surprising that many cadres reported feeling empty, disoriented, and depressed, like "stars that have left their tracks," after retirement.[70]

Such a dependent mentality rarely has its counterpart in contemporary non-Communist societies, nor was it the case in China's imperial past. When the cadres retire in these other cases, they start a different phase of life, reestablish old connections with their native places, live on their own savings, and are generally able to begin a different life. But Communist cadres presumably had no personal savings and few useful skills to cope as average citizens. They perceived themselves as belonging to a special category of people, and they expected the state to take care of them until they died. From their perspective, retirement was a euphemism for political death. The practices in many localities only confirmed their worst fears: in these cases, when the work units severed their relations with the retirees, they also refused to look after the latter's emotional or physical well-being.[71]

The Party's Incentives for Retirement

From the very beginning, the party appreciated how painful and unpopular the retirement policy was among old cadres and sought to soothe the transition through two main approaches. One approach was to rely on moral and spiritual mobilization. The other approach was to offer material incentives.

Spiritual Mobilization

The party's main technique of moral and spiritual mobilization was to conduct a massive and sustained propaganda campaign. The mass media, organizational channels, and personal contacts were all mobilized to appeal to the old cadres' sense of revolutionary dedication. This propaganda campaign conveyed several messages. The party praised old cadres for their ideological consciousness, farsightedness, and selfless dedication to the revolutionary cause. They were encouraged to fulfill a sacred historic mission and set an excellent personal example for future generations by yielding their positions to younger people. Their retirement was described as the most memorable contribution they could make to the nation in the twilight of their illustrious revolutionary careers.[72]

The party even tried to tap China's cultural tradition to bolster the self-esteem of the retirees, and it reminded the people of the need to show proper respect for the ''elders'' in their dealing with the retired cadres.[73] Retired cadres were referred to as ''national treasures'' who deserved the highest honor. In particular, middle-aged and young cadres slated to take over the old cadres' positions were admonished to emulate the latter's party character, personal virtues, and revolutionary styles. Middle-aged and younger cadres were further reminded that only by showing proper respect to the elders could the process of transition of power be carried out smoothly, and that they must continue to look after the well-being of retired cadres. The party school also created a special program for many high- and middle-ranking cadres to ease the pain of their retirement.[74]

Material Incentives

The party realized that spiritual mobilization by itself was not enough to induce old cadres to accept retirement, and that they had to be given more tangible assurances that they need not sacrifice the quality of their lives after retirement. The solution was to promise the old cadres that their ''political treatment will remain unchanged, living conditions will be improved, and attention will be paid to utilize their full potential'' after retirement. By guaranteeing ''political treatment,'' the party meant that retired cadres would continue to have the right to read internal documents, listen to reports, and attend meetings commensurate with their previous ranks. The party would organize them into party branches and allow them to enjoy many organizational privileges as if they had not left their jobs.

By ''living conditions,'' the party meant the conveniences and privileges cadres had been accustomed to for years, since a major concern for many old cadres was the possibility of losing these privileges and suffering a sharp decline of their living conditions after they retired. To assuage these anxieties, the party devised myriad methods to preserve or increase the tangible benefits of a retired life. Cadres willing to retire were often promised better housing for their families. Special funds were allocated by some agencies to construct new housing for retired cadres. Cadres willing to return to their native villages in the countryside were sometimes given hefty subsidies to build their own houses.[75]

Many work units offered to increase the number or frequency of routine physical checkups and other medical benefits for retired cadres. Special wards for retired cadres were sometimes set aside in hospitals. Detailed records were kept to monitor the physical conditions of retired cadres.[76]

Cadres were granted additional allowances of their daily necessities and given priority of access to scarce commodities. They were promised tickets to cultural or sporting events. Special household helpers were sometimes assigned to them, and the new party leaders of the old work units promised to visit them on a regular basis and attend promptly to their demands. Special recreational facilities, activities, and libraries were often set up for the benefit of only the retired cadres.[77] To insure the effective implementation of the policy on cadre retirement, special agencies were set up on all levels of the party and state to provide services to the retirees. By promising to utilize the full potential of the old cadres, the party was trying to address latter's fear that retirement would plunge them into a psychological void.[78]

The party contended that retirement was in no way intended to end the cadres' revolutionary activities. On the contrary, retirees could engage in a full range of activities to make their lives busy, exciting, and productive. To achieve this goal, the party instructed local organs to devise their own ways to allow the retired cadres to "radiate their residual heat" in retirement by making use of their talents, experiences, and energy. Many retired cadres were invited to help localities compile local gazettes, or to write personal memoirs to fill gaps in the official history.[79] Cadres with professional expertise were encouraged to conduct investigation and research for local communities, or to serve as consultants to economic enterprises on the lower levels.[80]

Social services provided another outlet for retired cadres' energy. Efforts were made to organize retirees into special committees to help the regular party organs provide social services to the masses in such areas as the maintenance of social discipline, management of rural markets, or inspection of public health conditions. Some places used retired cadres as part-time political instructors to teach party history and related political courses in schools.[81] Retired cadres were often asked to assume leadership over the residents' committees in their own neighborhoods, and to use their prestige and experience to serve as the masses' trouble-shooters, or as arbitrators of their quarrels.[82]

Retired cadres could become particularly valuable assets in the rural areas because they possessed a far better grasp of the party's policies than the average peasant and could help the existing rural party organs to interpret party programs or settle disputes. They could also serve as consultants to local party leaders on setting up collective enterprises and welfare programs.[83]

Finally, since many retired cadres had been the victims of political persecution, they were uniquely qualified to help other victims win vindication. Their participation in this respect could significantly lighten the loads of the party's regular investigative personnel in settling cases of rehabilitation.[84] In addition, retired cadres could be used to supervise the rural market, or help poor and illiterate farmers to learn new skills.[85]

The party press gave wide publicity to these possibilities in order to persuade the retiring cadres that they could expect more psychological fulfillment even after departing from their old work units. As a further concession, the party introduced the distinction of two types of retirement. The first was called *tuixiu,* which meant an irrevocable end of their careers. The cadres under the *tuixiu* arrangement would retire from their posts and completely sever their ties with their work units. The second type was called *lixiu*, which entailed a more ambiguous relationship. Nominally, the cadres would retain their official titles and only take a leave of absence from their posts for rest and recuperation, thus allowing younger successors to assume responsibilities. Technically speaking, the old cadres could still be called back to active service or to undertake special assignments from time to time, and definitely could keep their bureaucratic prerogatives. It was hoped that this arrangement gave the old cadres an additional measure of psychological guaranty that they still were associated with their work units even though they were expected to leave the official business entirely to their successors.

Generally speaking, *tuixiu* was enforced upon ordinary cadres, but *lixiu* was a special treatment reserved only for "old cadres." *Tuixiu* was implemented more mechanically: once a person reached the mandatory retirement age (sixty for males, fifty-five for females), he or she had to retire. But *lixiu* was applied more flexibly as the age restrictions were not strictly enforced. It became a bargaining process in many instances between the party and the cadres. *Lixiu* was required only for cadres in poor health who could not carry a normal workload. If they had good health, they could ask to be exempt from retirement.[86] In other words, ordinary cadres had to accept mandatory retirement, but leading cadres had a lot of leeway. The more powerful they were, the longer they could postpone their own retirement.

The Central Advisory Committee

While these accommodative measures were designed to appease the average cadres, the higher-ranking leading cadres required special treatment because they had much bigger appetites. On the material side, they were not moved by the promise of the standard treatment but were only interested in big-ticket items, such as spacious housing, automobiles, or jobs for their children. More important, leading cadres were generally exceedingly reluctant to relinquish power.

Deng and his associates were realistic enough to know that most leading cadres would not meekly give up their positions even when they were offered generous material payoffs. As a special concession to leading cadres, Deng proposed in August 1980 the establishment of a Central Advisory Committee that would be filled with aging national party and state leaders as a transitional arrangement before they went into full retirement.[87]

According to Deng's plan, the advisory committee was to exist only for the next ten to fifteen years, during which old leading cadres who joined the party before Liberation would be invited into these committees before being asked to retire. It was hoped that this advisory system would be phased out by 1995 or before the party's Fifteenth Congress, and that those cadres who joined the party after Liberation would go directly into retirement without this transitional phase.[88]

As soon as the Central Advisory Committee came into existence, however, its members began to demonstrate that they had no intention of limiting themselves to such tame tasks as doing an oral history of the revolution, conducting social investigations, or performing strictly advisory functions. Their personal prestige and stature in the party, networks of personal connections, and power bases all enabled them to remain active in politics.

In fact, in the first year alone, the committee's members occupied themselves with making major personnel decisions affecting the composition of the Sixth National People's Congress, the Sixth Political Consultative Conference, and, more important, the State Council. Its members continued to play active roles in the reorganization and institutional reform of the party and state, economic planning, party rectification, foreign policy, work against economic crimes, and other issues.[89]

Meanwhile, the party Secretariat announced that it would continue to rely on the Advisory Committee's input for a long time to come in major policy areas. Among other things, the members of the advisory committee would continue to enjoy the power to select and recommend candidates to the third echelon, to participate in the formulation and evaluation of the party's major policies and programs, and to direct the implementation of party rectification. Consequently, even after their nominal retirement and transfer to the advisory committee, the senior leading cadres' power over the party's programs and personnel was hardly diminished.[90]

Although these concessions were presumably made only to the most senior cadres, the Central Advisory Committee set the tone for the lower levels as well. Even though many younger cadres had been promoted to leadership positions, they must continue to defer to the opinions of the old leaders who had retired from their positions. The new leaders might issue the orders, but many old leaders still pulled the strings.

Progress of the Retirement Policy

In spite of the party's effort to make its retirement policy more palatable, the policy ran into fierce resistance almost immediately after it went into operation in 1982. Only a small number of senior leaders, including some from the Central Committee, actually volunteered to retire from their posts.[91] Most leading cadres promptly mobilized personal connections to seek exemption for themselves. Older cadres in poor health and with failing mental faculties insisted that they were fit to serve in office. In contrast, those cadres who had neither power nor connections became extremely depressed and stopped performing their official duties even before their turn for retirement arrived.

As the process of revamping the leadership was extended to the provincial and lower levels toward the end of 1982, the top leaders still expected that the old cadres would coexist with their younger apprentices for an indefinite period of time.[92] As Deng said at the time, "The old cadres must not be dropped abruptly. They must join forces and work together with the middle-aged and the young cadres."[93]

The party described this policy as "enter first, exit later," whereby new and younger cadres could be promoted first into leadership circles while the older cadres stayed in office. The party's plan was to give the older cadres time to transmit their experience to younger cadres before allowing the latter to take over the helm. In other words, the old cadres' main responsibilities during this transitional stage were to "teach, assist, and guide" the younger successors and gradually to delegate more decision-making authority to the latter.[94]

In fact, however, many older cadres interpreted this policy as the party's signal that they need not retire at all, and they exploited this policy as an excuse to hang onto their jobs indefinitely. Even cadres who had already consented to retire hastened to withdraw their applications and insisted on continuing their work.[95]

At the same time, the implementation of the policy for those who actually retired also encountered many problems. Since Chinese society was highly stratified and compartmentalized, coordination among lateral units was exceedingly poor. If old cadres retired from their own work units located in one neighborhood and moved into another neighborhood, they could not realistically hope that the latter would be attentive to their needs. It was even less likely that they would be invited into the leadership of the new neighborhood. The local organs simply had no interest in the retirees. In fact, they regarded the retirees as an unwelcome burden for them.[96] Stories of callous treatment of retirees by their new neighborhoods caused more anxiety among other old cadres who had yet to retire.

The idea of performing social service held little appeal for the retired cadres. The bureaucratic and condescending style that the cadres had acquired during their long years in office made them unfit to perform social services. Their haughtiness and airs of superiority rendered them ineffective and uninterested in mass-level work. Many leading cadres were accustomed to "listening to briefings, making comments on documents, and giving commands" but simply did not know how to conduct themselves once they were stripped of their trappings of authority.[97]

Since the promises of material benefits given by the national party or government carried little credibility, many cadres tried to squeeze as many concessions out of their own work units as possible with respect to housing, living conditions, and other perks before agreeing to step down. But for leading cadres, their best insurance for a comfortable life in retirement was to install their protégés as their successors. Some cadres even seized this last chance to extract promises from their work units to hire their children as replacements.

By mid-1983, old cadres by the hundreds and thousands had totally lost interest in their official duties, but devoted themselves to falsifying documents to lower their age and brighten up their medical histories so that they could avoid retirement. Many also misrepresented their residential status so that their children currently living in the rural areas could gain permission to rejoin them as urban residents and find good employment through the back door. Few cadres ever obeyed the party's orders to retire to their ancestral villages. The problem became so acute that the State Council had to issue an order (September 26, 1983) to ban these illegal arrangements. But since the ban was not retroactive, the more influential and resourceful cadres had already insured their arrangements and were allowed to keep them.[98]

Thus, the retirement system placed heavy financial demands on the individual work units and obliged them to grant preferential treatment to retired cadres long after the latter's departure from office. The financial burden could become particularly onerous if the current leaders had been hand-picked by the retired leaders, or if the units were marked by a high degree of camaraderie or hierarchical authority structure (such as PLA units). In many such cases, public funds were diverted as payoffs to retiring cadres, construction materials were taken from the units to build new houses for the retired cadres, and illegal commercial subsidiaries were set up to provide employment for retired cadres or their family members.[99] Overall, progress was slow in 1982–83 as many old cadres still resisted retirement. Only the less influential cadres were sent into retirement quickly, and by March 1983, only 423,000 "old cadres" had accepted *lixiu* from work.[100]

The party stepped up its efforts to revamp leadership on and below the provincial level shortly after the Twelfth Party Congress. During the revamping, considerable gains were made in reducing the size of the bureaucracy through eliminating superfluous positions and retiring their occupants. Consequently, by the spring of 1984, the number of provincial governors, deputy governors, and party secretaries was reduced by 34 percent, and the subprovincial and municipal leadership was reduced by 36 percent.[101]

Yet even in the spring of 1984, General Secretary Hu Yaobang was still dissatisfied with the pace of retirement and demanded that the Organization Department improve its work and devise better ways to make the lives of retired cadres more attractive and enjoyable.[102] As the party demonstrated its determination to make its retirement policy work, most cadres in their sixties were gradually reconciled to the inevitable outcome.[103] By November 1984, a total of 1.3 million old cadres had left state agencies and enterprises under the retirement policy.[104] This means that most of the less influential cadres had been sent into retirement directly, and that an increasing number of the more influential old cadres were also persuaded to accept the *lixiu* arrangement.[105]

In early 1985, the party announced that a major task for 1985 was to carry out further readjustment of leading cadres, and it promised that the principle of retiring old cadres and promoting new ones would be carried out resolutely.[106] In April 1985, Hu Yaobang indicated that the party hoped to retire two million old cadres by 1986.[107]

The retirement of old cadres gained momentum in the spring of 1985 when the party finally succeeded in persuading a substantial number of national leaders to step down. This was a remarkable accomplishment because previously many top national leaders, such as Ye Jianying, had rebuffed repeated pleas for their retirement. The fact that such a large number of powerful old leaders had finally agreed to retire gave a clear signal to the recalcitrant old cadres on the lower levels that they too must soon yield.

But the manner in which the national leaders were coaxed into retirement also revealed the extensive bargaining and persuasion necessary to gain their consent. According to Hu Yaobang, the Politburo had formed a special work team that spent more than four months of intense preparation before finalizing the lists of leaders to retire in 1985 and their replacements.[108]

There was no doubt that the retirement of these senior leaders was obtained with generous political payoffs. Ye Jianying's retirement was delayed until his son Ye Xuanping was promoted from vice-mayor of Guangzhou to governor of Guangdong Province. Marshal Xu Xiangqian's son was by this time a deputy chief of staff of the PLA, and Marshal Nie Rongzhen's son-in-law was the director of the Committee on National Defense Sciences, Technologies, and Industries.[109]

A quick review of the history of implementing the retirement policy also suggests an interesting sequence. When the policy first went into effect, a number of old cadres on the national level were prevailed upon to accept retirement to set examples for the rest of the party. In general, these were cadres who either were in very poor health or had little bargaining power. The more powerful old cadres were given membership in the Central Advisory Committee, but the most powerful senior cadres were unaffected by the retirement policy.

With unity on the national level intact, the party was able to compel leadership changes, first on the provincial and municipal levels in 1983, and then on the county level in 1984. The retirement policy had more teeth on the lower levels and was often carried out more forcefully. No advisory committee was created on the lower levels to soothe the pain of retirement for old cadres. On the contrary, not only were cadres in their sixties retired summarily, but even a vast number of cadres in their fifties were removed from leading positions or bypassed in promotion in favor of younger cadres.

Thus, according to the party's claim, the process of revamping the provincial-level leadership was "basically completed" by early 1983. Toward the end of 1983, when the rectification campaign got underway, the revamping process was also "basically completed" for subordinate organs under the provincial governments, as well as most municipal organs.[110] The leadership changes on the county level was accomplished in 1984.[111] By early 1985, the party was in a position to refocus its attention to the task of enforcing retirement of old cadres on the national level.

The Fourth Plenum of the National Party Congress, held in mid-September

1985, marked a triumphant chapter in the party's effort to implement the retirement system. The party announced that 131 old cadres, including 10 active members of the Politburo (Ye Jianying, Deng Yingchao, and several top PLA generals) had requested voluntary retirement from the party's top leadership.[112] As their replacements, 56 new full members and 35 alternate members were admitted into the Central Committee. Fifty-six new members were admitted to the Central Advisory Committee, and 31 new members were admitted to the Central Discipline Inspection Committee. All told, this reshuffle replaced 18 percent of the membership of the Central Committee and 24 percent of the Central Discipline Committee. It also sent 22 percent of the Central Advisory Committee members into complete retirement but increased the total membership slightly to accomodate new entrants.[113] After the plenum, Hu Yaobang was able to report that the revamping of leadership of all national party and government organs, provincial organs, and PLA units down to division level had been basically completed, and that future readjustment would bring only marginal reduction of the average age of leaders.[114]

Even at this time, however, the problem of resistance by old cadres had by no means totally disappeared. Overall, only about half of the old cadres had retired up to this point. Even some cadres who had already gone into retirement continued to doubt the abilities of the new younger leaders and wanted to give them unsolicited advice.[115] As a result, the party changed its position and suggested that old cadres should stop work as soon as they retired and allow their successors to make, and learn from, their own mistakes.[116] The year 1986 produced an even faster pace in the implementation of the retirement program and, by June, some 1.8 million old cadres had taken retirement.[117] Since China probably had a total of some 2.6 million "old cadres" in the country as of the mid-1980s,[118] this means that 70 percent of them had been retired by this time.

Yet the party did not relent its pressure. A national conference of senior party leaders was called by the Central Advisory Committee from June 30 to July 4, 1986, to discuss how old cadres could lend "positive support" to their successors. Urging the retired senior cadres to have confidence in the younger leaders, Bo Yibo stated bluntly that the "best practical action" old cadres could take to show their support for the new leaders was to refrain from interfering or obstructing the latter's work.[119] Thus, by the time the party's rectification campaign was concluded in mid-1987, it had also achieved the major objective of sending a whole generation of powerholders into retirement.

Gerontocracy had become a serious liability to the party and the state by the late 1970s. Yet, empirically, the CCP could not turn to any other socialist country for inspiration. One effective formula for solving the problem of aging leadership was Stalin's Great Purge of the 1930s, which erased an entire stratum of old revolutionaries to make room for younger ones. But the human cost was exceedingly high, and the party's own vitality was sapped for many years afterward. The Stalinist model was totally unacceptable to the Chinese, especially in

Table 1

Progress of the Retirement Policy, 1982–86

Month/year	Total retired to date
March 1983	423,000
November 1984	1,300,000
June 1986	1,800,000

Sources: RMRB, July 6, 1983, p. 4; November 9, 1984, p. 4; February 11, 1985, p. 1; September 19, 1985, p. 2; February 9, 1986, p. 1; June 29, 1986, p. 1; *Hongqi*, 1986, no. 12, p. 2.

the wake of the Cultural Revolution. Therefore, the Chinese devised their own policy of retiring their leaders through a combination of normative appeals and materialistic inducements. Has the retirement policy made any significant achievements? The answer is yes.

To be sure, implementation of the program encountered serious obstacles because there was widespread unwillingness among cadres to relinquish their power and positions. While the party bought off many old leading cadres with large sums of money and numerous privileges, it could not afford to extend similar treatment to the lesser cadres. Consequently, the latter often resorted to self-help, embezzling money or extracting promises of privileges from their work units as quid pro quo for accepting retirement. The retiring cadres' conduct was often so blatant that they significantly damaged the party's prestige in the public eye.[120]

Yet, in spite of these shortcomings, the CCP has scored an impressive success in solving the problem of gerontocracy. If nature had been allowed to bring about leadership changes in China, the old cadres would have continued their domination over Chinese politics until the end of the twentieth century, and even then they would be succeeded by other old leaders. The Chinese Communist Party eschewed the use of violent purges to drive old leaders from offices, but decided to pursue a patient, peaceful, and gradualist approach by introducing a retirement program.

By 1987, the party had succeeded in bringing about a peaceful transition process whereby power was taken away from a generation of old revolutionaries—with their distinct beliefs and experiences, social and educational backgrounds, policy orientations, and personal styles—and put into the hands of younger successors in leadership positions on all levels. In a bloodless manner, the party eased the old cadres out of the political stage at least a decade before nature would have taken its toll.

Has the retirement policy of the 1980s become firmly institutionalized in the

Chinese polity and freed China from the liabilities of gerontocracy in the future? The answer to this question is far less certain. Like many other reforms of the post-Mao era, the retirement program was enforceable only because many old leaders (e.g., Deng Xiaoping and Chen Yun) had stayed in power.

This glaring discrepancy between theory and practice could not fail to produce a cynical conclusion among many people that retirement only applied to people who had already lost their power, while the powerful cadres could either evade retirement or retire in name but not in fact. In a country where political power was not derived from the offices but from the political leaders themselves, everyone realized that retirement had different implications for different people. This point was amply confirmed by the political career of Deng Xiaoping since 1979. Although he never held the top office in either the party or the state, no one doubted that he was the most powerful leader in the country. Likewise, although many old cadres were retired from office, they had by no means relinquished their power.

The single most dramatic case to remind people of the power of retired leaders was Hu Yaobang's downfall in January 1987. As the party's general secretary, Hu had offended many old cadres precisely because he had been overenthusiastic in asking for their retirement. As soon as Hu took a political misstep, the old leaders were quick to descend upon him. It is significant that Hu's ouster was not initiated or voted by his colleagues in the Politburo alone, but was brought about in an "extended meeting of the Politburo" attended by seventeen semiretired leaders from the Central Advisory Committee, who offered harsh criticisms and tipped the balance against him.

On both the national and provincial levels, there still existed a sizable number of very old cadres in office after 1987. It seemed that if powerful cadres strongly refused to retire, they could manage to stay on. Consequently, in some situations, leaders in their seventies and even eighties were still in office.[121] Or they might retire in name, but keep their power in fact. This situation became most obvious in the aftermath of the Tiananmen Square incident in the spring of 1989, when the political center-stage was suddenly reclaimed by octogenarian party leaders, including the "semiretired" ones (e.g., Yang Shangkun, Li Xianian, and Wang Zhen) and the more fully retired ones (e.g., Deng Xiaoping, Bo Yibo, Deng Yingchao, and Hu Qiaomu).

How these facts will affect the future is difficult to determine, but it seems that at least three variables can have an impact on the future prospects of the retirement policy: personal prestige, the concentration of powers in one person, and the character of the party itself. The success of the retirement program of the 1980s owed much to Deng Xiaoping. Had it not been for Deng's personal stature, dynamism, determination, and effective control over both the party machinery and the PLA, Ye Jianying and many other leaders would probably never have agreed to retire. After Deng departs from the scene, it is not clear who will have the requisite personal qualities and political clout to enforce the retirement policy.

The character of the party is a crucial variable. As long as the party remains organized according to the conventional principle of "democractic centralism," then the leaders will ultimately decide if their own retirement is to be bound by the party's policy formulated in the 1980s. At this point, there is no way to predict whether future leaders will be swayed more by their respect for party precedent or by their insatiable appetite for power.

Building a "Third Echelon" of Revolutionary Successors

The Chinese Communist Party's control over the state and society was achieved by two major groups: its regular members and its cadre corps. The party's regular members were its front-line agents in the bureaucracy, economic enterprises, the military, public security forces, mass organizations, and throughout society. Not all cadres were party members, but, in any organ, cadres who were also party members usually wielded far greater influence than the nonparty cadres, and only the former could have a realistic chance to be promoted to leadership positions. Therefore, cadres who were also party members were the guardians of the revolution and the implementors of the party's programs. Cadres constituted the "backbone" (*gugan*) of the party's operations and were expected to possess higher political consciousness, greater ideological understanding, firmer revolutionary commitment, and superior organizational and professional competence.[122]

The Cadre System under Mao

The CCP began to develop coherent procedures and practices for the recruitment and utilization of cadres after Liberation. The cadre system that emerged was different from the civil-service systems in most other modern countries and had several characteristics. For one thing, being a cadre was a permanent occupation. Once a person was conferred cadre status, he would remain a cadre for life, because cadres were exempt from the mandatory retirement requirements that applied to ordinary workers. The putative advantages of this system were that it could foster a sense of pride in status and solidarity with the work unit, improve familiarity with one's work, stabilize career expectations, and assure personnel continuity. But it also had the potential of causing stagnation within the cadre corps and reducing the circulation between the cadre corps and the general population.

Second, the selection, allocation, and assignment of cadres on all levels and in all professions were processed exclusively by the party's organization departments on various levels. These departments selected the candidates who were submitted for approval by the party secretaries. But the staff in organization departments often performed their duties in a vacuum without consulting the masses, the cadres themselves, or the agencies that had vacancies to be filled.

Typically, the organization departments treated their duties as a paper exercise and relied heavily or exclusively on the dossiers of the individual cadres. They were preoccupied with reaching numerical targets rather than evaluating the personal or professional qualities of the candidates to match the cadres' talents to the job requirements.

In this closed system of cadre management, the party neglected to develop a set of precise, objective, and comprehensive guidelines for selection. At times, the party's cadre policy was dominated by a simple slogan or crude criteria, which provided little consistency over time.[123] The upshot was that although the party nominally had complete control over the cadres' careers, its management was quite chaotic. Since job assignments were often made for life, mismatches could result not only in reduced efficiency and waste of talents, but also in demoralization among the cadres.

Third, the avenues of upward mobility for cadres were both narrow and mechanical. The standard procedure was to promote cadres only from the next lower level within the same bureaucratic substructure. Thus, district cadres were picked only from the county level, provincial cadres were picked only from the district level, and so forth. This mode of selection and promotion automatically excluded certain cadres from leadership positions. Intellectuals in research and educational institutions, for example, rarely had the opportunity to be assigned to positions in the state bureaucracy or economic enterprises. Candidates to leadership positions were often promoted only from party and government organs.

Fourth, the party never institutionalized a system to conduct routine evaluation of the cadres' performance. Many lower-level organization departments had no rules to follow and were allowed to manage cadres in their own idiosyncratic ways. To gain entry into the cadre corps, one had to possess good social class backgrounds and demonstrate loyalty to the party. But thereafter, promotions and salary raises were made mechanically on the basis of seniority, without much regard for the cadres' competence or professional knowledge. Occasionally they were made on grounds of ideology or political activism. To the extent that evaluations were conducted, they were conducted sporadically and according to highly impressionistic factors. No feedback was sought from the masses. Since the party's organization departments in many places were chronically understaffed and typically isolated from the rest of the society, few of them ever actually possessed a sound understanding of the qualifications of cadres under their jurisdiction. This resulted in the promotion of many cadres who were unqualified for their positions, but the PRC tradition was such that once cadres were promoted to higher positions, they would never be transferred to lower positions.[124] One major exception to this extremely rigid system was the crucial role played by leaders in determining the cadres' careers. This means that personal connections (*guanxi*) and political pull could become the most important variables affecting cadres' careers.[125] This situation often enabled leaders to build personal factions or indulge in cronyism and favoritism.

Fifth, this system encouraged bureaucratic agencies to view their cadres and workers as their possessions. They would rather keep their cadres underutilized in their own units than allow them to be transferred to other agencies where they could make a greater contribution. Cadres assigned to one functional area rarely had a chance to move to a different functional area. In spite of the rational objective to achieve maximum utilization of cadres through centralized control and planning, lateral mobility of cadres was extremely limited.

Sixth, this system made it hard to control the size of bureaucracy. Many units engaged in inflating their need for cadres beyond their actual manpower requirements. This led both to bloated bureaucratic growth, as well as fertile grounds for factional infighting when the cadres' energies were not devoted to their work.[126]

Under this system, promotions were often made en masse, rather than on the basis of individual merit. The number of years of service or the year of graduation from school often constituted the only objective criterion for promotion. Cadres learned to gear their expectations for salary increase and promotion to their seniority instead of their performance records. Thus, cadres' basic concerns were to accumulate years in service, rather than merit points for performance. The smoothest way to accumulate years was to maintain harmony with colleagues, to curry favor with the superiors, and to refrain from making waves or suggesting innovative ideas in the work unit. Another by-product of this system was the sense of absolute equality. No one should be promoted unless everyone in the same age bracket was promoted.

As a practice, the cadres, particularly leading cadres, were never demoted nor dismissed for professional incompetence or dereliction of official duty. When they became extremely unpopular in one work unit, they were transferred to another work unit and maintained their leadership status. Since cadres were appointed from above, their superiors also developed a strong stake in saving their own face by refusing to admit that their appointees were deficient.

Throughout the decades of incessant political turmoil in Chinese Communist politics, lower-level cadres learned that self-preservation required that they observe closely the intentions and orientations of their superiors and not the masses. The more conscientious cadres might faithfully report the masses' sentiments to their superiors, but most of them could safely ignore the masses. It was always safer for cadres to defer completely to their superiors' decisions. Every time a decision was needed, it was best to seek instruction from above, step by step, often all the way to the central party or government.[127]

Evolution of a Policy to Groom Successors

The cadre system as described above obviously could not meet the needs of the new leaders, whose major objective was to accelerate the pace of the country's economic growth. To Deng and his close associates, the solution lay in the

Table 2

Correlation between Cadre Age and Education, 1983 (percent)

Age group	Below 20	31–40	41–50
College	20	22	20
Senior high school	64	47	34
College and senior high school	84	69	54
Junior high school	15	24	34
Primary school/illiterate	01	07	12
Junior high and below	16	31	46

Source: Jianghuai luntan (Hofei), 1984, no. 1, p. 38.

promotion of a large number of middle-aged and younger cadres to become successors (*jiebanren*), which could only be implemented by departing from the Maoist norms of cadre management. As Deng pointed out, the best safeguard for the party's new ideological and political line was to select quickly the right kinds of "successors" so that the Gang remnants could be prevented from restoring radical programs.[128] This earlier version of Deng leadership's succession plan also introduced several noteworthy features.

First, it put forward the idea that succession should be conducted not on an individual or personal basis, but in a collective manner. It was hoped that this could avoid many of the mistakes of personal leadership previously committed by Mao.

Second, it made clear that people tainted by previous association with the Gang of Four were to be denied eligibility as successors, because they would surely restore Gang politics.[129]

Third, it underscored the necessity to select successors while the old leaders were still capable of exercising power. In this way, the old leaders could groom the successors "for several years" to help the latter achieve maturity, and hold the Gang remnants in check and discourage them from attempting to seize power.[130] In line with this thinking, the succession policy was to be implemented in a staggered fashion so that the newly promoted younger cadres would coexist with the old cadres for a period of time. Although Deng was also in favor of implementing a retirement system, he believed that the issue of choosing successors should be given a higher priority at this time.[131]

Fourth, the party committed itself to a general timetable to complete the succession process. In late 1979, Deng estimated that it would take about three years to stabilize the leadership on all levels. During this interval, old cadres would continue to serve in the top positions of the higher-level party and state organs, while younger cadres should be promoted to the second and third positions. In lower-level organs, younger cadres could be promoted directly into the

Table 3

Age of Leading Cadres at Provincial, District, and County Levels for the Entire Country, December 1985

Year	Province	District	County
1982	62	56	49
1985	53	49	44

Table 4

College Education among Leading Cadres (percent)

Year	Province	District	County
1985	62	55	54

Source: RMRB, June 29, 1986, p. 1.

top positions. With respect to the successors' ages, Deng stated that although he preferred to see many college graduates below thirty years of age promoted to leadership positions, the most immediate objective was to promote enough middle-aged cadres into the leadership within the next five years.[132]

Finally, while the successors were to be selected on all levels, the party's strategy was to select them first on the lower to middle levels and then on the higher levels. Thus, for instance, young cadres could be promoted to be first or second leaders in middle and lower organs, second or third leaders in higher organs, and then gradually be promoted as first leaders.[133]

Deng gave succession policy a new dimension in his speech on August 18, 1980, in which he contended that the superiority of socialism must be demonstrated by economic and political performances. Deng said, "The major task at the present is to identify, promote, or even boldly promote middle-aged and younger cadres of superior qualifications" to carry out the economic and political programs.[134] This meant that successors were needed not only to prevent power from falling into the wrong hands (of the radicals), but also to employ power effectively to achieve the positive goals of socialist construction.

In spite of the increasing emphasis given to the succession issue after the Third Plenum, progress was very slow. Even by 1981, many provincial- and municipal-level organs had promoted only one or two "younger" cadres in token compliance with the party's policy, and usually placed them at the bottom of the leadership rosters. Since it was common for a party committee to have as many as seventeen or eighteen members in its standing committee, such accomplishments were quite meaningless.[135] As Chen Yun noted, many in the party still resisted the promotion of cadres in their fifties to leadership positions, while resentment against the promotion of cadres in their forties or younger was even stronger.[136]

These conditions convinced Chen Yun that the party had reached a critical juncture, for if the old cadres were allowed to serve until death, the party would one day be forced hastily to appoint unqualified people to succeed them, which would put the party in serious jeopardy. The only alternative was to plan ahead and promote cadres with both virtue and talents.[137] In mid-1981, Chen Yun estimated that at least ten thousand cadres should be promoted in a preliminary move, and that only this massive number could satisfy the needs for new leaders on the national and provincial levels and constitute a critical mass to overpower the attempts by the remnants of the Gang to sabotage the revolution.[138]

Qualifications for Successors

After the early 1980s, as the numbers and responsibilities of the successors were increased, their qualifications also received closer attention. The categories of people who were disqualified from candidacy to be successors became broader and more specific as time went by. At first, only people with close ties to the Gang of Four were disqualified. Later, the disqualification was broadened to include the "three types."[139]

The party also became more specific about the positive qualifications of candidates designated as successors. In the late 1970s, strong emphasis was still placed on the candidates' political ideological loyalty, revolutionary commitment, good discipline, and general ability to work.[140] In time, other qualifications were added and accorded equal importance. Education and professional expertise began to be stressed more often.[141] As the Commentator of *People's Daily* said on June 26, 1981, "Our leadership must consist of both statesmen and experts. We need comrades who are strong politically to be party secretaries, but we also need experts who have strong organizational ability to guide production."[142] Greater emphasis was also given to promoting intellectuals in leadership positions, especially college graduates of the 1950s and early 1960s.[143]

The age factor was given greater emphasis. Younger people were praised as having more energy, talent, and better capacity to learn; they could also afford to undergo longer periods of apprenticeship before assuming major responsibilities. In addition, younger cadres had lived through the turmoil of the Cultural Revolution as ordinary citizens and therefore were better able to uncover the diehards of the Gang of Four among the masses, and to prevent them from infiltrating the ranks of successors. For these reasons, Chen Yun expressed the hope in 1981 that 70 percent or more of the newly promoted cadres should be in their forties or younger.[144]

In conjunction with its retirement policy, in February 1982 the party also imposed age limits on office-holders on various levels. Thus, for example, it stipulated that ministers and provincial governors should not exceed sixty-five years of age, and that their deputies as well as division and section chiefs should not exceed sixty years of age. Even cadres below the age limit were encouraged to take early retirement if they were in poor health.

Both Chen Yun and Deng agreed that promotion and grooming should be conducted in an orderly and gradual fashion. Chen Yun personally suggested several different ways to institutionalize the system of succession. One way was first to send promising young cadres to the communes for a certain period of practical training, and then slowly to move them up the county, regional, and provincial hierarchy step by step. Another way was to promote younger cadres initially to become personal assistants to senior leaders so that they could develop their own leadership skills. After several years, they could become a "reserve force" as higher-level leading cadres in their own right.[145]

Yet, in spite of these refinements to the succession policy, progress was unsatisfactory. The party's decision in late 1982 to launch a rectification campaign the following year greatly increased the urgency of implementing the succession policy. If the old cadres refused to retire and younger cadres were unable to take over and invigorate the leadership, the prospects of a successful rectification might be severely reduced. The combined pressures persuaded the party that an even more ambitious and comprehensive succession plan was needed. The solution was to create the "third echelon."

The Concept of the "Third Echelon"

The plan to create a "third echelon" was unveiled at a Central Work Conference in June 1983. According to this new concept, China's leadership hierarchy would consist of three echelons. The first echelon referred to a very small number of senior leaders, such as Ye Jianying, Deng Xiaoping, Li Xiannian, and Chen Yun, who were all over seventy years of age and who occupied the top positions in the party, state, and the military. The second echelon referred to leaders like Hu Yaobang and Zhao Ziyang who were also above sixty years old and who exercised direct control over daily affairs in their respective fields of responsibility. The party believed that it needed to create a third echelon as well, consisting of better educated cadres in their fifties, forties, and even thirties whose function was to reinvigorate the leadership.[146]

The idea of an "echelon" was borrowed directly from military science, and it reflected the Chinese leaders' intellectual proclivity for long-term and grand-scale "strategic planning." The Chinese Communists had always assumed that a revolutionary force was needed to defend and carry on the revolution. It was quite natural for them to assume also that this revolutionary force should consist of several echelons. An echelon was not just a collection of individuals, nor merely a functional component or a branch of the whole army, such as the infantry or the artillery. Instead, the echelon possessed all the key components to perform its combat mission as an independent unit. The Chinese chose their term carefully, as *tidui* meant literally a ladder-shaped (different from a pyramid-shaped) formation, with each rung of the ladder performing identical functions to bring the realization of the goal closer. In a well-planned combat situation, the crucial question was the timing of deployment of the echelons to the front line. Ideally, the echelon in combat would be replaced by a fresh echelon before the former was exhausted. The battle would be won if there was an endless procession of echelons that could be sent into action.

In line with this thinking, the numbers, composition, and qualifications of members in each echelon must be in proper proportion and in full readiness before combat. In the revolutionary struggle, just like in war, echelons would also be deployed as the first line, second line, third line, and so forth. Each echelon was expected to execute its own duties and yield the field to the next echelon. Therefore, in the Chinese chart of succession, when one generation of leaders had fulfilled its revolutionary mission and reached retirement age, it would be readily replaced by the reserves on the next rung of the succession ladder, and so on.

This represented a radical departure from past thinking on the issue of revolutionary succession. Even during the Cultural Revolution, when Mao conducted massive purges in the party, he never entertained the idea of retiring all old cadres to make room for the younger cadres. He merely wanted to eliminate people who were disloyal to him, replacing them with reliable ones. His most innovative formula for revolutionary leadership was really just a combination of old, middle-aged, and young cadres in unspecified proportions.

The party's new succession plan also differed from its predecessors in several other important areas. In the first place, the third-echelon concept required the designation of specific individuals to be successors who would immediately begin their apprenticeship for the leadership positions. In contrast, earlier policies only indicated the desire to train people as potential successors, rather than to give them actual responsibilities prior to succession.

Second, the third-echelon plan was a concrete policy bound by a target date of completion in eight years, or by about 1990.[147] Previous calls for creating revolutionary successors were often mere expressions of intent with no timetables for implementation. Consequently, the party never developed an institutionalized approach to select and appoint successors or to decide how many of them were needed. Any grooming of the successors was performed haphazardly. Nobody was assigned the specific responsibility to aid and supervise the successors' progress. The policy was conducted in the style of a political campaign. Therefore, most cases of cultivating revolutionary successors ended inconclusively, and the party center rarely checked the accomplishments of lower-level organs.

Third, the qualifications for the candidates were different. Previously, the criteria for identifying revolutionary successors were either ambiguous or emphasized only political qualities. Class origin always played a critical role in the choice, as only people from the revolutionary classes were eligible. The third-echelon policy required candidates to possess not only good political qualities, but also youthfulness, education, and professional expertise. On the other hand, class origin was no longer explicitly emphasized, and intellectuals were given preferred status, at least nominally.

In addition to more stringent personal qualifications, the third-echelon policy also addressed the issue of collective attributes of the successors. Ideally, the number of people in different age brackets of the third echelon should be proportionate though not identical, and they should possess diverse yet complementary professional and educational skills. In this way, they could form a well-balanced reserve force ready to be promoted into leadership positions at any time. When the first echelon retired, the second echelon would move into top leadership positions, and the third echelon would also move one rung upward on the succession ladder. Thus, the plan did not mean that individuals replaced one another. Instead, an entire echelon was to be replaced by another, with younger and better-educated members.[148]

Finally, the policy of the third echelon represented a Chinese breakthrough in the Communists' thinking pertaining to revolutionary succession. No Communist Party has ever successfully institutionalized succession. Every succession poses a crisis of major proportions and is resolved on an ad hoc basis, often involving a considerable struggle for power or even violence. The succession struggle after the death of Mao was only the most recent reminder of this pattern in China.

The policy of the third echelon not only was designed to ensure a smooth and orderly transition of power and defend the regime's stability against the restorationist attempts of the remnants of Gang of Four, but also was expected to accelerate the pace of the country's political and economic development for years to come. Thus, in Deng Xiaoping's view, the party should continue to build its fourth and fifth echelons in the future, because only the building of these echelons could provide the personnel that would ensure the continuity of China's current policies.[149] Hu Yaobang also stated, "Our [economic takeoff] in the 1990s will depend on the current third echelon, and our takeoff in the next century will depend on our next third echelon."[150] These remarks showed that the third echelon was meant to become a permanent feature of the CCP's policy on leadership. Leaders must assume the responsibility to groom the third echelon at all times. Once the age differentials between the echelons were stabilized, then succession would occur at predictable intervals.

Accomplishments of the Third-Echelon Policy

In theory, the third-echelon policy seemed a marked improvement over the CCP's previous unsystematic ways of handling revolutionary succession. As originally conceived in 1982, the party's plan was to create the third echelon in three stages. First, a large number of qualified cadres would be quickly promoted into the leadership on all levels. Second, the new leaders would coexist with the old leaders until 1985 when the latter would have all been retired from office. Finally, during 1985–1990, the retirement policy would have become fully institutionalized, and the standards of cadre selection would be further tightened to ensure the quality of the new leaders.[151]

To meet this schedule, the party estimated that some 1,000 younger cadres were needed to fill the top leadership posts of the central ministries and the provincial governments; 30,000 cadres were needed by the ministries and provincial governments to fill leadership positions of organs on the district (*di*) and municipal (*shi*) or division (*si*) and bureau (*ju*) levels; and an additional 100,000 cadres were needed to fill leadership posts of organs on the county (*xian*) level. In other words, the party's plan called for the creation of the third echelon by the first quarter of 1985, and it needed to promote over 130,000 young cadres into leadership posts on all levels nationwide.[152] This new leadership would then be consolidated in the next five years.

Once the policy was decided upon, all organs throughout the country were required to draw up plans to reduce their size, to reduce the leaders' age and increase their educational qualifications, and to select younger cadres to enter the reserve corps to be eventually promoted into leadership positions.[153]

However, the policy still ran into considerable opposition during its implementation. A round of institutional streamlining had just taken place in 1982, during which most of the cadres promoted to leadership positions were in their fifties and sixties. These cadres had barely had time to enjoy their new positions when the third-echelon policy was adopted, which immediately placed their job security in jeopardy. Several arguments were quickly marshaled to oppose the third-echelon concept. One argument was that since a new leadership had only recently been installed, the party should allow it enough time to consolidate rather than rushing to create yet another leadership. Another argument was that the incumbent leaders had more pressing responsibilities to discharge than the creation of a third echelon. A third argument was that successors should be selected and trained in "due course" or at a "natural pace," and not in a contrived push.[154]

Even when leaders grudgingly accepted the rationale for creating a generation of younger successors, they believed that it was necessary to uphold the party's old conventions and practices, and they resented the ways in which the new policy was to be implemented. Many leaders regarded the principle of absolute equality and the seniority system as sacrosanct. They believed that all cadres in the same age brackets and with similar career backgrounds should be promoted simultaneously without exception. They believed it to be divisive and dangerous to promote only some cadres into the third echelon. They regarded it as even more unthinkable to promote younger and better-qualified cadres over the heads of the older and more "experienced" cadres.[155]

But, of course, the party could not possibly agree with these objections. The top leaders in 1983 had already become dissatisfied with the result of the institutional streamline of 1982 because it had promoted many cadres who were either already too old or unqualified. The leadership change of 1982 produced at best an interim arrangement.[156] The party rejected the proposal to allow succession to occur at a "natural pace" because it would take much too long and might still produce successors unqualified to undertake the tasks of the four modernizations. Consequently, the party made it clear that leaders must give high priority to the creation of the third echelon of successors while performing their other functions concurrently.[157]

Building the third echelon necessarily occurred in tandem with retiring the old cadres, since new leaders could move up only as fast as vacancies were made available on the higher levels. The retirement policy in general, however, made very slow progress from 1978 to 1983, and it moved into a higher gear only toward the end of 1983 when the party's rectification campaign was launched. But even then, the pace was sluggish. Although one round of leadership revamping on the provincial and district levels had been completed by the end of 1983, and many new cadres were recruited into the leadership, many of them were only slightly younger or better qualified than their predecessors, so the same problems might reemerge in a few short years. This led the national leaders to conclude that the creation of a third echelon of successors must be given a more vigorous push.[158]

The beginning of the party rectification campaign created additional incentives to accelerate the pace of succession, because the campaign provided an ideal setting to screen out the undesirables and to identify the really worthy candidates for succession. Many elder statesmen in the first echelon had already gone into retirement, and members of the second echelon were preoccupied with formulating political and economic reform programs. The national leaders felt an even more urgent need for a large number of capable, energetic, younger leaders to strengthen the party's organizational sinews, to implement their reform programs, and to ensure the continuation of the new political line since 1979.[159]

After about two years of intense work, Song Renqiong, the former head of the Central Organization Department (1978–1983), declared in October 1984 that "At present, from the national to the local level, party secretaries are engaged in the creation of the third echelon. This is a central task not only of the party's organizational work for this year, but also of the entire party's important work. Although the rectification campaign has just begun and there are many things to be done, the creation of the third echelon must not be delayed."[160]

Indeed, the party began a vigorous drive to cultivate the third echelon in 1984,[161] and by the year's end, Deng Xiaoping had become so pleased with the results of leadership rejuvenation on the national level that he characterized the current central party leadership as being "more mature, and more capable in managing a multitude of problems." He cited the performance of such third-echelon members as Tian Jiyun, Li Peng, Hu Qili, and Wang Zhaoguo to illustrate his point.[162] Deng also echoed Chen Yun's suggestion to promote more people in their thirties and forties, and he urged old comrades to abandon their reservations and offer more help to implement the succession policy.[163] Bo Yibo exuded even greater confidence when he observed that there was no longer any ground to worry about the continuity of party and state policies after the old leaders' departure from the political stage, because of the third echelon's firm hold.[164]

Under intense pressure from the top, both the policy of retiring old cadres and that of promoting younger successors had made great strides by 1985. In that year, the party released a body of statistics to show its accomplishments in building the third echelon. The top leaders of China's 107 central ministries and departments as well as its 29 provinces had been extensively overhauled.[165] Thus, for instance, on the national level, the average age of the 41 ministers and deputy ministers of the State Council declined from 65.7 in 1982 to 59.5 in the spring of 1985, while the ordinary cadres in these ministries with college-level education increased from 38 percent to 50 percent during this period.[166] Another survey showed that, in early 1985, the average age of the members of the third echelon promoted into the leadership of the ministries and provincial governments was forty-three, and more than 90 percent had college-level culture, while nearly 80 percent had special technical skills.[167]

A significant revamping of the national party leadership also occurred at the Fourth Plenum of the party's Twelfth National Congress in September 1985. About 18 percent of the membership of the reconstituted Central Committee (sixty-four full and alternate members) had joined the committee for the first time. The average age of these new members and alternates was 50.1 years, and 76.6 percent had college education. This group included the outstanding members who had recently been promoted to leadership positions in the central and provincial party, the government, and the military.[168] As Bo Yibo proudly noted, these results were brought about because of the party's faithful adherence to the formula of succession by "echelon."[169]

On the provincial level, by October 1984, the membership of party standing committees on the provincial and municipal levels as well as the number of governors and deputy governors had been reduced by 34 percent as compared with 1982–83.[170] Their average age dropped by seven years. Those leaders below 50 years of age increased from the previous 15 percent to 48 percent. Few leaders were in their sixties, but quite a number of the new leaders were only in their thirties. All new entrants into provincial party leadership since 1983 had education that was higher than senior high school level, and many had technical backgrounds. Those with college-level education increased from the former 20 percent to 43 percent. The number of department and bureau chiefs on the provincial and municipal levels was reduced by 36 percent. Their average age dropped by eight years, while those with college-level education increased from 14 percent to 44 percent.[171] There were also more females and members of national minorities in the newly reconstituted provincial leaderships.[172]

Extensive changes had been made involving the governors and party secretaries in all twenty-nine provincial units during 1984–85. Of the twenty-two provincial leaders who had reached mandatory retirement age, eighteen were actually retired. The average age of provincial leadership (including governors, deputy governors, and members of standing committees of provincial party committees) was reduced from 57 years to 53 years. The youngest governor was only 45 years old, and the youngest provincial party secretary was 42 years old. Those with college-level education had increased from 43 percent in 1982–83 to 60 percent. During this revamping, 126 young cadres were promoted into provincial leadership positions. Of this subgroup, 63 percent were below 50 years old, and another 27 percent between 50 and 55 years old. Also, 80 percent of this subgroup had college-level educations.[173] Among leading cadres on the subprovincial level (i.e., district, city, *zhou*, or major administrative departments and bureaus in the provinces), the average age declined from 58 years in 1982 to 50 years in 1985. The ordinary cadres in these organs with college-level educations increased from 14 percent in 1982 to 44 percent in 1985.[174]

Finally, the building of the third echelon on the county level and the reorganization of the county-level leadership throughout the entire country had also been basically accomplished by October 1984. The reorganization produced an 18 percent reduction in the number of members of the party's Standing Committee and in the county magistrates and deputy magistrates. Their average age was 42–43 years, and about one-third were below 40 years of age. The improvement of the county-level leaders' educational qualifications was equally impressive. While only 30.8 percent of these people had college education in 1982, after the reorganization in 1985 this was increased to 45 percent. As a result, in 80 percent of the counties, either the county magistrate or the party secretary had a college education. Furthermore, after the reorganization, some 15.4 percent possessed technical specializations, whereas previously none did.[175]

It is not easy to establish the exact number of young cadres who had been promoted into leadership positions, because different reports by the party or the press often referred to different categories of cadres or "leaders."[176] Probably in the broadest sense of the term of "leadership," the PRC had promoted 469,000 younger cadres into positions of "leadership" above the county/*qu* level between 1982 and December 1985, and more than 2 million young and middle-aged cadres to fill ordinary cadre positions in organizations above the county level before mid-1986.[177] Without a doubt, these younger cadres were able to move upward because a large number of vacancies had been created by the retirement of old cadres.[178] As party data suggest, the majority of the new cadres were under 50 years of age and had college-level educations.[179]

These data suggest that the party was able to make great strides in fulfilling the numerical objectives of its policy on the third echelon within the timetable it set in 1982. By September 1985 when the Fourth Plenum of the Twelfth Party Congress was convened, both Chen Yun and Deng Xiaoping were obviously quite gratified with the accomplishments of the orderly succession. Chen Yun said, "If we can maintain the ladder-shaped structure of the cadre corps, then we can be sure that the party's mission will be handed down from generation to generation. We have made considerable achievements on this issue."[180] Deng also said that "in the past several years, the cooperation and succession between new and old cadres have been conducted quite smoothly."[181]

Therefore, by late 1985 or early 1986, the results of the party's new policy of managing revolutionary succession were indeed impressive in quantitative terms. In only a few short years, the PRC brought into office an entirely new generation of leaders. The magnitude of the transfer of power was not only unprecedented in the PRC's own history, but also unrivaled in the history of modern China. The conception was a daring one, and the implementation was swift. Above all, the transfer did not entail any bloodshed, which was remarkable against China's historical background.

But what about the substance? How exactly was the policy implemented? What was the caliber of successors? Were they capable of fulfilling the original dual expectations of defending the regime and carrying out its programs? Has the CCP solved the issue of revolutionary succession once and for all? What long-term ramifications will the policy have on China's political development in the future? To answer these questions, it is necessary first to take a closer look at how the third echelon was actually formed, and what characteristics it possessed.

4

Major Attributes of the Third Echelon

THE CHANGE of leadership in a country can often have enormous political importance. The Chinese attempt to create an entire generation of "revolutionary successors" was a particularly dazzling event because of the sheer size of this new leadership. Before one can fully appreciate how this leadership might affect China's future, it is necessary to go beyond the official claims of success to examine some of its key human dimensions. The issues that are of special interest here include how the new leaders were selected, what personality traits they possessed, and how well prepared they were, educationally and professionally, to assume their leadership duties.

Candidate Selection

The new policy made the selection of the third echelon a joint effort by several groups. First, the candidates must have the support of the masses and win their nomination by "democratic means." Second, their credentials and character were to be investigated by the party's organization department on the same level. Finally, the recommendations must receive the endorsement by party leadership on the same level and the approval of the superior level.[1] The party vowed that it would not allow the candidates of the third echelon to be dictated by a small group of leaders behind closed doors and in great secrecy.[2]

On paper, the involvement of the masses represented an important departure from the party's previous cadre policy. Under the new policy, the masses were entitled to express their judgments on the candidates' qualifications.[3] If faithfully implemented, this would have marked a major improvement over the party's tradition of shrouding its cadre policy in great mystery, and it would have created a much healthier relationship between cadres and the general populace.

In actuality, however, the new policy was merely lip service paid to the mass-line theory: the masses were never given a chance to express their prefer-

ences in the choice of the third echelon.[4] Candidates were predominantly selected either by the organization departments with the leaders' approval, or by
the leaders directly.

The Role of the Organization Departments

To the extent that the organization departments were given the responsibility to
recommend candidates, the fairness and efficiency of the selection process was
affected by two factors. First, the organization departments on various levels had
barely been revived from the destruction of the Cultural Revolution. There had
been enormous personnel turnovers since 1976, especially among the younger
cadres with whom the organization department staff usually had less familiarity.
The need to promote a huge number of cadres into leadership positions occurred
suddenly and far exceeded anything ever experienced by the organization department hierarchy. Many of them still adhered to the old attitudes and practices that
were clearly not conducive to the rational selection of candidates to the third
echelon. The second factor was that cadres working in organizational, personnel,
and political-ideological fields who were primarily responsible for making the
selections had suffered a serious decline of their social prestige in the early
1980s. This decline was a big psychological blow that caused considerable demoralization and adversely affected the quality of their work.[5]

One of the problems of organization department staff was their propensity to
employ the old techniques of "political investigation" as the primary means to
select candidates. Strong emphasis was placed on people's political loyalty and
reliability so that their class backgrounds, social relationships, past histories, or
even personal idiosyncrasies and lifestyles were scrutinized exhaustively while
their talents and competence received little attention. This made it difficult to
conduct a rational search for talents.[6]

Another problem was the flexibility of selection. Early in the process, Deng
had expressed the desire to see the candidates for the third echelon possess a
diversity of talents.[7] But in practice, many organization departments adhered to
the traditional hierarchical view which assigned different political and ideological statuses to different professions in the country. There was a tendency to pick
candidates for the third echelon primarily from among leading cadres currently
working in the party or the government. Only these people were believed to
possess the requisite qualities to deserve promotion as leaders on the higher
level.[8] Likewise, in the economic field, a state-owned enterprise was regarded as
having an ideologically superior status to a collective enterprise, and therefore
promising cadres from the latter were generally regarded as unqualified to become leading cadres in the former. This status consciousness excluded a large
number of talented cadres, whose work units had inferior political and ideological standings, from being considered as candidates to party and state leadership.[9]

Bureaucratic compartmentalization also interfered with the succession process. Since there was no free labor market in China, and since very few organs had the authority to transfer personnel across geographical or administrative boundaries, succession tended to occur mostly within the individual work units or among work units under the same jurisdiction. This created a situation whereby some ministries or provinces might have a high concentration of talented cadres whose aspirations for upward mobility would be frustrated, while other ministries or provinces might suffer from a severe shortage of talents and yet might not be able to find the talents to fill their vacancies. This mode of succession was terribly inefficient in manpower allocation and utilization.[10]

Many organization departments also preferred to make selection decisions solely on the basis of people's personal dossiers, even though these dossiers were known to contain numerous inaccuracies, misinformation, and even false political accusations. The individuals concerned rarely had a chance to defend themselves because they lacked access to their own dossiers.[11] On the other hand, these dossiers also typically contained little reliable and objective information about the individuals' professional qualifications and competence, and they provided a poor and biased guide to the individuals' fitness to be leaders.[12] Therefore, the organization departments' indulgence in this paper exercise greatly increased the likelihood of their making unfair and unsound recommendations.[13]

The organization departments' unwillingness to conduct independent investigation of the candidates also reinforced their propensity to choose candidates in accordance with the old principle of mechanical egalitarianism and to give excessive weight to seniority. Hence, if one person in a given category was slated for promotion, then everyone else in the same category had to be promoted. Otherwise, no one would be promoted at all.[14]

The work of organization departments was plagued by other problems as well. They sometimes evaluated the candidates from their own narrow institutional perspective rather than looking at the broad needs of the party. Thus, for example, young cadres who had a controversial reputation or a questionable political past would be automatically excluded from consideration. Some organization departments falsified their recommendations to get rid of people they did not like, or to prevent those whose service they needed from being promoted out of their own work units.[15] Probably the most serious defect in the work style of organization departments, however, was their tendency to play it safe by implementing the party's policy in an excessively rigid and mechanical fashion even though it was clearly irrational to do so. The damage of this attitude was most evident in their frenzied effort to fulfill the party's targets of reducing the age and increasing the educational qualifications of the candidates to the third echelon.

To bring down the average age of the leadership, many organization departments promoted people exclusively on account of their age. They began the process by adopting a scale of descending ages for leading cadres on different levels under their jurisdiction and then set out to find candidates who would fit the age requirements, giving little consideration to the candidates' other qualifications. For instance, in 1983–84, the Beijing municipal party set down detailed targets to the effect that, before the end of 1985, at least one of the two top positions in all party or state organizations on the district, county, and bureau levels must be held by a person below fifty years of age, and that at least one-third of the overall leadership core on these levels must be below forty-five years of age.[16]

Many organization departments also resorted to mechanical implementation of the party's academic requirements to meet the goal of the "intellectualization" (zhishihua) of the leading cadres. Again, their method was to set quotas on holders of college diplomas first and then proceed to find people with the requisite degrees to fill these quotas regardless of whether they possessed any leadership skills, or whether their expertise was relevant to their new positions.[17] Again, to cite the example of Beijing, since the city could not find enough people with the required academic credentials, it decided, as a goal for 1985, to rush ten thousand cadres through training sessions to obtain the nominal equivalent of college-level education, and another eighteen thousand cadres to obtain the nominal equivalent of high-school-level education.[18]

The overemphasis on formal qualifications led many party units to became diploma-processing centers that tried to meet quotas by granting a certain number of certificates or diplomas. The academic requirements were so rigid that many young cadres were forced to falsify their educational credentials to meet the new requirement. But as long as education was a key requirement of the policy, it was much less troublesome for lower-level organs to accept formal degrees than to evaluate the substance of a person's education.

The result of this kind of mechanical implementation of central policy was that in many cases younger cadres who had the right age and educational degrees but the wrong qualifications were chosen for the third echelon. Graduates fresh out of schools were catapulted into leadership positions solely for the purpose of bringing down the average age of the incumbent leadership. Many work units ranked candidates according to the time at which they received academic degrees, joined the Communist Youth League, the CCP, or the cadre corps as the only relevant criterion.[19] On the other hand, the organization departments excluded many capable people solely because they were somewhat older. It was common practice in many places for the party organization to bypass for promotions people in their forties, and to force people in their fifties out of leadership posts to make room for younger ones.[20]

This overeagerness to fulfill the quotas enabled many party organs to give the appearance of accomplishing the goals of rejuvenating and intellectualizing the leadership, but actually it was at the expense of genuine leadership quality. Not only unqualified youths but sometimes even undesirable youths were hastily promoted into leadership positions in this way.

It is clear that the national leaders were as responsible for such mechanical implementation of the policy as the local organization departments. During the initial stage of the third-echelon policy, a number of national leaders had enthusiastically promoted the notion of a neat age structure for the new leadership without a careful examination of its full ramifications. They were attracted to the idea by its simplicity, and their endorsement of the idea offered yet another illustration of the Chinese leaders' fascination with totalistic planning. But it also revealed a serious problem of intellectual laziness and the propensity for impulsive actions. When the lower levels received instructions from above, their instincts of self-preservation easily led them to accept these instructions as inviolable truths, even when a purely mechanical implementation of the instructions would obviously produce harmful results. Nonetheless, many organization departments still insisted on achieving absolute uniformity through the method known as a "single cut" (*yidaoqie*) instead of implementing the policy innovatively and flexibly to promote the talented and deserving candidates.

The situation is but another illustration of the dilemma of policy implementation in the Chinese Communist system as a whole. Just as in the economic realm, reforms in general seem to be plagued by a vicious cycle. As the Chinese put it, "once the center relaxes, chaos will ensue, but once the center tightens control, stagnation will follow." In the present case, the organization departments followed the party's policy too literally. The primary concern of the lower levels was not to realize the center's objectives to improve leadership qualities, but to avoid criticism. Since age and academic requirements were the only tangible requirements, it was safe to adhere to them rigidly. In comparison, the political, ideological, and behavioral qualifications were more judgmental, and therefore could be safely ignored.

This manner of implementation was also criticized by the party's Central Organization Department, which urged the lower-level organization departments to give careful consideration to talented people who gained education through self-study, and to people who possessed professional experience and competence.[21] Yet in spite of such criticisms from above, the situation was not visibly improved.[22] The fundamental problem was that the party insisted, on the one hand, on achieving uniform results throughout the entire country, but expected, on the other hand, that the lower levels would exercise initiative and flexibility in selecting the candidates. Wedged between these instructions, the lower-level cadres chose to err on the side of safety by literally adhering to the formal requirements in spite of their harmful results.[23]

Domination by Party Secretaries

Although the party delegated the primary responsibility of screening and investigating the candidates to the organization departments and gave party leaders the right only to approve or reject the candidates, this division of labor was rarely honored. In many cases, the entire selection process of the third echelon was dominated by a few party leaders or even a single leader (such as the first party secretary) without consulting the organization departments.[24]

This means that a very small number of leaders in the party were able to determine the character and composition of the entire third echelon. Even if these leading cadres genuinely wanted to identify deserving talents, they still confronted serious difficulties because, as the leading cadres, they kept a long distance from their subordinates and the broad masses. The feedback mechanisms in Chinese party or state bureaucracies were usually so underdeveloped that leaders would personally know only a small number of people. As a result, they would exclude a large number of worthy candidates.

More seriously, these leaders' own attitudes toward young people; their intellectual proclivities, personal tastes, and subjective feelings; and their own self-interest all became important factors in shaping China's leadership group for the next generation.

Antipathy toward Young Cadres

Although a certain amount of mental distance between the generations is probably to be expected in any society undergoing rapid change, the situation was much more serious in China. Bias against young cadres was already apparent in the 1950s when young cadres who had both ability and education were accorded little respect.[25] Three decades later, many veteran leaders continued to harbor strong misgivings about delegating more responsibilities to younger people because they thought the latter "lacked experience." Many leaders regarded young cadres as poor successors because they could not project authority or inspire respect among the masses. The popular Chinese saying that "people who are not old enough to grow a beard cannot handle things maturely" was frequently cited to show their contempt for youth.[26] Such sentiments were by no means unusual in a country that had always put a high premium on age and seniority and that showed a tendency to equate the latter with wisdom.

The Chinese Communists' own practices reinforced this cultural antipathy toward youth. Since Liberation, many old veterans had become afflicted with an inflated sense of self-importance and intellectual smugness as a result of the party's propaganda. Revolutionary veterans were lauded as the "treasures of the party" and the repositories of "revolutionary wisdom" who must serve as the living models for future leaders. They acquired the conviction that only people who had been through the baptism of revolutionary fire were capable of shouldering heavy responsibilities. When carried to its extreme, this conviction created a circuitous logic that contended that young cadres did not deserve leadership positions because they had never borne leadership responsibility before.[27]

The Cultural Revolution was another factor that affected the old cadres' attitudes toward the younger comrades. As Chen Yun pointed out, many old cadres' personal sufferings during the Cultural Revolution convinced them that it was intrinsically dangerous to give young people too much power.[28] Of course, some old leaders also blamed the younger cadres as the direct cause of their being forced into retirement and regarded the later as hostile contenders for power and offices.[29]

The old leaders had a long litany of dissatisfactions with younger cadres. The harshness of the old leaders' criticisms and the whimsicality of their standards left no doubt that many of them were intrinsically hostile to certain types of young cadres. In the veterans' eyes, young cadres lacked "a comprehensive viewpoint toward things." Veterans dismissed articulate and outspoken young cadres as vain and publicity-hungry. They intensely disliked young cadres who did not have the capability to obey commands blindly or to "listen." They also disliked young cadres who called attention to the existence of problems and sought corrections. They criticized young cadres whose views or personal life styles differed from theirs as lacking in "organizational concept" or being possessed by "unhealthy ideology." Young cadres who dared to exercise their authority independently and who acted decisively were criticized as being "undemocratic." But if they consulted others regularly, they were criticized for "lacking leadership experience and capability."[30] Young cadres were also criticized widely for being "impatient" when they tried to take initiative, to change old practices, or were discontent with the status quo.[31] Young cadres who were smart, capable, energetic, resourceful, and purposive stood a good chance of being castigated as being "arrogant," "immature," "subjective," or "rash." Likewise, young cadres who showed boldness and daring, adventuristic spirit or creativity also were likely to be dismissed by the leaders as being politically unseasoned, and therefore incapable of becoming "ideal successors."[32]

Older leaders particularly resented young cadres who were also intellectuals. Their dedication to professional work only earned them the epithet "isolationists," that is, people who disdained to mingle with the masses. In this process, young people with bona fide intellectual capabilities were only assigned to a few relatively junior positions that required a high degree of professional competence (e.g., commissioners of science and technology). They got these jobs only because people with strong party career records were usually intimidated by these jobs and willingly yielded them to the intellectuals.[33] When younger cadres with good scholastic credentials failed to perform their work adequately, they only confirmed a common belief among old cadres that the younger people might have knowledge but no ability.[34] Many old cadres asserted that cadres without any scholastic credentials could be equally or more competent in their work.

When leaders applied such unreasonable standards of perfectionism against the younger cadres, it was not surprising that they should find the latter wanting in most respects. When they treated young people's personality traits and idiosyncrasies as "political defects," they could effectively kill the latter's prospects to move into the third echelon.

In general, old leaders preferred subordinates who were absolutely loyal to them personally, who did everything strictly according to established rules, who never voiced different opinions from their superiors, and who never attempted to be innovative.[35] They liked young cadres who were pliant and obsequious, did not have strong convictions on issues, but were particularly good at "knowing what the boss wanted."[36] The personal qualities that old leaders approved of were affability and docility (*wenshun*), obedience and subservience (*tinghua*), cautiousness and conservativeness (*wenzhong, laocheng*), and humility (*qianxu*).[37] In other words, young cadres who were most likely to win their leaders' endorsement as candidates for the third echelon were the "safe" cadres without strong personal convictions or outstanding abilities.

Ironically, even though the intent of the third-echelon policy in the 1980s was to bring about a thorough leadership transformation, it actually favored cadres with the same personality traits who had conformed to the image of the "good cadres" in the PRC's bureaucratic tradition since the 1950s.[38] In most cases, old leaders would rather pick young cadres who fit into their own mold. But the old leaders' attitudes toward the young cadres assumed a critical importance in the early 1980s because the scale of leadership change was so massive, and because the old leaders' domination over the selection process was so thorough. To the extent that the old leaders were repulsed by or attracted to certain personality traits among the young cadres, their selection would leave an indelible mark on the development of Chinese politics long after they were gone from Chinese politics.

Other Problems of the Selection Process

The major criteria used to pick young successors were not only highly idiosyncratic, but also closely tied to the leaders' personal relationships with the candidates. If the leaders had wanted to base their decisions on the young cadres' professional qualifications and performance alone, they could have employed objective and universalistic criteria and widened the circle of their search for candidates to include all qualified cadres. But by focusing heavily on the *personality traits* of the candidates, the old leaders limited the scope of their search to people they knew well. The organization department was often totally bypassed in the selection, as leaders chose only from people in their immediate circles of subordinates or acquaintances.[39] Highly qualified cadres who did not have personal contact with the leaders were severely handicapped in this selection process.[40] Particularly well-positioned to receive preferential treatment from the leaders were the cadres working in the leaders' personal entourage. In the early 1980s, many leaders' personal assistants (*mishu*) were promoted into the third echelon precisely because they occupied a strategic position in Chinese politics. Since many senior leaders were poorly educated, they had to rely heavily on their personal assistants to perform their official duties, which made them feel a particular bond with and confidence in these assistants.

Since this system of selection put excessive emphasis on the leaders' personal impressions and intuition—which were inevitably subjective and often downright whimsical—it created enormous potential for irregularities. Ambitious careerist cadres, who had no expertise or leadership qualities but who knew how to please their superiors, could move upward by ingratiating themselves to high-ranking backers through personal loyalty, personal services, gifts, or outright bribery.[41] But by far the most damaging impact of this selection process were the massive abuses of privileges by leading cadres to advance their family and factional interests.

The Impact of Factionalism

One major objective of the post-Mao leaders in the creation of the third echelon was to avoid the disruptive effect of factionalism. To achieve this objective, the party had issued guidelines to disqualify certain groups of known factionalists from candidacy as soon as the decision was made to launch the policy of revolutionary succession.[42] The Party Charter of 1982 also specifically forbade factional activities. In reality, however, the process of building the third echelon was overshadowed by factional calculations at all times.[43] Leaders' concern for their own bureaucratic and personal interests customarily took precedence over the party's interest to recruit new blood.

Old leaders wanted to hand-pick their protégés as successors so that they could exercise "remote control" over their work units even after their own retirement.[44] Leaders sometimes elevated the administrative status of an entire subordinate unit in order to promote their factional followers by default. Even when lower-level leaders were unaffiliated with a particular faction, they would pay close attention to the factional complexion in their organ so that they could ingratiate themselves to their superiors by promoting the latter's favorite candidates.

When factional cleavages already existed in a work unit, the leaders would break the impasse by agreeing on a spoils system whereby the favored candidates of all leading cadres would receive promotions.[45] But if the factional differences were not resolved quietly and cordially, leaders would then use more blatant measures to promote the insiders and exclude the outsiders. Rival factions often published competing slates of candidates or engaged in loud and disruptive activities to support their own candidates.[46]

The result of this selection system was that the successful candidates correctly concluded that they owed their new positions not to the party's policy, nor to the support of the masses, nor even to their own qualifications, but to the personal favor of their patrons. As one popular saying put it in reference to the selection process, "age is a capital, diploma is indispensable, past work performance provides a reference, but human connections (guanxi) are critical."[47]

Thus, even at their young age, many rising members of the third echelon had already become deeply mired in factional politics.[48] These young cadres felt an obligation to look after their patrons' interest, and to repay their favors with personal loyalty, obedience, and services. Their promotion only confirmed in their minds the indispensability of the "network of connections" in Chinese politics and gave them a chance to hone their skills in trading favors for their future career successes.[49]

Thus, instead of achieving the intended objective of infusing new blood into the party and state leadership, many new members of the third echelon acquired the mentality that it was now their turn to reap the benefits of power. A good number of these newly promoted cadres had serious flaws in moral character, incorrect thought, and poor personal styles.[50] Many of them felt emboldened by their factional backing to indulge in illegal activities.[51] Factionalism turned the succession policy into a highly divisive issue: it rekindled old hostilities, caused a decline of the party's prestige in the eyes of the masses, and blocked the career opportunities of a substantial number of capable young cadres who either belonged to the wrong faction or disdained to play by factional rules.

Family Connections and the "Party of Princes"

Familism under Chinese Communist rule has received far less scholarly attention in Western literature than factionalism. In its simplest form, familism existed when members of politically powerful families were accorded unfair and often excessive advantages in the opportunity structures of the society.

During their earlier years of revolutionary struggle, the Chinese Communists had made vociferous condemnations against familism. They won much popular support in the 1930s and 1940s because of their unrelenting attacks on familism under the KMT government. Chen Boda's analysis of powerful clans (*haomen*) in Nationalist China provided the Communists with invaluable political ammunition.[52] When the Communists came to power in 1949, they showed strong commitment to purge these "feudal practices" from Chinese politics.

In reality, however, familism was never totally absent from PRC politics but took many guises over the years. A brief historical review will suffice to trace its changing character and its specific impact on the policy of grooming the third echelon.

In the first decade after Liberation, familism was generally practiced in a subdued form. Since the first generation of revolutionary leaders like Mao and Zhou Enlai were still in their middle years and their children were young, the most noteworthy manifestation of familism was the sending of a small number of children of high-ranking cadres or revolutionary martyrs to pursue advanced study in the Soviet Union and other socialist countries.

In the 1960s, when the PRC required other urban educated youths to participate in the rustication campaigns, many cadres sent their own children to join the army instead so that they could avoid the hardship of physical labor in the countryside. Once in the army, their children were well taken care of by their old comrades-in-arms, quickly admitted into the party, and given pampered treatment. Most of these children eschewed the combat units. Young men usually were assigned as staff officers, technicians, secretaries, or to the rear services, while young women often joined the military medical corps or performing troupes. Upon demobilization, they were granted permission to live in the cities and assigned to good jobs. This method of entering the military through the back door and using it as a stepping stone toward fast advancement in civilian careers remained in vogue until the mid-1970s.[53]

Starting in 1970, the nation's colleges gradually reopened their doors for the first time since the beginning of the Cultural Revolution. But initially, college admissions were based not on examination but on recommendations, which gave preference to the so-called worker-farmer-soldier students (*gongnongbin xuesheng*). In fact, this policy gave many high-ranking cadres an opportunity to sneak their children into the colleges in numbers far exceeding those from genuine proletarian backgrounds. When the opportunity to study abroad emerged in the late 1970s, children from high cadre families were again among the first to take advantage of it with full government support.[54]

In addition to gaining privileged access to the best career and academic opportunities, the children of high-ranking cadres also contributed to the serious problem of elite inbreeding in the PRC. Both cultural and historical factors increased the frequency of marriages among children of high-level leaders of the party, army, and government in Communist China. Traditional Chinese norms gave the parents a strong influence in selecting the mates for their children more on the basis of social and economic compatibility than on the romantic sentiments of the young people themselves. After the Communist takeover, not only did the parental authority in this respect remain essentially undiminished, but class and family backgrounds became the overriding consideration. Theoretically, children from the working classes (including farmers, workers, military, and party and government cadres) should make equally acceptable marital prospects. In fact, however, the children of cadres or party members rarely married those of farmers or workers. Nor did they regard the children of intellectuals as desirable mates from the late 1950s until the late 1970s. In general, therefore, political considerations would lead children of cadre families to cement marital ties with other cadre families of comparable political status. This tendency was facilitated by two other factors.

One factor was the highly segregated residential patterns. While ordinary party members and cadres might live in a random geographical pattern, the high cadres' families usually lived together in compounds away from the masses. In Beijing, the provincial capitals, and many other cities, there were exclusive neighborhoods or housing projects reserved especially for high-ranking cadres, the military brass, and so forth. In such environments, the children of powerful cadres literally grew up together. Certain neighborhood schools were star-studded with children from the most powerful families and were lavished with the best teachers and facilities. They also provided fertile ground for fraternizing among these children. It was easy for romantic relations to develop among these children, usually with ample encouragement from their parents, who particularly cherished the idea of their children marrying the children of their close associates and comrades-in-arms.

The second factor was the further cementing of their bonds and identity during the Cultural Revolution. When high-ranking cadres in the same province or work unit got into serious political troubles, their children were often sent to the same village in a distant province to join the farm labor force as a means of protection. Far away from home and in deep emotional distress and physical isolation, these children only had each other to commiserate with and many of them developed lasting friendships or got married.[55]

These factors accounted for a large number of marriages linking together powerful party, army, and bureaucratic families, and fostered a strong group identity and feeling of superiority over other social groups. At the height of their political glory, before the disaster of the Cultural Revolution struck, the arrogance of members of high-ranking cadres families was most vividly illustrated by a saying popular among them: "Dragons beget dragons, phoenixes beget phoenixes, mice beget little mice who are good for nothing except digging holes."

Since the PRC was already the longest-lasting regime to rule over mainland China in the twentieth century, it is likely that the extent of inbreeding among its elite had surpassed that under any previous period. Whereas the Nationalist political elite's children regarded children from the families of landlords, merchants, and intellectuals as equally acceptable marital partners, the CCP elite's children had a much narrower range of options and ended up marrying each other. Given the political culture of China and the lack of institutionalization with respect to elite recruitment and circulation under the Communist regime, it was not surprising that members of high cadres' families should garner the lion's share of the benefits at the regime's disposal.

The timing of the emergence of familism as a rampant "political" problem in the late 1970s is not difficult to understand either. In the 1950s, most of the children of the top leaders (Liu, Deng, etc.) were only in high schools or colleges and could be easily satisfied with preferential educational opportunities. By the time they came of age in the 1960s to begin their own careers, their parents had suffered devastating political setbacks. It was not until the late 1970s, when their parents were rehabilitated that many of them returned to normal family life. But by this time, their careers had been sidetracked or ruined altogether for over a decade, and many had reached their thirties or forties. By the late 1970s, they had reached a desperate situation, for if they did not grab at the opportunities aggressively, life would soon pass them by.

Table 5

Family Connections of High Officials, 1985–88

National leader	Relatives	Position of relatives
Bo Yibo	Bo Xicheng (son)	Director, Beijing Tourist Bureau
	Bo Xilai (son)	Mayor, Dalian City
	Bo Quan (son)	General manager, White Peacock Art World
Chen Yi	Chen Haosu (son)	Deputy mayor, Beijing
Chen Yun	Chen Yuan (son)	Member, Beijing Municipal Party Standing Committee
Deng Xiaoping	Deng Pufang (son)	Chairman, Chinese Handicapped People's Welfare Association; President, Kanghua Corporation
	Deng Nan (daughter)	Chief, Bureau of Science and Technology, National Commission of Science and Technology
	Cho Lin (wife)	Working in the party's General Office
	Zhao Baojiang (son-in-law)	Mayor, Wuhan
	Wu Jianchang (son-in-law)	Vice-president, China Metals Corporation
He Changgong	He Quan (son)	Deputy chief of staff, PLA
He Long	He Pengfei (son)	Minister of equipment, PLA chief of staff
Hu Qiaomu	Hu Muying (daughter)	Head, Division for Registration and Supervision of Foreign Enterprises, State Administration for Industry and Commerce
Hu Qili	Hu Qihen (sister)	First vice-president, Chinese Academy of Sciences
Hu Yaobang	Hu Deping (son)	Deputy party secretary, Chinese Historical Museum
Jia Tingsan	Jia Chunwang (son)	Minister of national security
Li Fuchun	Li Changan (son)	Deputy general secretary, State Council
Li Peng	Li Yang (son)	Vice-president, Hainan Development Corporation
	Zhu Lin (wife)	President of a major South China corporation
Li Weihan	Li Tieyin (son)	Politburo member and head of State Commission of Education
Liao Chengzhi	Liao Hui (son)	Director, Overseas Chinese Office, State Council
Liu Shaoqi	Liu Yuan (son)	Former deputy mayor, Zhengzhou; deputy governor, Henan Province
	Liu Zheng (son)	Deputy mayor, Qingdao
Nie Rongzhen	Ding Henggao (son-in-law)	Director, Bureau of Technological Work, National Defense Ministry
	Nie Li (daughter)	Deputy director, Bureau of Technological work, National Defense Ministry
Peng Bai	Peng Shilu (son)	Minister of water and electricity

Peng Zhen	Peng Peiyun (daughter)	Director, State Birth Planning Commission
Song Renqiong	Song Ruixiang (son)	Governor, Qinghai Province
Tao Zhu	Tao Siliang (son)	Director, 5th Bureau (in charge of young intellectuals' affairs) in CCP Organization Department
Tian Jiyun	Tian Jizheng (brother)	Mayor, Xinxiang, Henan
Wang Zhen	Wang Jun (son)	Deputy political commissioner, Chengdu Military Region
	Wang Zhi (son)	General manager, Great Wall Computer Company
Wulanfu	Bu He (son)	Chairman, Inner Mongolia Autonomous Region
	Wu Jie (son)	Mayor, Baotou City (Inner Mongolia)
Xi Zhongxun	Xi Zhengping (son)	Party secretary, Ninde District, Fujian Province
	Xi Zhengning (son)	Deputy minister, Organization Department, Shaanxi provincial party
	Chen Guangyi (son-in-law)	Fujian provincial party secretary
Xiao Jinguang	Xiao Congce (son)	Party secretary, Datong, Shanxi
Yang Shangkun	Yang Baibin (brother)	Director, General Political Department, PLA
	Chi Haotian (son-in-law)	Chief of staff, PLA
Ye Jianying	Ye Xuanping (son)	Governor, Guangdong Province
	Wu Xiaolan (daughter-in-law)	Deputy mayor, Shenzhen City (also the daughter of Wu Yuzhang)
	Zou Jiahua (son-in-law)	Minister of munitions industry; member, State Council (also the son of Zou Taofeng)
	Ye Cumei (daughter)	Deputy director, Bureau of Technological Work, Ministry of Defense
Zhang Aiping	Yu Zhengsheng (son-in-law)	Mayor, Yantai City
	Zhang Haoro (son)	Bureau chief, State Council
Zhao Ziyang	Zhao Dajun (son)	President, Haihua Company, Hainan Island
	Zhao Liang (son)	Deputy general manager, Great Wall Hotel, Beijing
Zou Taofeng	Zou Jiahua (son)	Minister of munitions industry
	Zou Jingmeng (son)	Director, National Weather Bureau

Sources: China Spring (September 1985), p. 64; *World Journal,* April 24, 1989, p. 3; April 26, 1989, p. 9.

In this context, the party's decision to select the revolutionary successors became the perfect opportunity for these families to fulfill their long-delayed dreams to catapult their children into the elite. Thus, the age factor explains why familism had not become a conspicuous problem with a power dimension until the early 1980s.

The mode of selection of the third echelon opened the way for numerous irregularities. In general, familism was practiced with more subtlety on the higher level. National leaders rarely needed to take personal action to promote their own children; they need only acquiesce when their eager subordinates recommended their children for promotion over other, more qualified candidates. High-ranking cadres also could trade favors with each other so that they could arrange to promote each other's children without being accused of familism. Aggressive children or relatives of influential leaders could exploit their connections to press for their own promotion, which few bureaucrats would be stupid enough to object to. On the lower levels, the selections were often made more blatantly. Children of these leading cadres were relatively poorly educated, and some were manual workers. The horse trading on these levels was far more explicit, and, when necessary, leaders would not be reluctant to promote their own children.[56]

On the basic levels, the problems were equally serious. In many places, it was common for husband and wife, parents and children, and in-laws to work in the same unit.[57] After cadres had served in one locality for many years, they inevitably cultivated a complex network of personal connections. They had political debts to pay and protégés to look after. Numerous people were connected to them through marital ties, friendship, boss-subordinate relationships, and so forth. The longer a leading cadre had worked in a given locality, the greater the social pressure he was subject to and the less able he was to make a rational decision on the candidates of the third echelon. This was a particularly pervasive problem on the county level and below.[58] The leaders had wide discretionary powers to decide how to use the promotions to pay their personal political debts.

A related issue of familism that has received even less attention in Western literature on PRC politics was the extension of its scope to include the wives and daughters of powerful families. These cases are even more difficult to document because of the common practice among wives to use their maiden names or assumed names, and among daughters to take their mother's surnames instead of their father's. Under the imperial system, only the male members of the family were favored with official posts. Under the republican governments, more women became active in politics by virtue of their husband's position, but they usually were content with honorary titles, and few ever held high offices. Under communism, more women worked outside the family and successfully built their own careers. But a sizable number of them also benefited from their family connections to gain undeserved bureaucratic advantages.[59]

The problem of favoring family members with undeserved promotion to important posts was already quite widespread in the late 1970s. As early as 1980, the party had explicitly forbidden leaders to promote their own family members to leadership positions.[60] Yet such practices became more flagrant in the ensuing years as the third-echelon policy presented more temptations. By early 1986 the party center felt compelled to warn its leading cadres that they must observe proper procedures in selecting candidates to the third echelon. The party stipulated specifically that no children of leaders in top national and provincial positions (such as central party departments, National People's Congress, State Council and ministries, or provincial governors) would be promoted into the third echelon without the prior and direct approval of the party's Central Organization Department.[61]

Typically, such warnings forbade further violations but provided no corrections against past instances of wrongdoing. They therefore had no effect on the situation, because by this time the majority of children from the most powerful families had already been installed in the choicest positions in the third echelon. As in so many other instances, when the implementation of a particular policy ran into trouble, the party's solution was to recentralize power to plug up the loopholes. But this solution was ineffective because the party no longer commanded the organizational means to enforce discipline on the lower levels. At best, the party's belated reaction was a feeble post facto face-saving gesture that only confirmed most people's cynical conclusion that if one intended to commit misconduct, it was imperative to act expeditiously, before the national leadership had time to react. The abuses in the process of creating the third echelon were so pervasive that the people began to refer to the CCP as a "party of the princes," and the young leaders as the modern version of the "eight-banner corps."

Educational and Professional Qualifications of New Leaders

As has been seen, the selection process for the third echelon was plagued by a mixture of unimaginative and dogmatic applications of party guidelines by the organization department staff and highly irregular, subjective, and personalistic factors that influenced party leaders' decisions. Since the number of entrants into the third echelon was huge, and the reduction of age as well as the improvement of nominal educational qualifications among the candidates were both so substantial, the third echelon as a whole was definitely an improvement over the older, poorly educated elite. These positive gains, however, should not obscure the fact that the new third echelon fell far short of the party's original expectations and may have created serious new liabilities in their educational and professional qualifications.

The party had several options to improve the educational and professional competence of its cadre corps and third echelon. One was to promote into leadership positions cadres with good educational credentials. The other option was to select promising young cadres to attend party-sponsored training programs to upgrade their educational and professional proficiency and then promote them to leadership positions.[62] Since only a small number of party members met these criteria, the first method could not satisfy the party's need for new leaders, and the second method became the primary means by which the party cultivated its new leaders. Therefore, to appraise the qualifications of the party's new leaders, it is necessary to examine how the party conducted its training programs.

Cadre Training: The Historical Background, 1950–1978

During the years of revolutionary struggle, the party conducted only sporadic training for either party members or cadres. Little emphasis was given to the educational or professional qualifications of its members or cadres. There was little need for technical or professional and scientific skills during the years of protracted armed struggle. Although the party attracted a small number of college students to its ranks before Liberation, few had much opportunity to apply their professional expertise.

Therefore, when the party came to power in 1949, its ranks were filled with cadres who had strong political convictions but few skills to meet the technical demands of the state and society. Reluctantly, the party was forced to retain many experts and technicians who had worked under the Nationalist regime, even allowing them to work in highly sensitive areas such as communications and economic management.

During the early 1950s, the quality of cadres was partially improved by a thorough restructuring of the nation's higher education system according to the Soviet model, the sending of thousands of students to the Soviet Union and Eastern European socialist countries for advanced training, and the influx of a large number of experts from these same countries to China.

More directly, the party introduced a new system of training institutions including party schools, cadre schools, and workers and peasants accelerated middle schools to train cadres and selected party members. It also initiated the practice of sending a small number of young cadres to regular colleges and universities for retooling.

Although a cadre was ideally supposed to have a perfect combination of both redness and expertise, in practice, this was not the case. Starting at least with the Great Leap Forward in 1957–58, redness was often emphasized to the exclusion of expertise. Entire areas of the government's technical operations (e.g., statistical work) were abolished. Scientific methods (such as agricultural sciences) were scoffed at as being timid or nonrevolutionary. Under these highly charged political conditions, cadre training programs on anything other than political and ideological subjects were no longer considered useful.

When the Cultural Revolution erupted, party training was suspended altogether. Cadre schools, including the Central Party School, were closed, and cadres were sent to "May 7th schools" in the countryside so that they could enhance their ideological understanding and revolutionary commitment through physical labor.[63] In sum, except for the first six or seven years of its existence, the PRC basically made little effort to train its cadres and members.

The cadres had their own reasons to disdain training. Technical cadres seldom enjoyed the same status as those who specialized in "redness" or politics alone. Cadres who had technical knowledge were often derided as "white experts" and became the objects of suspicion by the party. They frequently found their career aspirations blocked. They were criticized for their alleged disdain toward ideological work, their "parasitic lifestyle," their disrespect for the innate intelligence of the peasants and workers, and their blind faith in bourgeois science and technology.

There also existed cleavages between party members and nonparty members in the cadre corps. Cadres who did not belong to the CCP usually had greater expertise, but they always had to work under the cadres who were party members. This highly discriminatory treatment of the nonparty cadres not only greatly undermined their effectiveness, but also created a notion that it would be wiser for people to choose a course of specializing in political redness than to hope to move up through the route of professional expertise.

In time, Chinese cadres developed a strong aversion to technical knowledge. The Maoist policy of overemphasizing class struggle but underemphasizing modernization only made matters worse. Consequently, for many years, the popular view of a model cadre was a jack of all trades, one who could handle different job assignments without adequate professional preparation. It was believed that as long as the cadres were imbued with ideological rectitude and political reliability, they should be able to work in all fields but needed to know little about any particular field. Many cadres actually took pride in being "nonexperts," and some of them went so far as to boast about their ignorance and lack of culture. Most cadres treated the thesis that "experts must be led by nonexperts" as an article of faith throughout the entire Maoist era.[64]

Revival of Party Training Programs, 1979–1982

Only with the Deng leadership firmly in control and the party beginning to address the issue of upgrading the quality of revolutionary successors was the cadre training system reactivated. By this time, the new leaders had concluded that the four modernizations could not be fulfilled unless the professional and cultural knowledge of the cadre corps were massively overhauled.

In 1980, the party made a decision to use "short-course training programs" to give one complete round of training to all cadres in the next three to five years.[65] The leading cadres of party and state organs, enterprises, and communes were all required to receive training.[66] The party also instructed all lower-level organs to conduct a thorough review of the educational and professional qualifications of its cadres and stipulated that henceforth only cadres with sufficient professional background would be promoted to leadership positions in their respective fields.[67]

But between 1979 and 1982, only some three million cadres reportedly had gone through short-term political and professional training sessions, the overwhelming majority of whom were trained in county-level schools where the quality of education was suspect.[68] This means that after three to four years of effort by the party, only one out of every seven cadres had received nominal training, a result that fell far below the original target of 1979.[69]

Thus, in spite of the party's desire to improve cadre and leadership qualities, the Chinese cadre corps in the early 1980s was burdened with at least three serious liabilities. The first and most conspicuous problem was the cadres' poor educational qualifications. As table 6 shows, 40 percent of the cadres in 1980 had junior high school education or less. A substantial portion of this group had only primary school education or were semiliterate or illiterate. On the high end, only 18 percent of the cadres had college education.

A second problem was the cadres' lack of even minimum professional knowledge to perform their duties. Those with only junior high school education or less had no professional expertise, and even those with senior high school education (who constituted 42 percent of the cadre corps in 1980) were scarcely better. The party admitted the existence of "a big gap" between the cadres' nominal educational credentials and the professional requirements of their work.[70]

Not surprisingly, some of the fields that were most crucial to the four modernizations suffered from the most severe shortage of qualified cadres. The shortage of cadres with financial or commercial know-how was particularly pronounced. Even in late 1984, the PRC's entire commercial system had only sixty-one thousand cadres with a college education. This constituted a mere 3.4 percent of the total personnel in commerce.[71] Even in the Beijing municipal government, which was one of the best staffed in the country, many key municipal agencies in finance and commerce had only one college graduate among their entire staff.[72] The situation was far worse in the rest of the country.[73] The specialized agencies hardly fared any better. Thus, for instance, 80 percent of the leading cadres across the nation in finance, industries, transportation, and commerce were reported as having no technical familiarity with their work.[74]

The third problem was the lack of both education and expertise on the leadership level. In many instances, the higher the level, the more pronounced the shortage of cadres who had a college education.[75] A 1983 survey indicated that leading cadres and average cadres working in party and state organs were among the worst educated.[76]

As table 7 shows, in 1982, the leading cadres on all levels and in all fields as a subgroup had a dismal education profile. Only 6 percent of leading cadres had college-level education, and 72 percent of this subgroup had only junior high school education or less. In contrast, 21 percent of the cadre corps as a whole had college-level education, and only 37 percent had junior high school education or less. The profile for the entire cadre corps was better than for the leaders because the former had many cadres who were not members of the Chinese Communist Party.

This situation was obviously intolerable. A cadre corps with such severe

Table 6

Improvement of Cadres' Education in the 1980s (percent)

	1980	1984	1987
College	18.0	19.0	23.6
Senior high school	42.0	41.0	46.5
College and senior high school	60.0	60.0	70.1
Junior high school and under	40.0	40.0	29.9
Total cadres (million)	19	21	22

Sources: RMRB, May 14, 1982, p. 1; February 21, 1984, p. 2; April 25, 1987, p. 4; *Liaowang*, 1983, no. 10, p. 9; *Banyuetan* (Beijing), 1984, no. 3, pp. 9–11; *Hongqi*, 1985, no. 7, p. 18.

Table 7

Educational Profiles of Leading and Ordinary Cadres, 1982 (percent)

Category	Leading	Ordinary
College	6	21
Senior high school	22	42
College and senior high	28	63
Junior high school or less	72	37
Total cadres (persons)	810,000	20,000,000

Sources: 1982 Population Census of China; Liaowang, 1983, no. 10, p. 9; *RMRB*, May 14, 1982, p. 1; February 21, 1984, p. 2.
Note: Leading cadres refer to those in charge of party, state, and economic organs on all levels.

handicaps could not possibly help the party to pursue the four modernizations. On the contrary, it could only totally defeat Deng's strategy of restoring the party's legitimacy through creating a thriving socialist economy. Something must be done about the cadres, and quickly.

A Bold New Approach: Regularization of Cadre Training

To correct these problems, the party adopted a new policy in October 1982 to put cadre training on a regular basis. It required all national-level cadres to bring their cultural and professional proficiency up to at least the equivalent of senior high-school or college levels, and it further demanded that all lower-level organs set appropriate standards for their own cadres. To accomplish these objectives in the next three to five years (or by 1987), the party required all cadres to take scheduled leaves from their work to engage in study.[77] It was hoped that, eventually, 60–70 percent of all national-level cadres would attain college-level education coupled with commensurate professional knowledge. Insofar as provincial-, district-, and county-level party and state organs were concerned, their leading cadres or successors were all required to attend the party school on the next higher level by 1990.[78]

An important change in the regularization policy was to crystallize the objective of cadre training and to lay down guidelines on target groups. Formerly, cadres were selected to attend party school for a variety of reasons and came from very diverse backgrounds and age groups. There were no consistent criteria to decide who should be given training. The new regularization program gave top priority to the members of the third echelon who had already been assigned to leading positions or who were candidates to leadership positions but lacked sufficient culture and/or technical expertise. Hu Yaobang suggested that the most effective way of training was to take these cadres off their jobs to undergo two to three years of training.[79]

The party also created a new institutional framework to support cadre training. It required all organs to conduct a thorough evaluation of their current cadres' educational qualifications, and to utilize their own resources to give their cadres remedial training. It also designated a number of regular colleges and universities (and some regular and professional senior high schools) to share the responsibility of cadres training. Lower-level organs were encouraged to experiment with such formats as evening courses, television schools, and correspondence courses to supplement their own training programs.[80]

But by far the major responsibility for cadre training was delegated to the regular party school system on various levels. Before 1982, party schools offered only short-term training to party members on rotational basis. Under the new policy of regularizing training, such short-term training became only secondary. The main mission of the party schools was to provide the majority of trainees with full-time training sessions lasting two to three years.

The Central Party School was presented as a model for all other party and cadre schools under the regularization plan. Although restored to operation only in the late 1970s, this school experienced rapid expansion in its enrollment and faculty to an extent unprecedented in its history. Whereas previously the curriculum in party schools consisted predominantly of political and ideological courses, such classes now constituted only about half of the total instructional hours. More "elective courses" in liberal arts, sciences, and management were offered.[81] In 1984, the party further standardized the curriculum of its cadre training programs to cover the subjects of political education, scientific and technological education, and managerial education.[82]

The party's decision to regularize cadre training was made in order to transform the Chinese cadres into people who would possess solid ideological as well as modern professional and technological knowledge.[83] The party contended that the new direction for cadre training had long-term "strategic significance" because cadres' quality and ability would affect not only the success or failure of socialist construction but the political future of the party and the state.[84]

The party also introduced several incentives to encourage cadres to take professional training seriously. It announced that all appointment and promotion decisions related to the third-echelon policy in the future should give as much weight to the candidates' academic credentials as their work experience. When prospective candidates to the third echelon had comparable qualifications in all other respects, preference would be given to those with superior academic records. Cadres who failed to meet the cultural and professional requirements of their current jobs would be removed and reassigned to lesser positions.[85]

These steps constituted a clear departure from the PRC's own bureaucratic tradition, which used to assign more weight to experience than to academic knowledge. The party's new position was that it preferred to err on the side of culture and professional know-how than experience. It even asserted that people who had abundant experience but little culture and knowledge would make poor leaders.[86] Under this new policy, credentials from training schools would become the critical factor for cadres' chances of being designated as revolutionary successors.

In late February 1983, the party decided to extend regular training beyond national-level cadres to include those designated as candidates to the third echelon on the provincial and local levels. To qualify for candidacy to leadership positions on these levels, cadres had to be under forty years of age, had to have worked for five or more years, and must possess the equivalent of senior high school education. Their training would last two years.[87] The party also instructed all state and party organs to develop a two-stage training schedule. The first stage would last from 1983 to 1985, and the second stage from 1986 to 1990, by which time all cadres throughout the country must be brought to realize fully the four goals set for cadres.[88]

Yet, in early 1984, the party set an even more ambitious goal to "complete one round of training within the next three to five years," not only for all leading cadres, but for all "basic-level cadres" as well as "basic-level technical personnel." The party even wanted county governments to extend training beyond the cadre corps to selected groups of rural educated youths and members of prosperous households.[89]

Thus, in 1982–83, the party had already devised a training program to give its cadres and new leaders adequate cultural and professional training so that they could perform their duties more competently. But how effectively was the policy carried out? What difficulties did it encounter? Were China's future leaders measurably improved because of this policy?

Major Issues in Implementation

The regularization program marked a momentous shift of the PRC's cadre policy. Its success must depend not only on a well-conceived plan by the national leaders, but also on the willingness of the sponsoring agencies on all levels to invest a tremendous amount of resources, and finally on the support and participation by lower-level leaders and cadres. As it turned out, the implementation of the program was seriously hampered by both physical resources and human motivations.

Availability of Resources

Training programs required resources such as funds, teachers, facilities, and teaching materials. At the outset of the regularization program, the party indicated that although it wanted to send millions of cadres to receive training, it wanted the individual work units to provide their cadres with full pay and fringe benefits while they were in training and away from work. Such an arrangement was decidedly unattractive to the work units because it imposed a heavy manpower drain and financial burden upon them.[90] Economic units were particularly reluctant to send people to training when they faced increasing workloads, in the midst of bustling economic expansion.[91]

In spite of the national party's repeated proddings, many leading cadres on lower levels remained unappreciative of the significance of regularizing cadre training and did not want to take the necessary steps to provide training to their cadres.[92] In other places, cadre training was handled in a highly formalistic style. These local party organs prematurely abandoned their short-term training programs in favor of higher-level and longer-term training even when they did not have the resources to do so.[93]

It was also common for many leaders on the local levels to make exaggerated claims about the accomplishments of their training programs. Training sessions that lasted a few days or consisted of self-study were reported to superiors as full-fledged training.[94] Many local leaders were only interested in gaining publicity or currying favor with their superiors, and their impressive statistics and fancy charts usually bore little resemblance to their actual work.[95] By early 1987, it was reported that there were a total of 5,700 cadre training schools in the entire country.[96] The data for the party's 1980–85 training programs claimed that one out of every two cadres receiving training ended up being classified in a higher cultural level.[97] Many training programs claimed routinely that 95 percent of their trainees got excellent grades.[98]

The quality of training they offered was suspect, however. Instructors from the old training schools were given new courses to teach without adequate retooling and were therefore incapable of helping the cadres to improve their professional and intellectual competence. A tiny fraction of the teachers were full-time professional teachers, while most instructors were amateurs who made only a few guest appearances.[99] The quality of instructors on the lower levels was even worse, and yet it was precisely in the lower-level schools that the overwhelming majority of party cadres were trained. Severe shortage of qualified teachers was a problem that plagued all the training programs.[100]

Although the party also required regular colleges and universities to train cadres, this option only provided limited relief.[101] These schools had limited excess capacity to train cadres when their existing facilities were already severely strained under the weight of rapidly expanding regular enrollment demands.[102]

The curriculum of cadre training institutions posed another major challenge. According to the party's resolution of April 1983, "the regularization (*zheng-guehua*) of party school education primarily refers to the regularization of the format of education as well as the content of curriculum. All party schools must gradually achieve standardization in academic requirements, curriculum, instructional materials, examination systems, and evaluation methods."[103] The major objective of regularization in this respect was to add requisite professional knowledge, modern sciences, and cultural topics to their basic staple of Marxism and the Thought of Mao.

Many schools, however, retained their obsolete curriculum and teaching materials and remained under the sway of traditional teaching methods.[104] Their classes often failed to address the current socioeconomic or political developments because texts had not yet been written, and teachers had little to offer with respect to professional or technical knowledge.[105] Furthermore, the teaching materials in all the schools tended to be alike regardless of their levels, making it pointless for cadres to advance their education from one level to another.[106]

Aside from the Central Party School, those schools that were conducted reasonably well usually existed on the ministerial or provincial levels. But these schools were few in number and had the capacity to accommodate only a small quantity of middle- and high-ranking cadres.[107] At such a rate, they could not play a major role in bringing about the fundamental transformation of the Chinese cadre corps.

Motivation of cadres

It goes without saying that the cadres' support was critical to the success of the regularization program. The local leaders and cadres had to recognize the value of the program and be willing to participate in it. The cadres' motivations, however, were sometimes colored by considerations that only defeated the original intent of the national leaders.

To begin with, as described previously, the process of selecting cadres as candidates for training was fraught with irregularities. In situations where training was considered profitable, only cadres with good relations with their superiors would have a chance to be chosen. But in places where training was considered a burden, cadres without good relations with their superiors would be drafted to fulfill the quota. Therefore, the training programs were often exploited to spread personal favors, and not to redress deficiencies.

Second, many cadres believed that the party's regularization policy was meant to give remedial education only to the poorly educated cadres. Consequently, cadres with better education smugly concluded that they had no need for the training programs. Many cadres tried to avoid training programs by arguing that they were too busy in their work, that the instructional materials had no bearing on their professional needs, that knowledge was not crucial to making revolution, or that training was a "soft" mission that deserved only a low priority.[108]

Third, the party's guideline to treat the cadres' scholastic credentials as one important factor in determining their job assignment, evaluation, and promotion was often interpreted mechanically and simplistically by lower-level leaders to mean that cadres must possess a diploma or certificate to receive favorable consideration in personnel matters.[109] Not surprisingly, this development caused considerable alarm among the less-educated cadres, many of whom flocked to training schools for the sole purpose of embellishing their academic credentials. Since the regularization policy was conducted in conjunction with the policy to pick cadres for the third echelon, many young and ambitious cadres signed up to undergo training in pursuit of a scholastic degree that they thought could enhance their prospects of upward mobility.

The cadres' motives inevitably affected the character and quality of the training programs. One common phenomenon was that many cadres had little interest in choosing training programs appropriate to their own educational level, but wanted to attend one at the highest possible level to earn the most prestigious diplomas. Thus, cadres who barely had junior-high-school-level education wanted to participate in "college-level" training programs.[110] In many places, cadres who wanted to go into college-level training outnumbered those who wanted to attend high-school-level training by a wide margin even when they were clearly unqualified to do so.[111]

The cadres not only wanted the training programs to give them more glamorous degrees, but also little work and easy examinations.[112] Many cadres had an inflated view about their own ability and believed that they only needed one or two courses to improve their knowledge.[113] While the original intent of the regularization program was to "put particular emphasis on improving cadres' professional standards,"[114] the cadres were unwilling to enroll in the more demanding courses on science and technology, resulting in a notable continued deficiency among them in these fields.[115]

The excessive emphasis on formal educational degrees had the effect of blocking the paths of advancement for many ambitious young cadres who had less than the required educational credentials. Their solution was to embellish their educational qualifications through falsification of their academic records, or to pressure their work units to grant them higher educational or professional classifications than they deserved so that they could retain their current jobs or be eligible for promotion into the third echelon.[116]

These ulterior purposes inevitably had a corrupting effect on the character of many training programs. They put tremendous pressure upon many schools to raise artificially their academic status beyond what their curriculum or faculty could support. Many schools found that the only way they could attract attendees was to offer degrees that would have been beyond the reach of these attendees under normal circumstances.[117] Many schools that were contracted by the party or state organs to train their cadres were not interested in the educational functions per se, but only in using training to generate extra revenues for the school or faculty through the sale of diplomas.[118] Even the regular colleges and universities participating in the cadre training programs were not above granting diplomas or scholastic certificates to make a profit or trade them for political favors.[119] These schools were notorious for their laxity in admissions policies and low academic standards.[120]

The upshot was that the regularization policy greatly increased the number of cadres with impressive academic degrees or certificates without meaningful improvement of their educational levels.[121] These problems were so prevalent that in early 1984, the party warned that the quality of cadre/party school education must be tightly controlled. Not only should the schools provide useful professional and managerial knowledge, but their academic standards must be kept high to prevent unqualified cadres from sailing through these programs.[122] Yet the mismanagement of these schools was never fundamentally corrected in the 1980s.

Meanwhile, numerous other cadres remained uninterested in training for other reasons. For one thing, cadres would have no interest in training when they believed their career prospects would not be visibly improved even if they attended the training program.[123]

Other cadres were unwilling to go into training for fear of losing their jobs.[124] This became a particularly realistic concern when the party pursued the policy of bureaucratic retrenchment during the early and mid-1980s.[125] Very few cadres felt assured by the party's avowed intention of upgrading their cultural level when they might risk the loss of employment at the end of their training period.

Third, for the huge number of cadres who were neither young and ambitious enough to qualify for the third echelon nor old enough to be threatened with compulsory retirement, training held virtually no attraction. As a result, many work units experienced great difficulty in delivering their quota of cadres to the training schools. By 1986 only a tiny number of party members who were slated to receive party training actually had done so, causing many party schools to have trouble filling their classes with trainees.[126]

Finally, the rigid requirements in terms of age and educational credentials of candidates to the third echelon forced some organization departments to seek relief from sectors that had the largest concentration of young and better-educated cadres—for example, in the technical fields or economic enterprises. The organization departments often raided these places and took away engineers, technicians, educators, and scientists to fill administrative posts so that they could fulfill the quotas imposed by their superiors.[127]

While the new leaders unquestionably had better qualities than the ones they replaced, they were not necessarily well-suited for their new responsibilities. They often bypassed so many administrative grades to reach the leadership positions that their organizational skills, their ability to grasp the complexity of their new jobs, or the compatibility of their expertise with their job requirements were completely untested. In Liaoning Province, for example, a survey of forty-five counties and cities showed that 71 percent of the 555 top party and government leading cadres nominally had college-level educations. But many of them never studied the professional knowledge related to their field of responsibilities, lacked modern knowledge, and lacked leadership skills. Of the 329 county-level leading party and government cadres, 82 (or 25 percent) had knowledge unrelated to their work. For example, engineers were put in charge of trade, metallurgists in charge of agriculture, and animal husbandry experts in charge of culture and education.[128] Not unexpectedly, many new leaders felt intimidated by their new responsibilities, decided to adopt a low political profile, and deferred to decisions made by older leaders.[129] This was entirely contrary to the original purpose of the third echelon, which was to inject a new spirit and style into the stagnant political environment and point to new directions.

The Difficulty of Correcting the Problems

As tens of thousands of young and middle-aged cadres were promoted into leadership positions each year on *xian* (county) level and above after 1982, the extent of incompetence and incompatibility soon reached serious proportions.[130] By 1985, the party felt the need to take additional remedial measures beyond cadre training to deal with the unqualified cadres.[131] The party demanded that lower-level party and state organs take prompt and decisive actions to reassign or demote the unqualified leaders in the third echelon, or to transfer them to more compatible professions. The party also demanded that misbehaving young leaders be dismissed outright.[132]

Once installed, however, the new leaders proved as impervious to attempts at removal as the old cadres. Several factors conspired to frustrate the party's efforts to correct the problems. First, the leadership and organization departments of many lower-level organs abhorred the idea because they were the ones who had promoted the young cadres into the third echelon in the first place. To take them from leadership positions would amount to an admission of erroneous judgment on their own part and would seriously damage their own image. Therefore, once young cadres were elevated into the third echelon, they had acquired a virtual lifetime ''guarantee'' to their positions.[133]

Second, the parents and factional patrons who had abused their influence to install their children and protégés in leadership positions would not supinely obey orders from above either. The careerists who had made considerable human or even monetary investments to acquire their new jobs would regard the loss of these jobs as utterly unacceptable.

Finally, even the young cadres who initially had not actively sought promotion into the third echelon found the thought of demotion or removal distasteful. For they had also internalized the long-standing assumption in the PRC's bureaucracies that leading cadres should never lose their positions unless they had committed terrible personal or political wrongdoings. It was this stigma that they strenuously refused to accept.[134] Their reaction suggested that even the new generation of leaders still operated on the traditional assumption of the bureaucracy that, once promoted, they had every right to keep their jobs regardless of their competence.

Consequently, many units remained in a state of turmoil even after the task of creating a third echelon was proclaimed to have been successfully concluded. When unqualified young leaders were targeted for removal, they would haggle with the party to ensure that their new assignments would carry pay, rank, prestige, and privileges comparable to the ones they were asked to vacate.[135] When these unpleasant problems arose in the work units, the other leaders were usually reluctant to force the issue, either because they wanted to maintain internal harmony or because the limited resources at their disposal would not allow them to satisfy the demands of the young cadres. Therefore, they preferred to let the problem drag on indefinitely in the hope that the party center would eventually lose its determination and let the unqualified leaders stay. Yet, as long as the latter remained in leadership positions, the rank and file would feel discontented.

Therefore, in many units, the well-intended policy to create the third echelon not only failed to revitalize the organization, to inject fresh air into the bureaucracy, or to bring about a new leadership style or an enhanced sense of solidarity, it actually produced emotional conflict, divisiveness, and further demoralization.[136] In his summation statement at the end of the rectification campaign in May 1987, Bo Yibo conceded that too many newly promoted cadres who had proven to be unfit for their jobs remained in their positions.[137] Although he continued to urge young leading cadres gracefully to accept reassignments, the third echelon had acquired a firm grip over the bureaucracy by this time, and the overwhelming majority of them will in all probability stay in office for the next generation.

In sum, the practices of falsification and exaggeration of academic records were so widespread that serious doubts could be raised about the accuracy of official data on the educational credentials of the third echelon. The mechanical insistence on formal degrees without regard to the substance of education also left unresolved the old problem of leaders possessing little or no expertise in their work, which was exactly what the party had wanted to alleviate by introducing the educational requirements for the third echelon in the first place.[138] The party secretary of Shaanxi Province, for example, candidly admitted in September 1985 that after two years of intensive training programs, the results still "lagged far behind" the needs of the four modernizations and economic reform, and the quality of provincial cadres and leaders remained unsatisfactory.[139] On a nationwide basis, *Hongqi* reported in 1985 that about half of the incumbent leading cadres were still poorly educated even after several years of personnel changes. The lower the level, the worse educated the leading cadres tended to be.[140]

A related complicating factor was the rate of obsolescence of knowledge provided by the Chinese educational system, a factor that aroused much public discussion during the implementation of the succession policy. Some national surveys estimated that, for those college students who graduated before the Cultural Revolution, the obsolescence rate of their knowledge in five years after graduation was 45 percent, and 75 percent in ten years after graduation. Yet, in many places, a large number of newly promoted cadres had left school many years ago and never acquired new knowledge after graduation. Therefore, even for those with nominal college degrees, the obsolescence of knowledge is a serious problem.[141]

The cultural and educational deficiencies were particularly serious among leading cadres in such specialized fields as finance and trade.[142] Prior to 1980, these fields had been neglected for many years in the Chinese educational system because they were considered inferior professions.[143] In 1985, a survey was conducted among 6,000 factory directors and managers in 120 large and medium-scale enterprises. It revealed that only 29.3 percent of these leading economic cadres had college-level educations. More important, the survey concluded that all of them lacked the requisite skills to promote the four modernizations.[144]

When one reviews the history of cadre training from 1979 to 1987 even on the basis of official claims, one realizes that the total of 6 million cadres trained was actually a very modest accomplishment. The party estimated in 1984 that it needed to train about 1.5 to 2 million cadres annually.[145] If actually implemented, it meant that almost 7 to 10 percent of the entire cadres corps would receive training on a full-time basis annually, an ambitious goal indeed. In reality, however, only about 0.75 million cadres were given any training at all per year during the 1980s. At this rate, the party would fall far short of its goal of giving every cadre training by 1990.

Finally, again taking official claims at their face value, the margin of educational improvement effected by training has not been impressive. During 1980–87, the number of college-level cadres increased by 1.7 million while the number of senior high-school level cadres increased by 2.25 million. But this total increase of about 4 million also included people, many of them nonparty members, who had entered the cadre corps in these years with better educational qualifications. The official report for 1980–85 suggests that only about 2 million cadres nominally improved their educational and/or professional credentials to senior high school and college levels through the training channels.[146] With a cadre corps of over 22 million in 1987, this was not a rate of improvement that had been originally envisaged by the architects of the regularization program.

Table 8

Numbers and Levels of Cadres Trained, 1980–86

Total number	5,560,000
Number whose cultural level was raised to:	
College equivalent	930,000
Senior high equivalent	1,020,000
Junior high equivalent	860,000
Other unspecified levels	2,750,000

Sources: RMRB, July 22, 1983, p. 1; April 25, 1987, p. 4; *Lilun yuekan* (Beijing), 1984, no. 5.

Conclusions: China's Leadership Changes

In democratic countries, transition of power usually occurs at predictable intervals as prescribed by their basic laws. Procedurally, the issue of who governs is decided by the electorate. The frequency with which the electorate exercises its right to choose leaders is usually less than once every four to six years, and sometimes much more often. On the other hand, except for a minimum age requirement, the candidates for leadership posts usually do not have to meet sex, age, or educational/professional requirements.

In contrast, the process of power transition in socialist systems is more unpredictable. Most Communist leaders acquire power through struggle. Without institutionalized procedures of leadership changes, purges become an effective and sometimes necessary way to accomplish such purposes. Purges allow the top leaders to replace those who have risen high enough in the hierarchy to become their potential rivals with more junior and youthful ones whose loyalty they can count upon. Purges can also enable a leader or a group of leaders to stay in power indefinitely; they can inject an element of perennial instability into the political system, keep everyone on his toes, and maintain the youthfulness and vitality of the leadership through constant personnel reshuffles.

In the Soviet Union, Lenin, the founding father of the revolution, only lived a few years after the Communists seized power. Lenin's death unleashed an intense succession struggle between Stalin and his rivals that did not end until the late 1930s with the thorough decimation of the latter. In China, the issue of transition of power at the very top never received much serious attention during Mao's lifetime, nor was there much doubt about Mao's right to hand-pick his own successor when he died. Until the Cultural Revolution, Mao's personal stature and the unity of the top leaders had made it unnecessary for the party to employ purges as a major instrument to produce leadership changes, even though several purges were conducted against Mao's opponents. In general, party leadership remained very stable from 1949 to 1965. This explains why the need to cultivate revolutionary successors never gained momentum during this period.

It was not until the 1980s that the leaders finally linked the policy of revolutionary succession with the policy of retirement of old leaders for simultaneous implementation. Yet in only five to seven years, the party succeeded in taking power away from over two million veterans and putting it in the hands of the first generation of post-Liberation cadres. The transition of power was carried out relatively smoothly because the veterans had already become quite advanced in age and had lost their combative spirit. Eventually, most aging leaders were realistic enough to haggle about the terms of their political exit rather than to fight to stay in power. From the party's viewpoint, this record was preferable to the enormous human and organizational cost inflicted upon the party when an earlier attempt to transfer power was made during the Cultural Revolution.

The policy of revolutionary succession of the 1980s undoubtedly changed the complexions of China's leadership stratum by enabling the party to rid itself of a leadership plagued by senility, professional incompetence, and ideological rigidity, and substituting one with youthfulness, better education, and more professional expertise.

An equally significant accomplishment of the party leaders since 1977 was their success in averting a potentially debilitating power struggle. Both Chen Yun and Deng Xiaoping had expressed deep concern over the possible political comeback by the leftists. The retirement policy enabled Deng and Chen to ease the important leftist leaders out of active service on the pretext of age without highlighting policy or factional conflicts. Then the third-echelon policy provided them with a convenient tool to exclude the younger leftists from the arena of power. All these tasks were carried out without precipitating an ugly confrontation. In this sense, the retirement of old leaders, the creation of the third echelon, and the victory over the leftists without a costly intraparty fight or a purge constituted the major accomplishments of the party under Deng since 1978 in leadership personnel.

But one must resist the temptation to overstate the accomplishments of the party's policy because the leadership changes of this decade have raised several important questions that should be considered in any balanced evaluation. What implications has the method of selection created? Has the leadership change brought about solutions to the problems of bureaucratic styles? Has the new leadership met the needs for manpower to carry out the economic reforms? Will the leadership change procedures be institutionalized so that one can expect continuity and change in a stable situation?

Implications of the Selection Methods

The specific ways whereby the third-echelon leaders were selected raised the very important issue of whether the selection methods constituted a significant step forward in China's political development. Under the imperial system, the norm of selecting members to the ruling elite was by the civil service system. The impartiality of recruitment by the examination method was buttressed by geographical quotas, and by stringent limitations on the scope of the "yin" system, so that aspiring young men anywhere in the country had a reasonable, if not an exactly equal, chance to gain admission into the ruling elite. After initial admission, bureaucratic careers were regulated by elaborate rules of performance evaluations. The Nationalist Government instituted its own civil service system. While abuses of privileges by powerful bureaucrats to give offices to their children certainly existed under the Nationalists, such abuses were constrained by the existence of a public opinion as well as a more pluralistic society in which children of powerful bureaucrats did not always want to pursue bureaucratic careers.

Insofar as the Communists were concerned, recruitment of leaders was not a problem during the revolutionary years because the party attracted people from all social strata and could afford to promote only those who excelled in military or organizational work. Nepotism and favoritism were not problems at all. The group that joined the revolution in the 1920s through 1940s basically stayed in power through the 1970s.

But the situation became distinctly different in the 1980s. The haste with which a huge number of new leaders had to be designated was unprecedented in the CCP's history and greatly exceeded the ability of the party organization departments to impose stringent quality control. The tens of thousands of incumbent leaders who took the selection of the candidates into their own hands only aggravated the problem tremendously.

The result was that, in countless instances, succession became a private transaction between the incumbent leaders and their personal favorites whereby hundreds of thousands of incumbent leaders literally selected their own successors according to their own personal preferences. In this sense, the selection process of the third echelon of the 1980s actually represented a regression from the previous processes under the Communists or their republican and imperial predecessors. The privatization of the succession process of the 1980s was so extensive that it constituted a serious setback in the path of China's political development and set a dangerous precedent for the future.

The third-echelon policy also raises the question of whether the party could realistically expect it to produce significant improvements to its leadership qualities. Since the old leaders were themselves unqualified to serve and therefore needed to be replaced, how could they be entrusted with the responsibility of picking the nation's leaders for the next generation? To put it broadly, how could the party expect the aging conservative leaders to bestow their blessings upon young, progressive cadres as their successors as their parting gifts to the revolution?

As it happened, the qualities and vision of the selectors left a decisive mark on the quality of the selected. Those leaders who had the authority to pick the third echelon invariably picked those whose intellectual propensities, political preferences, and personal styles were similar to their own. It also became a tactical necessity for the aspiring young candidates to foster such similarities to their seniors in order to catch the latters' attention.[147]

This means that the young cadres most likely to succeed were those who looked like carbon copies of their benefactors. In spite of the impressive appearance that China had effected a wholesale leadership change in the 1980s, the new leaders had not gone through the baptism of political fire on their own. The question of whether they are capable of handling the tough political challenges on their own can only be answered after their patrons are gone.

The Third Echelon and Bureaucratic Styles

One major original objective of the third-echelon policy was to inject new styles and mentality into the bureaucracy on all levels. On the basis of the available evidence, this objective was not fulfilled, and some of the most obvious defects in China's bureaucratic styles remain unabated or even have become worse. Evasiveness and shirking of responsibility are still widespread practices. The style of leadership has not become more democratic, and manifestations of commandism abound. Bureaucrats continue to labor under the burdens of "mountains of documents and seas of conferences."[148]

Traditional personnel practices have not shown any significant changes, as the rank and file of cadre corps continue to regard their jobs as their "iron rice-bowls." Even the third-echelon leaders who personally benefited from the recent retirement system believe that they are entitled to life-long tenure in their new leadership positions.[149] The old concept of mechanical egalitarianism still predominates, and bureaucratic "rank order" still plays a decisive role in determining salaries and promotions.[150]

But why did the promotion of a whole generation of new leaders fail to improve bureaucratic styles and efficiency? At least three reasons can be cited.

The first and most obvious reason is that the overwhelming majority of those young leaders who obtained their positions because of their personal connections had hardly any interest in improving bureaucratic efficiency. Since their objectives were self-serving, bureaucratic chaos and inefficiency actually provided them with a more favorable environment to make personal gains.

Second, even young leaders promoted on the basis of their merits had to learn to live with their environment. Many were promoted because the incumbent leaders needed to fulfill their quotas. In numerous cases, these young leaders were assigned to jobs outside of their fields of expertise, or to perform public relations work for their work units.[151] They were not delegated full authority to do their job, because the old leaders did not want to give up power. The younger leaders did not dare to contradict these seniors and often became willing stooges for the latter, rather than the innovators and reformers they were supposed to be.

Finally, the third-echelon leaders also felt pressured to cultivate cordial relations with their colleagues. Young leaders frequently found hostile reception in their work units because the veteran cadres were contemptuous of their youthfulness and inexperience. In some cases, veteran cadres actually conspired to turn public opinion against them. Such unsympathetic reception was enough to intimidate many younger leaders from recommending changes to the existing bureaucratic styles and practices.[152]

In a larger sense, the third-echelon policy exposed some serious problems in China's bureaucratic style. The policy was but one more reminder of the propensity of the leaders in a totalitarian system to indulge in grandiose designs and "strategic planning." This style of decision making was typically marked by intellectual sloppiness, wishful thinking, subjectivism, blind faith in their own efficacy, commandism, and impulsiveness. The drive for conceptual neatness easily led to the adoption of a mechanical and inflexible model. Thus, for example, by 1986, both the party and the State Council had issued numerous instructions on the exact age and education requirements for people to qualify for leadership positions on different levels. Often these precise standards were justified on the ground that only they could facilitate the four modernizations.[153] In some areas, this penchant for neatness and uniformity was carried to such extremes that the incumbent leaders even attempted to stipulate the specific attributes for the leadership of the 1990s and beyond.[154]

But the problem of leaders in a totalitarian system becoming addicted to subjectivism and wishful thinking could become especially costly when their ideas failed to win support from the majority of bureaucrats who controlled the party and state machinery. Even though Deng's 1980 intention of rejuvenating the leadership was basically a sensible one, the actual conduct of his subordinates in the provinces and localities in the following years amounted to a sabotage of his program.

This points to the complexity of political reform in China. The eagerness of top leaders to introduce reform was often met with reluctance and resistance by their subordinates, who were more interested in finding loopholes to advance their own interests, or adopting evasive measures to protect their vested interests from being adversely affected by the reforms. This phenomenon of the leaders setting new policies and the subordinates resorting to countermeasures became a recurring feature in the process of political reform and party rectification in the PRC. This process of wit matching hindered the progress of reform, dissipated its momentum, and vitiated its goals. The leaders were provoked by the subordinates' countermeasures to devise yet another set of remedial measures, which in turn only produced another round of countermeasures.

Thus, the third-echelon policy provides us with some insight into the general dynamics of policy implementation in the PRC as well as the conflict between the spirit and substance of a policy. The party has yet to solve the contradiction between the leaders' desire to initiate daring reforms and the mentality of lower-level leading cadres to play it safe to protect their own careers or to exploit the policies to serve their own ends.

The Third Echelon and Political Legitimacy

Leadership change should be evaluated by more than its ability to improve administrative efficiency. Leadership change offers the people an opportunity to reaffirm their trust in the political system. Therefore, the personal attributes and the mode of selection of the leaders can affect both their own legitimacy and that of the political system. The longevity of the imperial system was due at least in part to the ability of the system to sustain the political myth that it provided objective criteria and an impartial process for leadership selection. Even the KMT government tried to follow selection procedures that would lend legitimacy to its own rule.

This dimension of leadership change was especially important in the 1980s because the party's prestige had been badly damaged by the excesses and the exposés of the Cultural Revolution. The return of the old guard, with their old styles and practices, did little to ameliorate people's antipathy toward politics. The third-echelon policy gave the party an opportunity to create a brand new leadership unencumbered by the past so that it could win back the people's support.

But this opportunity was squandered when the party's policy enabled power and offices to be bartered like commodities. As numerous opportunists made off with enormous career or financial gains, the aspirations of really talented people for recognition and upward mobility were frustrated. The masses felt alienated as they were neither eligible as candidates nor consulted in the process of selecting others to leadership positions. The candidates came from an extremely narrow and unrepresentative segment of the party whom the masses did not know or support. The creation of the new leadership only served to undermine further the prestige of the party in the eyes of the masses.[155] By early 1986, popular discontent with the performance of the "third echelon" had become a serious problem.[156] The masses' distrust of, and disillusionment with, their leaders made them extremely suspicious of the leaders' reform promises in general. This sentiment in turn bred widespread cynicism, which became a major stumbling block to the party's reforms.

This phenomenon points to another fundamental dilemma in China's political development. In spite of the party's constant invocations of the mass-line principle during the first seventeen years of the PRC's existence, it had never intended to translate this principle into practice through democratic institutions and practices as they have been known in the West. The party merely wanted to mobilize the masses to serve its own policy ends, to demand the masses to give enthusiastic and unquestioning support to the policies dictated by the party. The mass line practiced in this fashion precluded the opportunity for the masses to articulate their own views or to aggregate their demands as policy options, for to allow this to happen would have endangered the principle of the party's leadership in everything as the Communists understood it. Although unintended, the disastrous experience of the Cultural Revolution only confirmed a widely held belief among many rehabilitated leaders since 1978 that the masses could become extremely dangerous if they ever got out of hand.

It is significant that party leaders in the post-Mao era not only swore off "political movements" but greatly reduced the prominence of the "mass-line" thesis as well. In fact, the party's loss of ideological monopoly and the creeping influence of Western democratic ideas in the 1980s gave leaders even stronger reasons to shun a mass-line approach. While the post-Mao leaders were undoubtedly eager to use reforms to shore up the party's sagging prestige, they preferred to implement reforms from above instead of inviting mass input and participation from below.

But under the circumstances of the 1980s, the leaders could no longer count on the masses to play out the party's script docilely and uncomplainingly. In actuality, an adversarial relationship soon developed between the leaders and the masses, with the former insisting on the principle of domination by the CCP, but the latter increasingly unwilling to comply. The suspicious circumstances surrounding the third echelon's rise to power and the repugnant conduct of some of its members greatly damaged the new leaders' own legitimacy to rule and rendered them incapable of performing the critical task of bridging the gap between the leaders and the masses, or restoring the latter's confidence in the political system.[157]

In time, even the official press frequently employed the term "feudalistic practices" to denounce the incumbent leaders' selection of their friends and relatives into the third echelon. Such practices had the effects of causing demoralization within the cadre corps, serious loss of confidence among the masses, and a further widening of the schism between the masses and the third echelon.[158]

The Third Echelon and the Institutionalization of Succession

From its very beginning, the concept of the third echelon was presented as a long-term solution to China's leadership problems.[159] Therefore, it is necessary to evaluate it as the party's innovative approach to institutionalize succession in the future. How long will the present third-echelon leaders stay in power? What is likely to happen to the transition of power during the next several decades? What conditions must exist to insure the faithful adherence to the third-echelon format in the future?

In his discussion in 1985 on the formation of the third echelon, General Secretary Hu Yaobang stated, "We will gradually select a group of people just over forty years of age to enter national leadership. These people will be only fifty-six to fifty-seven by the end of the century, and only sixty-six to sixty-seven by the year 2010.''[160] Hu had the reputation of being a most ardent promoter of the policy to rejuvenate the leadership. Yet these remarks implied that even he obviously assumed that the current third echelon would stay in power for the next two to three decades.

Will they relinquish power and retire voluntarily in due course? While it is obviously too early to answer this question with certainty, the conditions that made the post-Mao power transition possible can allow one to speculate whether such a format of power transition may continue in the future.

Earlier discussions clearly suggested that the key precondition of the third-echelon policy was the retirement of old leaders. This was brought about by a set of very unusual circumstances in the late 1970s and early 1980s, including Deng's extraordinary personal stature, the perception of possible collapse of the Communist regime, the excessive senility and physical frailty of some leaders, and the lurking of the remnants of the Cultural Revolution to seize power. Even under these multiple pressures, the leadership changes were successfully implemented only after huge payoffs were made to the retiring leaders.

Such conditions are not likely to occur simultaneously in the future. Nothing in the party's past history offers any assurance that the current third-echelon leaders will voluntarily relinquish power at the beginning of the next century. The completion of the third-echelon policy in the 1980s would not have been possible without the enormous pressure exerted by Deng, who had the authority and control over the party's apparatus and the military to enforce this policy. Deng was rare among Communist leaders in that he did not covet the highest office, which would have been his for the taking. It is unrealistic to expect the leader(s) of the next century to have comparable power and to be equally self-restrained in the exercise of power.

The adoption of the third-echelon approach to meet the leadership needs also grew out of the special circumstances of the 1970s, which might not arise again in the future and require the same kinds of drastic solutions. The history of implementation was fraught with so many defects and irregularities that the policy could hardly be considered as having been institutionalized.

In fact, even in a few short years, the party's own thinking on the third echelon has undergone some important changes. In August 1980 Deng Xiaoping criticized the old practice of orderly and step-by-step promotion as inadequate to meet the party's urgent need for new blood. Instead, he proposed that the party should boldly and quickly promote people who could meet the new challenges.[161] By 1986, most of the positions in the third echelon had already been filled. In August 1986, Tian Jiyun (Politburo member and deputy premier) announced that henceforth the party would no longer designate candidates for the third echelon first and then send them to receive more practical training. On the contrary, the new policy was to restore the traditional practice whereby graduates of colleges and professional middle schools would first serve on the basic level, and only those who excelled there would be promoted to higher levels in an orderly fashion.[162] By 1987–88, discussions about the third echelon had greatly diminished in both volume and prominence in the public media, while the continuing task of selecting the next third (or fourth) echelon also seemed to have lost its momentum.

One may wonder if there is not something intrinsically wrong with the third-echelon policy. Statements made by numerous party leaders left the impression that each new echelon would stay in power for fifteen to twenty years or longer. While individual members of this echelon may experience upward mobility at different speeds, the echelon as a whole will occupy all the important leadership positions until they reach their own retirement age, at which point they will be replaced en bloc by the next echelon.

Such a succession plan means that leadership may remain stagnant for as long as two to three decades. This is hardly an effective way to keep the leadership in a constant state of vigor, dynamism, and innovativeness. The scale of upward mobility across the entire system will be severely restricted. This mode of succession means that those cadres only ten to fifteen years younger than the top leaders will be denied the chance to be named successors, since the third-echelon members are supposed to be younger by twenty or more years. After every two or three decades, the process of creating the next "third echelon" will be mounted again and might even have to be relearned. To pick a new "third echelon" only when they have a realistic chance to succeed their elders may also create a mentality among the young cadres that they can afford to glide through many years of service with mediocre performance but concentrate on the few years immediately preceding the selection process to catch their leaders' attention. This mentality could then lead to the repetition of many of the problems that occurred during the early 1980s.

The implementation process of the third-echelon policy reveals another fundamental flaw in the policy's approach. To make the policy work effectively, the party told lower-level leaders in no uncertain terms that they had to step down and never meddle in the affairs of their old work units again. But the party's top leaders found it much easier to enforce the policy on their subordinates than to apply it to their peers. While most people benevolently accepted Deng Xiaoping's own failure to meet his repeated promises to retire, the failure of many other national leaders to retire on schedule or their failure to relinquish power entirely after retirement only aroused widespread resentment within the party and among the masses. Their motivation became even more transparent when Hu Yaobang was deposed by mostly the retired national leaders for trying too hard to carry out the third-echelon policy.

The succession policy offered a good example of the glaring discrepancy between what the party center preached and practiced, and another dilemma in CCP politics. In the contemporary context of Chinese politics, it may be entirely necessary for the top leaders to violate their own policy and continue to stay in power in order to force other aging leaders on the lower levels to abdicate power. But when the local leaders witnessed the conduct of their national superiors, it was not unreasonable for them to try to follow their leaders' example by either continuing their meddling in politics or treating their successors as lackeys. How can this contradiction be resolved? What are the prospects of a successful institutional reform when reform leaders feel compelled to violate their own rules?

In view of its numerous complications, the third-echelon policy can hardly be regarded as having become well developed in the 1980s. Its accomplishments to date have fallen far short of the goal to institutionalize revolutionary succession for the future. It is entirely conceivable that the policy was only an expedient solution to the party's special problems of the 1980s, and that it may never be applied again in the future.

The Party's Challenges

There is no question that the party inherited from the Maoist era an exceedingly defective leadership that desperately needed rectification. But while youthfulness and knowledge are preferable to senility and ignorance, it is questionable whether the party's mechanical prescriptions for the leaders' age and education constituted a meaningful solution. The attributes of good leadership are often culturally defined and must be tailored to the society's specific professional requirements at a given time. They are thus more complicated than the party had anticipated.

The process of leadership changes of the early to mid-1980s already revealed several major deficiencies that the party can address immediately to improve leadership qualities. These remedies are related to both procedural and substantive issues. It is imperative, for example, for the party to establish a cadre classification system that will specify the professional requirements of all jobs to be filled, and set criteria that are pertinent, reasonable, and impartial to identify and recruit qualified candidates to become cadres. The party can apply these standards to the existing cadres to retain the qualified ones and weed out the unqualified ones or give them additional training to improve their qualifications. In short, the party can develop a comprehensive set of rules that cover cadre recruitment, evaluation, supervision, reward and punishment, rotation, and retirement.

In fact, some party leaders had been aware of the need to reform the cadre system along these lines for a number of years.[163] In 1980, Deng expressed a desire to develop a new cadre system that included specific guidelines not only on the recruitment and promotion of cadres, but also on their tenure of service and retirement. Throughout the early 1980s, there were public discussions to reform the selection and appointment processes to include fixed-term appointments and selection by examination or other objective methods.[164] A major change was proposed by General Secretary Zhao Ziyang in mid-1987 to differentiate China's cadres into two categories: the executive and the clerical. According to this proposal, rules for the recruitment and management of the clerical cadres would become more fair, rational, competitive, and objective, while political considerations would presumably affect only the executive cadres.[165]

These steps are certainly in the right direction, and they may lay the foundation of a more open, flexible, and versatile system of leadership selection similar to the model of constant-flow and constant-replacement as employed in many other countries. Implementating these changes, however, has been extremely slow. By the summer of 1989, only two subministerial units in the central government had been designated to conduct experiments in this project. But even in these units, the policy encountered considerable resistance from the incumbents.[166] Only time will tell if the program will ever be implemented.

Even if these procedural changes are fully realized, the party still needs to tackle the broader issues of leadership selection. Traditionally, the party's organization department has specialized in personnel control techniques but not in the sciences of manpower allocation, utilization, and management. It is not enough for the party to decentralize the power of selection from the Central Organization Department to the local organization departments. Minimally, the party could try to transform the organization departments so that they could perform their "managerial" functions more competently. Better yet, the party could delegate more authority to the individual work units to make their own decisions regarding appointments and promotions.[167]

The party must rectify the highly "feudalistic" character displayed during the recent selection of the third echelon and broaden the scope of its search for qualified candidates to leadership in the future to include not simply people with privileged access to the incumbent leaders, but capable people from all potential sources.

Finally, the party must realize that the leaders' legitimacy depends directly on the active support of the people. The record of the past decade has conclusively demonstrated that the party is no longer capable of enforcing tight organizational control over its rank and file. The success of the reformist leaders' political agenda will be immensely enhanced if they can mobilize the power of the masses to supervise the performance of the cadres. The leaders' efficiency can be enormously increased, and the evils of commandism and bureaucratism may be significantly reduced, if they are made accountable to the masses. Democratization and the opening up of the political process for mass participation may provide the best long-term solutions to ensure a better, more honest, clean, and effective government.

In sum, the post-Mao leadership can be faulted as having once again fallen into the trap of totalistic thinking in handling the issue of revolutionary succession. The best way to produce a good leadership may be to let the political market factors decide the choices. These are decisions that can only be made in a decentralized manner. In this way, even if wrong decisions are made, they can be unmade quickly. The third-echelon approach of the 1980s undoubtedly produced a new leadership superior to the one it replaced in some respects. But the notion of scheduling a leadership change once every two or three decades seems to be the least effective means to achieve an otherwise highly laudable objective.

The measures taken to pick the third echelon were not merely technical matters but had enormous implications for China's political development. By the same token, to remedy the many problems created during the recent round of leadership changes, the party may need to transcend the search for technical improvements and ponder the need to restructure the fundamental relationships between party and government, between leaders and the masses, and, above all, reexamine the cardinal principle of party domination over Chinese politics. Will the party be willing to go this far?

5

The Recruitment Drive to Improve Quality and Relations with Intellectuals

MEMBERSHIP has worked as a crucial organizational weapon for the Chinese Communist Party. Whenever the party needed to mount a major military or political campaign or implement a major social or economic program, it nearly always expanded its membership to attract people with the requisite skills to join the party. This pattern of organizational manipulation was established during the years of revolutionary struggle and continued after Liberation. Therefore, the party's efforts of massive expansion of recruitment between 1949 and 1976 can be seen as closely related to the major campaigns during this period:

1. From the establishment of the PRC to the party's Eighth Congress (1949–1956). With rapid victory in the civil war, recruitment speed was also proceeding very fast. By 1949, the party had a total membership of 4.48 million. In the first few years after Liberation, the party's main work quickly shifted from country-side to cities. Under these conditions, the party cautioned repeatedly that recruitment must be handled with care, and it actually tried to contain the size of its membership by requiring all party members to go through the process of general registration after the second half of 1951. But starting with 1953, the party launched its program of land collectivization and issued a call to mount massive recruitment of party members from the rural areas in the next three years. As a result, by the time of the Eighth Party Congress in 1956, the party already had 10.73 million members, or 2.4 times the number of 1949.

2. The period of socialist construction (1956–1966). In 1957, recruitment was virtually suspended because of the antirightist campaign. Then in 1958, under the influence of Great Leap policy, and believing that the conditions for recruitment were better than in any previous period, the party instructed its units from top to bottom to make massive efforts to recruit. By the end of 1960, there were 17.4 million party members.

The Great Leap was followed by the "three years of hardship" when recruitment suffered as much as all other political activities. But the situations again changed after 1965 when the party believed that socialist construction in China had reached a high tide and therefore the party must aggressively recruit more members. The "four clean" campaign, and Mao's belief that there were capitalist roaders within the party who needed to be struggled against, heightened the perceived need for increased recruitment.

3. Cultural Revolution (1966–1976). During this ten-year period, political struggle on all levels was conducted at a feverish pitch. Contending factions needed to swell their own ranks to jockey for positions in the party hierarchy, and central organizational control over the recruitment process had virtually collapsed. As a result, the party admitted 17 million additional members.[1]

Given this kind of historical pattern, it is not surprising that when the party adopted a new agenda at the Third Plenum in 1978 to achieve sweeping modernization objectives, it must immediately face the task of finding enough members with the appropriate qualifications to do the job.

Since the CCP traditionally drew an overwhelming majority of its members from the rural areas and the urban industrial working classes, the limitations of such a membership had been obvious for decades. Any attempt to explain the backwardness of China must include the poor quality of the CCP membership as a key factor. By the early 1980s, party leaders realized that an indispensable measure to improve the party's ability to perform its tasks of socioeconomic construction was to "intellectualize" (zhishihua) the membership. Since the party had no intention to expel the existing members, its ambitious objectives could only be accomplished by attracting additional educated people as quickly as possible. The speed and magnitude with which this could be accomplished directly determined the party's prospects of serving as an effective modernizing agent for the country.

For these reasons, this chapter will trace the evolution and implementation of the party's policy to recruit intellectuals. But unlike even other socialist countries, there existed in China great tensions between the functional needs of the system and the actual policy of the party. Since Liberation, Chinese intellectuals had undergone drastic role changes. To understand how the CCP tackled the problem of recruitment, it is necessary first to address the key issue of the party's theory and policy on intellectuals.

The Party's Changing Theories on Intellectuals

A unique feature of Chinese Communist politics is that the party is supposed to have a "theory on intellectuals" at all times. It is a theoretical formulation to evaluate the nature of the social composition and orientation of the intellectuals; to prescribe their relationship toward the socialist state; and to decide whether they should constitute a part of the working class, a class by themselves, or only a status group. This formulation represents the party's attempt to define the role and functions of the intellectuals in the total revolutionary environment. Ultimately, it settles the question of whether the intellectuals are friends or enemies of the revolution and people, and whether intellectuals should be utilized or suppressed.

The "theory on intellectuals" provides the guidelines for the party to formulate specific policies toward these individuals. The policies are then implemented by the cadres and party members, who inevitably will have their own impact on how intellectuals are treated. As in many other policy areas, there usually exists some discrepancy between the party's policies and their actual implementation by party members and cadres. The theory, policy, and styles of implementation in turn can also profoundly affect the intellectuals' attitudes toward the party and perceptions about their political efficacy.

Historically speaking, the CCP used to be a party dominated by intellectuals, although it never felt entirely at ease with intellectuals inside the party. The first wave of anti-intellectual actions was mounted by Wang Ming after 1927 when he purposely tried to promote workers to replace intellectuals within the party. It was not until 1935 that the leftist policies were slowly rectified.

After the outbreak of the Sino-Japanese War in 1937, a large number of intellectuals flocked to Communist-controlled areas. In December 1939, Mao personally drafted a resolution to recruit intellectuals on a massive scale, arguing that revolutionary success would be impossible without the participation of the intellectuals.[2] Chen Yun, who was the director of the party's Organization Department at this time, also said that the mistake of discriminating against intellectuals must be corrected.[3] By late 1939, intellectuals constituted almost 85 percent of the middle-ranking cadres of the CCP.[4]

Shortly after Liberation, the party regarded the proper treatment of intellectuals as a high-priority issue. It adopted a scheme to divide intellectuals from Nationalist China into four broad categories. The scheme designated a small number of intellectuals as members of the reactionary class and the capitalist class. A third group included intellectuals who earned their living from mental labor in such fields as education, health, sports, industry, transportation and communication, commerce, and finance. They constituted the majority of intellectuals and were given the classification as "clerks" in August 1950. A fourth group included intellectuals who worked in the so-called liberal professions such as journalists, lawyers, writers, and artists. They were laborers, and were classified as "petty bourgeoisie."[5]

The PRC also introduced another system to classify China's intellectuals at this time. Intellectuals were divided into the "high intellectuals" and the "ordinary intellectuals." High intellectuals included higher-ranking college professors, medical doctors, senior researchers, engineers, prominent literary figures and artists, who numbered about 65,000 in the country. Ordinary intellectuals included junior faculty members in colleges, teachers of secondary and primary schools, ordinary medical personnel, engineering and technical personnel, and a number of scientists, writers, and agricultural experts. The total of both categories was a little over 2 million people. Less than 10 percent (or 200,000) of these pre-Liberation intellectuals had graduated from colleges and universities or had studied abroad. The overwhelming majority of them had graduated from high schools or even primary schools.[6] These figures suggest that the PRC in 1949–1950 adopted an extremely loose definition of intellectuals that included people who worked in the educational, scientific, medical, engineering/technical, and literary professions.

As Zhou Enlai pointed out, the intellectuals from the old society had the potential to serve the people in the new society but also maintained intricate affiliations with the old society. Therefore, the party's policy toward intellectuals should be to "unite with, educate, and reform" them.[7] This formed the basis of the party's policy toward the intellectuals for the first seven years after the creation of the PRC.

In January 1956, at a major conference to assess the accomplishments of the transformation of intellectuals since Liberation, Zhou Enlai delivered a famous speech entitled "Report on the Question of Intellectuals" in which he suggested that realization of the objective of socialist industrialization must depend on cooperation between those who labor with their minds and those who labor with their bodies. He announced the party's verdict that intellectuals had been successfully transformed and henceforth should be regarded as a part of the working class. On the last day of the conference, Mao himself gave his personal blessing to this newly legitimate status of intellectuals by urging the entire country to march toward science and technology.[8]

The party's benevolent theory on intellectuals took an abrupt turn soon afterward, however. During the antirightist campaign of 1957, numerous famous intellectuals were denounced as "rightists." Intellectuals were further accused of being members of the capitalist class who walked the path of "white and expert." Initially applied only to intellectuals from the old society, this new theory was soon extended indiscriminately to all intellectuals, including those who had been educated by the Communists themselves.

The party's theory on intellectuals was softened again in January 1962, when a meeting was convened to correct the leftist errors toward intellectuals since 1958. In February 1962, Zhou Enlai, Chen Yi, and Nie Rongzhen attended a Guangzhou conference and formally removed the stigma of "capitalist intellectuals" from the intellectuals' heads, conferring upon them the title of "people's revolutionary intellectuals." Intellectuals were again granted a status equal to the workers and peasants and were referred to as the "masters," and no longer the enemies, of the socialist system.[9]

The advent of the Cultural Revolution in 1966 brought about another precipitous decline of the intellectuals' status. They were again accused of belonging to the capitalist class, as "reactionary authorities" or as the "stinking number nine'' (meaning the bottom of the barrel as social outcasts). During the Cultural Revolution, knowledge itself was downgraded, and it was widely believed that ''the more knowledge one possesses, the more reactionary he will become.'' The radicals' theory on intellectuals as proclaimed in 1971 was embodied in the famous ''two assessments,'' which asserted, first, that the PRC's education system during the first seventeen years of its existence (1949–1966) was controlled by the capitalist class (otherwise characterized as the ''dictatorship of the black line''), and second, that therefore the majority of people who received education during this period were all, by definition, capitalist intellectual products. This view dominated the CCP's theory on intellectuals through Mao's death and Hua Guofeng's leadership.

Deng's Theory on Intellectuals

Major credit for the change in the CCP theory on intellectuals in the post-Mao era must go to Deng Xiaoping. At the time of the antirightist campaign in the late 1950s, Deng was the party's general secretary. He not only made personal denunciations against the intellectuals but oversaw their ruthless suppression. Therefore, Deng's view toward intellectuals as a social group was as hostile as that of other contemporary party leaders in the 1950s.

During the intervening years, however, Deng had obviously undergone a change of heart and developed both a new empathy for intellectuals' personal plight as well as a new capacity to appreciate their usefulness to socialist construction. Thus, shortly after the fall of the Gang of Four, Deng took the lead to proclaim his support for intellectuals when he said, ''we must create an atmosphere within our party to respect intellectuals and to respect knowledge.'' He contended that the party must once again remove the political stigma from the intellectuals' heads and crown them with the new title of ''people's intellectuals.'' He also volunteered to assume responsibility over the party's management of science, technology, and education, and he expressed his wish to serve as the director of the party's ''rear services'' to advance scientific and educational work.[10] These gestures indicate that Deng had become aware of the crucial importance of science and intellectuals even though other party leaders were neglecting them, and that he was willing to yield the political center stage to other leaders while making a more meaningful contribution in this particular area. Deng's personal involvement undoubtedly had a great impact in accelerating the change of the party's theory on intellectuals.

In September 1977, Deng Xiaoping began to refute the thesis of the ''two assessments'' advanced by the Gang of Four, maintaining that the PRC's education policy during 1949–1966 had been correct and that the majority of intellectuals were not class enemies.[11]

A major turning point of the CCP's theory on intellectuals came in March 1978 at the National Conference on Science when Deng Xiaoping reiterated a famous statement made by Zhou Enlai in 1956 that "the overwhelming majority [of intellectuals] have already become a part of the proletariat" and that they now constituted "a force that the party can rely upon." Deng put strong emphasis on the critical contribution that intellectuals could make to the task of modernization, arguing that the country must adopt a policy of respecting and producing more intellectuals.[12]

Deng's views set the stage for a new theory, or, more accurately, a revalidation of an old theory, on intellectuals that was quickly endorsed by many other party leaders. Thus, even before Deng had solidified his comeback, and while he was still cautious to conceal his views and preferences on many other sensitive political issues, he had decided to take a firm and clear position on the thorny question of intellectuals in direct contravention to the Maoist tradition.

Toward the end of 1978, when Deng emerged as the undisputed winner from the party's internal power struggle, his close associate, Hu Yaobang, announced that henceforth the party would cease to view the intellectuals as objects of the policy of "unity, education, and reform." The Organization Department promptly declared that the intellectuals had successfully acquired the qualities of being both "red and expert" after decades of socialist training.[13]

In the next several years, the party made numerous further efforts to refine, explicate, and extend the meanings of its new theory on intellectuals. At the Twelfth Party Congress, Secretary-General Hu Yaobang pointed out, "the policy on intellectuals that we strive to carry out is intended to make the whole party and whole society realize that intellectuals have become the same kind of forces as workers and peasants whom we rely on for our socialist construction. We are also determined to create conditions to enable the intellectuals to . . . enthusiastically and energetically contribute their strength to the people."[14] This new affirmation of the status of intellectuals was carried a step further in late November 1982 when Peng Zhen announced to the National People's Congress that "workers, peasants, and intellectuals are the three basic social forces in the construction of socialism."[15]

Under this new theory, science and technology received recognition as constituting integral parts of socialist productivity.[16] Intellectuals were credited with having made contributions to the creation of social wealth that equaled those made by workers and peasants. Hu Yaobang's statement that "all our wealth, in the final analysis, is the product of both physical and mental labor" legitimated the value of "mental labor" by intellectuals.[17] The party also concluded that intellectuals from the old society had been thoroughly reformed and reeducated, while intellectuals educated since 1949 were all products of the socialist education system. The commitment of both groups of educated people to communism was no longer doubted. In fact, intellectuals were now assigned to play an especially important role in the forthcoming socialist modernization programs. As Hu Yaobang said, "we needed both knowledge and intellectuals to overturn the old world, but we will need them even more in building a new world."[18] In the unfolding reforms of the 1980s, intellectuals were given increasingly important functions to perform. They were presented not only as the main force in China's spiritual construction, but also as the main force of reform in general.

The New Policy Toward Intellectuals

Once the theory on intellectuals was reformulated, the party's next task was to translate it into concrete policies. Starting with the late 1970s, the old policies of suppression and discrimination against intellectuals were officially abandoned and new ones developed. Broadly speaking, the party's new intellectual policy contained several major components.

First, the party removed all the stigmas previously imposed upon the intellectuals and restored the latter to a position of full social and political respectability. Many "progressive" intellectuals were selected for praise in the Chinese press and presented as models for the Chinese people to emulate. Intellectuals were eligible to become model workers, and delegates to the People's Congress on various levels.

Second, the government extended its policy of exoneration and rehabilitation to include intellectuals who had been unfairly treated during previous political campaigns. Although initially applied only to the victims of the Cultural Revolution, the policy was soon extended to cover even intellectuals implicated in the antirightist campaign of the mid-1950s. Since that campaign was conducted by some of the very same leaders who had returned to power since the late 1970s, the removal of the rightist stigma from intellectuals signified a sincere apology by the party for its past mistakes.[19]

Third, the party admitted that intellectuals had endured severe deprivations for decades and decided to make restitution. Extensive publicity was given to the plight of intellectuals (particularly middle-aged ones).[20] Numerous stories in the mass media depicted the intellectuals' misery to arouse popular sympathy. Intellectuals were designated as a special social group that deserved preferential treatment in job assignment, promotion, salary increase, and improvement of living and work conditions, including access to better medical services and better housing. Their children, who had often been barred from decent schools or desirable employment, were given remedial assistance. A large number of married intellectuals who had been forced to live apart due to conflicting job assignments received reassignments to allow them to be reunited.

Fourth, the party abandoned the former attitude of denigrating knowledge and intellectuals by mobilizing its propaganda machinery to emphasize the crucial importance of intellectuals to socialist construction and modernization. The leaders' new message was that the four modernizations campaign would not be realizable without the wholehearted support of the intellectuals. The perennial contradictions between "redness" and "expertness" were suddenly resolved when the party adopted a new thesis that the best "political contribution" that the intellectuals could make to socialism was to employ their professional knowledge to accelerate the four modernizations program. This meant that "expertness" and "redness" were most naturally combined among the intellectuals.

The adoption of these policies was intended to serve two purposes: for one thing, these policies represented the party's efforts to correct its past excesses against the intellectuals by offering them psychological and material compensation. They were also meant to remove all the old obstacles that had hampered efficient utilization of educated people in the service of the party's new socio-economic programs.

More importantly, they were designed to change the intellectuals' attitudes toward the party and to win them over as enthusiastic partners in the party's new grand design to achieve the four modernizations. What party leaders wanted most was to attract intellectuals to join the party's ranks in huge numbers, and to promote them to positions of responsibility.[21]

The party realized that its four modernizations program would be seriously impeded, if not rendered entirely unobtainable, without the active cooperation and support of the intellectuals. This was a crucial task because the CCP had been a victim of its own anti-intellectual policy of many decades to such a degree that by the early 1980s it had become a party marked by shockingly poor educational standards. In 1983, only 4 percent of party members had a college-level education, but those who had only a primary-school level or were illiterate constituted more than half of all party members. This educational profile made a mockery of the party's assertion of itself as the vanguard of the revolution in the new context of achieving rapid economic growth and socialist construction. The party desperately needed an injection of new blood. If a large number of intellectuals joined the party and placed themselves under its internal organizational control, they could dramatically upgrade its overall quality. Therefore, increasing recruitment constituted the ultimate test of the success or failure of the party's theory and policy toward intellectuals in the Deng era.

Different Groups of Intellectuals

China's intellectuals, of course, are by no means a homogeneous group. Even the term "intellectual" is fraught with conceptual ambiguity and confusion. One conventional practice is to determine a person's status by his/her profession. In this sense, "intellectuals" refers to those who "labor with their minds." Another common method of identification is by educational qualifications. But even official documents show wide variations on these qualifications. Usually, people with college education are automatically considered as intellectuals in China. But according to the 1982 census, there were only about 6 million people with the cultural level equivalent to a college education. Yet the number of "intellectuals" in China far exceeds this number. Thus, in late 1978 for instance,

Hu Yaobang said that there were over 20 million intellectuals in the entire country, 90 percent of whom had been educated since Liberation.[22] Several oft-cited estimates in the early 1980s put the total of China's intellectuals at 20 to 25 million.[23]

These estimates suggest that only a minority of China's intellectuals have college-level education while the majority have less education. In 1982, however, China had 66.5 million people with a senior high school cultural level.[24] Therefore, an intellectual in China is someone who falls between these two educational levels. The term probably includes all college graduates and a substantial number of professional high school graduates, as well as regular high school graduates.

A discussion of intellectuals can be facilitated by dividing them into four subgroups with reference to the time they received their education. The first group consists of those who completed their education before Liberation. The second group was educated during the first seventeen years of the PRC (before the Cultural Revolution). The third group was educated during the Cultural Revolution (including about 1.3 million college students), many of whom were the so-called worker-farmer-soldier students. The fourth group consists of those who entered colleges since 1977, but in larger numbers only after the full restoration of China's higher education system in the early 1980s.[25]

A balanced discussion of the party's recruitment drive must deal with these subgroups separately, not only because the party treated them as different targets, but also because different party members, schedules, and strategies were required to recruit them. In addition, the responses from these subgroups of intellectuals have been so different that they inevitably have had different implications for the long-term development of the party.

Old and Middle-Aged Intellectuals

The party's policy of aggressive recruitment of intellectuals went into full swing soon after Deng solidified his power in late 1978. Initially, the policy's targets were only the older intellectuals who had completed their education before Liberation. Many of these people had applied to join the party many times in the past but had been rebuffed as being unqualified. After 1979, the party decided not only to welcome them but actively to seek them out. The mass media gave extensive publicity to the party's recruitment drive as well as to the intellectuals' allegedly warm responses. In the early 1980s, the press praised numerous organs for having done good work in their recruitment drive.[26] Prominent coverage was provided in the newspapers when senior scholars and scientists were granted party membership.[27]

In September 1982, the party's Organization Department concluded that it was unnecessarily restrictive to recruit only the old intellectuals since about 45 percent of China's scientific and technological personnel in the early 1980s were

Table 9

Age and Educational Profile of Chinese Population, 1982

Age	College level[a]	Senior high
24 and under	1,273,000	40,219,000
25–39	2,090,000	19,462,000
40–54	2,213,000	5,600,000
55 and up	463,000	1,249,000
Total (rounded)[b]	6,039,000	66,530,000

Source: 1982 Population Census of China, table 47.
Note: In 1982, 55 year olds had graduated from college or senior high before Liberation. Those 40 years old had graduated during 1950–1966. People age 25–40 would have graduated during Cultural Revolution, and those below 25 would have graduated since 1976.

a. College level include both those with degrees and those who ever attended in college, those enrolled in college in 1982.

b. Rounded totals differ slightly from numbers in original source.

middle-aged intellectuals who had received their college education during the 1950s and early 1960s.[28] Overall, middle-aged intellectuals constituted over 60 percent of all the intellectuals in the country and had become the backbone of China's science and technology. Therefore the Organization Department instructed that henceforth the recruitment drive should be extended to the middle-aged as well.[29]

The Rank and File's Reactions to the New Policy

The party's new theory and policies on intellectuals marked a radical departure from tradition. Undoubtedly, some party members wholeheartedly supported the new policy and had no difficulty accepting the intellectuals as their equals. Many other members, however, especially those in powerful positions, continued to harbor strong anti-intellectual biases and opposed the party's benevolent new policy. Intellectuals of both age groups quickly found out that the worst stumbling blocks to their admission into the party were the leading cadres and party members in their own work units. While there are many possible explanations for such hostility toward intellectuals, three major reasons can be highlighted: leftist convictions, the clash of lifestyles and temperaments, and conflict of interests.

Residues of Leftist Thoughts

Old attitudes and perceptions toward intellectuals showed a strong resilience within the party. After more than two decades of incessant indoctrination, this should not be surprising. In addition, however, three issues fanned the leftist sentiments against intellectuals.

The first issue concerned the intrinsic value of knowledge. Even in the 1980s, party members with ultraleftist convictions still held the view that the bedrock of the Chinese revolution should be the poor and ignorant masses because only they were capable of harboring intense hatred against the old capitalist oppressive system. They stoutly believed that knowledge was "useless," or that knowledge could only make people more reactionary. The old epitaph of "stinking number nine" remained a favorite term used to refer to the intellectuals. Many cadres in economic enterprises believed that the most important factors of production were labor and machinery, not intellectuals with technical expertise. Some argued that the four modernizations would proceed just the same even without the participation of the intellectuals.[30]

A second issue was whether intellectuals should be treated as the political equals of other segments of the revolutionary masses. Many party members and cadres still adhered to the dogmatic theory of class struggle and regarded intellectuals as unqualified for party membership because of their undesirable "class background," "politically unreliable" family ties, questionable personal history, and social connections.[31] Many party members subconsciously adopted a "we versus they" mentality toward the intellectuals and viewed the latter as "outsiders," as the objects of the party's policies of "unity, education, and reform" with whom no bonds of trust could develop, or even as a "dissident group." They believed that while the talents of the intellectuals should be exploited, the intellectuals themselves should be closely watched but not trusted. Intellectuals, they felt, had no right to join the party: they should not think of themselves as being good enough to be part of the party, but should meekly accept guidance and reform by the party. Even those intellectuals who were already party members should not be treated as the equals of other party members.[32]

The third issue was whether intellectuals deserved to be regarded as a part of the proletariat. Many party members refused to accept intellectuals as a part of the working class, and some still regarded them as capitalists. They were convinced that only genuine working-class people could preserve the vanguard character of the party. They worried that the party's true character and the nature of the revolution might be dangerously compromised if too many intellectuals sneaked in.[33] Some party members feared that recruitment of intellectuals would change the sickle and hammer on the party's flag into fountain pen and eyeglasses.[34] These people refused to accept the new position that intellectuals had already become part of the working class. They justified their continuing mistreatment of intellectuals on the grounds that the latter were still the targets of proletarian dictatorship. Many leading cadres held fast to the belief that it was all right to "exploit" the intellectuals, and that one should not treat them with respect. Still others regarded intellectuals as parasites who lived off the labor of peasants and workers, or as "spiritual aristocrats" who disguised themselves in workers' garments.[35]

Clash of Lifestyles and Temperaments

Many of the intellectuals' personal and professional qualities were impediments to their acceptance by the party. Intellectuals' devotion to their professional work was seen as evidence of their determination to follow the "white expert's path" and to neglect their political responsibility. Their professional accomplishments were often dismissed as "individualistic pursuits" of fame and profit, or as "overeagerness to show off," which only betrayed their lack of collective spirit. Many party members and leaders were particularly upset by the intellectuals' propensity to develop independent viewpoints on issues that contradicted their own, regarding these differences of views as signs of the intellectuals' "arrogance," "conceitedness," or disrespect for leadership and organizational discipline. Intellectuals were also often faulted for their inability to tolerate abuses and swallow bitterness. They were said to be not "obedient" enough.[36]

Other qualities of intellectuals that were intensely disliked by existing party members included their alleged "aloofness from the masses," political apathy, "opinionatedness," "falsity and pretentiousness," and lack of proper deference to their leaders.[37] When intellectuals applied for party membership, the incumbent leaders expected them to show their humility and sincerity by submitting their applications year after year. If they gave up after a few tries, this was prima facie evidence that they did not deserve to be admitted.

There obviously existed a wide gulf between the intellectuals and the regular party rank and file with respect to their temperaments and lifestyles. Since the overwhelming majority of the party's current members had come from proletarian backgrounds and were poorly educated, they simply found it hard, or even impossible, to accept the value of the intellectuals' professional knowledge or their personality traits. On the level of social interactions, many party members felt ill at ease in the presence of intellectuals and tried to avoid contact with them. They were excessively suspicious of the intellectuals and imputed devious motives to the latter for wanting to join the party. They resented the intellectuals' individualism and their reputation for being difficult to get along with.[38] Even people who otherwise were considered good party members often harbored strong suspicion and dislike toward the intellectuals.

Jealousy and Conflict of Interests

In the early 1980s, the party's new policy emphasized the need to grant intellectuals "equal political treatment, full authority in work, and special consideration to their livelihood." This policy aroused much jealousy among party members, who believed that the party had shown excessive favoritism toward the intellectuals. Many in the rank and file believed that intellectuals had already reaped abundant economic benefits, and that they should not be granted equal political treatment as well. Many party cadres distrusted the intellectuals as being "malcontents" who were greedy for power and offices.[39]

People of peasant and working-class backgrounds were particularly offended by the preferential treatment accorded the intellectuals and complained bitterly that "the intellectuals had been promoted to the ninth sky while the peasants and workers had been cast aside."[40] They regarded the improvement of the intellectuals' status as leading directly to the denigration of the peasants and workers, and they believed that the intellectuals' improved life was at their own expense.

The alarmists raised the specter that the intellectuals' ambition was to grab political power from the working class and to subvert the Chinese revolution.[41] Many party members openly expressed their fear that the new policy might lead to a situation in which the party would "rely on a minority and desert the majority" and end up alienating the vast numbers of peasants and workers.[42]

Party members were gripped by the fear that their own interests might be jeopardized by this policy. Veteran party members and leading cadres felt wounded by the government's directives to give pay hikes and better housing to the intellectuals. While the government's action was merely intended to compensate the intellectuals for the many years of neglect and discrimination they suffered, many party members clamored for the same benefits and accused the government of turning the intellectuals into a privileged new class.[43]

The policy of promoting intellectuals to leadership positions was particularly upsetting to party members because it pushed both groups onto a collision course. Party members were never threatened by competition coming from contenders outside the party, but the situation was entirely different when intellectuals tried to join the party and to capitalize on their better education to replace the incumbents as the organization's backbone.[44] The possibility that some intellectuals might actually become leaders was overblown to look like an impending disaster of historic proportions. Some party members warned darkly that there was a possibility that the political power that workers and peasants had spilled their blood to seize decades before might be grabbed by the intellectuals in an insidious manner. These biases compelled the party to go out of its way to assure its members of peasant and worker backgrounds that the party never intended to desert them in spite of its policy to encourage more intellectuals to become members.[45]

These cases of conflict were often marked by a strong emotional dimension. Traditionally, it was common for the leading cadres and party members in many work units to lord over the helpless intellectuals for years. It was hard enough for these powerful people to see the intellectuals exonerated and given apologies, but it was extremely humiliating and utterly unthinkable to see them being courted to join the party and move up the hierarchy.

Not surprisingly, cadres and party members alike in many places were determined to block the new policy. One common way to accomplish this was to set arbitrary ceilings on the number of intellectuals who would be admitted. These low ceilings allowed leaders to argue that enough intellectuals had already been admitted, and that no more recruitment was necessary.[46]

Basic-level party organs also created numerous obstacles to make it almost impossible for intellectuals' applications to be approved. They usually put intellectual applicants under grueling tests to uncover faults with a degree of vigilance that was never applied to other categories of applicants. Intellectuals were subjected to excessively long periods of character observation and evaluation, or performance tests. Intellectual applicants were also subject to exhaustive critical review of their social and class backgrounds. Those with overseas or Taiwan connections were often automatically disqualified.[47]

During the application process, the intellectuals were expected to demonstrate their commitment by repeatedly submitting lengthier confessions and more humble pleadings.[48] Even then, many party secretaries still found numerous "defects" with the intellectuals. The whole exercise was designed to humiliate the intellectuals and force them to abandon their effort to join the party.

Policy Results

The CCP's Organization Department has released only a few figures on the recruitment of old and middle-aged intellectuals in the early to mid-1980s. On the surface, these figures seem to indicate a steady increase of such recruitment after 1978. In 1978, intellectuals constituted only 8.3 percent of the total party recruits of that year. They constituted 23.6 percent in 1982, 27 percent in 1983, and more than 40 percent for the first half of 1984.[49]

Although initially only the old intellectuals were recruited by the party, after 1982 the middle-aged intellectuals usually constituted over 70 percent of the intellectuals recruited in a given year.[50] Other official reports suggest that 580,000 intellectuals were recruited into the party during 1979–1984. If accurate, these figures mean that the average annual number of recruits was slightly less than 100,000 during this period.

Numbers aside, the recruitment showed very uneven geographic distribution. Indeed, there were places where enlightened party cadres implemented the party's policy conscientiously.[51] But even some of the successful cases were criticized by higher party leaders as suffering from a serious lack of cadre effort.[52] Overall, the isolated cases of success[53] could not conceal the reality of massive resistance and noncooperation by lower-level cadres and party members. In the early to mid-1980s, the press was filled with the party's stinging criticisms and dire warnings against noncompliance with its policy.

In general, the situation tended to worsen as one moved from the higher to lower levels, or from the more developed urban and coastal provinces to the less developed interior areas. In some places, the party's policy was virtually ignored, and an entire bureaucratic or even educational institution did not have a single party member who was an intellectual.[54] Probably the most dramatic illustration was Xuchang, a major city in Henan Province with the largest concentration of intellectuals in the entire province. Not a single intellectual was admitted into the party among the municipal cultural institutions there between 1958 and 1984.[55]

Lower levels resorted either to passive resistance or to open defiance of the national party if their own interests were seriously jeopardized. One powerful demonstration of this possibility was the case of Hunan University in Changsha where the administrators and party bosses put up a fierce and prolonged fight against the national authorities in refusing to carry out the policy on intellectuals.[56] This case came to light in 1983 only after several years of futile effort by the national party to impose a decision quietly. As Hunan's provincial party secretary, Jiao Linyi, admitted, the province had been under strong leftist influence, had a long history of mistreating intellectuals, and was plagued by intense factional struggles in many agencies. Many party members and cadres who had abused intellectuals for decades were still holding important offices in the early 1980s. To ask these cadres to welcome intellectuals into the party was to ask them to repudiate their own past convictions and to admit personal wrongdoing to the intellectuals which they found impossible to do.[57]

Party leaders soon began to be aware of the problem of nonenforcement of their policy and to voice their concern. For example, Chen Yun was particularly candid in expressing his dissatisfaction. He complained that it was common for many intellectuals' applications to be rejected year after year, only to be granted posthumously as a consolation to the deceased person's family, thus spreading the ironic impression in the society that a good intellectual was a dead intellectual. He suggested that the party might need to create a special agency under the Organization Department to enforce the recruitment policy.[58]

In early 1983, the party press also began to admit that the policy toward intellectuals was "far from being completed."[59] In July 1983, the commentator of the *People's Daily*, after noting widespread obstacles to the intellectuals' admission into the party, demanded party leaders on all levels to make a thorough investigation of their own units' performance record, and to make an all-out effort to implement the policy.[60] Throughout the early to mid-1980s, the media kept up a sustained propaganda campaign denouncing notorious cases of discrimination and oppression of intellectuals.[61]

The recruitment drive was intensified in 1984 as many provincial party secretaries made frank admissions with regard to the unsatisfactory results of the policy and introduced a variety of measures to expedite the recruitment of intellectuals.[62] Deng Xiaoping also repeatedly lent his personal prestige to promoting the party's new policy. At the National Day (October 1) ceremony in 1984, for example, Deng said, "the whole party and society must sincerely respect knowledge, and give intellectuals the opportunity to develop their talents fully." On the next day, he said again, "China's intellectuals issue is a very unique one that we have not properly resolved to date. It is both urgent and important that we resolve this issue."[63] In late October, Deng spoke at a meeting on the party's recently formulated "Resolution on Economic Institutional Reform," a document that marked a milestone in Deng's reform agenda. Deng singled out Article 9, which stated the importance to "respect knowledge, respect talents" as the linchpin of the entire economic reform program.[64] To underscore its commitment, the party also indicated that cadres' work performance in the future would be evaluated partially on their success or failure in implementing the new policy.

Even in late 1984, party leaders still complained loudly about resistance to the policy of recruiting intellectuals in many places.[65] The Organization Department found it necessary in November 1984 to convene yet another national conference to discuss ways to recruit more intellectuals. It admitted that propaganda work to date had yielded very unsatisfactory results and demanded that the lower levels make even greater efforts to overcome the obstacles blocking the intellectuals' entry.[66] In compliance, some provinces actually dispatched large numbers of cadres to the basic level to pressure them to recruit more intellectuals.[67]

But none of these measures produced appreciable changes in the anti-intellectual mentality among the lower levels of the party. Since the CCP's Charter stipulated that recruitment had to be conducted on the basic level, it was hard or even impossible for intellectuals to enter the party as long as cadres with an anti-intellectual mentality continued to hold power.[68] As the party's own survey revealed, widespread discrimination, exclusion, and oppression of intellectuals continued.[69] Numerous basic-level party secretaries continued to ignore the national policy, and the national party was able to intervene directly in only a small number of cases. Not surprisingly, many intellectuals concluded that it was futile to submit their applications.[70]

The conditions were not visibly improved in 1985.[71] The national party's response was to set yet another deadline—in this instance, the next party congress scheduled to be held in October 1987—for the thorough implementation of the policy.[72] Under such intense pressure from above, some lower-level party organs reluctantly allowed more intellectuals to enter the party in 1985–86. But by this time, even many more old and middle-aged intellectuals had gotten the message that they were unwelcome and lost interest in party membership.

Conclusions

The recruitment of old intellectuals was never a numerically important issue. Of the some two million intellectuals left on the mainland at the time of the Communist takeover in 1949, no more than half a million survived to the early 1980s.[73] Their admission into the party in their twilight years would not have made a significant contribution to the party's future mission as a modernizing agent.

The political treatment accorded to the old intellectuals was viewed, however, as a bellwether of the party's sincerity in fulfilling its new pledge to respect intellectuals in general. Many of the old intellectuals had chosen to stay in China and work for the new regime instead of leaving with the Nationalists for Taiwan. A sizable group had actually returned to China from their study or professional careers overseas. Therefore, their emotional commitment to the motherland and sympathy for the Communists were beyond doubt. If, after over thirty years of mistreatment, they still could not win complete political trust and genuine respect, then the middle-aged and younger generations of intellectuals should have good reason to doubt whether their own fate would be any better. In this sense, the actual manner of implementation of the CCP's policy, rather than its rhetoric, would have enormous symbolic significance for the vast number of other intellectuals that the party must still court in the decades to come.

In contrast, the middle-aged intellectuals were much larger in number. There were about 2.2 million Chinese in 1982 between 40 and 55 years of age who had a college-level education. These individuals constituted about 37 percent of all the college-educated people in the country. There were another 5.6 million people in the same age bracket who had senior high school level education. Together they form the backbone of China's educated and scientific manpower pool and will remain in active service for at least the remainder of this century.

By the mid-1980s, many older and middle-aged intellectuals had abandoned any illusion about joining the party. This change of attitude came about partly because of the declining prestige of the party, but chiefly as the result of the intellectuals' own realization that there were just too many insurmountable hurdles in their efforts to gain full political respectability.

The exoneration and rehabilitation of intellectuals from past injustices were highly emotional issues, both for the intellectuals who were the victims and for the lower-level cadres and party members who were the culprits. Not surprisingly, the latter resisted every effort by the party to change the old political verdicts. Intellectuals had to expend enormous amounts of energy to overcome the obstruction of cadres and party leaders in their effort to clear their political records, which in many cases occurred only posthumously.[74] That most intellectuals should encounter even greater difficulty in their attempt to join the party was easily understandable, but even those who succeeded in joining the party sometimes found, to their dismay, that the crucial paths to power and responsibility remained secretly sealed off to them.[75] Thus, for instance, it was extremely rare for intellectuals who joined the party in the 1980s to be appointed as party secretaries in their work units. The few intellectuals who managed to reach nominal leadership positions found themselves under ceaselessly hostile scrutiny by party veterans and became the latter's favorite targets of criticism.[76] These intellectuals often felt isolated and insecure and were made to feel like ''guests'' or ''outsiders'' not entitled to exercise the full authority of their offices.

While it is true that the intellectuals' social status improved noticeably in the 1980s, this was achieved independent of, and sometimes in spite of, the hostility of lower-level party members and cadres. Intellectuals' property losses incurred from previous decades of political persecution were never satisfactorily compensated. Meanwhile, their work and living conditions were only marginally improved. They continued to toil under heavy family burdens, poor health, serious financial difficulties, terrible housing, and a plethora of other handicaps. Their energy was consumed primarily by trying to make ends meet in their daily struggle for survival.[77] Yet even in the mid-1980s, new instances of oppression of intellectuals continued to occur, such as when they were forbidden to engage in scholarly activities, or to publish research articles.[78] The general treatment that intellectuals received from lower-level party organs was either neglect or disdain.

Both politically and professionally, many middle-aged intellectuals concluded that they had reached a dead end. Under these conditions, it was hard for intellectuals to feel inspired by the party's new policy. Most of the promises made by the party remained unfulfilled. On the whole, intellectuals were the most overworked and underrewarded segment of Chinese society.

The anti–bourgeois liberalization campaign of late 1986 and early 1987 was a poignant reminder of how fragile the intellectuals' new status actually was under the party's benevolent policy. This campaign delivered a particularly heavy blow to the old and middle-aged intellectuals, as they were the primary targets of denunciation and expulsion. Some had only recently been courted by the party, but as soon as they deviated from the party line, however slightly, they were promptly and mercilessly persecuted. The message of discriminatory treatment against intellectuals could hardly be missed by most observers of party politics in recent years. When nonintellectual party veterans committed egregious acts of negligence, incompetence, or corruption and caused heavy losses of physical resources or human lives, they could escape unscathed or be mildly reprimanded by the party. But if the intellectuals articulated their own views, then the whole party's propaganda machine and disciplinary mechanisms would descend upon them to humiliate and punish them.

Even though some party leaders made great efforts to restrict the scope of attack, such incidents could not fail to cause serious setbacks in the party's attempt to win the intellectuals back, and their chilling effects could take years to heel.[79] Conversely, the party's own prestige declined because of its inability to win the support of the old and middle-aged intellectuals.

In the decade since the CCP adopted a new policy toward intellectuals, therefore, the disparity between its rhetoric and reality remained as great as ever. There is no doubt that many national leaders were eager to tap the resources of the intellectuals, but their intentions were constantly frustrated by a sizable portion of the party's own ranks. As a result, the intellectuals' hearts were not won over by the party, and their talents were not fully utilized. The estrangement between the party and the old and middle-aged intellectuals remains a stark reality that has yet to be rectified.

6

Recruitment of Youths

DURING its early revolutionary years, the CCP had been highly successful in attracting large numbers of idealistic youths, including young intellectuals, to its ranks. Not surprisingly, the party was marked by youth and vitality when it became China's ruling party. In 1950, for instance, 26.6 percent of the total party membership (some 4,488,000 at the time) were young people below twenty-five years of age.[1]

The founding of the PRC also fostered a tradition whereby successive generations of Chinese students and young people set their sights toward joining the party. This process usually required years of dedication and hard work on the part of the individuals through the Young Pioneers and the Communist Youth League to cultivate the necessary qualities to deserve party membership. Due to the low priority given by the Party in recruiting young intellectuals, the number of applicants among senior high school and college students for membership always far exceeded the number actually admitted in the early 1950s.

The antirightist campaign of the mid-1950s, and the subsequent emphasis on class struggle in Chinese politics dealt several further blows to the young intellectuals' chances of gaining party membership. Not only was the recruitment of educated youths relegated to an even lower priority, but many young intellectuals who had already won party membership were expelled. Throughout the Maoist era, however, young people's enthusiasm to join the party remained high at all times.

The situation began to change after Mao's death. The party's initial policy in the late 1970s was designed specifically to recruit older, well-established intellectuals. But soon it also adopted a more encouraging position toward the admission of younger intellectuals. Nonetheless, the party's efforts were met with a lukewarm response from the younger population in general, and younger intellectuals in particular. To be sure, this lack of response was partly the fault of the party organs on many campuses, which were slow to recover from the shock of the Cultural Revolution and failed to make a meaningful attempt to recruit students into the party. But the more fundamental reason was that many young people and young intellectuals had simply lost interest in party membership.

This phenomenon had become quite obvious at the end of the 1970s. Many schools had so few party members among their students that many classes, especially among freshmen and sophomores, did not have a single party member. It was not uncommon for a whole school to have a few cells, but not enough of them to form a branch (*zhibu*). This created a crisis in many schools because the academic and extracurricular activities in schools used to be conducted under the leadership of students who were party members. But, by this time, often there were not enough student members even to participate in such activities, not to mention assuming leadership over them.

Starting with the early 1980s, the party's organizational weakness in the areas of youth work in general and educated youth work in particular had become impossible to ignore. According to the party's own survey, only 1.9 percent (about 23,000) of the roughly 1.2 million students enrolled in China's higher educational institutions at the end of 1982 were party members.[2] The party's declining appeal to young intellectuals was accompanied by an equally alarming trend among young people in general. Between 1950 and 1983, the total party membership had increased ninefold (from 4,488,000 to 40,950,000). But during the same period, the party had experienced a sharp loss of its youthful elements. In 1983, party members 25 years of age and younger constituted only 3.34 percent of the party's total membership, a drop of more than 21 percent from the high point in 1950.[3] Party members in the age bracket of 26–30 years old constituted only another 10 percent. This means that more than 86 percent of the CCP's members in 1983 were older than 30 years of age.[4] In many areas, the percentage of young people among party members was virtually nil, and an entire administrative district might have only a few young party members.[5] After several years of concerted efforts by the party to remedy the situation, by the end of 1986 party members below age 25 still constituted only 5 percent of total membership, while those younger than 45 constituted slightly over 50 percent. This means that nearly one out of every two party members was above age 45.[6]

These comparisons indicate that, by the early 1980s, the party had lost considerable ground in maintaining its once youthful composition and began encountering serious difficulty in replenishing its ranks with young people and young intellectuals.[7] The potential danger of this trend cannot be overemphasized: without routine injection of youthful elements, the vitality of the party could become sapped. In a country where 62.71 percent of the population in 1982 was under the age of 30, the party must find ways to win back the support of both ordinary youths and young intellectuals.[8] Otherwise, there is little reason to be optimistic about the party's organizational health in the forthcoming decades.

In the following discussion of the party's recruitment, the main focus will be on the recruitment of educated youths, because they could make the most critical contribution to improving the party's human qualities. Some attention will also be given to the recruitment of young industrial workers. Since many of these workers had senior high school or vocational education, they were located on the lower end of China's group of educated youths but constituted an important subgroup that deserves attention. The recruitment of rural youth will be addressed in a later chapter on issues related to the rural party.

The New Policy toward Students

In the early 1980s, party leaders finally confronted the problem of the party's declining appeal to educated youths and formulated policies to step up recruitment of more educated youths. In 1982, the CCP's Organization Department set the goal that in the next three to five years, all freshman and sophomore classes in all colleges must have party members, and that all junior and senior classes must have enough party members to form their own party cells. Between 1983 and 1985, the Organization Department issued many more directives to colleges and universities to intensify their effort to recruit students into the party.[9]

But the implementation of the party's policy on the lower levels was fraught with problems. In a way, these problems were different from those that hindered the recruitment of old and middle-aged intellectuals. Party cadres on college campuses had no reason to fear the students as potential rivals for either their jobs or their power. But many of them nonetheless harbored the same disregard for the intellectuals' value as leading cadres in other professions and had little interest in helping young intellectuals to apply for party membership. This was understandable because most party cadres on college campuses were not intellectuals themselves, but were political specialists or demobilized officers from the People's Liberation Army. Furthermore, the party's decision in 1983 to launch a three-year rectification campaign also became a major distraction since educational institutions were generally hardest hit during the Cultural Revolution and had many scores to settle. As many party cadres on college campuses became preoccupied with their own well-being during the rectification campaign, recruitment work was often neglected.[10]

When college cadres came under pressure from their superiors to deliver results, they often went to the other extreme by trying exclusively to fulfill the numerical quota without paying sufficient attention to the applicants' motivations or qualifications. As Bo Yibo candidly pointed out, some colleges conducted indiscriminate recruitment and took a large number of careerists and opportunists into the party.[11] One indication of this formalistic approach toward recruitment was that dramatic increases in recruitment usually occurred just prior to the students' graduation because this afforded the party cadres the last chance to embellish their recruitment record before the students were gone. This mode of operation also spread the impression among many students that the only reason why some students joined the party was to obtain good jobs.[12]

In the mid-1980s, the official press published a number of reports on recruitment, but their validity is often suspect. Not only were officials' claims sometimes padded, but the terms used were also confusing.[13] It has been reported, however, that in 1984 some 30,000 students from China's 902 graduate schools, colleges, and professional high schools gained admission into the party.[14] At the end of that year, the party claimed as party members some 68,000 students on college and university campuses throughout the country.[15] Even if the latter figure were accepted at face value, party members still accounted for only about 5 percent of the nation's college students. All indications are that the situation did not dramatically improve in the following years. In most places, young party members continued to constitute a much smaller percentage of party members than in the 1950s and 1960s.[16]

Since the number of students being admitted into the party was quite small, it is possible that the national totals were bolstered by heavy recruitment on a few campuses. In the city of Beijing alone, for instance, college recruits accounted for more than 10 percent of the national total in 1984.[17] A few universities, such as Beijing University, Qinghua, Shanghai Jiaotong University, and Huazhong Polytechnological Institute, were given special praise in the official press as progressive models in recruiting students.[18]

Yet while praising the few schools, the official press cited more schools to illustrate the widespread disinterest of students in party membership. Sometimes a whole school did not have a single party member in a particular class. For instance, Zhongshan Medical College in Guangzhou, one of the nation's leading medical schools, did not have a single party member in its 1983 entering class.[19] A teachers' college in Jiangxi had only 23 party members among its 1,976 students in 1984. Twenty-one of the 38 classes in the school did not have a single party member. The 23 party members were so scattered that only one class had enough members to form a cell, which was also the only cell in the entire student body.[20] At the Hengyang Normal College in Hunan, party members constituted only 0.32 percent of its student body in 1984 and 1.8 percent in 1985.[21]

National figures on college students' recruitment into the party appeared much less frequently in the press after 1985. This may be an indication that the recruitment effort directed at college students had peaked, because the CCP's recruitment policy had traditionally been conducted like a campaign. Party functionaries in the schools took recruitment seriously only for as long as the party kept up the pressure on them. Once the pressure was relaxed, the recruitment momentum on the campuses would also subside. The policy to recruit young intellectuals probably produced the best numerical results during 1983 and 1984, returning to routine operation thereafter. One indication of this trend was that, as early as 1985, the Central Organization Department had already begun to complain about the slackening of recruiting drives among graduate students, college students, and professional high school students. The department expressed the wish that young intellectuals should be recruited while they were still in school, and that recruitment efforts should be maintained at all times rather than only before the students' graduation.[22]

In fact, the recruitment of intellectuals as a whole, not just young intellectuals, probably lost its momentum after the mid-1980s. Thus, for instance, the head of the Beijing municipal party's Organization Department complained in early 1985 that the policy of recruiting intellectuals had been implemented very unsatisfactorily. Intellectuals were not given any special attention; their applications were processed not according to the applicants' merit but according to their age, job seniority, or even date of filing.[23] The deputy provincial party secretary of Henan province also complained in early 1985 that, even after years of prodding from above, the provincial party lagged "very far short of fulfilling the national party's goal" of recruiting intellectuals into the party, and yet many lower-level party leaders already felt that too many intellectuals had been admitted and wanted the party to halt the recruitment process right away.[24] Similar complaints about the obstacles of recruiting intellectuals were published in the press of Jiangxi, Anhui, and many other provinces after 1984–85.

Declining Proportion of Young Intellectuals

Youths used to flock enthusiastically and in large numbers to the party prior to Liberation as well as in the 1950s and 1960s. During 1976–1983, the party recruited between 700,000 and 900,000 new members each year.[25] But in 1983, only 1.4 million (or 3.34 percent) of party members were below 25 years of age.[26] The most precipitous drop in the admission of youths occurred after Mao's death. Why did this happen? How does it affect the party?

To answer these questions, an investigation must be conducted on two different levels. First, it is necessary to understand why the party failed to recruit young educated people (both college and high school students) aggressively. Second, one must ask why young students no longer valued party membership as much as before.

Recruitment of Young Intellectuals

Many of the reasons for the party's failure to attract young people are already familiar enough. Many party leaders in educational institutions had no conception of the long-term strategic significance of the party's policy to recruit intellectuals. Rather, they regarded the policy as a marginal issue that they needed to address only when pressured by their superiors. Many were upset by the youths' behavioral style and thought of educated youths as not obedient or disciplined enough to be party members.[27] Many of these leaders felt justified in relaxing their recruitment work because they felt the party had already reached an optimum size and should not expand any further. To the extent that they engaged in recruitment at all, they found it more rewarding to spend their effort on a few prominent figures (scientists, professors, etc.) than on the average student.[28]

On the other hand, some of the factors that impeded recruitment of old and middle-aged intellectuals did not apply to the young intellectuals. For one thing, the personal animosity and complicated history of interpersonal friction that poisoned the incumbent party cadres' relations with older intellectuals did not exist between them and the younger intellectuals. The question of class contradictions was less relevant because the younger people were brought up under the socialist system, and some actually came from cadre families. The leading cadres not only did not have to swallow their pride to welcome the younger people in, they actually had a chance to play the role of political benefactors to these inexperienced young people. Presumably, such factors should have made it easier for the party functionaries to win the young intellectuals over.

Therefore, the party's failure of recruitment must be explained primarily in terms of the younger intellectuals' unresponsiveness to the party's courtship. This line of inquiry will enable one not only to understand the difficulties the party encountered, but also to evaluate the party's prospects of ever becoming a modern, progressive political force in the future.

The Broken Link: The Declining Role of the Communist Youth League

The Communist Youth League (CYL) used to be a crucial linkage between the party and the country's youth. The party had traditionally relied upon the CYL to supply it with new blood. This responsibility was reaffirmed in the new Charter promulgated by the Twelfth National Party Congress. The Charter revived the tradition of the Eighth Party Congress by characterizing the CYL once again as the party's "assistant and reserve force."[29] The intent of stressing a close relationship with the CYL was to charge the latter with the responsibility to "send new blood to the party, train them, supply the party and the state with young cadres, and groom successors for the Communist movement."[30]

The league's general membership was open to people between the ages of 14 and 28. In 1982, a quarter of China's population (250 million) belonged to this age bracket. About 30 percent of them lived in the urban areas and in turn made up over half of China's urban industrial working force. On the other hand, about 70 percent of China's youths in this age bracket resided in the rural areas.[31] Together, they formed the population that the CYL's organizational activities were designed to politicize and propagandize. The best and brightest among the CYL members were sent to the party.

Even more important is the fact that China's intellectuals were highly concentrated among the younger population. For instance, more than three-fourths of Chinese who had senior high school education in 1982 were less than 30 years of age. About one-third (2 million) of the 6 million Chinese who had college-level education were in the same age bracket. In the decades to come, as educational facilities and enrollment expand, Chinese youths will become an even larger share of the country's total educated people. This means that in terms of the long-range development of the party's membership, the recruitment drive must be directed toward the country's youths.

It is easy to understand why the party had placed high expectations on the CYL's ability to attract large numbers of promising young people into the party. Many of the rising stars in Chinese politics in the 1980s were themselves elevated from the ranks of the CYL (including Hu Yaobang, Hu Qili, and Wang Zhaoguo). But, like other branches of the party, the CYL was also totally suspended from operation during the Cultural Revolution and revived after 1978. Between 1979 and 1982, the CYL's mission was gradually transformed from training young people to wage class struggle to making them better equipped to shoulder the responsibility of the four modernizations.

According to a report by the CYL's First Secretary, Wang Zhaoguo, in the four years between 1979 and 1982, the CYL had recruited 26 million new members.[32] In December 1982, when the CYL held its Eleventh National Congress, it claimed to have a membership of 48 million.[33] CYL membership reportedly increased to 50 million by mid-1986.[34] Wang reported further that during 1979–82, the CYL had supplied 2.7 million members to the CCP.[35] Wang's figures suggest that during 1979–82 the number of CYL members who joined the party averaged about 700,000 per year, a figure that roughly corresponds with the previously estimated number of recruits taken in by the party each year. This implies that the CYL was the major supplier of the party's new members.

With the total party membership already at 40 million at this time, this means that the CYL could infuse new blood into the party only at the rate of less than 2 percent of the party's membership per year. It also implies that, each year, the CYL was able to persuade an even smaller portion of its own members to seek party membership. A reasonable inference from these figures is that the overwhelming majority of CYL members simply declined to take advantage of their special qualifications to seek party membership. It must be noted that only a small group of CYL members had a chance to attend colleges where they would be subjected to another recruitment drive. For the majority of CYL members, the commitment to seek party membership must be made while they were in school. If the CYL failed to politicize them sufficiently, if they were uninterested in accumulating a "good record," and once they graduated from junior or senior high schools and became employed, their chances of becoming party members would be much slimmer.

In view of these factors, how can one explain why many CYL members failed to follow the beaten path like their predecessors? How was it possible that a sprawling organization such as the CYL delivered such a modest number of young people as party members?

One obvious answer was the erosion of the CYL's control over China's youths. The CYL was supposed to be a mass organization, and should enjoy the most extensive contact with the target population. The CCP Charter had characterized the CYL as the "mass organization of progressive youths, the training ground for the study of Marxism through practice for the large number of youths, and the assistant and reserve force of the party."[36] Yet even at 50 million members, it reached less than 20 percent of the population in this age bracket (14–28). Therefore, there existed a problem of the span of control between CYL members and the general youthful population in the country. At the CYL's Eleventh National Congress on December 20, 1982, Hu Qili expressed dissatisfaction over the number of members and said that much remained to be done to increase the total membership of the CYL.[37]

But the total CYL membership was not so small that it could not supply the party with more youthful members. After all, by 1982, the CYL had already grown to be a hierarchy with more than 180,000 full-time cadres and several million part-time basic-level cadres. These people formed the backbone of the CYL and should have been the most qualified candidates for party membership and the cadre corps.[38] But apparently only a small number of this backbone force actually joined the party each year.

A more relevant factor was the CYL's organizational weakness. As Hu Qili pointed out in 1982, a substantial number of existing CYL members had poor qualifications, and the CYL's organizational work in the vast rural areas was in shambles and in urgent need of repair.[39] Wang Zhaoguo also admitted on December 31, 1982, that the CYL was unable to fulfill its responsibility as the leading core of China's youth because "at present, the CYL constituted a very weak link in this process. Many basic-level organizations, especially rural and urban street-level organizations, are in a state of laxity and paralysis. This has seriously undermined the CYL's political progressiveness and organizational capabilities."[40]

The close relationship between the party and the CYL was given much lip service but no serious attention in the 1980s. Most party leaders were uninterested in league activities and paid little attention to the league's development. Nor were they concerned about rewarding outstanding CYL members with party membership. As a result, by 1984, in some places, only a minority of the CYL branch secretaries were CCP members.[41] In some places, the CYL also experienced difficulty in finding young intellectuals to serve as local branch leaders.[42] Even when some CYL branch secretaries were also party members, they were often neglected by the regular party cadres and were not invited to participate in regular party activities. Many party leaders held a low opinion of the league and did not believe it was capable of fulfilling its mission as the party's assistant. This weak organizational linkage between the CYL and the regular party bureaucracy directly contributed to the declining interest of younger people in joining the party.[43]

But at the heart of the CYL's difficulties was the change of the moods and attitudes among the country's youth. When the CYL was first revived in 1978, many people who had allowed their relationship with the league to lapse during the previous decade were returned to power. In their eagerness to build up the league, many new members were indiscriminately admitted. This explains why the CYL experienced such impressive growth during 1979–1982 that by the end of 1982, 54 percent of its members had joined the organization in the last four years. But this growth was less a sign of the CYL's organizational vigor than the result of its lax admissions standards. In those initial years, youths still regarded CYL membership as a political asset and eagerly went after it. Furthermore, the CYL's target populations in the urban areas were captive groups, the overwhelming majority of whom were either in schools or factories, and therefore were subject to various forms of organizational pressure to join. Thus, for instance, some colleges reported that 60 percent of their students were members of the CYL.[44]

But this situation began to change as the 1980s progressed. As league leaders were quick to point out, their work among young people became more difficult to promote after the new policy of opening China to the outside world and the new economic reforms in urban areas were introduced. CYL leaders complained that many young people acquired a "selfish mentality," and a "propensity to use unscrupulous methods to seek pleasure." In the rural areas, CYL work experienced serious obstacles after the introduction of the individual responsibility system, which diverted young people's attention toward the pursuit of new economic opportunities. The league's work was hindered because many youths began to feel the impact of new concepts, values, and practical problems, for which the CYL workers could not provide convincing answers or solutions. The CYL ran the risk of becoming gradually irrelevant to its client population.[45]

These factors led to a noticeable slowdown of the recruitment rate. The figures cited above suggest that the CYL's membership increased by an average of 6.5 million a year during 1979–1982, but slowed down to an average of only 500,000 a year during 1982–1986. In the process, the CYL found it necessary to change its tactics to appeal to the youths, and to allow a change in the meaning of league membership as well.

As stated earlier, the biggest attraction offered by the League during Mao's time was that CYL membership would give the youths a headstart over their peers in the application for membership to the CCP. Often, CYL membership was a prerequisite for party membership. Under the conditions of the 1980s, party membership itself was no longer an effective inducement to young people. For its own survival and organizational health, the league had to change its image and present new appeals to young people on their own merit.

This need led the league leadership to modify its old emphasis on rigid discipline and indoctrination and to adopt more flexible, enlightened, and educational approaches to win over youths. Instead of transmitting messages with a high political content, the league in recent years tried to cultivate a new image as a provider of valuable services to its clientele. Thus, the new accent was put on seeking employment for young people, offering training schools or evening classes for their self-improvement, providing recreational facilities, and hosting such activities as sport events, fashion shows, concerts, social dancing, drama club, and even serving as match-makers and marriage counselors.[46]

Although a number of CYL activists had breezed through the party's admission process and enjoyed a meteoric rise on the cadre ladder in recent years, these successful careers had not triggered a wave of emulation among other young people. Whenever CYL branches were popular, it was primarily because their activities had become less political and more recreational and service-oriented to meet the genuine needs of young people. By the same token, to the extent young people joined the CYL voluntarily, they did so less to groom themselves to become lifelong political activists and more to enjoy the nonpolitical rewards at the moment. In this sense, the CYL's effectiveness as the spawning grounds for party membership had become less important than before. In fact, the CYL's ability to shape the values and attitudes of youth in the 1980s had decreased sharply.

Thus, while it was easier for youngsters to accept CYL membership without much thought, it was a more serious decision to seek party membership since the latter signified a lifelong political commitment. By the mid-1980s, most young people had been exposed to entirely different social and intellectual environments, and many variables had intervened to cause them to recoil from the prospect of becoming party members.

Young Intellectuals' Attitudes toward Politics and the Party

What factors, then, account for the young intellectuals' disinterest in party membership? This question can be answered analytically by examining the profound changes in the objective environment around young people and their subjective moods and attitudes in recent years.

The Academic Subsystem: Old and New

Theoretically, the party could either make its membership so attractive that the highly educated wanted to join it voluntarily, or make the access to educational opportunities so difficult that only people with good political conduct were allowed to enter schools. In fact, of course, the PRC had employed both mechanisms in previous years, either simultaneously or alternately. Party membership was a highly valuable asset in China throughout the Maoist era and was eagerly sought by all youth. On the other hand, the party also developed elaborate mechanisms to restrict education to desirable youths. Within the academic subsystem itself, the government traditionally controlled the fate of students at three critical stages: the admissions process, the years students spent in school, and their job assignments upon graduation.

During the admissions process, preferential treatment was given to children with solid revolutionary backgrounds, to political activists, and to party members, while children from undesirable social backgrounds or with poor political performance suffered discrimination or exclusion from certain schools. This policy reached its extreme during the Cultural Revolution when only children of peasant and working-class backgrounds were admitted into the colleges and universities, with little regard for their capacity to learn.

China's education used to be fully socialized. Therefore, after students were admitted, they became completely dependent on the state for their expenses. This dependency became a powerful lever in the hands of the party to ensure the students' conformity with its political line.

Finally, when the students graduated, the party and state had absolute control over their job assignments. Students who possessed strong political credentials (party membership) invariably enjoyed an enormous advantage in getting good jobs and entering the fast track of career advancement.

All these practices began to change in the 1980s and significantly weakened the party's ability to control students. The institution of open and uniform entrance examinations made the students' political qualifications increasingly irrelevant to the admissions process. The academic process had become a much larger, self-contained subsystem that could confer greater stature and more satisfaction on a larger number of people and had been quite successful in insulating its members from blatant political manipulation.

Compared with the Maoist era, the speed of educational expansion had been nothing short of dazzling. Colleges and universities were revived in large numbers only in the late 1970s. College enrollment expanded impressively in the following years (from 565,000 in 1976 to 1,280,000 in 1981).[47] In May 1983, the State Planning Council and the Ministry Of Education unveiled a plan of educational expansion for the next five years. According to this document, the annual admission of students in colleges and universities would increase from 315,000 in 1982 to 550,000 in 1987, or a 75 percent increase. This means that the total enrollment of colleges and universities would increase from 1,153,000 in 1982 to 1,760,000 in 1987, or an increase of 53 percent.[48] By 1987, China actually had 1,063 institutions of higher learning, and a total college-level enrollment of 2,060,000 students.[49]

The Chinese government restored graduate programs in 1978 and created yet another important outlet for talented and dedicated students. Within the next four years (1978–1982) alone, they admitted 1.7 times more graduate students than the total for the decade 1955–1965.[50] Doctoral programs were established for the first time in PRC history in 1982.[51] Even though graduate programs were of very recent origin, by the end of 1982 there were already 21,284 students in such programs, and the rate of increase for the following several years was phenomenal.[52] By 1987, China had 396 graduate programs, enrolling 120,000 doctoral-level students.[53]

Ultimately, China's youth aspired to study in the Western world, a thought that would have been regarded as far-fetched or subversive a mere decade ago. By mid-1984, some 33,000 Chinese had gone abroad for study, surpassing the total number of students and scholars sent abroad during 1950–1977.[54] Before the Cultural Revolution, a trip abroad was a political privilege, and only one out of every ten people China sent abroad was a student. Students could only go to socialist countries. But in the early 1980s, intellectuals began to earn the right to study abroad on the basis of their academic excellence, and almost eight out of every ten persons China sent abroad were students. In fact, by the mid-1980s, intellectuals had a better chance to visit foreign countries than any other segment of the Chinese population except very high-ranking bureaucrats.[55] This trend steadily gained momentum over the years until 1988, when over 30,000 Chinese students and scholars were studying in the United States alone. In 1988–89 there was a new wave of enthusiasm among Chinese youth, especially from South China, to go to Japan for study. It is fair to say that by the late 1980s, the best, the brightest, and the most ambitious educated youth in China aspired to study abroad, preferably in a Western country.

Therefore, the early 1980s marked the beginning of a distinct academic track separate from the political track. This new track was accessible to most young educated people in the urban sector. Like the political track, the academic track required an early decision on the part of the students or their families, strong commitment, and years of hard work. But the requirements of these two tracks were so conflictive that young people often had to make a choice between them at an early age. The intense competitiveness of the college entrance examination had an enormous impact on the quality of life in lower-level schools as well. For most people, the choice had to be made no later than the junior high school level, but many made up their minds (or their parents made up their minds for them) as early as primary school.

In the urban areas, schools' rank and prestige were now decided by their ability to send their graduates to colleges. To accomplish this, many schools even chose to do away with the regular curriculum in order to prepare students for college entrance examinations. Subjects not covered in the entrance examinations (e.g., music, drawing) were ignored; weekends were abolished. Courses and activities that had political content were either suspended or drastically curtailed because they were considered a waste of time and were opposed by the students' parents. CYL activities fell victim to this trend as well.

There emerged a hierarchy of "keypoint schools" (zhongdian xuexiao) that devoted virtually full time to drilling their students to pass the entrance examination at the next higher level. The schools were rewarded financially and administratively for their students' successes in these examinations. For the students, performance at each successive level of entrance examinations would decide how far they could travel on this new ladder of upward mobility.

Roughly 50–60 percent of high school graduates planned to go to college, but only one out every ten might succeed.[56] While this may seem like a very restricted opportunity structure by the standards of other developed countries, it represented a great leap forward for China's youths. A successful academic career would also give the students an opportunity to gain modest control over their lives, free from political complications, because the students' academic record was the ultimate determining factor for their future. Even the most favorable evaluation and recommendation by the CYL or party secretary would not be enough to give students the opportunity to be admitted into a graduate program in China or in a foreign country. Education again became a respectable and desirable commodity in its own right. It provided a career alternative to politics and a degree of insulation from politics that had never before been possible in China. On the high school and college levels, therefore, there usually emerged a division between the academically committed students and the politically-oriented students.

Altered Campus Atmosphere

The college students' financial situation underwent significant changes in the 1980s. Previously, the major share of their educational expenses were borne by the state. But starting in the early 1980s, the government introduced more flexible methods of student financing of higher education. Although the original intent was not to give up the state's control over education but to cut costs, the effect was gradually to reduce the state's ability to hold students hostage by the threat of financial reprisal. At the same time, many high schools and colleges became interested in generating more revenues and were willing to admit students above their official quota (sometimes illegally) as long as the students had the ability to make substantial contributions or pay high tuition.

As the students' own financial burden increased, they had to turn increasingly to their families or to their own ingenuity for help. By the mid-1980s, it was estimated that each college student needed to spend about 3,000–4,000 RMB of their own (or their family's) resources during the four years of schooling. Many college students now earned substantial incomes from sideline activities, such as giving private tutorial lessons or peddling small wares. The number of self-supporting students in colleges and universities grew steadily. As the students were asked to underwrite a larger portion of their educational expenses, the school administration had less leverage to pressure them to join the party.

Political Convictions

The campus had always been an important arena for political socialization in China. There are two important elements in this socialization process: explicit political messages, and social norms and values that produce serious political implications. Both can influence the students' attitude toward party membership.

Chinese college campuses were traditionally tightly controlled by the party.

Ideological uniformity had been sternly enforced since the antirightist campaign of the late 1950s. Political indoctrination was intense, and ideological orthodoxy was far more vigilantly maintained on campuses than in production units. Social norms and values had to conform to the correct political line, and social life on campus was puritanical and monotonous. Friendships were warily maintained, and romantic ties were forbidden. The intellectual atmosphere was marked by rigidity, dogmatism, and intolerance. Political workers (party secretaries) occupied a dominant position in this academic setting. Philosophical curiosity and pluralism were the most deadly political sins.

In the 1980s, however, political work on college campuses began to lose its effectiveness. Many students resisted political indoctrination and refused to participate in political activities.[57] But most important of all were the profound value changes that swept across the campuses and created new political difficulties for the party.

College campuses gradually became the spawning grounds for iconoclasm in recent years. By the mid-1980s, a serious "crisis of faith" had spread among college students. This crisis manifested itself in two major issue areas.

First, there were doubts about the validity and explanatory power of Marxism itself. Some students believed that Marxism had outlived its utility as a political ideology, or that it had been disproved by modern realities.[58] There were those who regarded communism as "pie in the sky," as being "visible but unreachable," or as being "remote and opaque" (p. 283). Some conceded that communism might contain some good ideals for the future, but that it offered no viable solution for present problems (pp. 286–87).

Many students questioned the fundamental communist premise on the "collective good" and believed that since human beings were by nature selfish, communism was nothing but a utopia. Others rejected the validity of all "isms" and political philosophies (p. 296). The most negative among the students contended that all ideals were lies, and that all faiths and pursuits could only bring disillusionment. They maintained that all human societies were irrational regardless of their form, and that societies were governed by ruthless forces that rendered their human constituents powerless to shape their own destiny (p. 298).

It was only a short step from doubting the validity of the communist ideology to questioning the role of the CCP. While some students conceded that the CCP had played a constructive role during the revolutionary stage, they argued that the party had become "superfluous" during the stage of socialist construction because it had done more harm than good to the revolutionary cause in recent periods (p. 258). They believed that the principle of leadership by the Communist party had lost its historical relevance as China marched toward greater democracy (p. 227). Some rejected as erroneous the assumption that socialist construction had to be conducted under the guidance of a single Communist party, arguing that this assumption was potentially in violation of the theories of Marx, Engels, and the model of the Paris Commune. Many cited history to raise doubts about the CCP's ability to handle the challenges of socialist construction (pp. 267–68, 275).

The theoretical justification for the principle of proletariat dictatorship also came under fire. Many students could not understand why China still needed proletariat dictatorship when the country had presumably been under socialist rule for several decades (p. 41). Others rejected the traditional class struggle thesis which focused exclusively on the contradictions between the capitalists and the proletariat. Instead, they contended that the new class contradictions in contemporary Chinese society occurred primarily between the ruling "bureaucratic class" (actually an indirect reference to the CCP) and the masses (p. 98).

Second, socialism in contemporary China also became a target in this intellectual turmoil on the campuses. Many students viewed Chinese socialism as "agrarian socialism," "backward socialism," or "socialism with very strong feudalistic characteristics"(pp. 18–19). Many people suggested that conditions in China might have been better if it had not chosen the socialist approach to begin with (p. 75). Much controversy surrounded the party's assertion of the putative superiority of socialism. Some went a step further to question the realizability or even relevance of socialism. The recent economic reforms also generated heated debate concerning the socialist credentials of these reforms. For instance, the new individual responsibility system in the rural areas was cited as irrefutable proof of the inadequacy of the socialist collective economic system (pp. 109, 121).

If these students did not like communism or socialism, nor the leadership of the party, then what alternatives did they see for China?

While no consensus emerged, many showed personal preferences for Western solutions. Many students argued that socialism could not stand a comparison with capitalism insofar as materialistic construction was concerned, and they believed the latter had conclusively demonstrated its superiority over the former with its far higher standards of living and sustained vitality of economic growth (pp. 62, 67–68). Still others pointed to the many commendable features of capitalist societies in contrast with the dark sides of socialist China, the most commonly cited examples of which included the cult of personality, bureaucratic arrogance and inefficiency, corruption, and crime (pp. 68, 70). Some went so far as to argue that had China not followed the socialist path but had allowed the Nationalist party to govern with capitalistic policies, the country might have fared better and the catastrophe of the Cultural Revolution might never have occurred (p. 21). Still others insisted that socialism might be superior in purely theoretical terms, but "ideals make empty talk, only capitalism can bring tangible benefit" (pp. 286–87).

The students' favorable attitude toward capitalism as an economic system was also extended to Western political systems. Some students openly expressed admiration for Western democracy with its electoral process, representative system, separation of powers, and political pluralism (pp. 68–69). Many favored the adoption of the multiparty system in capitalist countries to replace the one-party system in China on the grounds that it would be more conducive to the realization of "socialist democracy" (p. 234).

The party proved utterly impotent to stem this tide of political skepticism on campuses. Needless to say, the party's own prestige and appeal suffered in direct proportion to the spread of these "heretical" ideas.

Social Norms and Personal Values

Concurrent with the crisis of political faith, there was a quieter but no less profound reevaluation of long-held moral standards, values, world outlooks, and ideas on the meaning of life among educated youths. The once monolithic value system on campuses had given way to diversity. Students found themselves fascinated by new ideas. Many students turned their attention to discovering their "true self." They regarded society and collectivity as being detrimental to personal well-being and self-fulfillment, and they believed that "socialism was a graveyard for individuality." They were attracted to a motley of Western thoughts, among which Sartre's existentialism and Dewey's pragmatism were belatedly rediscovered by a new generation of Chinese students (pp. 177, 295). The writings of classical Western thinkers (Rousseau and Montesquieu among others) were also eagerly devoured (p. 268). While no single dominant new philosophy or creed emerged, more and more students came to the conclusion that communism's emphasis on altruism and selflessness was but "a lot of air and empty talk" (p. 268).

Students' attitudes toward politics and the party also changed. Many students now became openly contemptuous of political activists, dismissing them as people without integrity or scruples. Extracurricular social work, which previously had been highly praised, was now regarded as a waste of time and a detriment to one's academic performance. Some students refrained from seeking party membership for fear of becoming the objects of ridicule and verbal attacks by their peers. Instead of winning admiration, people who showed an interest in party work were viewed as "opportunists" (p. 184). Female students became particularly reluctant to seek party membership because nowadays boys preferred girls who were politically inactive and did not want to marry girls who were party members.[59] The return of many pre-Liberation social values, including the desire to avoid political complications, made party membership a liability rather than an asset for many young intellectuals.

The changed social values affected not only campus life, but also students' career plans and strategies. In Maoist China, the ultimate career goal for most ambitious young people was to be made a cadre assigned to party or government work. Assignment to a political or administrative job was considered more prestigious than assignment to economic enterprises or technical fields. Another top preference for young people was to join the PLA. Cadres and PLA soldiers would have topped any popularity poll in young people's career choices, followed closely by industrial workers. Only a minority of students would have aspired to be intellectuals for life.

In the 1980s, however, a significant shift of the rank order of different professions occurred in the eyes of Chinese students. While the young people's top choices might fluctuate from one year to the next, the new top favorites were the engineers, medical doctors, technicians, journalists, and other professions that required a good education. Cadres and PLA soldiers both suffered a substantial depreciation in prestige. Many people sneered at political workers because "they did not produce social wealth" and their jobs were dispensable. They were generally regarded as a bunch of ignorant people whose careers would lead to dead ends, and who were totally unworthy of respect. Laborers, once considered sacred, lost their luster and dropped even further than cadres or soldiers in the eyes of the students.[60]

The expansion of economic opportunities in recent years brought significant changes to the employment relationship between the state and the students. In fact, a substantial number of the jobs still under the exclusive distribution of the party or state were no longer deemed as desirable jobs. An increasing number of college graduates refused to accept the jobs assigned to them by the state. Well-educated people with certain kinds of skills (foreign languages, computer science) were aggressively recruited by the more lucrative professions which offered higher salaries and greater professional mobility (both upward and lateral) than the party or state ever offered. The new commercial opportunities in the 1980s created a semifree labor market that kept expanding and made it possible for intellectuals not only to lead a less complicated political existence but also to gain greater personal and professional gratification.[61]

What was the impact of the students' changing values on the party's recruitment of young intellectuals? The most obvious was that most of the educated youths of the 1980s were not as interested in joining the party as their predecessors. College students now preferred to shape their own lives and to mold their own future, rather than allow the party to dictate how they should live.

Broadly speaking, the college students of the 1980s could be divided into three major groups. One group consisted of those who were determined to pursue academic excellence in school so that they could scale the ladder of scholarly success in China or abroad. They wanted to devote themselves fully to academic work and considered political activities a nuisance and party membership a liability.

A second group consisted of the great majority of students who felt assured that they would obtain their diplomas in four years and find jobs either through the state's assignment or by themselves. They saw little reason to take academic work seriously, nor did they believe political activities were worth the trouble. It was students with this mentality who contributed to the widely observable worsening of discipline on campuses after the mid-1980s. Their major goals while in school were to have a good time and to make money through sideline activities. All they wanted was to maintain minimal grades, graduate, and find a job free from political pressures.[62]

Finally, a third group consisted of students who opted for the political track. But unlike college students of the 1950s and 1960s, few of them felt inspired by political idealism and took genuine pride in party membership per se. Instead, most had lost ideological zeal or purity of motives and regarded the party as a launching pad for a successful bureaucratic career.[63] Even in the 1980s, party membership could make a crucial difference when a person aspired to become a cadre in the party and state structures.[64] They went after party membership for the very substantial benefits it could bring them.

Young people from cadre and party member families might be particularly attracted to the third option. Against the backdrop of the show of disinterest by the overwhelming majority of China's young intellectuals toward party membership, the chances were greatly enhanced for the small minority of people who had chosen the political path to move ahead. Party cadres charged with the responsibility to recruit young intellectuals sometimes found themselves in panicky situations because not enough young people voluntarily sought party membership. The few who did so were eagerly grabbed without much attention to their motivations or qualifications. These new recruits could expect to make headway precisely because there was little competition from their peers. If they also had strong family connections, they might even be quickly elevated into leadership positions, as often was the case during the process of selecting the third echelon.[65] In this sense, the party's recruitment policy in the 1980s might also have exacerbated the tendency toward the self-perpetuation of its own elite.

On balance, however, the party's attempt to improve the educational and professional qualities of its members through the recruitment of educated people had yielded limited success. Realizing the resistance it had encountered from intellectuals, the party in 1985 stipulated that all historical problems (unfair and unjust treatment) concerning the intellectuals must be resolved before the convocation of the Thirteenth Party Congress in 1987.[66] Also, the party urged more aggressive recruitment of intellectuals after 1985. Although a number of intellectuals whose applications had previously been rejected were now accepted, the value of party membership in the eyes of intellectuals depreciated even further after 1985. Among China's universities, the People's University in Beijing was supposedly the most politicized. Yet in the late 1980s, even students at this university either refused to apply for party membership or declined to serve in party organs when assigned to do so upon graduation.[67] Intellectuals' sense of frustration with Chinese politics and alienation from the party deepened during 1987–88, and many took pride in not being party members, or even in being expelled by the party. By this time, intellectuals' confrontations with the party became increasingly open and frequent, as they made speeches and published articles critical of party leaders and policies. The desertion of the intellectuals from the party had reached avalanche proportions.

Other Categories of Youths

Outside the school compounds, there existed in urban China a large number of people working in party and state organs and in industrial enterprises. They had finished high school or vocational school. While they would not qualify as intellectuals in other advanced countries, they were located at the lower end of the intellectual scale by Chinese standards. Those among them who possessed special skills were called "technical personnel" or even "experts"; the younger ones were also called "educated youths."

Statistics released by the CCP's Organization Department reported that "technical personnel" accounted for only 8.3 percent of the party's recruits in 1978 but increased steadily to 27 percent in 1983.[68] Other reports claimed that of the some 4 million new members recruited into the party from 1979 to mid-1983, only 460,000 (about 11 percent) were classified as "experts in various professions."[69] In 1983, about 150,000 "technical personnel" were recruited into the party. In 1984, this category increased to 340,000 new recruits.[70] It was also claimed that a large number of "model workers" and activists were recruited into the party.[71] Another report claimed that between the end of 1978 and mid-1988, about 2.3 million people with technical skills of all kinds had been admitted into the party.[72]

These figures were offered to create the impression that the cream of the crop in society was being recruited into the party. But these figures can be misleading because they seldom indicated the level of education of these new recruits. Since it is known that party organs and party members on all levels indulged in inflating their educational credentials or performance records, these figures should be viewed with suspicion. Furthermore, when units were under pressure to recruit a certain category of people, they were more interested in the body count than the quality. Finally, even accepting the annual number of recruits at face value, such numbers were too low to make a tangible difference for a party with over 48 million members in 1988.

The CCP has not released figures on the number of intellectuals by profession. It is known, however, that the recruitment drive was plagued by uneven coverage with respect to professions and geographic areas. The new recruitment occurred primarily in the few professions that already had a large concentration of better-educated people, such as in central government organs, national defense units and heavy industrial sectors, and well-established work units. On the other hand, organs on the local level, civilian enterprises, light industries, collective enterprises, and work units with a short history tended to have fewer recruits who were well-educated. Professions such as education, science and technology, medicine, journalism, and literary work had large numbers of intellectuals but very few new party members. Therefore, while the overall number of intellectuals within the party increased modestly, many organizations still suffered from a shortage of party members who were also intellectuals.[73]

The recruitment policy also showed uneven geographical coverage. The recruitment of young intellectuals in a given locality depended on a number of factors, including its geographical location (coastal or interior), political atmosphere, quality of existing leaders, and level of economic and educational developments. Numerous reports in the press suggest that the party's success was made possible by the good performance of a few places while serious problems persisted in many other places.

Yet even reports of successful recruitment must be treated with a grain of salt. For instance, the province of Hebei was widely praised for its recruitment success far above the national average during the 1984–86 period.[74] But the official press revealed that in many places in the province, people in the target professions (such as intellectuals and technicians) were indiscriminately recruited for the sake of fulfilling quotas regardless of their personal qualifications. Even people who had no intention of becoming party members were pressured to join. Cadres' own friends and relatives were frequently sneaked in and recorded as intellectuals to pad performance reports.[75]

In looking at the CCP's recruitment history since 1977, one can see two distinct phases. During the seven-year period between 1977 and 1983, the party admitted about 5 million new members, or less than 1 million per year. Many places either ignored recruitment work or restricted the proportion of recruitment in relation to existing members or put an arbitrary lid on the total. But between 1984 and 1987, the party admitted about 8 million members, averaging 2 million per year. By the spring of 1989, the CCP claimed a total membership of 48.3 million people. All told, in the nine years between the end of 1978 and mid-1988, the CCP admitted 12.85 million new members.[76]

Yet this dramatic numerical increase not only should not be taken as evidence of the party's dynamism, but should be perceived as a symptom of the party's recurrent problems with recruitment. For ever since Liberation, every major expansion of recruitment has been accompanied by serious flaws. In the twenty-eight years between 1949 and 1977, the CCP experienced eight years of "massive recruitment" (in the 1950s and early 1960s) and ten years of "abnormal recruitment" (during the Cultural Revolution).[77] But almost without exception, the party's own verdict at the end of each period of exceptional membership growth was negative. Thus, for instance, at the Eighth Party Congress in 1956, the party demanded that the quality of recruits be guaranteed even at the cost of slowing down recruitment. During the Great Leap, many places resorted to surprise attack tactics in recruiting party members in order to "produce (numerical) miracles," to "increase party members by several-fold," and so forth, and caused the quality of party members to decline visibly.[78] Those who were admitted during the Cultural Revolution were of even worse quality and prompted

Deng Xiaoping to say in 1980 that they were "unqualified."[79] During the Maoist era, whenever the party urged the lower levels to conduct aggressive recruitment, the latter responded by paying attention to numerical quotas and ignoring quality.

This tendency resurfaced during the 1980s as well. When the party became unhappy with the slow progress of recruitment during the early 1980s and demanded more aggressive action, the lower levels responded by brushing aside the party's prescribed admissions procedures.[80] Local recruiters did not bother to develop or screen progressive candidates. In their eagerness to conform to the party's directives to attract educated people, many units paid exclusive attention to the applicants' formal education or professional skills without due regard for their political qualifications. Many party organs were in great haste to approve applicants to become probationary members and then consider their work done, but never did any further work to make sure that the new members were qualified. The superior organs showed interest only in receiving impressive quantitative recruitment reports from below but not in exercising quality control over new recruits.[81]

Under these conditions, the recruitment drive after 1984 was conducted very unsatisfactorily. Some leading cadres regarded recruitment as a way to build up personal power or to reward relatives and friends. Many basic-level organs put great pressure on reluctant people to apply for party membership. If they did not show interest, they would be criticized. Even people who openly said that they did not believe in Marxism, that they did not want to participate in party activities, and that they regarded party work as a waste of time were forced to join the party.[82]

Not surprisingly, this kind of recruitment work could hardly improve the party's ability to fulfill its historical mission. On the contrary, many new members were perceived to have qualities worse than the average masses, and their admission into the party caused the organization's prestige to decline sharply among the masses.[83] By the spring of 1988, the damage done by the recent recruitment drive had become so serious that there emerged a chorus of criticisms in the official press calling for a quick rectification of the situation.[84]

In spite of the party's effort to recruit aggressively, various party publications admitted that many people still did not want to join the party, including youths, students, and intellectuals, and that the proportion of party members among people in science and technology, literary work, athletics, and health work was still very small in 1988.[85]

Young Industrial Workers: A Special Subgroup

Urban industrial workers constitute an important subcategory of youth in China. These people supply the new blood to the country's industrial manpower. To maintain its image as the vanguard of the proletariat, the CCP must try hard to recruit these young workers, especially the better educated.

Traditionally, one indicator of the party's effectiveness as vanguard was the large number of party members occupying critical positions on the floor in the production process. These people, who were said to be located at the "front line" of industrial production in the plants, formed the backbone of the labor force in these professions. In the earlier decades of Communist rule, it was common for 20 percent, 30 percent, or even more of the "front-line workers" in plants to be party members. Since these plants were ranked along the ideological scale, there was a typically high concentration of party members on the front lines in state-owned plants, followed by the collective plants, and cooperative plants. But a disturbing situation developed in the 1980s with a dwindling number of party members on the front lines until, by the end of 1985, only 9.8 percent of the front-line workers in the most advanced socialist economic units— the state-owned industrial enterprises—were party members. The percentage in other industries, such as construction or mining, was even lower.[86]

This was indeed an alarming phenomenon, and there were at least two reasons for it. One was the reluctance of existing cadres in the plants to recruit young workers who might threaten their own positions in the party because of their better qualifications.[87] Some party leaders in plants still regarded party membership as a plum that people should come begging for, and they were in general contemptuous of young workers' immaturity and inexperience. These aging party leaders felt repelled by the mentality, sentiments, and life-styles of the younger workers and regarded them as unfit to be party members. By and large, however, the party in many industrial plants lost its organizational vitality and did not spend much energy to expand membership. This led directly to the decline of party membership among the young industrial workers.[88]

The second reason was the demographic and attitudinal changes brought to the work force itself. In recent years, many workers had left demanding jobs on the front line, sometimes through illegal means, for more comfortable desk jobs or retirement. Their departure caused a noticeable reduction of the numerical strength of the party on the basic levels of the work force.[89]

The atmosphere in most industrial plants in recent years had changed substantially. On the plant level, unlike on higher levels, "let economics take command" had become widely accepted as the modus operandi. Younger workers were more interested in earning bonuses and considered political work an interference with their economic pursuits. If given a chance, many workers would probably leave the state-owned enterprises to work for more "capitalistic" collective or individual enterprises. In any event, many workers, even in state-owned plants, now had side occupations and made additional money by doing extra work at home or in other enterprises after their regular shift. Their life-styles had also changed substantially: they were more interested in sensual pursuits, material acquisitions, and recreational activities and less in political activities. In short, the socioeconomic structure and the values system of urban educated youth had undergone such a tremendous change that it is hardly surprising that few were receptive to political mobilization and motivation or wanted to work hard for party membership.[90]

The upshot was that even though workers below age 35 continued to constitute the overwhelming majority (sometimes over 70 percent) of the work force in many plants, only a small portion of them were party members. In one well-publicized case of a major industrial plant in Beijing with a work force of about 4,500 people, for example, the party recruited only 26 members during the period 1979–1985. Consequently, older people (above age 35) constituted a commanding majority of party members in the plants. The party's stagnant growth in many industrial plants in recent years meant that it began to experience difficulty in extending its tentacles into all aspects of plant operations. As the work force in a plant was typically divided into teams of workers on the floor, sometimes as many as 40 percent of the teams did not have a single party member, which rendered it almost impossible for the party to assume a leadership role among them.[91]

The party took this development seriously and tried to reverse it by giving high priority to recruiting industrial workers after the mid-1980s. Yet the decrease of party members among industrial workers and the lack of party members on the front line in all kinds of work remained uncorrected during the late 1980s.[92] At the national conference of Organization Department directors on August 21, 1989, the party's new general secretary, Jiang Zemin, reported that he was terribly disturbed by the fact that there were few party members among productive workers, especially among the first line of production. He reported that there were plant sections or workshops that did not have a single party member.[93] Although the CCP called itself the proletariat's party, it had less than eight million members who were industrial workers. Thus, industrial workers constituted only 17 percent of the party's total membership at the end of the 1980s.[94] The party obviously regarded this as a serious problem.[95] If this process of organizational erosion persists, the party's control over industrial workers may become even more tenuous in the future.

Long-Range Implications

Why has the party's recruitment drive fallen so short? As discussed in the areas of recruiting old and middle-aged intellectuals, the major stumbling block was the unwillingness of party cadres on the lower levels to carry out national directives faithfully, which eventually drove intellectuals to the conclusion that they were not welcome in the party. But the failure to recruit younger intellectuals and educated youth can only be partially attributed to the incompetence or resistance of lower-level cadres. A more fundamental reason is the unwillingness of young people to join the party. This phenomenon has far more ominous implications for the party's long-term well-being than the declining recruitment of older and middle-aged intellectuals.

The discussion of the party's recruitment drive to upgrade its membership quality ultimately raises two fundamental issues about the party's future. One is the ability of the party to perform its vanguard functions effectively. Can party members conduct themselves as the modernizing agents to achieve China's four modernizations? The second issue is the ability to win the trust and good will of intellectuals and to maintain political stability. Will the intellectuals support the party or resist it?

The CCP as a Modernizing Agent

On the basis of the above discussion, the most generous estimate would put the number of "intellectuals" and "technical experts" recruited into the party during the 1980s at less than 2 million. When measured against the party's own membership of about 48 million during the late 1980s, this was a very small portion of the total size. Even if this pace had been sustained, it would take the party several more decades before it could produce a fundamental change in its educational profile. But as mentioned before, this pace of recruitment was probably not maintained after 1985.

What kind of educational profile did CCP members have in the 1980s? At the end of 1983, according to party statistics, intellectuals with college cultural level constituted only 4 percent of the over 40 million party members, and those with senior high and vocational school level constituted 13.8 percent.[96] In other words, less than 20 percent of CCP members had the educational equivalent of college, middle professional school, or ordinary middle school. On the other hand, about 30 percent had junior high school level, 42.2 percent had primary school level, and illiterates accounted for 10 percent.[97] At the end of 1986, the party's data showed about 25 percent of total membership had senior high school level or above, 25 percent had junior high school level, about 42 percent had grade school level, and 8 percent were illiterates.[98] Another set of party data suggested that at the end of 1988, about 30 percent of members had senior high school education or above, and about 70 percent had junior high school level or less.[99]

These figures should not be regarded as accurate, but rather as being suggestive. It is highly doubtful whether the purported improvement between 1983 and 1988 actually happened, because it is known that a large number of people falsified their educational credentials to gain career advantages.

Nonetheless, even these figures seem exceedingly inadequate to allow party members to perform the role of modernizing agents for such a huge population. To justify its role as China's revolutionary vanguard, the party must be composed of the most progressive elements in the country. This need gained further urgency since Deng's decision that the party's historic mission for the next several decades was to build up socialism both spiritually and materialistically. Neither task seems realizable without enrolling a large number of the country's better-educated young people in a common endeavor.

While it is impossible to decide how many intellectuals should be recruited into the party, the situation in another socialist country, the Soviet Union, allows an interesting comparison. There, in the 1980s, one of every three technical experts in the country with high school or college education was a party member, and one out of every two doctorate degree holders was a party member.[100] Although the Soviet Union had a much smaller population, it had a much larger Communist Party proportionately. It also had a far higher percentage of people who had received higher education. In fact, China was one of the major countries in the world with the lowest number of well-educated people in per capita terms. Again, as a measure of comparison, in 1983, for every 10,000 population, there were 58.4 college students in India, 106 in Soviet Union, 210 in Japan, and 507 in the United States, but only 11.6 in mainland China.[101] This extremely unfavorable ratio suggests that even if all college students were recruited into the Chinese Communist Party, it would be still a long way from being an effective modernizing agent.

Of course, the potential candidates for membership in the CCP were not restricted to people with college degrees. A more reasonable way to assess this issue is to measure the number of recruits against the number of potential candidates in the general population. In 1982, among Chinese people in the bracket of 18–29 years, there were about 1.75 million people who were either currently enrolled in college or had college-level education, and another 40.5 million people with senior high school level (including higher professional and vocational schools). In other words, there were about 42 million people who had the equivalent of senior high school level or better, all between 18 and 29 years of age.[102] Since over half of the CCP members in the 1980s had junior high school education or less, these 42 million people constituted the logical targets of the party's recruitment drive in the 1980s. But against this huge source of supply, the number the party actually took in annually in the 1980s seems highly insignificant.

In any event, the party itself realized that the low educational qualifications of its members had already become a major hindrance to the promotion of its economic programs. In urban areas, the party members who worked in plants and enterprises could not assume leadership because they could not absorb new technology or handle new equipment. In the countryside, the situation was much worse. Party members often could not understand the content of political directives issued by higher levels. When the party called on Chinese peasants to "use scientific methods to till the field," party members were unable to assume leadership because they did not have the education to do so.[103]

It is entirely conceivable for the modernization of China to proceed without much meaningful contribution from CCP members. While the general population (particularly the urban population) takes advantage of the expanded opportunities to improve their educational qualifications, the party's efforts to recruit the best educated may lag far behind. If the party insists on the principle of leadership by maintaining control of all key positions in the state and economy, then the progress of modernization will be impeded. If, on the other hand, the party loosens its grip and allows more nonparty intellectuals to assume greater responsibility, then the economy may become more diversified and dynamic. In such a case, however, there may emerge serious animosity between party members and ordinary people. It is the latter who will create wealth for the country and make the greatest contribution to the realization of Deng Xiaoping's ambition of economic development, but it is the former who will control power and may use their privileges to rob the latter of their economic gains. It is also questionable whether in the long run the creators of wealth can remain content without asking for a greater share of power. The resentment of the wealth-creators against the power-holders may become more serious.

Relations with Intellectuals

An equally serious concern for the party is how to soothe the intellectuals' distrust and resentment toward the party, and win back their good will. This task has not been accomplished even a decade after Deng's return to power, and the party still appears to most intellectuals as an oppressor and not a friend.

The disillusionment of China's intellectuals with the party and with politics in general was movingly expressed by Liu Binyan, one of China's most respected intellectuals, when he said:

> Starting in 1957, the road in front of Chinese youths and intellectuals became increasingly narrow. . . . If you try to be a straight person in politics, then you will be branded an antiparty, antisocialism element. This road has been effectively blocked. If you think of yourself as being somewhat talented, interested in science or the arts, and wish to make some modest contribution, then the accusations of being a "white expert" or "bourgeois individualist" will quickly be heaped upon you. Thus, this road, too, is basically blocked. . . . As a result, there is only one road left for China's intellectuals, a road that is relatively safe and easy. That is to try to be a political opportunist, or a fence-sitter.[104]

The party not only must have the intellectuals join it, but also needs their full confidence and genuine cooperation. Whereas the party's relationship with old and middle-aged intellectuals in the early 1980s was a transient issue arising out of a peculiar historical background, its relationship with young intellectuals remains an ongoing concern for as long as the party wishes to survive. It is ironic that at the precise historical juncture when Chinese Communist leaders are professing their deepest appreciation for the value of intellectuals and welcoming them to join the party, the intellectuals' enthusiasm for political activism through party membership has waned.

As long as the reasons for the young intellectuals' lack of enthusiasm to join the party are ignored, the party's chances for sustained recruitment success look dim. In the 1980s, however, even national party leaders seemed to have developed an ambivalent attitude toward the young intellectuals' political apathy. On the one hand, they lamented the students' unwillingness to join the party, but on the other hand, they probably preferred that the students remained apathetic rather than seeing them becoming highly politicized for the wrong causes. By and large, the party had conceded the futility of using mobilizational means to rekindle the students' political activism. In other words, the party's attitude amounted to benign neglect as long as students refrained from causing disturbances. The party was content to keep things quiet on campuses and to tolerate the students' hereticism and idiosyncrasies.

But it could be dangerous for the party to grow complacent about the quietude among educated people in China. Students and young intellectuals have been the most volatile element in Chinese politics both before and since Liberation. Time and again, politicians and seasoned observers have been lulled by the surface calm on the campuses to conclude that China's students had lost their political dynamism, only to be rudely awaken by a new round of angry outbursts. The volcanic eruptions of student protest in 1986–87 and the spring of 1989, which quickly spread to many major cities, should serve as a warning that students' docility should never be taken for granted.

The party can afford to lose touch with the students and young intellectuals only at its own peril. The students' grievances might be poorly focused and ineptly articulated, but they are deep-seated. Dissidents such as Fang Lizhi are not so much the shapers of student opinions as the effective synthesizers of ideas that have percolated among them since the beginning of the 1980s. The political suppression of Fang and his colleagues might give the party a respite, but it does not solve its problems with the students and intellectuals. In the long run, China's hope for orderly political development hinges on the party's ability to pay close attention to the political orientations and aspirations of the young and better-educated people and to develop a cooperative relationship with them. Prolonged alienation of the intellectuals and educated youth and their exclusion from the mainstream of Chinese politics could bring inestimable harm to the party itself.

The party faces a monumental task in fostering a more constructive relationship with intellectuals. As a minimum, it must realize that it cannot reinstate its monopolistic domination over the education system without doing enormous damage to the country. The party may have to learn to tolerate and respect the trend toward a gradual depoliticization of education. If it is genuinely committed to enhancing its appeal to the intellectuals and attracting them to join the party voluntarily, then it must mend its ways. It would help if the party could address the ideological reservations of the intellectuals, and shore up its own image to make them proud to be party members. Above all, it must tighten discipline within its own ranks to enforce its new policy toward intellectuals. Better cadre attitude, more genuine respect for intellectuals, greater delegation of authority to intellectuals, and more freedom for them to develop their talents and career objectives inside the party could probably gradually soften the intellectuals' resistance.

The party's challenge, of course, does not cease after the intellectuals are recruited. New strains will emerge even after they are in the party. Initially, and for quite some time to come, intellectuals will constitute an island of knowledge surrounded by a sea of ignorance. Intellectually, the party faces the challenge of blending these two extremes into a coherent whole to fulfill its responsibility as the shaper, catalyst, and enforcer of China's modernization plans.

Possibly for decades to come, the party will be confronted not only with the problem of smoothing the major intellectual differences between the better-educated minority and the poorly educated majority, but also with the potentially even more troubling emotional and psychological cleavages within the party. Given that the overwhelming majority of existing party members come from peasant and working-class backgrounds, it is not surprising that there already existed many signs of serious incompatibility between them and the intellectuals. The increase in the number of intellectuals inside the party might only aggravate this situation in the short run. Even many party members who had friendly attitudes toward intellectuals subscribed to the view that they possessed certain "defects" (such as vanity, narcissism, and temperamentalness) that must be rectified to make them better party members.[105]

The implications of this psychological cleavage can be further explored on two different levels. On the macro level, it seems that the party may have to endure considerable growth pains to find the means to reduce mutual distrust and internal strains between the new intellectual recruits and veteran party members. In this sense, the party must make fundamental decisions on how its organizational character is to be shaped. Will the CCP remain under the shadow of a predominant majority of peasants and workers decorated by a perpetual minority of intellectuals? Or will it reduce the influence of the peasants and workers to transform itself into a truly elitist party in the technical sense? The party may need years to decide on these broad issues and must exercise extreme caution at every point of the process to avoid provoking a backlash.

On the micro level, the party may need to do much more to inject confidence into the intellectuals. Intellectuals in China come from a small segment of the urban population. As long as class remains a discriminatory factor in the PRC, the intellectuals cannot feel completely secure. The party redefined the intellectuals' status in the 1980s through a reinterpretation of an old ideology. But a decade later, this reinterpretation has yet to meet the full approval of the party's rank and file. As the antirightist campaign and the Great Proletarian Cultural Revolution amply demonstrated, the atmosphere could change abruptly. This apprehension is a main reason why so many intellectuals decided to stay out of harm's way by refusing to join the party.

Empirical data indicate that those intellectuals who have joined the party do not feel entirely comfortable in their new surroundings. The distant and suspicious attitude with which other party members treat them, and the supercritical yardsticks against which their conduct is measured, can be quite intimidating. Consequently, many intellectuals tend to become even more cautious and self-effacing after they join the party. They sense that even when they are treated courteously by other party members, they are being treated "differently," and they have trouble mingling with the rest of the party. Their intuition counsels them to shy away from taking the initiative or assuming leadership, to withhold their opinions, and generally to avoid making waves. These conditions inevitably raise the question as to how the intellectuals' presence in the party can contribute positively either to its revitalization, or to the full realization of their own potential.

In sum, more than a decade after adopting a new policy toward intellectuals, the CCP still faces monumental obstacles in fostering a more constructive relationship with intellectuals. The pace of progress has been exceedingly sluggish, and the resistance from the party's rank and file is still widespread. It may take decades more for the party to acquire a critical mass of intellectuals as members to fundamentally alter its intellectual as well as technical character, even assuming that the present commitment is kept. But the tasks of the four modernizations cannot be held in abeyance. The party can either persist in and accelerate its recruitment of intellectuals or learn to share power with nonparty intellectuals for the sake of socioeconomic progress. If it chooses to do neither, but jealously guards its power, then it may run the risk of deferring the realization of its own socioeconomic goals.

7

The Party's Crisis in Discipline

ALTHOUGH party leaders began to notice a serious discipline problem very early on, their initial analysis put the blame on the remnants of Gang of Four and the bad and confusing influences of the Cultural Revolution. Therefore, their prescription was to expose and remove the remnants who "incited troubles," and to thoroughly repudiate the Cultural Revolution to clear up the confusion in the ideological and behavioral realms. It was hoped that with these twin measures, the rank and file would not be misled by erroneous conduct or ideas.

But the party's problems continued to multiply between 1979 and 1982. Finally, two factors affected the timing of the party's decision to seek a comprehensive solution. One was the leaders' eagerness to create favorable conditions for an economic "takeoff" in China. The failure of the campaign to smash economic crimes and other forms of misconduct led the leaders to believe that economic reforms would be jeopardized unless the party could improve its performance and tighten its discipline.[1] There was an emergent realization among some top leaders that fulfillment of the party's mission of socialist modernization was contingent upon a disciplined and competent membership.

But by far the most important factor was the heightened sense of danger to the party's survival. The staying power of leftist ideology, the insubordination and repugnant conduct of party members, and the paralysis of organization caused great alarm among the leaders. If these deviances were not checked promptly, then the party might lose control. Therefore, the leaders believed that a rectification campaign was not only "necessary" but "urgent." Finally, at the Twelfth Party Congress on September 1, 1982, Hu Yaobang announced the party's decision to launch a three-year rectification to commence sometime in late 1983.[2]

The Rectification Campaign, 1982–87

Once the decision was made, the CCP followed its tradition of conducting a test run of its policy on a smaller scale before extending it to the entire party. The

170

units that would conduct the test (called "experiment points" or *shidian*) were carefully selected. These preliminary tests would give the party a chance to find out the real conditions on the lower levels, to detect the flaws in the policy's conception and execution, and to verify the effectiveness of new methods before they became guidelines for the rest of the country. The tests also gave the party a chance to create success stories for its propaganda so that the policy could begin in an auspicious manner.[3]

Tests became particularly important in the current rectification because many methods employed in earlier rectification campaigns had to be rejected due to their "leftist" character. The party needed a dress rehearsal to make sure that the policy could cope with as many contingencies as possible and could be carried out smoothly.

By early spring of 1983, a number of test points in the provinces had been chosen and were encouraged to conduct rectification "with a new and creative spirit." The party urged members at these points to be bold and innovative, and to formulate a new strategy for the rectification campaign on the national level. The Secretariat sent more than a hundred cadres to these points to supervise their rectification.[4]

But even during this experimental stage, the rectification was already met with a cool reception. Many units loathed to be designated as test points because they doubted that the rectification would accomplish anything. Many party secretaries were uninterested in rectification, set lenient standards, and had no desire to confront the wrongdoers, particularly when the latter were colleagues or superiors.[5] The fact that an institutional reform was being carried out simultaneously also reduced the effectiveness of the rectification work since many cadres were unsure about their own jobs and paid little attention to the requirements of rectification.[6]

Notwithstanding these problems, the party pushed through the experimental stage and formally initiated the rectification in the entire party in October 1983.

Objectives

The party's "Resolution on Rectification" set four major objectives to be accomplished in three years:

First, party members must reject both rightist and leftist tendencies and achieve a higher level of ideological and political unity by a total acceptance of the party's line and objectives since 1978.

Second, party organizations must be purged of the "three types." Leadership on various levels must be reconstituted and a third echelon of successor must be promoted to leadership positions to provide an organizational guarantee for the continuity and stability of the reforms.

Third, party styles must be improved by combating bureaucratism and the abuse of privileges by members, and by restoring the latter's revolutionary commitment.

Fourth, party discipline must be tightened and the principle of democratic centralism reasserted to reverse the party's organizational ineffectiveness.[7]

Besides the second objective, which was intended to change leadership to ensure against the possibility of the seizure of power by the Cultural Revolutionists (discussed in a previous chapter), the other objectives of the campaign were all related to various aspects of discipline, namely, party members must obey the party line, must conduct themselves properly, and must not commit misdeeds. The party noted that cases of misconduct had aroused enormous popular indignation. These instances must be prosecuted, and the culprits severely punished.[8]

Sequence and Methods

The party's strategy called for rectification to be carried out in successive stages, each of which was directed at a different subgroup of its membership. The first group consisted of national and provincial members, the second of district and county-level members, and the third of members below the county level, or on the basic level. Originally it was estimated that each subgroup would devote about one year to rectification, and the whole campaign would be wrapped up by the end of 1986.[9]

The resolution also stipulated identical procedures for all subgroups, starting with the study of political documents, followed by investigation and verification of individual members' thoughts and deeds, and concluding with general registration for qualified members and denial of membership to unqualified ones. Each of these procedures or "phases" would last three or four months. For the first phase, "political study," the party also issued lists of standard reading materials, which consisted of four volumes of documents numbering about half a million words.[10] During the second phase, "examination and verification," members were required to identify defects in their personal conduct and problems in their work units, and to suggest concrete ways to correct them. The actual correction of these problems would occur during the third phase, "correction and rectification."[11]

After the individual members completed their effort at self-improvement, it was the party's turn to take "organizational (disciplinary) measures" against members who had committed serious misdeeds, followed by a "general registration" to decide which members deserved to stay in the party. All members were to be judged against the relevant articles (articles 2 and 3) on membership qualifications in the party's Charter. But the decisive factor was the members' actual conduct since 1978. Members who failed to meet this test might be given a chance for additional education at the end of which the unfit ones would be denied the opportunity to renew their party membership.[12]

Finally, before each work unit concluded its rectification, it was required to make an overall evaluation of the results of rectification and to suggest areas for future improvements.

To supervise the rectification, the party also created a Central Rectification Guidance Committee. This committee's chief responsibilities were to collect information, supervise implementation of policies, provide guidance and propaganda, and shape broad decisions. The actual rectification work was delegated, however, to leadership in the individual work units. Superior-level units would not send work teams to manage rectification directly in the lower-level units, but superior levels had the responsibility to stay informed of the progress in the lower units.[13]

Special Features of the Campaign

This campaign differed from most previous rectification campaigns in several major respects. First and most obviously, its scope was much broader than previous campaigns. The campaign was not restricted to problems in a single area, but aimed at tackling simultaneously all major problems confronting the party. The party's ideology, style of work, and organization, as well as its members' personal conduct were all to be rectified. Furthermore, it ranked as one of the most sustained efforts by the party to rectify its problems, lasting longer than many previous campaigns. The campaign was to be conducted in stages according to carefully prescribed procedures and in sequential manner.

Second, the rectification was to be conducted strictly within the party itself. Other democratic parties or mass organizations were not required to undergo their own rectification. However, they were invited, along with the general population, to make suggestions and criticisms to help the CCP implement its rectification.[14] Since the majority of nonparty people were only too glad to be spared the political tensions, the recent rectification was one of the few campaigns conducted solely within the party's own organizational confines.

Third, whereas many previous rectifications were directed only at errant members, this one required every member to go through the screening process to prove his or her worthiness for party membership. Also, unlike some previous campaigns that set quotas on deviants to be punished, this one presumably applied the same stringent criteria to screen all members but adopted an open-ended position on how many members would eventually be punished. The categories of members that might be refused registration included not only people who had committed serious economic misconduct or criminal acts, but also those who failed to possess the necessary requirements for being party members or who refused to participate in the rectification.[15]

The remainder of this chapter examines how effectively the party implemented its plan, and how well it achieved its objectives.

The Escalating Character of Misconduct

The most striking feature of poor discipline in the 1980s is that its tempo and nature changed over time. Poor discipline occurred in several major waves during this time. The first wave occurred prior to the launching of the rectification campaign and showed several general characteristics. First, the main reason for abusing privileges in most cases was to gain modest advantages to make life slightly more comfortable for a member's family. This desire was most force-fully displayed in their attempt to grab more housing spaces. The more audacious and resourceful ones built their own houses by embezzling public funds, confis-cating land or purchasing it at nominal cost, and stealing construction materials.

Second, they also abused their privileges to gain modest favors for their relatives and friends and, occasionally, peddle them for a small fee. Their goals usually involved the bending of administrative rules to help people gain employ-ment, admission into a college, or a change of residential status so that they could leave the rural areas to move into towns or cities.[16]

But even during this period, it became clear that the cadres and members had already acquired the habit of trying every conceivable way to circumvent the party's disciplinary measures. For instance, when the Central Discipline Com-mittee made it illegal to use public funds to build expensive housing for party members in February 1983, the latter quickly found loopholes in the new regula-tions so that they could use public funds to "subsidize" the members' purchase or construction of their own residences. Since housing spaces were distributed not according to family sizes but based on official ranks, leading cadres not only grabbed huge living space for themselves, but often hoarded several apartments for their children as well.[17]

The second wave of misconduct began roughly in the second half of 1984 and dwarfed the misconduct of the previous years in both scale and frequency. Illegal economic activities, complex in nature, now became routine operations for some public agencies. Such activities were masterminded by the agency's leaders, participated in by most of the staff, and conducted under the pretext of carrying out reform or promoting employee welfare.[18] A large number of public organs took advantage of the party's new policy of encouraging economic entrepreneur-ship to form private companies even though the laws had specifically forbidden them to engage in profit-making activities. These "attaché-case companies," as the Chinese called them, were all phantom companies because their capital, production facilities, warehouses, vehicles, and so forth were all taken from the government at no cost. Company employees were all bureaucrats who drew salaries from the state but conducted company business during their regular office time. Children of prominent leaders often played key roles in these attaché-case companies, and influential and well-connected retired cadres were retained as consultants or board members. Cadres and staff members became "stockholders." Their official and commercial roles became indistinguishable, but the company's profits would be split only among themselves. When losses were incurred, however, they would shift the cost entirely onto the public organs. In less than a year from the fall of 1984 to mid-1985, more than twenty thousand such commercial enterprises had sprung up.[19]

With time, forms of misconduct became more inventive and sophisticated, even as the rectification campaign was being carried out. Companies could purchase commodities from the state at centrally controlled prices and resell them in the market for substantial profits. Commodities like steel, automobiles, chemical fertilizer, color television sets, bicycles, and woolen fabric were in short supply in 1984–85. The reason was that many producers of these commodities told the government that they were unable to fulfill production quotas set by the state while they actually supplied their products to their own phantom companies to sell in the market for much higher prices.[20]

Tax evasion and document falsification became common practices. Large quantities of merchandise were written off as gifts or free samples from their producers while in fact they had been sold to evade taxes. Producers who had earned foreign currencies from the sale of their products concealed their revenues from the state so that they could sell the currency in the black market for higher prices. State and collective enterprises sometimes lent their business licenses, contract forms, and bank account numbers to criminal elements for a fee. Factories often sold high-grade products through their own outlets while delivering their inferior products to the state's distribution system. State and collective-owned enterprises also concocted schemes to sell or transfer resources or merchandise to cooperative or private economic entities at concessional terms on the pretense that they were helping these less advanced forms of economy but actually to split the profits with them.[21]

Cases of fraud, deception, and swindling began to mount. By late 1985, the national party acknowledged that there had been a notable increase in the frequency of major cases of economic irregularities. The perpetrators of such schemes usually were able to enlist leading party or state cadres to be their partners and swindle money from other gullible customers (usually other public agencies), sometimes amounting to millions of renminbi.[22] Also, some of the public agencies whose leaders were unfamiliar with economic activities often entrusted their business operations to charlatans who advertised their connections with high-ranking officials or overseas Chinese and their ability to open doors and make deals. These people promoted themselves as the new breed of entrepreneurs, people who were capable of "striking it rich." In their capacity as managers or sales representatives for these phantom companies, they were sometimes able to swindle large sums of money out of their employers and customers.[23]

In this new atmosphere of economic free-for-all, many people acquired an expectation to be paid off. Public agencies routinely demanded commissions, kickbacks, or service charges for services they rendered. Numerous organs of the party, state, military, and economic enterprises converted their public authority into an economic asset and exploited it to enrich themselves. Every public service agency had the potential of becoming a "hegemon" who could hold the people hostage and demand a ransom. As these agencies were located on the basic level and away from the party's disciplinary control, they could do practically anything they pleased and the people were totally helpless.[24]

Of course, cadres and leaders could not perpetrate their schemes without the support or acquiescence of their colleagues and subordinates. To retain the latter's loyalty and collusion, bureaucratic agencies and economic enterprises concocted numerous excuses to pay hefty bonuses out of public funds, ranging from cash, to uniforms and household wares, to washing machines, refrigerators, and television sets.[25]

Some units were even more inventive in finding pretexts to pay their leaders and staff with public funds. Some paid a "walking fee" to those who walked to their workplace. Some leaders were paid an "organization fee" for doing their office work. Some units under the Nanjing Bridge Administration paid out more than a million RMB to their staff to compensate for their working on weekends during the previous twenty-seven years, allowing some people to make off with nearly RMB $3,000 in one swoop.[26]

A substantial number of public agencies and economic enterprises also established contact with criminals or foreign businessmen to engage in bribery, hoarding, smuggling, black-marketing, evasion of taxes and customs duties, manufacturing of counterfeit medicine and liquor, sale of pornographic materials, and prostitution.[27] Some of these activities were conducted on a truly grand scale and involved a network of colluding organizations over great geographical distances.[28]

Thus, although China was a socialist state in name, the wanton abuse of privileges by cadres and party members suggest that property rights in China had really fallen into the hands of those who held power. People who held public offices or managed economic enterprises acquired the mentality that they actually owned the resources and could do whatever they pleased with them, with total disregard for the public trust placed in them.

The Decaying of Cadres' Lifestyles

The worsening work ethic inevitably affected the personal lifestyle of party members and cadres. Conspicuous consumption and ostentatious living by cadres and members on all levels became even worse than in the preceding period. The number of illegal activities among cadres and party members to grab better housing and to arrange better jobs for their children and relatives had subsided only because the desires of the overwhelming majority of influential people in these respects had already been satisfied, and not because the party had scored any success in halting them.[29] But their tastes for expensive travel and social entertainment had grown.

One clear indication of this trend was the use of automobiles. Throughout the Maoist years, the domestic-produced "Shanghai" sedan or even a converted military jeep was the ultimate status symbol for only a few ministerial or provincial-level leaders, and "Red Flag" limousines were reserved for only the very top national leaders.

Automobiles were first imported into China in the early 1980s to modernize the urban taxi fleets and earn foreign exchange from tourists, but they soon became the most cherished possessions of party cadres and members. There began a wholesale effort to upgrade their vehicles. The top leaders abandoned their once awe-inspiring "Red Flag" in favor of foreign-produced stretch limousines that had more features as well as tinted windows to shield their identities from pedestrians. By 1986, black Mercedes-Benzes had become standard issue for even middle-level bureaucrats in Beijing and cruised the city streets in large numbers. As some Beijing residents sarcastically commented, the only thing the cadres in this socialist republic had not yet dared to ride in was a Rolls-Royce. Those not resourceful enough to acquire an imported sedan for personal use would accept the second best—an imported van for group riding.

Beijing, as the nation's capital, was always a trend setter for the rest of the country on matters related to political pomp. Before long, provincial and even municipal and county-level officials were all eagerly acquiring foreign cars to preserve their dignity in transport. By 1985–86, only ineffectual petty bureaucrats would ride in Shanghai sedans, which now aroused more pity and scorn than envy. The rush for imported automobiles became so frenzied that in 1985–86 many public agencies gladly paid five to seven times the fair world market price for them. Of course, cadres were unperturbed by their high costs because they used public funds to pay for automobiles that they used for personal transportation.

Cadre travel expenses also skyrocketed. As before, their favorite locations to hold business meetings were the major cities or famous vacation spots.[30] The number of fact-finding missions to lower levels proliferated. Both visitors and hosts were afflicted with the disease of rising expectations on these occasions. Visiting dignitaries were given the best accommodations. The official guesthouses that had been built years ago at great expense specially for visiting cadres were no longer good enough. Instead, the visitors now preferred to stay in tourist hotels patronized by Westerners for their modern amenities.

Lower-level hosting units competed with each other to set higher standards of lavishness in their entertaining and gifts to show their "sincerity" and "enthusiasm." Visitors were customarily presented with "local special products" (*tuchan*, which could be anything from a product with genuine local color to an expensive camera) as euphemistic "souvenirs." Even in the midst of the rectification campaign, the rise in the scale and expense of these acts was unabated.[31] The signs of the return of the mandarin styles were unmistakable.

As China's economy became more lively and diversified, feasting and gifts became indispensable lubricants between public agencies and their leading cadres in transacting official business. These acts were defended as necessary to "smooth relations," "make human emotional investment," and "broaden one's (business) horizons.'' The situation became so bad that rarely anything could be accomplished in terms of official business unless accompanied by an expensive and elaborate dinner.[32]

A new code of conduct in the transaction of official business quickly gained wide acceptance among cadres and party members. This code had to be honored by economic enterprises that wished to obtain supplies or sell their products, and just as much as by academic and research units that wanted to have their funding requests approved. In spite of repeated warnings from the national party, the tendency only became worse with time. China's administrative expenses doubled during 1982–87, and the use of public funds for personal gifts and entertainment accounted for a substantial portion of this increase.[33]

Common Characteristics of Misconduct

What generalizations can be made about the worsening disciplinary problems after 1983? Were they different in nature from the previous years?

The waves of erroneous styles of conduct that emerged after 1983 had several common characteristics. First, after 1984, the main objective of misconduct shifted from ''personal conveniences'' to ''economic gains,'' to the amassing of fortunes, sometimes of great magnitude. The ongoing economic reform undoubtedly created numerous opportunities for illicit activities. Many cadres and members justified their misconduct in the name of promoting ''economic reform'' or ''innovations.'' One favorable excuse widely used by the perpetrators of illegal economic activities was that they were committed to increasing the masses' or their work unit's interests, and not to personal enrichment.[34]

There was a steady increase in major cases of economic crimes. By early 1986, nearly 90 percent of the major criminal activities investigated by the party's Central Discipline Inspection Committee were economic in nature.[35] Even in an economically backward province like Gansu, for example, economic criminal cases involving more than RMB $10,000 increased from four in 1983 to thirty in 1985. The number of public organs on the county level and above that were implicated in economic crimes increased nearly three times between 1985 and 1986. By 1985, party members accounted for over a quarter of all criminals within the province, an astonishingly high percentage in view of the fact that party members constituted less than 4 percent of the general population. Dramatic increases in the number of major economic crimes during 1985–86 occurred in many other places.[36]

Second, there was a visible increase in the number of participants in economic irregularities. Misconduct became a standard part of business operations. When these schemes bonded together partners in joint ventures, their organizational resources were considerably increased. They often involved entire organizations or even chains of organizations, with the leading cadres working as the moving forces behind these schemes and party members, cadres, and even the entire staff as the supporting cast, all trying to fatten their own pockets and defraud the state. The sheer numbers of people implicated in some cases made it virtually impossible for the higher level to prosecute them. Frequently, high-ranking cadres extended their "protective umbrella" to shield lower-ranking criminals.[37]

Third, the nature of misconduct became much more elaborate and complicated. Even in the early stage of rectification, it became clear that national leaders and party members and cadres were locked in a classic cat-and-mouse game. Cadres and members learned to anticipate their leaders' inclinations. Whenever the leaders introduced a more liberal economic measure, lower-level cadres and party members would detect the loopholes in it and hasten to commit certain acts before the leaders had a chance to pronounce them illegal and close the loopholes. As soon as one kind of activity was banned, the smart perpetrators would shift to a new area of criminal activities. High-ranking cadres and their children were always a step ahead of the government because of their access to inside information. Only lower-level people who made a slow start would get caught.

Misconduct became more deliberate, calculated, and collectively engineered. Laws and regulations were diligently combed to detect loopholes for exploitation. Influence, money, and sex were employed to build connections. Secret channels were cultivated to launder money, including opening accounts in foreign banks. Criminal tactics had become more refined. There was also a clear spillover effect: once an act was committed by a daring few, it would be quickly imitated by others.[38]

Combating Poor Discipline

From the above description, it is clear that mounting a rectification campaign did not stem the tide of worsening discipline among party members. On the contrary, in 1985, the frequency of major cases of economic crime showed a noticeable upward trend.[39]

The party's battle against the rising tide of misconduct took several forms. First, it continued to issue warnings to members, sometimes two or three per month, to halt erroneous conduct.[40] Routine warnings were augmented by threats of severe punishment. In late January 1985, Hu Yaobang said that in spite of the party's earlier promise not to use harsh measures to punish errant cadres, discipline had declined so much that he had changed his mind.[41] At the party Congress of September 1985, discipline was again a major issue for discussion. Shortly afterward, the party and government issued more joint criticisms against misconduct among cadres.[42]

Second, special warnings were issued to high-ranking cadres to desist from committing misconduct. The party admitted that a major deficiency of the rectification campaign's first phase was its failure to prosecute cases of misconduct among higher-ranking party cadres. In 1985, the Central Rectification Guidance Committee promised that this problem would be corrected during the second phase of rectification.[43] Bo Yibo suggested that the party needed to prosecute several major cases involving high-ranking members to deter the lesser people from committing crimes. He said that the party should not hesitate to dismiss high-ranking errant members from jobs, expel them from the party, and expose them in the press.[44]

Third, and probably the most noteworthy feature of the party's assault against poor discipline in 1985, was the gradual assumption of a more aggressive role by the party's Secretariat. Previously, the Central Discipline Inspection Committee had been charged with the main responsibility to direct the rectification campaign. But the first two years of the campaign had produced negligible results.[45] Therefore, by late 1985, Hu Yaobang personally assumed leadership and gave the Secretariat the authority to mount a new attack against corruption and poor discipline. In conjunction with the State Council, the Secretariat announced its determination to eradicate the major forms of corruption and boldly set a deadline for the completion of this task as no later than the spring of 1986.[46]

On December 31, 1985, the Secretariat launched yet another denunciation of a wide range of erroneous conduct and demanded that national party and government organs rectify their style within the next six to twelve months and set examples for the rest of the country.[47]

Toward the end of 1985, the campaign to denounce economic crimes was escalated dramatically as a flurry of prosecutions were conducted to show the party's resolve. In December 1985 alone, large numbers of cadres in Beijing, Foshan (Guangdong), Fuzhou (Fujian), and elsewhere were exposed for their crimes.[48] The timing of and wide publicity given to these notorious cases were clearly orchestrated to heighten the political atmosphere against poor discipline.

The Last Offensive—1986

According to the party's resolution issued at its Twelfth Congress, 1986 was to be the last year of rectification. The leaders were understandably frustrated by the failure of the campaign to reverse the party style and decided to make one last concerted effort to solve the problem.

In January 1986, the party and the State Council convened a huge gathering of over eight thousand cadres to announce a new policy of cracking down on misconduct. They urged the national and Beijing municipal cadres to serve as the models for the rest of the country. The top leaders vowed that each of them would exercise personal supervision over the prosecution of several cases of major crimes. Deng Xiaoping lent his weight by delivering a personal warning that the anticrime campaign must be directed primarily against the high-ranking cadres and their family members in order to achieve positive effects for the rest of the country. He said that the success or failure of reforms hinged on the resolution of this problem.[49]

Deng's warning was quickly echoed in an article in *Hongqi* that asserted, "the most pressing task at the present is to concentrate our effort to investigate and prosecute the major cases. In the near future, we must focus our attention on prosecuting several representative cases that have produced a very negative and wide-ranging impact in order to achieve the effects of warning against potential future offenders, educating the masses, and deterring the bad elements."[50]

Secretariat member Wang Zhaoguo admitted that misconduct among some party members had reached intolerable proportions and indicated that the Secretariat would play an increasingly active role in setting stiffer guidelines for cadre conduct. He also vowed that henceforth the Secretariat would concentrate its efforts to prosecute major cases of misconduct no matter how high the perpetrators' positions might be.[51]

During the next six months, a number of "major cases" were prosecuted.[52] But they were far from sufficient to restore the Chinese people's confidence in the party's sincerity to stamp out crime. The people were convinced that crimes existed on much higher levels and waited in vain for the party to fulfill its promises. By this time, the party's image had become so tarnished and its credibility had dropped so low that the few exposed cases only confirmed the popular suspicion that they were scapegoats to cover more serious crimes among even higher leaders.[53]

By late 1986, the rectification had come to the end of its urban stage and moved into the rural stage. With this, the new move by the Secretariat to smash crimes also lost its momentum. A new wave of student unrest erupted in Beijing and many other cities in late December. When the party decided to mount the anti–bourgeois liberalization campaign in early 1987, the leaders were completely distracted from the rectification work. The power within the Secretariat was badly shaken up with the resignation of Hu Yaobang. For practical purposes, the rectification campaign was over by late 1986, although it was not until May 1987 that it was formally concluded.

Results and Evaluation

On May 26, 1987, Bo Yibo delivered the party's verdict on rectification at its termination. Predictably, he asserted that the campaign had made many accomplishments, and that "each stage was an improvement over the preceding one." While conceding that some units had not done their work thoroughly to correct discipline, he insisted that the overall results were positive. He noted with particular satisfaction the party's success in not using ruthless methods or a "mass movement" format, and preventing the repetition of leftist mistakes and excesses committed in previous campaigns. He also noted the success in keeping a proper perspective with respect to the relationship between rectification and economic reform so as to avoid any disruption of the production process.[54]

Bo concluded by saying that "party construction is a long-term historical developmental process. It is impossible to resolve all problems within the party through one single rectification campaign."[55] Yet, right after the official conclusion of rectification, the party dismantled all agencies set up specifically to implement rectification throughout the country and announced that it would enter the new era of routine party construction work. In effect, the entire party had returned to normalcy.[56]

Should the party's report be accepted at its face value? Can an independent judgment be made on the success or failure of the rectification? Observers of recent political phenomena in China can readily appreciate the difficulty of interpreting the official data on misconduct. The data's credibility is tempered by at least two factors. First, the party had a strong incentive to conceal the facts in its possession to save its own face. Since there is little likelihood that the CCP will open its archives for research any time soon, it will probably not be known how much information was deliberately concealed from public view. Second, there was also a strong possibility that the party did not have a good grasp of the full extent of misconduct by its members because of poor organizational control and the deliberate falsification of reports by lower levels.

The absence of a free press posed the most serious obstacle to an accurate assessment of the true extent of poor discipline. While the official press occasionally admitted the existence of strong popular discontent, the masses had little impact in checking misconduct by cadres or members. The masses learned to endure petty corruption as a way of life, and they often reluctantly served as accomplices, if only to get things accomplished. As usual, the masses were poorly informed about the party and government functionaries' illicit activities beyond their personal experiences. The masses became sufficiently aroused only when egregious misconduct was committed on a sustained basis and led to human suffering or property losses of major proportions. Only then would these acts become the targets of "mass indignation."

There existed many hurdles between the unorganized expression of the masses' indignation over criminal deeds and the actual official decision to launch an investigation of these deeds. Much of the time, the leaders were kept in the dark about the misconduct by their subordinates. The number of cases prosecuted represented only the tip of the iceberg. Given these factors, it would be fair to say that the party's efforts to rectify the discipline and style of work of its cadres and members had largely failed.

During the second phase of rectification, the national party dispatched seven roving teams of inspectors across the country to conduct interviews and conferences with leaders and to assess the accomplishments of rectification on the district and county levels. Their reports revealed that in a substantial number of local party organs, the rectification campaign produced mediocre results, and in a minority of cases, the campaign was conducted very unsatisfactorily.[57] The results were also uneven geographically and across institutions. Many units simply went through the motions, allowed the major cases of wrongdoing to go uninvestigated or unresolved, and allowed them to creep back as soon as rectification was officially concluded.[58]

The fact that, even in 1986, the party had to issue directives to criticize repeatedly the same activities that had long been outlawed was eloquent testimony of the failure of rectification.[59] This assessment was supported by occasionally candid reports from the provinces. In May 1986, Wang Ning, the deputy provincial party secretary of Guangdong, presented a bill of complaints about the breakdown of discipline in his province that included all the items listed in previous years.[60] The provincial party secretary of Heilongjiang pointed out in December 1986 that in the previous two years, many leading cadres remained unconcerned about the dangerous decline of party discipline. They treated rectification as a marginal task, took a laissez-faire approach, and let things drift.[61]

When the party focused its efforts to combat one or two specific targets, it usually was able to achieve some temporary results. But this would only give other forms of misconduct a field day. Besides, when the party turned its attention to other forms of misconduct, then the old forms would reappear. Thus, the overall pattern was for old problems to worsen and new problems to keep emerging.[62] There was also a tendency for misconduct to disappear briefly when a work unit was scheduled to conduct its own rectification, only to resurface after the rectification was over.[63] Misconduct in one area might disappear when all the opportunities to make illegal gains had been exhausted (e.g., housing assignments), but party members and cadres would soon apply their ingenuity to other, newer, more lucrative areas.

Even at the end of 1986, a substantial number of organs within the party's national hierarchy, the state bureaucracy, provincial and municipal governments, as well as over six hundred county-level organs had not even begun the rectification campaign.[64] As the rectification campaign proceeded, many people developed the pessimistic view that many basic-level party organizations had become weaker and more paralyzed. Addressing this issue in the spring of 1987, Wang Zhaoguo had to admit that 5–10 percent of the party's basic-level organs indeed still remained in conditions of chaos and disarray. This was definitely a gross underestimation, but even if taken at face value, this meant that as many as 200,000 basic-level organs fell into this category.[65]

The popular view was that party style was not improved. The masses believed that "rectification means to go through the motions with an appearance of all seriousness," or "rectification is worse than no rectification," or "rectification has aggravated the problem of misconduct."[66] Even *Hongqi* was compelled to admit in 1987, "In spite of the amount of work we have done, many people remain dissatisfied with the status of party style. Party style has not been fundamentally improved. Actually, many forms of erroneous style are resurfacing repeatedly after being dealt with."[67] At the end of rectification, it was hard to point to any form of misconduct that had existed in the late 1970s and been effectively eradicated since. In fact, the magnitude of corruption, abuse of privileges, and other forms of misconduct had become far worse and more pervasive than ever before. By early 1988, not only were the Chinese masses bitterly complaining about poor party discipline, but even many people within the party admitted that discipline had become worse than in any previous periods.[68]

Changing Perceptions on Rectification's Efficacy

When the decision to launch a rectification was first made, the party confidently stated that three years would be sufficient to bring about a "fundamental improvement" of members' conduct. During the first year of implementation, the party optimistically reported that the most common forms of abuse of privileges and bureaucratism were being successfully halted in the units currently undergoing rectification, and therefore the rectification should be completed on schedule in 1986.[69] But the first phase of rectification involved only a small number of carefully selected units to show impressive results. The optimism disappeared quickly as rectification entered its second phase. In January 1985, when the party took stock of the rectification after only one year of implementation, it admitted that many problems and deficiencies existed.[70] The Central Rectification Guidance Committee drastically lowered its expectation by saying, "Overall, the present rectification campaign can only resolve *some* of the major and serious problems that urgently demand resolution, but cannot resolve *all* the problems."[71] It began to suggest that party building was a long-term process. The rectification campaign was no longer billed as one to provide a "fundamental solution" of the party's disciplinary problem, but instead as only "the starting point" of a prolonged process.[72]

The party's more somber estimate of the length of time needed to rectify discipline was coupled with the gradual loss of saliency of the discipline issue itself. It is recalled that Chen Yun in 1980 had darkly warned about the possible collapse of the party and state if poor discipline persisted. But by mid-1984, Hu Yaobang was able to say, "Our party at present does not have any crisis. On the contrary, we have restored our vitality! Full of vitality!"[73] When Chen Yun addressed the Fourth Plenum of the Twelfth National Party Congress on September 23, 1985, he merely said that correcting party style "still remained" a major task, but he no longer defined the issue in apocalyptic terms.[74]

It is quite possible that the leaders' assessment of the danger brought about by the breakdown of party discipline had undergone a subtle change during the 1980s. In the beginning, the party was gripped by a sense of mortal danger: Without prompt rectification, the party might collapse. To rectify was the only way to save the party. But by the end of 1984, the top leaders had gained a new confidence in the stability of their rule. This confidence certainly was not based on improved party discipline but came from two other related developments: the successful purge of the "three types" and the installation of the second and third echelons into leadership positions.

Reflecting the leaders' sense of subsiding danger, Bo Yibo, the deputy director of the Central Rectification Guidance Committee and the operational leader of the campaign, introduced a new argument at the beginning of the second stage of rectification that the purpose of rectification was to remove the obstacles from the path of reform, to create favorable social and political conditions for reform, and to promote and guarantee the healthy development of reform. Whether these objectives could be achieved had by now become the major criteria in evaluating the accomplishments of the rectification in the future.[75] Hu Qili, another deputy director of the Central Rectification Guidance Committee, also argued that the central purpose of the rectification was really to ensure that the economic reforms could be effectively carried out.[76]

Since poor discipline had ceased to be a matter of life and death for the party, its existence became much more tolerable. It was viewed as an unpleasant reality but by no means a terribly threatening problem. In a major speech on July 8, 1986, Bo Yibo sounded a guarded note on the efficacy of rectification when he said, "It would be impossible for the darker sides of the party to be eliminated in a *single* rectification campaign. . . . As conditions evolve, new types of unhealthy things will occur in the party even as older types of unhealthy things are overcome." [77]

By 1986, the leaders had definitely grown more sanguine about how much time it might take to combat the many problems of party styles and poor discipline. It was no longer considered feasible to give bad styles and poor discipline a quick fix once and for all. Instead, it was believed that "a prolonged battle" had to be waged. The party concluded that the strategy of using an occasional rectification campaign to combat poor discipline only exacerbated the problems and produced a vicious cycle.[78] For these reasons, Hu Yaobang suggested that the task of rectification must be conducted with the "spirit of the foolish old man who wanted to move the mountain." This meant that the overcoming of erroneous party style would require both "determination and perseverance" over a long period of time.[79] An article in *Hongqi* flatly said, "The rectification of the party's style cannot be accomplished overnight, but will remain as a long-term political task."[80] In other words, three years after promising a fundamental solution of its poor discipline through a rectification campaign, the party finally admitted, albeit obliquely, that the problems of poor discipline were not solvable by the campaign approach.

The CCP certainly did not embark on the rectification lightly. The party took ample time to work out the rules and procedures to conduct the rectification properly and effectively. The campaign was carried out in three separate phases. The first phase, although affecting only 388,000 members from the national and provincial levels, took more than a year to carry out. This immediately created pressure for the following phases to be rushed through. The 13.5 million members in party organs on the district and county levels had only six months each to go through the second phase of rectification. Finally, the 28 million members in organs below the county levels had even less time to rectify themselves in the third phase of the campaign.

Why did the party spend so much time on a few members and so little time on the overwhelming majority of members during rectification? There are several possible explanations. First, the party might have considered it important to score impressive successes during the initial phase of rectification, to debug the system and refine the rules, in order to lay a sound foundation for subsequent phases of rectification. Second, the party's original intent might have been to concentrate on the leadership on national, provincial, and regional levels, and it might never have had a strong desire to rectify the entire rank and file of the party. Third, the party might have wanted to bring about a fundamental improvement on all levels but encountered so many difficulties that it was unable to keep its schedule and had to settle for much less.

Of these three reasons, it seems that the most plausible explanation is the third one. To be sure, the party wanted the first phase of rectification to be as successful as possible. But the ground work had already been laid prior to October 1983 at the experiment points. After all, rectification was nothing new to the party as it had conducted campaigns many times before. But once rectification actually began, the problems turned out to be far more intractable than were originally expected. Even though only 1 percent of party members were undergoing rectification in the first phase, the party was simply unable to bring it to a successful conclusion. After many uncontrollable delays, the party had to allow the first phase to come to an end with few accomplishments to show. In spite of the extension of the campaign's length by more than six months, the roughly 32 percent of members on the district and county levels and the 66 percent of members on the local levels hardly had time to undergo a serious rectification.

If the party's original intent of conducting a successful rectification on the top level had worked, then the good discipline enforced there could have served as a model for the lower levels, and the time required for rectification on the lower levels could have been reduced significantly. But precisely because the leaders were unable to rectify discipline on the highest levels, they defeated their own purpose. It may be argued that once the rectification on the higher levels failed, it was doomed to fail on all lower levels regardless of how much time was devoted to them.

Probably the most important damage that resulted from the party's failure to rectify discipline was that poor discipline destroyed the bond of trust between the governors and the governed, caused widespread cynicism, lowered standards of political ethics, and eroded the basis of legitimacy of the leaders, which inevitably had a deleterious impact on other aspects of the political life in the country. But exactly what factors contributed to the party's underestimation of the magnitude of the problems, and why were its methods of rectification so ineffective?

8

Factors Impeding the Rectification Campaign

DESPITE an awareness of the disciplinary problems that existed among party members, the rectification campaign failed to produced the expected results. In the following pages, five different factors contributing to the campaign's failure are examined, including the loss of organizational control, the inadequacy of rectification techniques, the lack of leadership resolve to enforce discipline, the confusion generated by the decision-making process, and the difficulty of balancing political and economic interests.

Control of Organizational Resources

Rectification is a major endeavor. The rectification of the 1980s was an even more massive undertaking than many previous ones because it aimed at correcting a multitude of problems throughout the entire party membership. For such a campaign to work, at least two conditions must be met. First, there must be a consensus within the party on the need for rectification. This consensus is most important at the highest levels. Second, the party must possess an organization capable of implementing the rectification faithfully.

Failure to Achieve a Consensus

A successful rectification is possible only when there is a consensus on its necessity that permits the party to concentrate its energy, shape a coherent strategy, and devote the necessary resources. Unfortunately for the CCP, there existed wide differences of opinion on the desirability of rectification.

A significant number of party leaders believed that a large-scale rectification campaign would do more harm than good. Many cadres viewed the breakdown of discipline as the culmination of a multitude of factors that had existed for years. Others believed that rectification might reopen the old wound within the party and could be a blow to its unity and prestige. Many thought that the current level of misconduct was regrettable but not serious. These people felt that a rectification campaign could be counterproductive because it would attract too much public attention to misconduct and might actually exacerbate its magnitude.[1]

Much opposition to rectification grew out of concern for its potentially negative impact on the economy. Some leading cadres believed that vigorous prosecution of economic misconduct could retard economic growth and dampen the innovative spirit. They believed that it was imperative for the party to improve economic conditions as quickly as possible, but they regarded the party's own organizational work as a far less important issue.[2] Personal interest was also a significant factor in the opposition. Leading cadres who had committed misconduct opposed rectification for fear that their own skeletons might be dragged out of the closet.[3]

Even among those who accepted the need for rectification, there were strong disagreements with regard to its proper scope. Many cadres believed that rectification should be selectively applied and narrowly focused. They wanted it directed only against specific categories of misconduct whose severity warranted such drastic actions and not against the entire membership.[4] Others believed that the rectification should be targeted only against leading cadres and not against the rank and file. Still others thought that only those who had committed "political errors" should be dealt with rather than those who had committed only nonpolitical mistakes. Many leading cadres thought that the rectification campaign had nothing to do with them at all. This feeling was strong especially among cadres who had suffered during the Cultural Revolution and had recently been rehabilitated. They believed their suffering had automatically proven their credentials as "good party members." Finally, the retired members thought the rectification should only be applied to members still in active service.[5]

On the other hand, the overwhelming majority of the rank and file were apathetic toward the rectification campaign for two additional reasons of their own. First, many were apprehensive about the "*zheng*" aspect in the concept of rectification (*zhengdang*). The Chinese word "zheng" has two entirely different connotations. The proper connotation for the rectification is to "sort out" (*zhengli*) or to "set straight" (*zhengdun*). But the more sinister connotation of the word is to be "punitive" or "vindictive," suggesting a deliberate scheme to abuse people for the purpose of inflicting pain and suffering. People were afraid that the rectification would be overshadowed by the second connotation and produce intense personal animosity in a leftist backlash. Second, many people also doubted the leadership's ability and determination to carry rectification to its logical conclusion since the latter had committed the lion's share of misconduct.[6] Many party members believed that since they had done nothing wrong, they should be spared the rectification process. In other words, rectification should be conducted against those who had committed serious offenses, particularly those in high places.

This diverse set of reasons for opposing the rectification not only hampered the party's initial decision to launch the rectification but also created serious disunity during the campaign.[7] The contrary views led to different impressions of the campaign, based on what different groups saw as its proper goals. For instance, there were two diametrically opposite assessments of the success of the first stage of rectification. One group thought that the campaign had achieved its original objectives, while another criticized it as neither harsh nor thorough enough because it had not purged enough people.[8] Such diverse opinions meant that throughout the rectification, the campaign's advocates and enforcers were forced continually to battle its critics, detractors, and saboteurs. This inevitably undermined the campaign's effectiveness.

The Organizational Format

The rectification campaign required the mobilization of over forty million party members for three years. The second requirement of a successful campaign, therefore, was that the party possess effective control over its organizational resources. Analytically, the party had three options to improve discipline. First, it could rely on agents from an independent branch of the party armed with broad investigative and punitive powers to enforce proper conduct among members. Second, it could rely on regular party organs to carry out rectification within their own units. Finally, it could allow public opinion to exert outside pressure on party members to rectify their conduct, or allow the state's legal system to expose and prosecute criminal cases.

An Independent Disciplinary Arm

The use of a special and independent apparatus to enforce discipline is a favorite method in many totalitarian systems. Both Hitler and Stalin effectively employed their secret police to eliminate political rivals and maintain the loyalty of subordinates. In Communist countries, the use of political commissars in the army also has a long tradition. In all these cases, the format is to use a small group of special agents to control the behavior of a much larger group of people. The institutional separation minimizes the possibility of collusion between supervisors and supervised.

Shortly after Liberation, the party had experimented briefly with the approach of creating a separate hierarchy of committees to enforce discipline. But the party soon gave up this system because it did not believe it important to maintain surveillance over its members.[9] In the intervening years, whenever disciplinary issues arose, the party's favorite solution was to form ad hoc teams of agents on the higher level and send them downward to solve the problems on the lower level in a typical "campaign" style.[10] But the empirical records suggest that these teams often did not understand the local situation and showed a tendency to take things into their own hands and use brutal methods to enforce policies.

At the outset of the current rectification, the party decided to eschew the "special team" approach in favor of creating a system of separate discipline inspection committees on the national, provincial, and local (county) levels. In addition, a Central Rectification Guidance Committee (Zhongyang Zhengdang Gongzuo Zhidao Weiyuanhui) was created to coordinate the work of all the discipline inspection committees. Thus, guidance for the policy was to be provided by the Central Guidance Committee, and the actual rectification work was to be performed by the discipline inspection committees.

Initially, the leaders intended to give the committee broad powers over rectification. Thus, during the first phase of rectification, the Central Guidance Committee divided the country's professions into ten fields and dispatched a team to each field to guide, assist, supervise, and evaluate the rectification work in that particular field.[11] But this method of direct central supervision was abandoned in the second phase and the local discipline inspection committees were given the primary responsibility to conduct rectification in their respective organs or localities.

Although the Twelfth Party Congress required the members of the discipline inspection committee to be elected by the Party Congress on their own level, and to make them accountable to both the party secretary on the same level and the discipline inspection committee on the superior level,[12] the discipline inspection committees never evolved into an independent vertical hierarchy. The members of discipline inspection committees were invariably personally hand-picked by the party secretary from his subordinates who owed their allegiance primarily to him. Therefore, throughout the rectification, the party did not have a separate channel of information or enforcement with respect to disciplinary matters.

Regular Party Organs

Under this system, the major responsibility for rectification was borne by the regular party organs themselves. The party organ in each work unit, whether a state agency, economic enterprise, or the military, would form its own discipline inspection committee whose responsibility was to make sure that the party members conduct rectification faithfully, and to investigate and prosecute misdeeds. Originally, the party had intended to send inspection teams to certify the results of rectification before allowing lower levels to bring their rectification work to a close. But in 1984, the party notified the provinces that it would not conduct an inspection and verification of the results and allowed the lower levels to make their own judgments if their rectification had been successfully concluded.[13] This hands-off policy of the party center made the local committee's structure and personnel crucial factors in its success or failure.[14]

In general, very few members of discipline inspection committees were qualified for their jobs. They were not selected for excellence in their ideology, work style, or personal conduct. Some might even have been unsympathetic to rectification altogether. Few had received any prior training on how to deal with discipline problems.[15] In most cases, they were just average party members appointed by their party secretary to fill the posts.[16] Not surprisingly, many of them showed passive attitudes and preferred not to take the initiative to uncover wrongdoing. But an even more serious impediment to their work was that they were already deeply enmeshed in the complicated personal relations in their own units or had acquired a strong factional leaning, and therefore were unable to maintain an objective or impartial attitude in discharging their duties.

Even if they were courageous enough to enforce discipline on their subordinates, few would dare to touch their peers, and it was even more unthinkable to expose the wrongdoing of their superiors because of the many avenues for retaliation by the two latter groups.[17] In addition, when the discipline personnel committed their own wrongdoing, there was no other internal mechanism to check them.

These problems became particularly acute after 1984 as economic crimes often involved the participation of entire organizations.[18] These organizations could count on their in-house disciplinary personnel to keep quiet and could form collective security pacts to stonewall investigative efforts by their superiors.

Therefore, both the structural arrangement and the personnel of the discipline inspection committee system hindered its effectiveness. Even the party's own press sometimes could not conceal its frustration over the quality of discipline work. Discipline personnel were criticized as passive, demoralized, and inexperienced. Some were accused of being criminal elements themselves. Some discipline inspection committees were so paralyzed that they allowed lawlessness in their work units to reach alarming proportions.[19]

The disregard for discipline was but a reflection of a broader problem. As the party press of the 1980s repeatedly pointed out, there was a widespread tendency for many party organs to abdicate their responsibility to manage the party's internal affairs. Party leaders preferred to devote more time to administrative or economic affairs than to the party's own organizational development. This situation was probably inevitable for a totalitarian party because it faced no competition from other groups and therefore had no incentive to improve itself. As long as it enjoyed unchallenged, monopolistic control over the country's political, military, economic, and social resources, it could afford to neglect the issue of maintaining organizational effectiveness.

The party's organizational weakness became worse after 1978. Following the declaration that economic construction was to be the major mission of the new leaders, party members rushed to engage in economic activities and neglected political and ideological duties altogether. The prestige of "party work" suffered a sharp decline, and capable cadres shunned "party work" because it neither rewarded them financially nor conferred power or respect. The popular view was that "party work" cadres had no future. Many party leaders treated "party work'' as a chore, and had little interest in developing the party's organization or strengthening its style of work.

The points of direct organizational contact between the party and its rank and file at the lowest level were the basic-level branches. The party's Charter defined these basic-level branches as the party's "fortresses." They were relied upon to educate its members, guard against deviant thoughts and deeds, support official programs, and maintain the party's organizational purity. If the rectification campaign was to succeed, the basic-level branches must perform their assigned functions.

According to the party's own survey in 1986, however, only about 30 percent of the branches were judged as able to perform these "fortress functions" satisfactorily. More disturbing, 50 percent of the branches were judged unsatisfactory, while the remaining 20 percent were judged to have failed to perform their functions at all. Since the survey indicated a close correspondence between the number of branches and the number of party members, one can conclude that 70 percent of party members could not meet the party's criteria for good members, including 5 percent who were said to have committed serious errors or crimes.[20]

The party also presented a long list of defects common among the leading cadres of basic-level branches. These branch leaders followed a middle-of-the-road course to avoid offending anyone, neglected to enforce discipline, and failed to set examples for their colleagues. They were incompetent, unwilling or unable to do political work, paid no attention to party documents, did not observe democratic procedures in internal relations, and had no interest in the recruitment of new members. They neglected to hold party meetings or conduct training classes as required. Finally, they continued to behave in a commandistic way toward their subordinates and deliberately concealed true conditions in their units from their superiors.[21]

Given the poor quality of leadership in the basic-level organs, it was hardly surprising that the rectification campaign produced unsatisfactory results. The overwhelming majority of discipline inspection cadres failed to perform their duty. Moreover, when some did discharge their duties determinedly and conscientiously, they were poorly received by the rank and file. In some cases, they were even physically assaulted.[22]

The Role of the Masses

From the very beginning, the party had decided that the rectification campaign would be restricted to the Communist Party. While the democratic parties or the masses were welcomed to help the party rectify by expressing their views, all problems were to be resolved within the party itself, and the masses were not allowed to interfere with the party's own organizational process.[23]

The reasons behind this decision were twofold. One was that the party never believed that nonparty elements were qualified to tell the party how to handle its disciplinary affairs. The last time the masses were allowed to interfere with the party's internal problems—during the Cultural Revolution—the party's organization and legitimacy had been delivered devastating blows. The second reason was that the party also wanted to assure the masses that they had nothing to fear from the rectification campaign. Previously, campaigns were conducted in the fashion of mass movements and often ended up hurting the ordinary citizens. This time, the party was determined to confine rectification to a methodic housecleaning operation without affecting the broad masses. Of course, if the masses were victimized by acts of corruption and abuse of privileges by party cadres and members, they were encouraged to expose the offenders and seek justice.

In reality, the non-CCP groups and the broad masses were totally excluded from the rectification process. Their grievances and criticisms were not given a chance to be articulated through regular channels. Party members and cadres were able to ignore completely unfavorable opinions coming from those outside the Communist Party. Those among the masses foolish enough to expose the misconduct of party members were retaliated against.[24] If superiors acted on such complaints from the people and initiated investigations, the perpetrators inside the party could block them by causing the investigations to be inconclusive. Even when the superiors made specific judgments against them, their protectors could still refuse to carry them out.[25]

Since the party delegated the authority of self-policing and self-evaluation to the lower-level units, this means that the leading cadres of the latter were primarily responsible for the units' rectification work. They had the authority to decide whether a particular unit had successfully implemented its rectification campaign. Once they claimed that their unit had successfully completed its rectification, their superiors usually simply endorsed their conclusion. At this point the unit could terminate its rectification and return to normalcy.

Since very few leaders ever wanted to admit deficiencies and make their own unit look bad, and since they were usually under tremendous pressure from colleagues to conclude rectification as quickly as possible, there were clear incentives for them to cheat and falsify the results. The superior-level organ had to accept these glowing reports from below at their face value because they usually had neither the ability nor the inclination to verify their accuracy independently. It would be simpler just to transmit these reports to still higher levels. Consequently, even when serious defects were uncovered, everyone along the chain of command had an interest in concealing their own negligence.

In such a setting, it was extremely difficult for victims of wrongdoing committed by party members or cadres to seek justice through regular party channels or the court system. Their only recourse was to appeal directly to top leaders or to the few journalists who had a reputation for exposing crimes. In the popular parlance, these people were called the modern-day "Minister Bao."[26] As a consequence, a few conscientious leaders were overworked while most discipline personnel blithely neglected their duties. This process placed an enormous burden upon the few leaders who realized that only their personal intervention could produce tangible results. As Hu Qili once described, ''Our leaders seldom have free time for themselves. They do not have vacations or holidays, and they often stay up late at night to read a massive volume of documents and letters from the people.'' By his account, during 1980–85, General Secretary Hu Yaobang personally read and acted on more than two thousand pleas for justice from the masses and visited more than fifteen hundred of China's twenty-two hundred counties, during which he intervened in numerous cases involving miscarriage of justice.[27] It is ironic that after more than three decades of socialist ideological indoctrination and political development, the Chinese people still found it necessary to seek justice in the traditional manner.[28]

One organizational resource that might have facilitated rectification but did not was the system of neighborhood party organs. Normally, party organs were attached to work units (such as factory or office). In contrast, the neighborhood organs were divided along residential boundaries. These units had traditionally been effective in providing surveillance over practically every aspect of daily life. Neighborhood organs could be particularly effective in monitoring poor discipline because even when misbehaving cadres or members were able to escape the scrutiny of colleagues at work, their life-style changes could hardly escape the vigilant eyes of their neighbors. The neighborhood organs were also valuable because they could bring the party structure into direct contact with mass opinion. Composed of party members living in close proximity with the average citizens, the organs could accurately gauge the people's reactions toward misconduct in general as well as transmit information concerning specific acts of misconduct to their superiors.

Despite their potential, however, important socioeconomic changes on the neighborhood level during the 1980s reduced the party organs' effectiveness. The most basic change was that the average neighborhood became larger and more complex. Before 1978, a typical urban neighborhood was largely composed of individual families, with only a few collective (small-scale) factories, and several outlets of ordinary merchandise. In the 1980s, however, a host of privately owned shops, hotels, restaurants, road-side stalls, and new factories or workshops sprang up.

Many neighborhoods also experienced a greatly increased turnover. While Chinese neighborhoods had traditionally been very stable, in the 1980s a large-scale internal migration occurred. Many retired party cadres moved out of the compound of their work units into neighborhoods. Many party members were transferred back to the cities from political exile in the countryside. Massive housing reassignments of old residents and the construction of new housing projects added to the confusion. In many places, neighbors were total strangers. The increased numbers, varied backgrounds, and different life-styles increased the difficulties of neighborhood surveillance.[29]

Unfortunately for the campaign, however, the quality of neighborhood-level cadres did not increase in conjunction with the increasing complexity of their responsibilities. For years, the quality of neighborhood-level party cadres had been low, but as long as the party's prestige was high, neighborhood party organs were able to wield great authority. By the 1980s, however, as the party's prestige plummeted, many people regarded assignments to neighborhood organs as dead ends and worked hard to avoid them. As a result, neighborhood organs became even less able to make meaningful contributions to rectification.[30]

On balance, a fundamental reason for the failure of rectification was the party's insistence that poor discipline of its members was strictly its own business. The party preferred to use its own machinery and apply its own rules to impose its own solutions. But the party actually no longer possessed an efficient machinery to implement rectification in the 1980s. Had the masses been invited to play an active role, many aspects of poor discipline would have been exposed more easily. Yet this was perceived to be a threat to the party's legitimacy and was rejected. In the end, the complete exclusion of the masses from the rectification process deprived the party of a golden opportunity to improve its discipline with the masses' assistance and supervision and accentuated the masses' sense of alienation from the party.

Techniques of Rectification

Criticism and Self-Criticism

A critical phase of the campaign occurred when each individual member's political record came under "examination and verification." During this phase, according to Directive no. 7 (March 4, 1984), the party organ must encourage a frank, thorough, and penetrating dialogue between the leading cadres and the regular members. Leading cadres were required to take the lead in making criticism and self-criticism to set examples for ordinary party members. As the directive made clear, "the process of examination and verification is the process of criticism and self-criticism. Criticism and self-criticism are our major weapon to expose the dark side in our party, to correct mistakes that exist among our party members and cadres, and to improve their style."[31]

In conducting either political movements in general or rectification campaigns in particular, the CCP has had a long tradition of putting a heavy reliance on criticism and self-criticism as its key techniques to resolve intraparty problems. There exists a large body of literature on the theory and practice of criticism/self-criticism. Many party leaders, including Mao and Liu Shaoqi, have written extensively on this topic. The intent of this section is not to provide a detailed analysis of their history, but to assess their effectiveness in the current rectification. Therefore, this discussion will only highlight the key points in the Chinese Communist theory of criticism and self-criticism, focusing primary attention on their practice in the current campaign.

Chinese Communist leaders have always believed that whenever contradictions exist within the party, it is better to expose them, to urge errant members to criticize themselves first, and to encourage other party members to assist the errant comrades by criticizing them as well. If properly conducted, Chinese Communists believe, criticism and self-criticism can achieve many positive results, including clarifying thought, rectifying conduct, and unifying with the comrades to make greater progress in resolving contradictions and improving personal conduct, interpersonal relations, work efficiency, and so forth. Therefore, criticism and self-criticism have two broad objectives: to cure the disease and save the patient on the individual level, and to attain a higher degree of solidarity for the party on the collective level.

Communist leaders have devoted considerable attention to establishing proper ways of conducting criticism and self-criticism. Thus, for example, party members are told that intraparty problems must be resolved only by peaceful and democratic means. The criticisms must be principled and deal with "political" issues and not "personal" attacks, and must be guided by uniform standards of right and wrong. The criticizers must respect facts and rely on reason to persuade people, to render full assistance to errant comrades, and to help them improve.[32]

Party members not only have the duty to criticize others, but also the obligation to engage in self-criticism, to reveal their own shortcomings or wrongdoing, and to share their soul with their comrades, especially the leading members. This can be done by engaging in informal heart-to-heart talks, or by making a confession in a formal session. Just as the concept of privacy has no legitimacy in the traditional family, it has no legitimacy in the party either. A member who has committed an error is expected to engage in a full self-exposure and self-criticism. If so, his comrades will help him correct his mistakes, forgive him, and reembrace him into the party.

Ideally, party members are to "uphold truth, correct mistakes," and guide all their criticism in accordance with the principle of "unity–criticism–unity." If party members engage fully in criticism/self-criticism, what they lose will only be shortcomings and mistakes, but what they gain will be progressiveness and improvement.[33]

Results of the Current Campaign

Criticism and self-criticism were assigned key roles to play in the rectification campaign of the 1980s. The original expectation was to expel only a small minority of antiparty elements while helping the remainder rectify their deficiencies in the areas of political thought, style of work, and discipline. This was expected to help the party achieve a higher degree of solidarity and strength.[34]

Despite the party's intentions, however, the actual implementation of this policy ran into trouble almost from the campaign's inception. It became obvious in early 1984 that criticism/self-criticism sessions were encountering enormous resistance even among the small group of high-level units preselected to conduct a trial run for the rectification work.[35]

Many party members were afraid that enthusiastic participation in the campaign might later be criticized as "leftist errors" if the political wind should shift directions. Many declined to engage in criticism because they believed that a rectification campaign would always be followed by another round of rehabilitation when those who had been criticized would be exonerated, while those who made the criticisms would themselves be criticized. Others declined to criticize their colleagues or their leaders for fear of disharmonizing their relations or inviting retaliation. Self-criticism was resisted because people did not want to lose face, or to suffer other unpleasant consequences. On the contrary, those who made mistakes did their best to conceal them.[36]

To soothe such anxieties, the party promised that it would not use members' criticism or self-criticism against them in the future, nor would it record such data into their dossiers. The party assured members that they were entitled to the right to revise or retract their statements, to defend themselves against accusations, to correct their own mistakes voluntarily, and to challenge other people's judgments on them at a later date.[37] Despite these assurances, many doubts were not assuaged, and the results were disappointing. In January 1987, toward the end of the rectification campaign, Wang Zhaoguo, speaking on behalf of the Central Secretariat, complained:

> In some of our party's organizations, it has become difficult to engage in self-criticism, and even more difficult to engage in criticism. Frequently, criticism either hardly scratched the substance of problems or degenerated into unprincipled squabbles. In these organizations, the leading cadres are afraid of contradictions, are avoiding contradictions, and are unwilling to apply organizational measures to solve their problems. In worst cases, even after the contradictions have already been exposed by other people, and after the party members have been instructed by their superiors to resolve them, they would still procrastinate or conceal the contradictions. This is a serious dereliction of their duty.[38]

What factors account for this bleak verdict by the Secretariat? Why did the majority of party members decline to heed the party's instructions to conduct criticism/self-criticism sessions with more zeal and commitment? To answer these questions, it is necessary to examine briefly the factors that must exist to enable criticism or self-criticism to work as intended, and whether these factors were indeed present during the campaign.

Factors Necessary for Success

Although criticism and self-criticism have had a long history within the party, their success is contingent upon the existence of a particular set of favorable factors. Motivational factors are critical for individual party members both to begin and to carry through a process of criticism/self-criticism. Environmental factors are also important because criticism/self-criticism must be given a chance to produce the intended impact on members.

Certain motivational factors must be present for criticism/self-criticism to work. First, party members must value the opinions of their peers and the approval of their organization. They must regard themselves as totally integrated into the party, without which life would become empty and meaningless. Second, they must be driven by a strong desire to externalize their errors and to be reaccepted by their group, because this group is their only psychological anchor. In other words, they must see that they are given a chance of absolution and return to grace by performing certain deeds or rituals.

Third, they must have deep convictions in the morality of the party and the revolutionary cause, and believe their admission of mistakes is a small sacrifice to make by the individuals in order to accomplish a far greater good for the collectivity. Fourth, they must have faith in the efficacy of criticism and self-criticism as methods to accomplish the party's objectives and be ready to guide their conduct by the script. As Mao once said, criticism and self-criticism must be conducted "with the expectation that it will bring about unity to the party, that it will bring good results to the individuals concerned, that it 'punishes the violators only for the sake of warning against potential violators in the future, and cures the disease in order to save the patient.' "

In sum, for party members to engage fully and successfully in criticism/self-criticism, they must identify with the party, embrace its cause without reservation, be ready to do anything for the good of the party, and believe in the efficacy of criticism/self-criticism to accomplish good ends.

Even when party members are motivated, they still need a supportive environment for criticism and self-criticism to realize their full potential as methods of controlling human behavior. Ideally, sufficient time should be allotted to criticism/self-criticism sessions so that people can make exhaustive and penetrating analysis of their thought and behavior. The individuals must be sufficiently isolated physically and psychologically so that they are vulnerable to organizational and peer-group pressures. They must believe that they have no place to escape and can enjoy no peace of mind until they thoroughly surrender their hearts to the party. Their colleagues must also faithfully play out their assigned roles and make the necessary investment in time and energy to promote criticism/self-criticism.

Were These Conditions Present in the 1980s?

If the above reasoning is sound, then it follows that much of the failure of the rectification campaign can be attributed to the absence of many of these factors.

Motivational Factors

First, there was a serious erosion of party identity among members in the 1980s. Party members could find alternative sources of psychological support. The Cultural Revolution, more than all previous political campaigns, produced a paradoxical effect. On the one hand, ideological and organizational means were ruthlessly exploited to assault families and social relations in a systematic manner. On the other hand, such methods also helped many people to rediscover the enduring bonds of family and friendship that transcended political loyalty.

Previously, people who broke such bonds for the sake of politics were praised by the party for possessing a high level of revolutionary conscientiousness. Good party members presumably should have no hesitation to divorce their spouses to uphold a political position. Yet the Cultural Revolution reminded people, including many high-ranking leaders, that when the party disgraced and abused them they could still count on the support and comfort of their families and close friends. Thus, a fundamental value change took place after the death of Mao. People who cherished their family and social ties no longer needed to feel guilty or apologetic about harboring such "feudalist thought" or "petty bourgeois sentimentalism." Even party propaganda ceased to glorify people who would "betray the family for a righteous cause," conceding a person's right to value his family and social relations.

This change was, of course, part of the general relaxation of party control over its members' existence. The new atmosphere of the 1980s had devalued membership in the Communist Party. The former messianic zeal and unswerving faith in the righteousness of the party's cause evaporated. Many true believers turned cynical after witnessing too many destroyed careers and shattered lives around them. Many party members lost the appetite for becoming activists or progressive elements. Such activists are now rather pejoratively called "campaign specialists."[39] As a result, the party's ability to exert psychological pressure upon its members has greatly diminished. This resulted in one of the loudest and most frequently heard complaints of the party, that many members had become self-centered and lost their regard for the party's welfare.[40]

One of the most damaging consequences of this change was a profound distrust of what criticism/self-criticism could accomplish. The party, not unaware of this problem, chose to put the blame solely on the Cultural Revolution and the Gang of Four.[41] A quick review of history, however, reveals that the only period when criticism and self-criticism played a constructive role was during the early 1950s when the party allowed the people to bare their thoughts without suffering overly harsh consequences.

But after the antirightist campaign, the damage that criticism and self-criticism could bring to party members steadily outweighed their benefit. In the following years, both criticism and self-criticism began to lose their voluntary character. People were forced to fabricate charges against colleagues to meet the quota of identifying a certain portion of them as "rightists" (usually 5 percent). Previously, self-criticism was supposed to lead to forgiveness. According to the party's slogan, "confessors will receive leniency, resistors will be dealt harsh punishment." Increasingly, however, the information extracted during self-criticism was regarded as a "club" to be used against the confessor in future campaigns. The cost of self-criticism reached its nadir during the Cultural Revolution when the standard practice was to reach a verdict and then coerce people to make self-criticism to incriminate themselves.

Neither was criticism used to help an errant comrade reform, but "to smash the counterrevolutionary's dog-head." The criticizers realized that their own conduct was under close watch by other people. If they did not criticize their targets harshly enough, they would be suspected as coconspirators and become the targets of the next round of criticism. The typical criticism/self-criticism session became a vindictive and ruthless process, dominated by unrelenting abuse and humiliation of the victims' bodies and spirit. Criticism and self-criticism became tools of waging personal vendettas and factional warfare. It did not take long for members to conclude that criticism was vicious, and self-criticism suicidal.

Not surprisingly, when the rectification campaign was announced in 1983, many people's most immediate reaction was to view it as yet another round to abuse and torment people. They were opposed to criticism because they viewed it as a bludgeon whose only function was to hurt people. This meant that those who were criticized believed they had been unjustly and unproductively vilified rather than helped.[42] Consequently, although the party's proposed solution to overcome these popular misgivings was to ask leading cadres to set an example by boldly and vigorously engaging in proper criticism and self-criticism, it encountered widespread difficulty in promoting these practices on all levels.[43] Even when people had concrete issues to criticize, they did not dare to do so because their targets would no longer take criticism meekly and objectively but wanted to fight back. Many units that employed criticism discovered that once started, it could not be stopped or even contained within constructive limits, but simply degenerated into uncontrollable chaos.[44]

An additional impediment was that by the 1980s, the CCP's numerous campaigns had turned its members into experts on self-preservation. Through experience they were now armed with an elaborate set of defense mechanisms against the dangers of criticism and self-criticism. The most prevalent strategy was assuming a low profile during a campaign and waiting for it to lose its steam. Although the party sought to reassure the rank and file that the rectification of the 1980s would "not be conducted as another campaign," most members were unconvinced and were determined to sail through this one unscathed.[45]

As a consequence, in the 1980s, most members approached criticism/self-criticism sessions with the strategy to "plant flowers, not thorns," behave congenially, and heap praise upon their colleagues. They did not want to be the first to disturb the conditions of peaceful coexistence. When pressured by the party to criticize, they would indulge in harmless abstractions or generalities but avoid naming specific persons or facts. They disliked making judgments on right and wrong and would take a detour as soon as contradictions emerged. They would make vague recommendations for improvements or limit their discussion to trivial issues.[46] Smart people learned to keep their ears cocked for hostile innuendoes but keep their true feelings to themselves.[47] Although most party members did not have the courage to refuse to attend criticism/self-criticism sessions, at least they tried to make them as tension-free as possible.

Many leading cadres also wanted to maintain harmony within their units and actively discouraged serious criticism for fear that things might get out of hand. Some leading cadres actually let it be known that they would not tolerate any mention of concrete events during criticism sessions. Leading cadres who had committed mistakes were especially anxious to put a lid on criticism. They set the tone for evasiveness in the hope that others would follow suit and not expose their faults.[48]

Likewise, party members who had caused harm to others during previous campaigns were understandably nervous and wanted to guard themselves against retribution by their victims. Intense bargaining between rival individuals or factions sometimes preceded criticism and self-criticism sessions. Implicit rules of conduct were worked out so that they could exercise damage control. Often they would agree to refrain from exposing wrongdoing by the other side. Most members learned that it was in their interest to honor these deals, as the result of a breach could be costly retaliations and recriminations.[49]

Environmental Factors

Not only were the motivational factors absent to inspire individual party members to participate actively in criticism and self-criticism, the environmental factors necessary to make them work were also lacking.

First, the time allotted to rectification was short: some units had only a few weeks to go through the phase of "examination and verification." This length was insufficient for criticism/self-criticism to uncover the problems, sort out the complications, mobilize psychological pressures, and resolve the contradictions. The entire process was rushed through while people were distracted by the need to carry on normal professional activities.

Second, China in the 1980s was experiencing multiple changes in life-styles, values, and socioeconomic patterns. The party was no longer the all-encompassing community for its members. The party could no longer place an errant member in total isolation, or exert unrelenting pressure on him or her until he or she capitulated. On the contrary, party members could turn to their family, economic pursuits, or even religion when they felt rejected by the party.

On previous occasions of party rectification, a political hysteria filled the air.

There was a sense of urgency and crisis that pervaded the entire society. The targets of rectification would feel the entire world closing in on them, and they must capitulate to the party's dictate. In the current case, there was also supposed to be a sense of crisis within the party, but in the outside and larger world, it was business as usual. This was an unprecedented situation. The atmosphere of normalcy in the outside world tended to give the crisis within the party an air of artificiality. It was difficult to get people tensed up, agitated, and attentive. This social tranquility took much steam out of the party's effort to exert psychological pressure upon individual members.

It should also be noted that the party's top leaders were themselves uncertain about how harshly the rectification campaign should be conducted. This ambivalence was reflected in their directives. On the one hand, they prodded members to engage in thorough self-analysis, to be courageous in revealing their own weaknesses and mistakes, and to "conduct a sincere, in-depth, and truthful self-criticism." On the other hand, they wanted to avoid the excesses so characteristic of previous rectifications and advised party members that, when making criticism against others, they need not always strive for an immediate verdict in every case. Instead, the critics should allow the criticized persons to correct their mistakes in their own time "after a certain amount of examination has been made." In some places where the party secretaries were overeager in carrying out the rectification by forcing people to make full confessions, the party quickly stepped in to forbid this practice for fear that it would create another reign of terror.[50] Realizing that criticism could lead to such inconclusive results, many members could not help wondering why they should bother to make either criticism or self-criticism at all.

In the 1980s, it was no longer possible for the party to recreate the atmosphere of total dedication and omnipresent tension that characterized political meetings of the earlier years. For instance, the party's routine organizational-life meetings were intended to provide party members with opportunities to engage in broad-ranging criticism and self-criticism regarding the constituent members' ideological, political, and personal problems. But this purpose was defeated when many units crammed such meetings with discussion of office business and professional issues, or tried to kill time with innocuous chitchat.[51] At some work units, the afternoons set aside nominally for serious political matters were actually converted into free time for people to read newspapers or do their shopping. Given such lackadaisical attitudes by party members, it was unrealistic to expect criticism/self-criticism to accomplish anything.

Conclusion

Traditionally, the Chinese have always placed a premium on maintaining harmony. Since Liberation, generations of Chinese have been indoctrinated to believe in the virtues of conflict and struggle. Yet even as Chinese were told to make criticism in a political setting, they were still brought up to maintain harmony in their social relations. Therefore, there always existed a psychological tension between cultural preferences and political duties. The primacy of politics over culture was maintained for as long as the party's authority and wisdom were deemed to be beyond question. Thus, the chief reason why criticism and self-criticism lost their effectiveness was the lost credibility of the CCP among its members.

The decline of political influence opened the way for traditional cultural norms to regain their standing. Many party members now valued harmony and conviviality above political obligations. They preferred to be perceived as "nice guys" who would see and hear no evil, rather than the humorless and totally dedicated revolutionary firebrands that they used to admire. As the popular saying goes, "if you insist on principle, you will provoke many criticisms; if you act like a nice guy, you will get many votes; if you fraternize, you will have many friends; and if you engage in eating and drinking, you will obtain many benefits."[52]

In the 1980s, criticism/self-criticism failed to improve the discipline of party members. The physical, psychological, and political conditions in China had changed so much since the death of Mao that there appeared to be very little hope of reviving the effectiveness of these traditional techniques. The party's continued reliance on these traditional techniques and failure to develop new ones was another main reason why the rectification failed to accomplish its goals.

The Determination to Punish Offenders

To enforce discipline, the party must demonstrate convincingly that misconduct did not pay. It must demonstrate both the resolve and the ability to punish misbehavior so that the rank and file would realize that they could ignore party commands only at their peril. One factor that reduced the party's ability to do this, however, was the discrepancy between the top leaders' desire to maintain harmony with colleagues on their own level and their determination to enforce discipline on lower levels.

The desire to maintain harmony at the highest levels is easy enough to understand. There were so many other important policies that needed to be implemented that leaders could ill afford to antagonize their colleagues unnecessarily. In contrast, however, top leaders often criticized lower-level cadres for failing to make hard decisions. For instance, Chen Yun in 1982 accused many members of a lack of moral courage to distinguish right from wrong. Chen lamented that a prevalent problem within the party was that too many people were reluctant to expose other people's wrongdoing for fear of provoking retaliation, or spoiling their professional connections, or losing their popularity, and that their favorite stance was to be unobtrusive and evasive, which in turn made it very hard to carry out the rectification campaign.[53] Yet the very same leaders like Chen who failed to practice what they preached inevitably set poor examples when they wanted discipline to be thoroughly enforced among their subordinates.

This behavior was not uncommon. Throughout the CCP's history, top leaders showed a tendency to put the blame on basic-level cadres when things went wrong. This was done for different reasons. First, when there was a policy dispute among the top leaders, one group would engage in the tactic of "accusing the birch by pointing to the mulberry tree" by criticizing cadres on the lower levels who faithfully implemented their opponents' policies. Second, the lower-level cadres were in the closest daily contact with the public. By criticizing or prosecuting them, the top leaders hoped to deflect anger from themselves. Finally, when wrongdoings were committed by members on all levels, the leaders could employ the tactic of "killing the chicken to warn the monkeys." They hoped that prosecution of a few low-ranking wrongdoers would deter the wrongdoers on higher levels and thereby save the party from the embarrassment of high-level scandals.

But by the 1980s, the sociopolitical atmosphere had changed so much that enforcement of discipline became more difficult than ever. The leaders were reluctant to prosecute misconduct for a number of reasons. Some were worried that if too many members were punished, it would only confirm the public's worst assessment of the party's degeneration. Others were worried that the rectification campaign might detract from economic tasks. But probably the most powerful factor affecting the party's attitude was the ghost of the Cultural Revolution.[54]

Several aspects of conducting political struggle during the Cultural Revolution had become particularly repugnant to party members. First, the Cultural Revolution relied heavily on the use of "big exposure," "big criticism," and "elevation of minor issues all the way into fundamental principles" in dealing with party members' alleged ideological or behavioral defects. Second, the Cultural Revolution adopted not only a militant, but also a militaristic, attitude in resolving intraparty differences. It deployed "combat regiments" to smash its opposition. Party members were picked to form the "backbone," and activists from the masses were enlisted as "gunners" to fire barrages at their targets. They employed coercive and sometimes brutal tactics (generally referred to as "armed struggle") to extract confessions from, or to silence, opponents. Standard procedure during the Cultural Revolution was to pass judgment first and collect evidence later. Finally, the Cultural Revolution emphasized the format that "everyone must pass through inspection," thereby creating an atmosphere of panic among the entire membership.

In fact, however, many of the same methods had been used by the party in numerous previous political campaigns, except that their combined impact was most painfully felt only during the Cultural Revolution, particularly by the leading cadres at that time. In their attempt to restore the party's sagging legitimacy, post-Mao leaders tried to do two things simultaneously. On the one hand, they thoroughly repudiated the Cultural Revolution and conveniently attributed many of the party's long-standing defects to it. On the other hand, they promised to restore the pristine image of the party and revive its "good tradition." But when they vowed to reject the Cultural Revolution approach, with all its associated attributes, they also removed from their arsenal some of the most effective techniques to extract conformity from deviant members.

To underscore the difference between the current rectification and the Cultural Revolution, the leaders assured the members that the former should be viewed as a "gentle breeze and soothing rain." The premium was put on harmony and unity. The rectification was to be conducted in a civilized manner wherein members would assist each other to rectify by relying on the individual members' self-awareness and self-enlightenment. The leaders told members that the party did not intend to scrutinize their past in detail, nor would it coerce them to accept its verdict. They also promised that the party would be thorough in conducting its investigation and precise in making its accusations. As one provincial leader said, the most important objective of rectification was to give the whole party an education and not to achieve the "unrealistic goal of making everyone perfect," or to correct completely all past wrongs. Finally, the party vowed not to tolerate the return of the Cultural Revolution method of "kicking aside the party secretary to wage revolution." Instead, it wanted rectification to be conducted under the tight control of the party secretary at all times.[55]

While the intent of these restraints was to avoid widespread panic and to facilitate an orderly improvement of discipline, the effect was to take the teeth out of the rectification. For, once the misbehaving members realized that the rectification would not be conducted harshly, they concluded that they need not cooperate at all. In the ensuing process, the party never worked out a formula to make punishment commensurate with the offenses regardless of the perpetrator's rank and status.

It may not be easy for people unfamiliar with Chinese Communist affairs to understand why a totalitarian party like the CCP could find it so difficult to enforce discipline among its own members. But in fact, the party had always been highly discriminatory in disciplinary matters. While it was always ready to be ruthless toward the nonparty population when the latter committed misdeeds, it had been much more reluctant to enforce discipline upon its own members, especially higher-level cadres.[56]

This reluctance to enforce the rules was one reason why discipline failed to improve. Before the 1980s, the party rarely allowed the courts to have jurisdiction over members' criminal activities. Although the public procurate and the court system both existed, they had to defer not only to their superiors in the government, but also to the party organs on their own level. Judges and public prosecutors who failed to defer to the party secretaries would be quickly dismissed or transferred.[57] The Chinese Communist party never subscribed to the principle of rule by law, including the constitution. It was the party's view that laws were instruments to control the people and should be used as it saw fit—not to restrain the party itself.

Traditionally, when members committed crimes, the party preferred to treat them strictly as internal matters. But whether a case was prosecuted or not was often a matter of personal discretion. Very few cadres wanted to offend their colleagues. Aggressive prosecution of such cases could create personal enemies. The prosecutors and investigators were surrounded by complex networks of personal relations that were mobilized by the offenders to seek leniency. When the offenders were connected with other powerful figures in the party or government, then it would be foolhardy for lower-ranking cadres to pursue a case too aggressively.

Even when party sanctions were imposed, they were lenient as long as the members' deviations were not of a political and ideological nature. There was a prevalent view among many leading cadres that economic misconduct need not be taken too seriously. Thus, it was downplayed as the result of the errant members' ''misunderstanding of policies'' or their having made ''technical indiscretions.'' No crime was considered to have been committed if no money entered a person's own pocket, or if the act was committed in the name of a public office. Any transfer of funds that had the blessing of a leading cadre or was endorsed by a bank or other industrial or commercial enterprise automatically acquired the aura of legitimacy.[58]

As a result, only a tiny percentage of cases of misdeeds ever became the subjects of disciplinary inquiry. An even smaller number of cases resulted in a judgment against the offenders. Even then, the penalties usually amounted to a slap on the wrist, involving a warning or a reprimand within the party. Out of the huge numbers of misdeeds, only a minuscule fraction resulted in dismissal from office, expulsion from the party, or imprisonment.

It is almost impossible to know exactly how many party members had been disciplined during the rectification campaign, for what offenses, or how severe were the punishments, because the party has never released detailed figures on this subject. The disciplinary system imposed several forms of punishment, the severest of which was expulsion. But in his summary report marking the end of the rectification campaign in May 1987, Bo Yibo did not provide figures on the number of members who had been disciplined. The available information suggests, however, that only a small number of members were ever punished. For instance, during the much publicized campaign to smash economic crimes from March 1982 to October 1983, only some 9,000 members had been expelled from the party, and another 18,000 had received lesser forms of intraparty disciplinary actions.[59] They constituted only 0.07 percent of the membership (of some 40 million) at the time. In May 1985, General Secretary Hu Yaobang indicated that no more than 20,000–30,000 members had received more serious disciplinary action and criminal prosecution since the beginning of the 1980s.[60] In October

1986, Hu Qili revealed that the number of party members who had received any form of intraparty disciplinary action in any given year during 1981–85 was merely 0.2–0.3 percent of the entire membership. Finally, at the Thirteenth Party Congress in 1987, the party claimed that during 1982–86, it had taken disciplinary action against 650,141 members, of which 151,935 had been expelled.[61] The most recent data released in 1989 by the CCP Central Organization Department claimed that in all, more than 320,000 party members had been expelled from the party since Mao's death. This total included 130,000 people who had entered the party through irregular methods during the Cultural Revolution and were the followers of Jiang Qing. It also included another 130,000 expelled during the rectification campaign of 1983–87. Finally, another 60,000 party members had been expelled or persuaded not to renew their party membership during 1987–89 in conjunction with the party's anti–bourgeois liberalization campaign.[62]

It is uncertain whether these figures have been padded post factum to give the impression that the party had been stern to violators of discipline. It is also unclear whether the figure of expulsions included those people who voluntarily allowed their party membership to lapse. But even accepting these figures at their face value, they were out of proportion with the enormity of misdeeds committed by party members during the 1980s. Furthermore, an extremely small number of them were ever prosecuted criminally.[63] Typically, when serious economic crimes had been committed, the offenders would at most be asked to return their loot, or be temporarily denied their bonuses.[64]

These measures only confirmed the popular belief among party members that they could realistically get away with any misconduct except antiparty activities.[65] In spite of the party's tolerant attitude toward poor discipline, its members still accounted for an inordinately large portion of the official statistics of crimes. For instance, 25 percent of the economic criminals prosecuted by the city of Beijing in 1985, and 36 percent of them in 1986, were party members. Nationwide, one out of every four economic criminals in 1986 was a member of the Chinese Communist Party.[66] These numbers appear particularly significant when it is recalled that party members constituted only 4 percent of China's population. Therefore, the combination of the party's own tradition, the lack of respect for laws, the absence of clear rules to guide personal conduct, and the reluctance of leading cadres to enforce discipline all contributed to the deterioration of party discipline even in the midst of rectification.[67]

If the number of errant members had been modest, and the nature of their misconduct had not been egregious, the party would have been able to shield its disciplinary problems from the public view. In the 1980s, however, the increasing scope and magnitude of misdeeds made it impossible for the party to conceal them. As public indignation mounted, the party promised that it would become more aggressive in prosecuting errant members.[68] But the party's reactions failed to mollify the public. The more astute observers noted that it hardly prosecuted anyone during the first phase of rectification when it affected the higher-level party organs, but began to threaten aggressive prosecution only during the second phase when rectification was carried out on the district and county levels.

Ever since the late 1970s, the public had become convinced that misconduct on the higher levels was far more rampant and egregious than misconduct on the lower levels, but that the latter were used as scapegoats to create the impression that rectification was working. This prompted many regular party members to observe sarcastically that "when the leaders suffered from poor health, the rank and file were forced to swallow the medicine."[69]

If it was painful enough for the party to punish the average members, it was doubly painful to direct rectification against the leading members. By the early 1980s, incidents of misconduct involving high-level leaders and their children had multiplied substantially. Many leaders or their children had abused power to gain access to the state's confidential economic data for personal speculative use, establish liaisons with overseas businessmen, set up secret bank accounts in Western countries, or sign exclusive deals to import or export certain commodities (ranging from minerals to weapons). Many children of powerful leaders had gone abroad, mostly to the United States, through the back door. Those staying in China quickly became an important part of China's emerging entrepreneurial class. If the party had been serious about launching an exhaustive investigation into their activities, it could have found a staggering amount of wrongdoing at the top, but it also would have created intense conflict within the leadership and possibly caused significant economic confusion and instability, neither of which the party wanted.

Occasionally, there would be an outburst of denunciations and threats from a leader against high-level abuses of privileges, but no concrete action would follow. In general, there was a conspiracy of silence on this subject. If a high-ranking leader's misconduct was detected, tremendous pressure would be marshaled to let him go free with a plea of ignorance of the law, or that punishment should not be applied to first-time offenders, or that the party should treat it as "a unique case" or accord the offender "special consideration," "make an exception," or "apply the laws with flexibility" to get the offender off the hook.[70]

It was not until late 1985 that some party leaders became sufficiently aroused by the magnitude of misconduct on the high levels to acknowledge it as the root of the party's problems with discipline. By this time, the masses had become far less concerned with the remnants of the Gang of Four than with the inexorable decline of discipline. They believed that the Gang's followers no longer had the power to cause further trouble, and therefore that the party's continued emphasis on the "three types" was misguided. In contrast, the masses had become deeply disillusioned with the widespread corruption and deterioration of the quality of government. Many people were convinced that no improvements could be expected on the lower levels unless the top leaders cleaned up their own act. The masses' distrust of top-level cadres was so widespread that rumors about high-

level misconduct would gain wide and immediate circulation. Even the traditionally docile deputies to the lower-level People's Congress would openly cite these
rumors. By 1985, high-level corruption had become the number one complaint
of the people.

As Wang Zhaoguo recounted it, the top leaders came to the conclusion only
around September 1985 that the party must set good examples for discipline, and
instructed the Secretariat to draft plans for implementation.[71] During the remainder of 1985, the party made increasingly open and threatening denunciations in
the hope of stemming the worst wave of economic crime, but to no avail.

Finally, the party mounted a new major offensive at the beginning of
1986. Between January 6 and 9, 1986, some eight thousand leading cadres from
the national party, state, and military organs as well as the municipality of
Beijing were summoned to hear a series of denunciations delivered by top party
and government leaders against high-level wrongdoing.

At the January 9 session, General Secretary Hu Yaobang, after reciting a long
list of misconduct by high-ranking cadres, said, "For a long period of time, there
has been a tendency within our party to put the blame on lower levels whenever
the party encountered problems, instead of looking for causes among the leading
organs." This was a perversity that must be corrected. Hu called upon "the party
organs of national agencies . . . to set examples for perfecting internal party life,
overcoming [organizational] weakness and laxity, promoting healthy criticism
and self-criticism, paying heed to the voices of the masses, and accepting the
supervision of the people and lower-level organs."[72]

Wang Zhaoguo warned that there was another common tendency among party
organs to allow new varieties of misconduct to emerge even as old ones were
being rectified. He further observed that there was much misconduct on the part
of leading cadres on the national level, and some of which were outright criminal
deeds.[73]

This meeting seemed to mark a high point in the rectification because it was
one of the largest assemblages of high-ranking cadres in the party's history.
Unfortunately, the party's proposed solutions were unimaginative and ineffective. The party and the State Council jointly issued a number of instructions to
the national leading cadres on how to set good examples for their subordinates. It
is interesting to note that the injunctions were related more to the leading cadres'
public image than to the substance of their misconduct. In other words, the party
seemed more preoccupied with image manipulation than with the essence of
wrongdoing.[74]

Shortly after the conference, the party's Central Discipline Inspection Committee declared that the top leaders would assume personal supervision over the
drive to eradicate erroneous party style, and that the party would prosecute
several major cases of economic crimes involving high-ranking people in 1986
to show its determination. The special commentator of the *People's Daily* issued
a specific warning to high-ranking cadres and their children not to test the

resolve of the national leaders. As he said, "Our party does not allow the existence of 'special party members' who place themselves above party rules. As long as a rule has been violated, we do not care whether you are high-ranking cadres, or children of high-ranking cadres, or famous people. We will sternly prosecute you."[75]

But the overall results of this much publicized offensive were disappointing. From January 1986 until the official termination of rectification in June 1987, only a handful of middle-level people were prosecuted. In the cases involving children of powerful figures, the latter had either retired or died.[76] A few more incumbent officials were given unspecified forms of intraparty sanctions.[77]

Probably the highest-ranking cadre to receive expulsion from the party, public disgrace, and full criminal prosecution during the entire process of rectification was the governor of Jiangxi Province, who in 1987 was accused of a moral offense and the embezzlement of some U.S. $600,000.[78] But these cases hardly scratched the surface of the problem of high-level misconduct and were totally inadequate to soothe the cynicism of the party rank and file or the masses.[79]

It is recalled that one major reason why the leaders decided to launch a general rectification campaign was to provide the party with a chance to weed out all unqualified and undesirable members. This was to be done at the time of general registration, which was required of every party member. But in the end, the leaders did not have the resolve to implement this objective.

Several surveys indicate that even the party acknowledged that it had many unfit members. A survey conducted in Beijing in June 1985 showed that only 36 percent of the members within the city's jurisdiction could meet the party's new demands, and 52 percent had mediocre qualities. But 10.5 percent of them failed to carry out their duties as party members, and 1.5–2.0 percent had committed serious criminal deeds. Another survey conducted in urban areas of Hebei Province revealed that the better party members and party organs constituted 35 percent, mediocre members and organs constituted 45 percent, while unqualified party members and paralyzed and nonfunctioning party organs accounted for 20 percent. Finally, a much broader national survey (encompassing nineteen provinces, autonomous regions, and municipalities) in 1986 indicated similar trends among party members and organs in the rural areas. These data reveal that after two to three years of the rectification campaign, only about 30 percent of party members and organs possessed the necessary qualifications to implement its policies faithfully and effectively, identify with its line, and actively support its reforms. Fifty percent of party members and lower-level organs were judged to have mediocre commitment to party programs and even less ability to carry them out. Nearly 20 percent actually failed to meet the standards set by the party. Finally, 5 percent of the party members were judged to have committed serious errors, and 5 percent of the party organs were in a state of paralysis. As there were 42 million party members in 2 million basic-level party branches at the time of these surveys, the above data mean that at least 8.4

million party members and 400,000 party branches were in very poor situation. Worse still, 2.1 million party members had committed serious offenses, often economic crimes. But they all managed to pass the campaign's last hurdle—the general registration process. Even *Hongqi* had to admit in May 1986 that "a substantial portion of party members possess relatively low political and ideological qualifications, some even have very low moral qualifications. After repeated efforts of rectification, the problem of erroneous party style and poor discipline has not been fundamentally resolved."[80]

These figures were indeed alarming and raised serious doubts about whether the time and energy devoted to the rectification campaign by the entire party was justified. The thinking of the top leaders had not really changed despite the fanfare of early 1986. The same methods were prescribed in the face of mounting evidence of their ineffectiveness. The leaders could not muster the moral courage to do the one absolutely essential thing— mete out just penalties to deserving offenders on the highest level to restore the party's credibility. As long as high-level cadres demonstrated that they could get away with misconduct, no rectification measures could have much effect on the rest of the party. The party's inability to change this situation created more serious long-term political liabilities than any other conceivable factors.

Policy-Formulation Approaches and Poor Discipline

Throughout the 1980s, and particularly during the rectification, party complaints concerning poor discipline invariably focused on the individual members. The official press routinely criticized members for not understanding the meaning of central policies, for their lack of commitment to implement the policies faithfully, and, in the worst cases, for deliberate attempts to resist and sabotage the policies. While many of these charges were accurate, an analysis of the causes of poor discipline would not be complete without taking into account the party's policy-making practices.

To maintain a high level of discipline, it is essential that standards of good conduct must be both explicit and reasonable. They must be explicit so that the boundaries of permissible acts, whether in implementing policies or in personal behavior, are clearly demarcated and understood. They must be reasonable so that it is possible and practical for people to observe them.

How did the party's policies contribute to its members' poor discipline? Analytically, they suffered from three major shortcomings. First, many were so obviously unreasonable that they offered little choice but to violate them. Second, many policies were so poorly crafted and the standards they set so vague that they often misled people into acting improperly. Lastly, many policies were so unstable that people had no reason to respect them, believing, with good reason, that they would soon be replaced by a new standard.

Reasonableness of Policies

The ability of people to engage in proper conduct is, in part, a function of the reasonableness of the rules. If the codes of conduct are sensible, fair, and practical, then the probability of observance will be high. If, however, the rules are insensible, unfair, and impractical, then people may be forced, or at least be more willing, to break them. In China, many policies were so unreasonable that their violations became inevitable.

Yet why were there unreasonable rules? While every bad rule had its peculiar origins, many of them bore the imprint of the same mentality and style of work of the leaders who formulated them. Chinese decision makers had long been conditioned to think in totalistic and strategic terms. They had unfailing faith in the superiority of central planning. Other modes of policy making were believed to lead to chaos, confusion, and waste. Chinese leaders not only wanted to plan everything, they preferred rigid and simple methods of implementation so that the results could be as neat and uniform as if they were strands cut "with one single slice of the knife."

The compulsion for total planning produced many unreasonable policies. For example, for many years, promotion and pay raises were not decided by performances but by a single criterion such as birth date or date of graduation from high school or college. Likewise, where people could reside, what kinds of job they could hold, and where they could attend schools were not decided by ability and free choice but by place of birth.[81] A more sweeping example occurred in the 1980s, when Chinese leaders concluded that the country had a severe population problem, the solution to which was to limit all families to one child. Such simplistic and indiscriminate policies were resented as they created enormous injustices and drove people to rely on whatever self-help measures were within their reach if they were to survive under the system.

As party members and cadres had far greater access to the limited resources and opportunities in China, they were in far better positions to satisfy their own needs than the average citizens. A considerable amount of "abuse of privileges" occurred on the basic levels of the party and state because people with influence decided to use the prerogatives at their disposal to escape the miseries and injustices of daily human existence. Even when they got caught, their superiors were sympathetic and understanding and often let them go free.[82] Cadres and party members could also peddle their influence to help others for a fee. The necessity of doing things "through the back door" was directly related to the party's propensity to impose totalistic controls over all aspects of people's lives. Cadres and party members were afforded ample opportunities to indulge in misdeeds precisely because they were given the opportunity to hold numerous strangleholds over people's livelihood and careers. As long as there remained a large number of such unreasonable policies, it would be difficult to improve dramatically members' discipline.

Policy Formulation

Poor discipline can also result when people, despite an intention to behave properly, do not have clear guidelines on which to pattern their behavior. Sometimes people may commit illegal acts unknowingly because the policies are ambiguous. In this manner, the policy-making process and the clear articulation of policy can significantly affect party discipline. Several aspects of the Chinese policy-formulation process made it difficult for cadres and party members to know and stay within the limits of proper conduct.

First of all, the mode of policy formulation was often dominated by one or a few leaders on any given level. Many top leaders in China showed a tendency to act impulsively because they were not held publicly accountable for their acts and because they subscribed to a political cultural proposition that put a premium on the leaders' ability to act "decisively." Once a top leader gave his blessing to a project, neither his peers nor his subordinates would want to contradict him. If a policy became identified with a top leader, then it was unlikely to be reversed even when found to be in error.[83]

Second, the actual policy-formulation process was often marked by intellectual sloppiness. Many decision makers possessed no professional expertise related to their work. They seldom visited the basic levels to gain firsthand understanding of the actual conditions, relying instead on briefings by subordinates to form their judgments. Decisions were often made without adequate deliberation. Debate, even behind closed doors, seldom took place. The masses almost never had input into the process. As a result, many of their policies were heavy on rhetoric but skimpy on substance. They were plagued by the lack of conceptual rigor, intellectual fuzziness, and sloppy staff work. Half-baked ideas were frequently rushed into implementation without working out the operational details. Policy directives often were couched in ambiguous terms and left to lower levels to make sense of them.

The confusion created by this style of policy making was exacerbated in the context of fast-paced economic reforms. The problem was particularly acute in China because of the reform's intellectual process. In many Western liberal democracies, reforms are frequently preceded by intense intellectual agitation and public debate, allowing many policy nuances and ramifications to be aired. When the reform ideas are legislated and put into operation, lower-level bureaucrats and even informed citizens are quite familiar with both the spirit of the reform and the guidelines for its implementation. When disputes arise, the concerned parties can turn to an independent court system for impartial adjudication.

But China's reforms since 1979 displayed an entirely different type of dynamics. They were prompted by two sources: one was the people who took things into their own hands and forced the leaders to acquiesce and coopt them. The second source was the leaders who formulated their own reforms. The first source played an active role primarily in the rural areas in the late 1970s, while the second was dominant in the urban industrial areas in the 1980s.

In many cases, conditions in the rural areas changed because peasants decided to take unilateral action in opposition to the directions of socialist agriculture. The pace of peasant action was often far ahead of the party's, as the party remained undecided about its basic policy orientations. The party's failure to cope with situations as they arose and to provide direction created much confusion among basic-level cadres and members who did not know what to do.

As it happened, the party eventually acquiesced to many of the peasants' practices, systematized them, and incorporated them into its own reform package. This pattern had a strong impact on the lower-level cadres and members, for what they witnessed was that the peasants had clearly acted in contravention to the party and gotten away with it. Soon many of them also decided to exploit the party's indecisiveness to their own advantage.

The phenomenon of the leaders' indecision continued into the 1980s even after the reforms had moved into the urban areas. The best illustration of this problem was the party's failure to define precisely the term "private enterprises" between 1982 and 1987 as applied to urban private economic activities. Could a private enterprise employ more than five workers without being accused of exploitation? The party's silence on this issue caused policy to drift and created anxiety and confusion on the basic levels. This issue was finally settled in 1987 when the party formally announced that it would not set any limit on the number of employees.[84]

In contrast to rural reforms, the reforms in the urban-industrial sectors were usually under much tighter party control. Because the leaders wanted to retain maximum flexibility, however, reform ideas were often shrouded in secrecy during the germination stage. This meant that lower-level cadres and members knew little or nothing of the new policies until they were formally adopted. As a result, the bulk of party members who were responsible for their implementation often lagged far behind their leaders in understanding the spirit of the reforms or the rationale of specific policies. The lower-level cadres and members were put in a situation of having to second-guess their leaders. Yet this was not possible because often even the leaders were uncertain of where and how fast their reform policies would go. As some leaders candidly admitted, the reforms were a process similar to "crossing the river by touching the stones underneath the water," and the reformers only knew as far as the next step.

The fact that even the leaders were uncertain placed the average cadre or member in an even more precarious position because of the long party tradition of blaming lower-level cadres whenever policies went awry. When failures occurred, higher-level leaders rarely acknowledged that their own conceptual flaws, careless planning, or misleading directives were contributing factors. Instead, the responsibility was always placed squarely on the average cadre or member, who was said to have an incorrect understanding of central directives or to have committed unauthorized acts. Without an independent judiciary to appeal to, lower-level cadres and members were completely at the mercy of their leaders.

Possibly the case that best illustrates the risk of this style of policy making was the Hainan automobile smuggling case, which ranked as one of the biggest scandals to break during the 1980s. This case involved massive corruption and illegal acts committed from January 1984 to March 1985. It implicated nearly the entire top echelon of the Hainan Administrative Region, including the deputy party secretary, Lei Yu. These people acquired huge amounts of foreign exchange and bank loans to finance the importation of 89,000 automobiles, numerous television sets, VCRs, and motorcycles, all for the purpose of reselling them to other parts of China for a profit.[85]

It is telling that during this fourteen-month period, the party and State Council had repeatedly asked Hainan to halt its practices. Yet the island's leaders persisted in the belief that they were conducting a bold economic reform for the benefit of Hainan's economic development and not for personal enrichment. Eventually, the party branded this operation as a case of gross indiscipline and "illegal" acts and shut it down. Yet strangely, the architect of this operation, Lei Yu, was only transferred to a lesser post in Guangdong Province and was allowed to enjoy a political comeback in less than three years.

This case illustrates the types of misunderstanding possible between national and local leaders regarding the limits of permissible conduct to promote reforms. Hainan officials claimed that national leaders, including Zhao Ziyang and Deng Xiaoping, had given them broad discretionary powers to develop the island's economy, and that they had acted within their mandate.[86]

This case points to a major hazard of conducting party rectification in the midst of economic reforms. When the reform's guidelines were ambiguous, it would become doubly difficult for the lower-level cadres and party members to know the precise boundaries of legitimate innovations. In addition, the definition of proper conduct was subject to change as a result of the leaders' change of moods, or of power struggles on the higher levels.

In the 1980s, the pace of change was so fast and its scope so broad that many people suffered from conceptual disorientations. In a totalitarian system, the leaders were accustomed to issue policies without the benefit of feedback from below. The result of conducting reforms from above could be a serious cognitive gap between the leaders and the lower ranks as the former could not possibly hope that the latter would fully grasp what they wanted.

Chinese Communist cadres and members were indoctrinated to obey orders blindly. This was both safe and feasible in a well-structured situation. But the 1980s witnessed a reorientation of the country's political and economic programs of unparalleled magnitude. Given the characteristics of the policy-formulation process discussed above, a significant amount of the poor discipline by cadres and members can be attributed to the policy process that imposed reform from above by administrative fiat unaccompanied by popular education, mass participation, or open debate. This process left a large number of cadres and party members genuinely perplexed about the applicability of the new rules to their own situation and created an almost irresistible urge to violate the party's policies.[87]

Stability of Policies

Poorly conceived and poorly crafted policies contain loopholes that tempt people to exploit them. In China, many half-formed ideas were hastily formalized into policies. When leaders realized their mistakes, they would abandon them and try something different. The Chinese Communists euphemistically called these mistakes indispensable "tuition" paid to improve their performance. They even proudly asserted that "we Communists always correct our own mistakes"; except, of course, they never paid for their mistakes by losing their own jobs, nor would the CCP ever relinquish power as parties in democratic countries would.

Wastefulness, however, was by no means the only adverse effect of this deficient policy-making process. A far more damaging effect was the disrespect and distrust it bred among the public toward policies. Although policies were routinely accompanied by vows of determination to carry them out thoroughly when they were first introduced, the public's expectation was that policies had a short lifespan. To vast numbers of Chinese, as a popular saying goes, "Communist policies are like the moon, they are different on the first and the fifteen day of the month." This changeability of policies easily eroded people's confidence in policies in general. An illegal act at one time might become legal after enough people had committed it. On the other hand, a legal act at one time might be banned later after too many people had abused it.[88]

By the 1980s, party policies had lost so much credibility that no sooner had one been introduced than it became fair game to undermine its effectiveness. People might want to avert its potential harm, to circumvent its restrictions, or to exploit it for personal gains. The government, in turn, would react by introducing qualifications, withdrawing certain provisions, or canceling the whole policy.

The constant flux in policies and rules of proper conduct created an opportunistic mentality among the people. People tried to get ahead as soon as a policy was announced because this was usually the time when both the language and rules of application of the policy were at their loosest.

This mindset bears a resemblance to that held by people in the throes of economic inflation. Every remedial measure taken by the government to alleviate the public's anxiety only prompts the public to take measures that defeat its purpose. The more goods a government puts on the shelves to assuage the public's fear of shortage trigger more panic buying and exacerbate the shortage. Of course, the major difference in China in the 1980s was that it was not only the official currency that had suffered serious depreciation, but the party's basic credibility. The result was a circular policy trap. Although the party (government) could announce a decision to relax control over an issue, the public, having no faith in the promise, would still try to take maximum advantage, even by resorting to illegal means. The government, in turn, would become alarmed and decide to retighten control. The public would further refine their counter-measures to circumvent the new restrictions.[89]

Thus, the party/government and the public, or the top leaders and the rank and file, were locked in an incessant battle of matching wits, which caused many people to view their relationship as an antagonistic one. Whereas in the early years the misbehaving members only tried to evade regulations and discipline by hiding their activities, they had become much bolder by 1984–85, when many of them openly defied the party's policies by saying, "the top leaders have policies, but the lower levels have counterpolicies."[90] For instance, the reform principle that a minority should be allowed to get rich first became the justification for some leading cadres to form their own companies to do business. The party's decision to smash the iron rice bowl and abandon absolute egalitarianism was used by some to give excessive bonuses to their favorite people. The new princi-ple of "pay according to labor" was exploited by some leading cadres to give themselves large salary increases, better housing, and special subsidies. All these acts were justified as implementation of reform.[91]

With these attitudes, the cadres and party members had become the worst obstructions to the party's own programs. The demoralizing effect among basic-level cadres and members was unmistakable. Many of them had lost their dedi-cation to serve the people. Instead, they concentrated on exploiting their privileged positions to make personal gains and completely violated the public trust. Meanwhile, the masses also became more cynical and concluded that re-forms only made cadres richer, and the "individual responsibility system" al-lowed cadres to make windfall profits.

This discussion suggests that flaws in the policy-formulation process played a key role in precipitating poor discipline among party members. Many instances of misconduct were created because either the reform ideas were so new that they created genuine misunderstanding among cadres or they were so full of loopholes that unethical cadres found it easy to exploit them.

A factor that fundamentally exacerbated the problems of poor discipline in China was that the CCP's reforms of the 1980s were primarily introduced by administrative fiat rather than through the long and deliberative legislative route. Often a new policy was introduced by a leader in a speech and became the new law without due process. As is typical of totalitarian societies, many Chinese laws or policies were made not with the intent to conform to the standards of rationality but only to meet the transient needs or whims of the leaders. Their impatience with the legislative process means that Chinese leaders introduced reform often by breaking existing laws. A good example of this pattern is the fact that nearly all the agricultural policies of the early 1980s were introduced in explicit violation of the constitution at that time; the leaders thought it necessary to carry out reform in this manner. If lower-level leaders introduced their own reforms in the same manner, however, they might be punished. This created the strange situation whereby both genuine reformers and criminals had a similar need to break or disregard laws. This political setting made it difficult to draw the fine line between reform and lawlessness. Party rectification presumably should hinder lawlessness, but it also hindered reforms.

But this point was never candidly admitted in the rectification. Many leaders remained convinced of the soundness of their policies but acknowledged the need to increase the volume and frequency of their political exhortations. Hence, their solution was to resort to verbal overkill, using the same format and sending the same messages, but doing so more loudly and more often in the hopes that sheer shrillness would make errant members snap to attention. This approach toward rectification, however, only desensitized the party members' respect for laws and policies until they eventually became oblivious to the empty threats from the leaders.

Conflict Between Rectification and Economic Growth

From the beginning of the rectification campaign, party leaders were caught in a dilemma between politics and economics: how to tighten party members' discipline while encouraging them to be bold and innovative enough to achieve economic growth. There were two aspects to this problem: one had to do with whether politics or economics should have first claim over the time and resources of the participants; and the other had to do with whether the requirements of party rectification were compatible with, or inimical to, the requirements of economic growth.

Theoretically, these two tasks should be complementary. Rectification should help eliminate such liabilities as the party's erroneous style of work and its internal contradictions so that the party might acquire the strength to realize its economic reforms. Conversely, reform could ameliorate many problems in the economic system, erect a new socialist economic order, and put a new gloss on the party's legitimacy.

In reality, however, tension between rectification and economic reform soon came to the fore. This tension was caused by three factors: the subtle shift of the leaders' sense of crisis; the leaders' aversion to potentially destructive political campaigns; and the popularity of a new variant of economism opposed to the rationale for rectification.

Shifts in the Leaders' Sense of Crisis

In the beginning, party leaders placed strong emphasis on rectification on the assumption that the party would face an irreversible decline unless measures were taken promptly to correct poor discipline. But by 1983–84, top leaders' attention was increasingly drawn to the exciting prospects of great economic strides. This shift inevitably affected their priorities.

In late 1983, the party took the position that "no work unit should allow production and work to be interfered with by party rectification."[92] During a visit to Sichuan in early 1984, General Secretary Hu Yaobang began to define the party's "central mission" as economic construction. Throughout 1984, Hu continued to underscore the fundamental importance of economic objectives and referred to rectification as only one of many measures designed to achieve the overriding economic end of creating wealth, rather than as an end in itself.[93]

Hu also became fascinated with the concept of a "third takeoff" in this century and urged cadres in his many inspection tours to experiment with new methods, to liberate their thoughts, and to continue the policy of opening up to the outside.[94]

Hu Yaobang's high expectations about China's economic prospects were shared by Deng Xiaoping. In October 1984, Deng stated that China's political and economic situation had reached a level of unity and stability rarely surpassed in PRC history. He also stated confidently that the economic reform policies would remain unchanged through orderly leadership successions in the future, and that China was capable not only of realizing the goal of quadrupling the GNP by the year 2000, but of achieving parity with other economically developed countries by 2030 or 2050.[95] To both Hu and Deng, the main ingredients for economic success were leadership unity and stability and improved "professional" qualities of the cadre corps, rather than a disciplined party rank and file.[96]

These leaders' preoccupation with economic issues was also reflected in the party's agenda. At its Twelfth National Congress, the party's leaders unveiled an ambitious economic plan for the next twenty years. It expected major economic structural readjustments, reorganization, and technical improvement to be completed during the Sixth Five-Year Plan (1980–1985) so that the country could concentrate on achieving rapid growth during the Seventh Plan period (1986–1990).[97] The party also passed an important resolution on comprehensive urban economic institutional reforms.[98]

At the beginning of the second stage of rectification, Bo Yibo made an important speech outlining the rectification's direction. He said, "Whether rectification can be conducted successfully would critically affect the success or failure of the reforms [of urban economic institutions]. If the party style is improper, if discipline is not tight, then reform will not work." Consequently, the purpose of rectification was to remove the obstacles from the path of reform, to create a favorable social environment and political conditions for reform, and to promote and guarantee the healthy development of reform. In Bo's words, whether the above could be achieved would constitute a major criterion in assessing the accomplishments of the second stage of rectification.[99]

These measures made it clear that even as the rectification was proceeding, the top leaders' imagination was gripped more by their excitement over the potential for economic growth than by the mundane tasks of tightening the party's own discipline.

Economics above Politics

Given this frame of mind among the top leaders, it is natural that they were determined not to allow the rectification campaign to be turned into another destructive mass movement. In this respect, the anti–spiritual pollution campaign of early 1983 served as a reminder of how easily a campaign could get out of control. Originally directed only against such abstract concepts as "alienation" and "humanitarianism," the campaign soon veered against concrete manifestations of Western life-styles. Before long, even the party's current economic theories and practices were attacked as spiritual pollution. As these attacks placed the policy innovations in the vast rural areas under imminent danger, the leaders quickly stepped in to contain the damage. But they also learned that they must vigilantly guard the fruits of their economic progress, even in the midst of rectification. Clearly, while the leaders wanted to solve the party's discipline problems, they also wanted to make sure that rectification would not plunge it into chaos again.[100]

As a result, party publications released at the outset of the rectification campaign in late 1983 made it clear that lower-level party organs must not allow rectification work to impede their normal professional operations or production process. The commentator of the *People's Daily* reiterated the point that the purpose of "all" party activities (including rectification and the anti–spiritual pollution campaign) was to promote economic activities. Revealingly, he asserted that the obverse was also true: if a work unit had made commendable economic gains, then it should be regarded as having performed satisfactory work in rectification as well.[101] Hu Yaobang was quoted as having said in September 1984 that "party rectification will promote economic performance, economic performance will serve as the standard to evaluate the accomplishment of party rectification."[102]

In reviewing the accomplishments of the first year of rectification in December 1984, Bo Yibo expressed gratification that it had been conducted correctly precisely because it had not degenerated into a highly emotionally charged political movement. He quoted Deng Xiaoping as having said that the four modernizations program was not merely an economic program but "the most important political program," and that it should constitute the major criterion to evaluate work in all other areas. Bo made it clear that rectification must complement economic reform, and that the pursuit of economic growth should take precedence over all other missions for the present generation.[103]

The national leaders' attitudes set the tone of how provincial and lower-level party leaders viewed the interrelationship between rectification and economic reform. For instance, Sichuan's first party secretary, Yang Rudai, instructed all provincial party units to pay particular attention to their professional operations during the rectification in order to achieve economic reform and growth.[104] A Jiangxi provincial leader stated in 1985 that rectification's function was to remove obstacles from the path of economic reform, and economic reform was the major content of party rectification. From these two propositions, he easily reached the conclusion that "economic construction should be the *sole criterion* in evaluating party rectification and reform."[105] Likewise, a Hubei party leader (Xin Congzhi) restated the party's position that "the general purpose of the current rectification is . . . to realize the target of quadrupling national industrial and agricultural production by the end of the century."[106] Probably the most forthright statement of this position was made by Xiang Nan, first party secretary of Fujian Province, when he said in January 1986, "What is the objective of our conducting a party rectification? It is to facilitate our economic work, to realize the goals of quadrupling our GNP and achieving the four modernizations, but not for rectification's own sake."[107]

Such interpretations of the meaning and objectives of party rectification led many lower-level organs openly to downgrade their rectification work. These party organs allotted little time to conduct rectification on the grounds that it would interfere with their normal productive work. They conducted rectification only intermittently, or waited to do so only during holidays and vacations. In 1983, the party had instructed all units undergoing rectification to divide their leadership into two separate sets so that one set of leaders would take charge of normal professional operations or economic production while the other would devote their full attention to conducting rectification.[108] But although rectification was supposed to affect all party members in the work units, many work units were willing to assign only one or two second-string cadres to take charge of rectification for the sake of window-dressing, so that the majority of the staff could carry on with their normal business operations without interference. Even when higher-level party organs sent supervisors downward to provide guidance on rectification, they often ended up helping the local people solve their technical and production problems and paid scant attention to their rectification needs.[109]

Overall, rectification was accorded marginal attention wherever it was felt to be competing with normal economic activities for time and resources. Again, Xiang Nan of Fujian offered his frank confession in this connection. In 1986, he noted that after more than two years of the campaign, his province had not spent much effort on rectification because top priority had been given to economic work.[110]

Economics Against Politics

But many lower-level leaders and members went beyond the leaders' desire to conduct rectification, albeit subordinate to the economic reforms, and argued that rectification was actually inimical to economic reforms. For those party members who had committed mistakes and feared that they might become targets of rectification, economic reforms offered a convenient protective cover. Some argued that rectification interfered with economic work and therefore should be called off. Others argued that economic progress was tantamount to good party work, and therefore their performance should be measured by economic gains and not by their work in rectification.[111]

But a much larger number of regular party members were unpersuaded by the argument that reforms were possible only after the party had been rectified. These people genuinely regarded economic performance to be intrinsically more important than rectification, and they believed that members currently engaged in meaningful economic work should be immune from the rectification process. According to this logic, as long as party members performed useful economic functions, they were fulfilling the objective of the party's rectification, and their other faults should be glossed over. Some local party secretaries went so far as to suggest that the most reliable way to evaluate rectification accomplishments of a particular locality was to look at the income level of its people.[112]

Others asserted that rectification and economic reforms were inherently incompatible with each other, and that insistence on party style and discipline could only stifle individual initiative and innovation, retard the reforms, and shackle the reformers. In the mid-1980s, the "relaxation" (*songbang*) thesis gained widespread currency among leading cadres in many provinces. They contended that there actually existed an inverse correlation between discipline and reform, and they maintained that the success of reform was contingent upon the relaxation of discipline. These advocates argued that "party style must be relaxed if the economy is to develop," or that "wealth can be created only when the party style is improper." Still others argued that party style would be self-correcting after the economy had improved. The most extreme position held by some reformers was that discipline was restrictive, and that reform and progress had to break out of old straitjackets, and therefore rectification was a counterproductive idea.[113]

Although many party leaders vehemently denounced these views about the dichotomy between party discipline and economic growth and the accompanying demand for relaxation,[114] they gained much popularity among many party members, particularly in the coastal areas, which had experienced robust economic activities in recent years. Citing their economic achievements as evidence, party members argued that it was only natural for these areas to have a higher incidence of misconduct. Their proposed solution was for the party to give them preferential treatment by relaxing standards of proper conduct in these areas.[115] On the other hand, whenever economic enterprises encountered stagnant growth, they tended to point to the rigid party rules as the main culprit, alleging that it was the party's insistence on discipline that prevented the reformers from taking bold initiatives.[116] Although the party leaders rejected all these contentions, a substantial portion of party members remained convinced of the validity of their views and adopted a hostile attitude toward rectification on economic grounds.

Conclusion

Economic progress had been expected to become a major pillar in the party's strategy to bolster its legitimacy since 1979. If the prospects for economic growth and improvement of quality of life for the masses were threatened, it was feared that serious political turmoil might follow. Therefore, the Deng leadership wanted to do everything possible to avoid disruption of economic development. Another major foundation of Deng's power was his pledge to banish ruthless political oppression from China forever. These two commitments set the parameters within which the party must conduct its rectification.

The above discussion suggests that there were three stages in the interrelations between rectification and economic reform. During the first stage, rectification was perceived to be more important than reform, because without the former, the party might collapse. During the second stage, the two were perceived to be complementary and interdependent, with economic reform gradually gaining the more prominent position and rectification assuming the role of supporting reform. But during the third stage, a sizable group of lower-level leaders and members took the position that rectification and economic reform were mutually contradictory, and that the latter could be achieved only at the expense of the former.

It is recalled that when the rectification campaign first began, the party had issued a directive demanding lower-level organs to pay attention to the development of a proper "professional" work style in conjunction with a proper "party" work style. But many units seized this directive as an excuse to focus attention only on their professional work to the nearly total exclusion of other efforts to improve party character, discipline, or political work.[117]

As the rectification proceeded, there was an increasing tendency for many organs to substitute strictly economic criteria for the party's political or disciplinary standards. Party members who performed their professional work competently were automatically assumed to possess the proper "party character." Economic efficiency and the ability to generate material wealth for the society were particularly valued. According to this logic, a competent economic worker was by definition a good party member.[118]

In comparative terms, the rectification of the 1980s was very different from many of its predecessors. On earlier occasions, the party usually could afford to conduct rectification without much concern for its economic impact. But throughout the entire process of the recent rectification, the party had to tolerate evasions and subversions on the lower levels because it did not want to risk enforcing harsh disciplinary measures that might slow down the momentum of economic development.

The leaders' anxiety to protect economic reforms against political interference was most vividly exhibited by their handling of the major crisis during 1986–87. By Chinese standards, the student unrest in the winter of 1986 was a major disturbance that called for stern disciplinary measures. When the "conservatives" made their move to change the political course, Deng was willing to sacrifice Hu Yaobang but stood fast to protect his economic reforms. It is important to note that the very same Politburo resolution announcing Hu's resignation also included a guaranty that the policy of economic development and opening to the outside would not be affected by this leadership change.[119] Shortly afterward, Prime Minister Zhao Ziyang tried to lay to rest the popular anxiety that the new policy of opposing bourgeois liberalization might turn into another political movement when he said, "On behalf of the CCP center, I want to tell you in a responsible manner that we will definitely never mount another political movement." He then proceeded to place severe limits on the scope of the policy of opposing bourgeois liberalization: it would be conducted strictly within the party itself, primarily in the ideological realm. Specifically, he excluded the rural areas and promised that the policy would be implemented by "positive education" instead of negative criticism and punishment.[120]

In his summation of the three-year-long rectification campaign, Bo Yibo admitted that one important defect of the campaign was the tendency of many leading cadres to employ their professional operations as a shield against rectification.[121] By either asserting that their professional work was the equivalent of rectification work, or by holding up the specter of economic collapse if the party should push too aggressively on the disciplinary front, many units, especially economic enterprises, managed to exploit the leaders' eagerness to maintain the momentum of economic development and escaped the brunt of rectification. But the price the party paid to protect its economic gains was the worsening of discipline that swept the country in the later stages of the rectification campaign.

It can be safely said that all the disciplinary problems that emerged during the late 1970s persisted into the end of the 1980s as new forms of corruption and poor discipline came into existence. At the time of the party's Thirteenth Congress in late 1987, General Secretary Zhao Ziyang reported that, "At the present, the trend of abusing privileges for personal gains is still rampant. First, the level of wrongdoing has been raised and the number of higher-level cadres implicated has increased. Second, the scope has been expanded so that gifts become essential in either seeking personal favors or conducting official business. Third, the style has become blatant. Instead of hinting at an expectation (of bribery), they now make direct demands. Instead of feeling guilty about such abuses, they now become cavalier about them. Instead of negotiating deals behind the scenes, they now engage in public discussion about them." [122]

In 1988, party publications complained that organizational discipline had continued to decline, as evidenced by the increase of the so-called three-no's members, referring to those who did not perform party work, participate in party activities, or carry out their basic obligations.[123] By mid-1988, Song Ping, the director of Central Organization Department, again threatened that the party might have to expel some unqualified members.[124]

In the midst of renewed party threats to tighten discipline, however, it is interesting to note that a new thesis about corruption also gained considerable circulation. According to this thesis, corruption in the party was a "historically inevitable" development in the sense that it was a by-product of a process whereby China changed from a closed to an open society, from a natural economy to a commodity economy, and from underdevelopment to development. The implication was that corruption in Chinese society would last for a long time and might in fact function as a lubricant in China's imperfect economic system.[125]

9

The Rural Party's Special Problems

THE RURAL wing of the Chinese Communist Party is a huge collection of people and organizations. Roughly speaking, about half of the party's members and basic-level organs are located in the rural areas. While many of the principles and practices that guide the party in general certainly are applicable to the rural areas, the rural party also has many special features and problems.

Therefore, a balanced view of the transformation of the party in the 1980s must include some attention to the trials and tribulations of the rural wing of the CCP. This chapter is not intended to offer a full treatment of all the issues confronting the rural party, but only to offer a measure of comparison of how the rural party fared during the 1980s. It also highlights how the rural party coped with the same issues that plagued the urban party. Finally, problems unique to the rural party are discussed.

Ideological Confusion and Erosion

Ideological training in the countryside never acquired the level of intensity or sophistication that it did in the urban areas. The rural party members' extremely low educational level made it impossible for them to comprehend intricate ideological issues. Their ideological convictions consisted of a few simplistic notions about communism which they held dogmatically and applied mechanically.[1] The recruitment of large numbers of people with radical thinking and poor qualifications during the Cultural Revolution only exacerbated the rural party's ideological rigidity.[2]

Rural cadres and members were the first group inside the CCP to be rudely confronted by a challenge to the validity of their ideological convictions. They realized that many key features of the party's so-called reforms introduced in the late 1970s were actually concessions to the fait accompli that already existed in the countryside because the peasants had taken things into their own hands.

When the party tried to save face by claiming credit for these practices as "reforms," the rural cadres and members became terribly confused and reacted in two very different ways.

The dogmatists refused to accept the legitimacy of the reforms and regarded the introduction of the "individual household responsibility" system as signaling a restoration of old institutions, and a retreat from socialist goals. As they put it, "for thirty years we have toiled hard (to build socialism), but overnight things went back to their pre-Liberation conditions." Whenever possible, they continued to apply the old standards to undermine the new reform programs.[3]

Although by the mid-1980s the dogmatists' ability to do actual harm was severely limited, their destructive potential remained substantial. Even after years of economic reforms and visible accomplishments and transformation of the countryside, considerable ideological tension persisted in 1986–87 among the rural party cadres and members. It was not inconceivable for these people to overturn the reforms and revive the orthodox socialist policies when favorable conditions arose, such as after a conservative return to power at the top. It is precisely this fear that has dissuaded many prosperous peasants from making long-term capital investment in their land or new enterprises. Even the government admitted that in a number of places, this ideological confusion had already seriously hampered the reforms in the countryside.[4]

In contrast to the dogmatists, a far larger number of rural party cadres and members had simply lost their faith in the ideology and regarded it as irrelevant to current economic realities or as being fallacious by nature. For years, rural party members were accustomed to exercising ideological leadership over the masses. But the experience since the 1970s showed them that the peasants who reaped material benefits were precisely those who had defied socialist norms. The introduction of the individual responsibility system and the dismantling of the commune system occurred with such speed that the majority of party members experienced a profound crisis in faith and confidence. They soon began to question the superiority of socialism and regarded communism as being too remote or too impractical.[5] As a result, many rural party members neglected ideological training work and turned their attention exclusively to economic work. In many places, political education was entirely removed from the party's agenda.[6]

Many leading cadres also erroneously believed that they could neglect collective enterprises or collectively managed operations such as irrigation networks, water conservation projects, or collectively owned forests. In some cases, members simply divided up and took home the collectives' capital, savings and properties.[7]

The more resourceful party members quickly abandoned their political ideals and loyalty in favor of their own plots of land or money-making schemes.[8] The less competent ones had to achieve their aspirations through illegal means.[9]

There was also an alarming increase of rural cadres engaging in "superstitious" or religious activities. By the 1980s, the revival of religion in the countryside had become far more widespread than in the cities. In Gansu Province, for instance, about 20 percent of rural cadres routinely participated in religious activities and possibly as many as 50 percent of them believed in a god.[10]

The upshot was that by the mid-1980s, socialism and Marxism had lost their hold upon the majority of rural party cadres and members. Such ideas could no longer attract new blood into the party. Except for the minority of ideological diehards, ideology had been rendered nearly totally irrelevant to life in the countryside.

Qualities of Rural Leadership

A key reason for the party's traditionally firm control over the countryside was the quality of rural leadership. Without exception, rural leaders were drawn from the most solid socioeconomic background, namely, poor peasants. For many years, the basic requirements for rural party branch secretary consisted of good political background, seniority in age and party membership, and ability to control the masses.[11] They were indispensable to the party's paramount goal of imposing political control over the countryside, even though their ability to promote production was limited.

This rural leadership had enjoyed more longevity and greater homogeneity than the party's urban leadership. Whereas the urban party had a sizable number of better educated members who were branded "rightists" during earlier periods but who returned to active political life after Mao's death, no comparable group existed in the rural areas. Comparatively speaking, the rural leadership strata remained more stable throughout the decades and consistently exhibited more rigid ideological propensities than the urban areas. By the early 1980s, transformation in the rural areas put several new strains on the party's rural work. First, the primary mission of the rural party changed from one of conducting class struggle to one of achieving economic growth. Second, previously the party's economic responsibility was only to ensure the production of grain, and to guarantee that state taxes and compulsory purchase quotas were fulfilled. Now the party needed to provide leadership over a wide range of productive activities. To provide leadership over these new activities, the rural party cadres needed to possess far greater scientific and managerial knowledge than before.

Third, the rural party's clientele had changed. Previously, the rural party was coterminous with the production units. The jurisdictional boundaries of both political and economic controls were virtually identical. In the new situation, the party must try to reach the individual households or individual peasants directly. The party could no longer lead by issuing administrative directives. Instead, the leaders must possess a good grasp of policies, offer services to the peasants, and use economic incentives to provide leadership.[12]

But few of the party's incumbent basic-level leaders in the 1980s were capable of coping with these changes. There were two reasons for this deficiency.

First, rural leaders in the early 1980s were uniformly old, poorly educated, and unmotivated. For instance, a survey of rural branch leaders revealed that out of a provincial total of 230,000 rural branch leaders in Hebei in 1985, 41 percent were above 46 years of age. Some were even over 90 years old. Some 63 percent either were illiterate or had only primary school education. An additional 20 percent of the rural branches did not have a single member with a high school education.[13]

The conditions in Hebei were typical of those existing in most other provinces. In many instances, the local party leaders were first appointed to their posts in the late 1940s or early 1950s. Overall, only a tiny minority had been promoted to leadership positions since 1979.[14] In backward regions, illiterates could be over one-fourth of the party secretaries, and an additional 50 percent had only primary school education.[15] Such people simply did not have the professional knowledge or administrative skills to implement the increasingly complex new economic programs.[16]

Second, the rural leaders of the early 1980s were also too ideologically rigid to meet the new needs of the time. Many old cadres still believed in the paramount position of grain production over all other farming activities. They could not comprehend the commodity economy, manufacturing, or other key components of the new rural economy. Consequently, they insisted that "farming means tilling the fields," and they rejected other pursuits as heretical.[17] Many of them never dared to entertain the thought of getting rich, nor would they tolerate other people's becoming rich. Their egalitarian dogmas made them hostile to prosperous rural families.[18] Needless to say, such mentality made them serious impediments to the government's economic policies.

Therefore, by the early 1980s, the party already realized the urgent need for a new group of basic-level leaders who possessed different qualities. It wanted people who unquestioningly accepted its reform package since 1979. It also wanted leaders to be young, energetic, better educated, and innovative. Better still, it wanted leaders who possessed scientific expertise, some managerial ability, and familiarity with commerce. These leaders must be smart enough to excel in their own economic work and help the masses to get rich. Lastly, they must be able to command respect among the masses by virtue of their personal rectitude. In other words, the party had adopted a drastically different model of the "good cadres" in rural areas. It now put the primary emphasis on the rural leaders' ability to be efficient economic operatives to achieve the twin goals of spiritual and material civilization.[19]

Leadership Changes during the 1980s

In general, the issue of rural leadership changes was not placed on the party's agenda until 1985, when the party took steps to revamp rural party branch leadership with younger and better-educated members.[20] Unlike the earlier leadership changes on the higher levels, the party did not set specific age or educational requirements to be met on the rural level, but gave the provinces the flexibility to set their own standards of implementation. The "third echelon" model was consciously not applied to the rural areas.

Actually, only a short time was devoted to revamping rural leadership. Because of the numerous organizational difficulties plaguing the party, most basic-level organs did not have the ability to make their own leadership changes, but had to rely on superior party organs to tell them what to do. But these superior organs on the district and county levels had only recently gone through their own rectification and were hardly in a mood to assume the new task of supervising the change of leadership on the village level.

Not surprisingly, progress was exceedingly slow.[21] At the conclusion of the rurai phase of the rectification campaign in April 1987, the party reported that only between one-fifth and one-third of all rural party branch had undergone some degree of leadership change.[22] Even if the party claim were accepted at face value, it meant that some three quarters of a million (or more) rural party organs had been untouched and basically retained their old leadership.

Obstacles to Rural Leadership Changes

The results of the rural leadership changes were inconclusive for two reasons: for the policy to succeed, the incumbent leaders must be willing to give up power, and a pool of better qualified candidates must exist to become new leaders. Both conditions were absent in rural China.

Attitudes of Incumbents

Although there was a general recognition that rural basic-level leadership needed strengthening, many people resented the proposal of a massive replacement of the incumbents by more qualified leaders as unnecessary organizational overkill. Many party leaders argued that rural party leaders did not formulate policies or enjoy discretionary power in implementation so that they should not be made the scapegoats for troubles in the party. Many people favored a more moderate approach to improve the incumbents through training. Others believed it desirable to keep the old leaders in office and feared that a wholesale replacement might produce chaos and weaken the party. They believed that only the old-style leaders had the power to keep things under control, and that the young and inexperienced leaders might not win the respect of the masses.[23]

In addition, several other powerful forces also worked against the proposal of an extensive overhaul of the rural leadership. First, as long as the party claimed to be the vanguard of the proletariat, it was difficult to take power away from those who had solid class backgrounds and long service records. The majority of incumbents had been picked on account of their political credentials.[24] Party leaders were genuinely worried that wholesale replacement might trigger vehement resistance from the incumbents.[25]

Second, the special character of rural life made retirement far less palatable than in the urban areas. The party could not afford to offer rural leaders the preferential treatment it gave to urban retirees. It essentially told the rural party organs to handle the problem in their own way.[26] But the rural organs had few resources to placate the leaders. Most leaders had nothing to retire with, and they dreaded the prospect of having to return to toiling in the field after years of comfortable office work. Understandably, they regarded retirement as utterly unacceptable.

Third, since the party specifically exempted the rural organs from the duty to expose the "three types" in their midst, rural leadership changes did not have the same degree of political urgency as those in the urban areas. In other words, they were not viewed as an issue that affected political power.

Finally, many rural leaders had extensive family and clan power bases in their locality. The party could arouse serious communal trouble by trying too hard to remove leaders from offices.

Together, these factors created a natural tendency for many rural party organs to procrastinate and evade the issue.[27] Consequently, the results were extremely uneven among the provinces.[28] Even in places where leadership changes had presumably occurred, such changes only brought a reduction in the new leaders' average age, but not much appreciable improvement of their other qualifications. Many of the new leaders lacked experience in rural work, could not command the respect of the masses, showed commandistic styles, and inadequate education to deal with the agricultural problems on hand.[29]

Lack of Qualified Replacements

Traditionally, all rural party members shared a strong desire to become leaders, and for good reason. Leaders were not only exempted from working in the fields, they also enjoyed a host of other privileges.[30] But the rural economic reforms of the 1980s led many people to reassess their views about the attractiveness of rural leadership positions. It was widely assumed that the party branches had lost their usefulness after the responsibility system was extended to the individual households. Some rural leaders even believed that their positions were a liability that effectively prevented them from enjoying the full benefits of economic improvement for themselves.[31] This was most obvious with respect to the incomes of rural leaders. Traditionally, rural cadres' salaries were paid out of the funds of the production units. But the introduction of the individual responsibility system of rural production immediately threatened this payment system because much of the resources at the party organs' disposal were taken away. As a result, rural cadres in some provinces were without a stable source of income even as late as 1986, creating a strong disincentive for party members to stay away from party assignments.[32]

In the 1980s, rural and urban party members viewed the implications of promotion to leadership positions very differently. The pace and extent of privatization of the economy started late in the urban areas. Since the party still commanded tremendous organizational and material resources in the urban areas under the centralized form of ownership, leadership positions were attractive because they allowed the occupants to indulge in extensive economic activities and abuse privileges. In the rural areas, in contrast, the scope of party domination over the economy was fast receding. It was apparent to most party members that political activities were not nearly as profitable as economic activities because the avenues of making money through private enterprises were far broader than through the party or state hierarchy, and because upward mobility through party channels seldom went beyond the village level.

The kinds of party members that the party wanted the most to appoint as the new rural leaders were members of the "keypoint families" and "specialized families" who had already convincingly demonstrated their economic proficiency. Other sources of better-qualified candidates included educated youths and demobilized soldiers.[33] But in general it was easier to find people to reduce the average age of existing leadership than to improve significantly its professional and educational qualifications, or ideological and political credentials.[34] The party encountered a serious problem in trying to induce its members to accept promotion into basic-level leadership positions. Worse still, by the mid-1980s, even some incumbent rural party branch secretaries wanted to resign their posts so that they could devote full time to personal economic pursuits.[35]

By the early 1980s, China's countryside was plagued by three serious problems of manpower shortage: it had trouble attracting qualified people to work in the rural areas, those who were assigned to rural work did not want to serve, and those who came refused to stay.[36] In many areas, there was actually a brain drain from the rural areas to the urban areas, aided by the relaxation of economic conditions and political control in the countryside. Legally or illegally, millions of people left the villages to establish permanent residence in the cities in the early 1980s.

The emigrants included several major groups of the better-educated people in the rural population. One group consisted of the educated youths who had been sent to the villages as part of the regular rural rustication programs in previous decades. A second group consisted of the family members of rightists and other categories of political offenders who had been exiled to the countryside. A third group consisted of the children of high-ranking cadres who had volunteered to settle in the countryside to show their political loyalty during the Cultural Revolution. Together they constituted the core of the best-educated people in the countryside. Particularly alarming was the outflow of agricultural technicians and teachers which produced immediately visible decline in the quality of basic-level technical services and education. Often, the more backward the regions were, the harder they were likely to be hit by the brain drain.[37] Their exodus seriously depleted the pool of qualified people to replace the incumbent leaders.

In some instances, when qualified party members could not be found on the basic level to fill branch leadership positions, higher-level party and government organs felt compelled to send cadres from their own units to do so.[38] But such measures were seldom effective because few county-level cadres had any desire to serve on the grass-roots level on a permanent basis.

Lastly, the party's decision to make leadership changes at the higher levels first also produced unintended, detrimental effects. Since young and well-educated people had always been in short supply in the countryside, those who excelled were quickly snatched away by the higher-level party organs to fill their needs, leaving the basic-level organs with few, if any, qualified people to meet their needs.[39] All these factors created great difficulties for the party's attempts to upgrade rural leadership.

The reform of rural party leadership was a gigantic task. With over a million rural basic-level party organs (*zhibu*), each staffed by three or four cadres (secretaries, deputies, etc.), a thorough implementation would affect at least three to four million rural leaders.

The party's objective was to replace them with a new generation of leaders. But the rural party needed both an effective organization and a large number of qualified candidates to realize this objective.

It soon became clear, however, that the party had neither the organizational strength nor the human resources to produce the intended results. The party's organizational problems have already been discussed and need not be repeated here. Insofar as the manpower supply was concerned, the rural party leadership was a collection of the least competent people among China's entire rural population with respect to their educational and professional standard. Throughout the 1970s and early 1980s, the rural party had consistently failed to upgrade its membership in these respects. Therefore, when the party decided to implement leadership changes, the rural party was already handicapped by a severe shortage of qualified candidates.

The policy stalled during the implementation stage between 1985 and 1987. On the one hand, many old and incompetent leaders knew that their standard of living would suffer a serious decline if they left their party positions, because they had few other skills. On the other hand, the younger and more enterprising people were no longer interested in climbing the party's ladder of career success and were reluctant to take on party work. In between these two groups there were a number of incumbents who were willing to vacate their leadership positions, but for the wrong reasons. These leaders viewed their personal interests as being hampered by their party duties and wanted to devote their full energy to economic activities.

Even when leadership changes occurred, the process was often a haphazard one. Often higher-level leaders simply replaced old leaders with younger ones within the same branch without paying attention to their ability. Overall, the rural leadership changes produced only marginal improvements in terms of the leaders' age and educational composition, but these changes had little impact on increasing the party's efficiency and leadership in its rural work.

As a group, the new leaders had a much weaker commitment to the party and the ideology than their predecessors. Many younger replacements accepted their new jobs because they realized that they could not compete with others in the purely economic realm, or because they thought that their personal economic interests might be enhanced by their official connections. Their ability to revive or improve the party's rural work was suspect.

The above discussion thus points to an interesting problem in the current context. For according to Communist theory, the party is supposed to be separate from the state and supervise the state's functions. In the 1980s, as the state intensified its rural economic reform and gave local-level governments greater autonomy, the basic-level party organs were also expected to play a greater role to ensure that the party's economic, political, and ideological programs would be faithfully and creatively carried out in the countryside.[40] But in fact, the rural leaders' capacity to serve as the party's transmission belts had deteriorated to an alarming degree. Even the rural rectification campaign failed to arrest this trend, and it is highly unlikely that it will be reversed in the foreseeable future.

Factors Contributing to the Party's Organizational Decay

Traditionally, the party's control over its members and the rest of the population relied heavily on two mechanisms. One was its ability to restrict the latter's spatial mobility, including both the location of residence and the right to travel. The other was its monopolistic control over people's work assignments and incomes.

Spatial and Occupational Mobility

When party members were bound to a residential area or a work unit, it was impossible for them to evade the party's organizational reach. This kind of control was particularly strong in the countryside, where the peasants were confined to a single village for their entire life, and their livelihood depended on a rigid system of rationing and travel permits.

From the late 1950s to the early 1980s, the party's rural organizations corresponded closely to the relatively simple economic organizational chart of the commune system. Under this system, a party committee, headed by a party secretary, existed in every commune; a branch was established for each production brigade; and a party cell existed in every production team. For the purpose of imposing control, this policy of making party and economic organizational units coterminous made sense and worked well under the traditional mode of agricultural production.

The party initiated a massive reform of the rural administrative structure in the early 1980s. The policy to separate the commune from the government, and to establish the *xiang* government, was completed by February 1985. Before this reform, China had 54,000 people's communes, and 2,800 *zhen* (administrative townships) in the countryside. After the reform, there were 91,590 *xiang*, and 9,140 *zhen*. Before the reform, there were 700,00 production brigades; after the reform they were replaced by 948,600 villagers' councils.[41] The party also made its own adjustments in conjunction with this administrative reform. Under the new conditions, party committees existed on the *xiang* level, *zhibu* existed on the villagers' council level, and party cells on the level of villagers' cells.

But soon even this system was rendered impractical by the new rural economic conditions and employment patterns. As production decisions were made increasingly by the individual households, the many economic combinations formed by these households, or numerous *xiang*- and *zhen*-sponsored enterprises, the whole rural economy rapidly moved away from self-sufficiency toward a merchandise economy, from traditional labor-intensive agriculture toward agriculture with more modern technological inputs, and from uniformity and simplicity toward diversity. The administrative jurisdiction of *xiang*, village, and villagers' cells no longer corresponded with their constituent members' economic activities, and these units were sometimes rendered ineffective either as instruments of control or as instruments to promote economic development.

In this new context, party members also acquired greater spatial and occupational mobility, just like the rest of the peasant population. Many new rural enterprises had sprung up, such as construction work teams, transportation and hauling, repairing, or sales. Since the geographical coverage of their activities was extensive and their work schedules unpredictable, it was difficult to require party members in these professions to participate in regular party activities.[42] For instance, a study of the rural party members in Gaoping County (Shanxi Province) in 1984 showed that over 50 percent had left farming to engage in industry, trade, transportation, or other professions, with many of them traveling to distant places to do sales or construction work.[43] Another report from the province of Hebei indicated that, by the spring of 1987, of the more than 1.5 million rural party members in Hebei Province, one-third actually were employed in collective economic enterprises, in cooperatives, or in business by themselves, away from their native villages.[44]

Across the country in the early 1980s, more and more rural party members engaged in long-distance trading or obtained employment away from home. Many even ignored the ban on rural migration to the urban areas and flocked to new occupational opportunities in the cities.[45] Such expanded economic horizons shattered the party's once rigid geographical and occupational control over rural life. Many new enterprises defied old categorization because they crossed not only administrative jurisdictions, but also occupational lines.

Many party members found themselves in an organizational vacuum because they still belonged to the old village party organs, which were too far away to control them, and had not been organized into new party organs by their new occupations. This created a situation in which many old party units could not retain enough members to participate in their activities, while at the same time many party members could not locate new party organs with which to affiliate.[46]

As more village-level economic enterprises multiplied in the mid-1980s, the party's loss of organizational ground worsened progressively. In some cases, these new rural economic enterprises had no party branch or cell at all, and most of their leaders either were not party members or were members who had no party organs to answer to.[47]

The party was slow to react to these developments. Up to 1985, party organs had not been established in the majority of the newly created collective enterprises, and virtually none had been set up in individual businesses. As a result, numerous party organs practically lost physical contact with their members. Party organs could not extend their tentacles over members to control their schedules, to enforce discipline, or even to notify them to attend branch meetings. In some cases, itinerant rural party members paid their monthly dues by mail and participated in organizational activities only when they returned home for New Year's holidays.[48]

Needless to say, when so many newly established economic enterprises failed to form their own party organs, the party also lost contact with the vast rural masses in these enterprises. The party was being quietly excluded from decisions affecting rural production and distribution. In other words, it gradually ceased to exercise leadership over many key aspects of China's new rural life.[49]

But many party members undoubtedly savored their newly gained unattached status and guarded it jealously. There emerged a new group of rural party members who were dubbed by the party as the "four-no's party members" because they deliberately tried to "maintain no organizational ties, participate in no intraparty life, pay no party dues, and perform no party functions."[50]

The Party's Response

Although the widening gap between the old structural arrangements and the new rural economic developments had become obvious throughout the early 1980s, it was not until the spring of 1985 that the party turned its attention to this issue. In December 1985, the party decided it was necessary to improve its basic-level organizations.[51] Over the next two years, it gradually formulated a number of new guidelines. Party members who had left farming to join rural enterprises were required to transfer their organizational affiliations from their natural villages to their enterprises. Members who remained in farming and still lived in their old neighborhoods were to be regrouped into new branches or cells. If the party members had joined an occupation that necessitated prolonged absence from their home villages (e.g., transporters or contract laborers), they were required to form their own special party organs. Party members who were self-employed and needed to be absent from home would be loosely attached to a home party organ. Finally, members who belonged to the individual responsibility households had to be combined into party *zhibu* or cells.[52]

But basically, the party put the burden upon the lower levels to experiment with new organizational formats to fit their local situations. Although the press reported a number of local experiments in connection with the reorganization, no uniform national model was announced.[53]

On paper, the party's plan represented a flexible attempt to bring the party to the members rather than the other way around, by setting up new party organs according to the party members' residential neighborhoods, professions, employment location, or other needs. It also appeared to be an effort to decentralize power in the rural areas by reducing the size of basic-level units. The typical rural party unit tended to become smaller and have fewer members, as each *xiang* or *zhen* created more branches to cover the multitude of new enterprises, and each village created more cells.[54] While this appeared to be a more rational approach to recapturing the newly mobile members than was the old format, its impact was suspect for several reasons.

First, the magnitude of the task of restructuring was beyond the rural party's organizational capabilities in many places. Even the party itself conceded that it would be impossible to reassert even nominal control over certain categories of its members.[55] In many places, the party organ was readily sympathetic to the members' work needs and refrained from enforcing the party's requirements. This enabled the economically more active members to evade the party's control, while those who were tied to farming the land found themselves more vulnerable.

Second, the significant increase in the number of basic-level party organs necessitated a corresponding increase in the number of rural leading cadres. But traditionally the rural party leaders had regarded farming as a more important occupation than the enterprises in the rural areas. Therefore, there was a long-standing practice of assigning the least competent party members or cadres (often the old, infirm, or handicapped) to manage party work in the enterprises, which produced relatively ineffective party work in those units. This situation was exacerbated by the sudden increase in the number of rural enterprises, and the slowdown of rural party recruitment in recent years. Many new enterprises simply did not have enough party members to form a party cell, resulting in the absence of party work in a significant number of these enterprises.[56]

Third, even when the rural party organs conscientiously implemented the party's directives, their control over members was probably significantly reduced. The cornerstone of the rural party's organizational strength used to be the tightly knit cells. Members of these organs shared similar life-styles and out-looks, common interests, and enduring friendships. But this kind of solidarity gradually disappeared in the 1980s; now a branch might consist of members who had different social or geographical origins and personal interests, and might be so busy with their economic pursuits that they hardly had the time or inclination to interact with each other in the party's organizational context. In other words, the network of crisscrossing social ties and peer group pressures that used to lend great strength to the smaller and more permanent party organizations had been eroded by the reconstitution.[57]

As rural discipline and organizational strength continued its downward slide, the task of restructuring the rural party was never energetically implemented. The party conducted a number of surveys to find out the conditions of rural party organizations and members. The results for the three Northeastern provinces (Liaoning, Jilin, and Heilongjiang) indicated that only 33.8 percent of rural party branches were regarded as in a "healthy" situation, while 48.5 percent were judged as mediocre, 15.1 percent as poor, and 2.6 percent as "paralyzed." The province of Jiangsu evaluated its own rural party members and concluded that only 40 percent were qualified, 50 percent were mediocre, and 10 percent were unqualified.[58]

These regional survey results were corroborated by a national survey con-ducted by the Central Organization Department covering nineteen provinces, autonomous regions, and municipalities. The national survey concluded that only about 30 percent of rural party branches and members were in a sufficiently healthy position to implement the party's policies and perform the party's normal functions in the countryside, while 50 percent of them suffered from low spirits and could not effectively perform their duties, and another 20 percent could not function at all.[59]

The rural party's organizational decay was not appreciably arrested by the rectification campaign. By late 1986, the *People's Daily* admitted that a large number of the mobile rural party members were still not affiliated with either the home village party organs or the party organs at their workplace.[60] Many branches still did not possess a full complement of leaders, and nobody was in charge of convening party meetings, collecting party dues, or conducting party activities.[61] After the spring of 1987, the rural party leaders' attention was in-creasingly distracted by the fall of Hu Yaobang, and the uncertainties created by the anti–bourgeois liberalization campaign. For practical purposes, the effort to restructure the rural party had simply lost its saliency.

In sum, the decade following Mao's death was a tumultuous period for the party's rural organization. During much of the PRC's early history, the party's organizational needs always took precedence over other considerations. Party members were assigned to party organs according to the party's needs, and the members were never asked about their preferences. Traditionally, the party simply set up branches on the brigade level or cells on the team level and instructed members to gravitate around these organs to conduct party operations.

But the post-Mao rural developments greatly reduced the party's organizational initiative. They posed new obstacles to the party's traditional organizational format, management system, and educational methods in the rural areas.[62] The spatial and occupational mobility acquired by vast numbers of party members inevitably loosened their party affiliation. The enormous increase of new economic activities far exceeded the party's ability to establish leadership over them. By the mid-1980s, the party was being increasingly pushed to the sideline in many places.

In this connection, two recent developments may be of particular interest. According to State Statistics Bureau, in the five years between 1983 and 1988, about 20 million Chinese rural people had moved to another location in search of new economic opportunities. Of this number, about 14 million rural people had moved into urban areas. The rate of migration in 1987 was double that in 1982.[63] In addition, according to Song Jian, the PRC's state commissioner of science and technology, the product output of *xiang* and *zhen* enterprises had reached RMB $460 billion in 1987. This marked the first time that such enterprises' output exceeded the output from growing grain and other commercial crops. He estimated that about 80 million peasants had shifted from planting crops to industrial jobs. Furthermore, private individuals also ventured into the business of setting up scientific and technical enterprises in the countryside. In 1988 alone, some 12,800 civilian-owned (nonstate) enterprises were registered with the county governments.[64] Both were important signs of the vitality of the private economy. As these trends continue, the prospects for the party to regain its organizational control over rural party members may grow progressively dimmer.

Rural Party Recruitment

As noted previously, the CCP's rural recruitment activities in the 1950s were undertaken only intermittently to meet the specific political needs of the time, such as the land collectivization campaign and the Great Leap Forward. In the 1970s, the rural party's primary interest was to recruit virtually all the cadres working in the production teams to become members.[65] While the party pursued these special targets energetically, its recruitment of ordinary peasants slackened off considerably. Rural recruitment during the Maoist era gave top priorities to the poor, lower, and middle peasants because they had the proper class credentials.[66] But the new economic reforms created new conditions that brought a fundamental change to the party's rural recruitment policy in the 1980s. The party now believed that it was no longer enough for good party members to have the ability to do solid political work, but they must also be young, better educated, and possess technical knowledge, managerial skills, and a more pragmatic and scientific leadership style.[67] Since the progressive models of productivity were the specialized households, keypoint households, and economic combines, the party instructed that rural recruitment policy must put the emphasis on these people as well as educated rural youths and village school teachers.[68]

Slowdown of Recruitment in the 1980s

Notwithstanding these fundamental policy changes, their actual implementation was far from satisfactory. Highly publicized cases from many rural places suggested a general pattern of conspicuous slowdown of recruitment activities since the late 1970s. As the *Farmers' Daily* admitted in early 1985, basic-level party organs in many rural places had actually suspended their recruitment work entirely by the early 1980s.[69] In this general decline of rural recruitment, the lack of infusion of youth and women became a particularly serious problem.

By the early 1980s, the shrinking portion of youth in the party's overall membership had become impossible to ignore. But this problem was possibly far graver in the rural areas than in the urban areas. Indeed, the party press publicized a number of cases in which people below age 25 constituted a mere 2–3 percent of the rural party membership. In some cases, only one of every ten new party members recruited since the late 1970s was a rural youth, while in other cases no youth was recruited at all.[70]

The decline of recruitment of women was equally noticeable. For many years, women had been praised as "holding up half of the sky" under the PRC. In China, a much larger portion of women worked outside the households in a greater variety of professions than in most other underdeveloped countries. In addition to being active in the political work of their own work units, they were the targets of political mobilization by a number of women's organizations. Recruitment of women had always been a major task for the CCP. Therefore, employment outside the home made women susceptible to politicization but also gave them the incentive to join the Communist Party. But in recent years, there has been a noticeable drop of female recruits into the party on the village level. Sometimes, not a single woman would be recruited by the lower-level party organ in a year. As a consequence, the overall portion of female members declined in the rural party.[71]

Factors Contributing to Declining Rural Recruitment

How does one explain the decline of recruitment work in the rural areas? Analytically, there are two sets of factors, one related to the rural party's inability to conduct recruitment aggressively, and the other related to the peasants' falling interest in party membership.

The Party's Loss of Effectiveness

Insofar as the rural party was concerned, the main problem was the decline of its organizational resources and commitment. Sometimes, the organization department for an entire county had only three or four recruitment workers, which was hardly enough. Many party secretaries had no desire to mount an aggressive recruitment drive but preferred to wait for applications to come to them.[72]

Many rural party cadres and members were preoccupied by their own economic pursuits and did not regard recruitment as a high-priority task. The rural party's own operations were also hampered by the trend of commercialization that swept the country, and many rural party workers were only interested in tasks that carried bonuses or promised promotions. Since recruitment work was not rewarded with these benefits, there was almost no incentive for party workers to invest their time to do a good job in recruitment.[73]

Many party cadres and members were particularly unenthusiastic about recruiting rural youths, especially educated youths, for additional reasons. The existence of a serious generation gap between the party veterans and the rural youths was a readily observable phenomenon. The veterans were offended by the youths' faddish life-styles, or their fascination with new ideas, or the fact that they had more money to spend. They were equally upset by the more prosperous members of the "two households" (specialized and keypoint households) and regarded their economic activities as unscrupulous profiteering. Members of these households were frequently looked down on as inexperienced in revolution, immature in ideology, and unreliable in politics, and therefore unworthy for party membership.[74]

Jealousy was widely felt by party bosses and members toward educated rural youths. Many party secretaries were afraid of losing their leadership positions if more talented people were admitted into the party.[75] This fear was most palpable in the village-level party organs because of their simplified structure. With about twenty members in a typical branch, a single better-educated youthful member could outshine the rest and put the ignorant leader in a very uncomfortable position.

The decline of the Communist Youth League in the countryside also reduced the party's ability to attract youths. The CYL's effort to strengthen itself in the rural areas in the early 1980s quickly lost steam. The percentage of rural members in the CYL's total membership continued to shrink, until by mid-1986 the number of rural-based CYL members in some provinces was even smaller than the number of CCP members in those same provinces.[76] Deprived of an effective CYL as its assistant, the party's ability to reach the rural youths was substantially reduced.

Finally, many traditional concepts also hindered the party's rural recruitment. Many rural party cadres still regarded proper class backgrounds as essential for membership and confined recruitment to people from "poor, lower, and middle peasant" backgrounds. Incumbent cadres and factory workers were also favored candidates, resulting in the neglect of the progressive and youthful peasants.[77] Since many rural party bosses assumed that the party's rural functions would decrease in correspondence with the expansion of the individual responsibility system, they concluded that there was no longer a need for aggressive recruitment.

Peasants' Loss of Political Interest

Yet such rigid and ineffective recruitment policies constituted only half of the story. In an earlier age, even these multiple handicaps could not have discouraged peasants from applying for membership. The most important difference in the 1980s was that many rural people had lost interest in party membership. Among the reasons for this new mentality were the precipitous decline of the party's prestige, the loosening of its grip over the key aspects of rural life, and the corresponding decline of both the spiritual gratification and material advantages that party membership used to confer. Many people now actually viewed party membership as a detriment to their economic interests.[78]

There had been a particularly pronounced change of the values held by rural youths. To them, party membership was not a status symbol, but a social liability. In some cases, rural youths who filed applications for admission felt compelled to do so surreptitiously so that they would not be ridiculed by their peers. By the mid-1980s, the disinterest of rural youths in party membership had reached an alarming rate and prompted a number of articles in the party press highlighting the plight of rural areas. In many such cases, less than 1 percent of rural youths (defined as below 25 years of age) ever submitted applications for party membership.[79]

The decline of recruitment of females also had its special reasons. The economic changes since the late 1970s had caused politics to lose its saliency in many rural women's minds. When given the option to manage their own labor input, many households showed a preference to send the men to the field and keep the women at home to attend to household duties or manage other sideline activities (such as raising poultry). As a result, women became more insulated from party functionaries, and less susceptible to political mobilization and indoctrination. This trend was also accompanied by a subtle change of rural values whereby politically active women were viewed as undesirable marriage prospects for the young men in the villages.[80]

These factors explain why it was common for many rural party organs to experience stagnant recruitment. In some cases, village party organs actually had no recruits for several years in a row, and some even suffered negative growth.

Age and Education Profile of the Rural Party

The rural party's inability to maintain a high recruitment pace means that the party has so far failed to free itself of some of its most severe liabilities. Two such liabilities that may have long-term impact on the party in the countryside are the members' age structure and their educational qualifications.

The neglect of the recruitment of rural youths into the party has had a direct impact on the age structure. Many cases reported in the Chinese press painted a similar picture of the aging of the rural party. For example, a survey of 56,570 village-level party members in the Chengde region of Hebei in 1984 showed that 53.3 percent were above 46 years of age. In Nantong District of Chongqing Municipality, 49 percent of the party members were above 46 years of age in 1985.[81] In many rural places, the party members' age resembled an inverted pyramid, with half or more of the total members above 46 years of age, members in their forties and thirties in decreasing numbers, and members between 18 and 25 constituting only 2 or 3 percent.

The slowdown of recruitment also denied the rural party a chance to reverse the problem of poor educational qualifications, which had plagued it since Liberation. By November 1984, only 0.4 percent of the 22.65 million rural party members (or about 90,600 people) had college-level culture. On the low end, in contrast, 68.4 percent of the rural members (or about 15,490,260 people) had only primary-school level or were illiterate. This leaves 31.2 percent (or about 7,066,800 people) of rural party members with either junior or senior high school level. Since about 120 million people in rural China had a junior high school level or better, this means that only 6 percent (7 million) of these educated rural people were party members, while the remaining 94 percent were outside the party.[82]

In using these aggregate national figures, one must be aware of the existence of enormous geographical extremes. While a small number of rural areas near the big cities and along the east coast might have a better educational profile, many other places, especially the interior and mountainous regions, would have far worse profiles.[83]

Long-Term Implications

The current age structure of rural party members not only widened the generational gap within the party itself, but also lengthened the intellectual and emotional distance between the party and the rest of the rural population, which was considerably younger. The contrast becomes stark when the party members' age distribution is juxtaposed to that of the rural adult population. Equally important, but often not adequately discussed, is the fact that many rural party members were already too old and too frail to perform normal party work.[84] If the party should continue to fail to reverse this trend for another decade, as was the case between 1977 and 1987, the consequences could indeed become enormous.

The available data leave no doubt that the party did an extremely poor job in equipping itself to facilitate a technological transformation of rural China. The overwhelming majority of its present members were the political type (ignorant but with solid class backgrounds), while large numbers of rural teachers, cadres, young peasants, and skilled producers in many professions were not party members. Yet the latter groups included precisely the people who in the 1980s had become the backbone of rural economic growth. It was they who had culture, knew about science and technology, possessed managerial talent, and were entrepreneurial and resourceful. Their exclusion from the party or their disinclination to join can only raise an embarrassing theoretical question about the party's credentials to occupy the vanguard position, and a practical question about its ability to play the role of modernizing agent in the countryside. If the present trend persists, the rural party not only may have to abdicate its "leading role," but may not even qualify to play an "active role" in China's rural modernization. As noted in chapter 5, the party put tremendous pressure on the basic-level organs to conduct recruitment more aggressively. The result was that recruitment was conducted indiscriminately to fulfill quotas at the expense of the quality of the membership.[85] On the basis of the rural party's past track record, one can reasonably assume that the recruitment drive of 1985–88 was conducted in a far worse manner in rural areas than in urban areas. Very possibly, large numbers of unqualified or even unethical people (opportunists, friends and relatives of rural party bosses, and even local bullies) exploited this opportunity to enter the CCP, further damaging the reputation of the party. On the other hand, there were also indications that the recruitment drive failed to attract enough people who were in the front line of rural productive work.[86] This, then, raises the serious question of what may be the future of the Chinese Communist Party.

Rural Party Discipline Problems

Misconduct by rural party members is nothing new in the PRC. During the Maoist years, however, the highly centralized economic system severely limited the access of rural cadres and party members to resources. Consequently, their misconduct usually took the form of unfair distribution of work and grain, with the minority of powerful cadres receiving disproportionately larger shares of the benefits from the production unit than the majority of toilers. Such unjust production relations were one contributing reason for the low productivity of Chinese agriculture.

Noneconomic forms of misconduct usually included physical brutality toward peasants, the forceful seizure of their property, or the raping of their wives and daughters by party bosses, especially when the victims belonged to the wrong social classes. The privileges enjoyed by rural cadres and party members amounted to a heavy burden upon the peasants and were a powerful factor contributing to the growth of the size of rural party and government bureaucracies over the years. By the 1980s, every three or four peasant families in many places were required to support one cadre who did not participate in farm labor.[87]

The party over the years had tried many formulas to tighten rural discipline, but they never produced any lasting successes.[88] During the Cultural Revolution, the vast countryside was not nearly as adversely affected as the urban areas. Rural areas even served as the haven for numerous persecuted party leaders and intellectuals in exile. Mao also let it be known that grain production should not be affected by political upheavals. Consequently, the rural leaders were not affected by the power struggles that swept through the urban areas and stayed in office into the 1980s.

Overall, therefore, rural party members' misconduct was different from the urban areas in nature and magnitude. As long as the conditions of a subsistence agriculture prevailed, the rewards of misconduct were limited. Basically, the most common forms of misconduct by rural party cadres and members were their high-handed leadership styles (commandism), irregularities in work-point assignments or grain allocations, and petty larceny.

Misconduct Stimulated by Initial Economic Reform

The situation began to change after the late 1970s. Many old forms of corruption and unethical conduct reached new levels of intensity, and new forms of misconduct began to emerge. The embezzlement of public funds through what was euphemistically called "personal loans" increased. By the mid-1980s, party data indicated that a large number of cadres and members all over the country were pilfering public funds as "personal loans," with sums ranging from several tens of millions of RMB in some provinces to as much as hundreds of millions of RMB in other provinces.[89]

The building of fancier and taller houses, excessive feasting and drinking, and other forms of conspicuous consumption became routine events among rural leaders.[90] They not only collected illegal taxes and levies, and extorted money from the peasants, but even encouraged gambling, revived clan conflict, and participated in superstitious activities.[91]

A new and illegal activity experiencing a sharp rise was the sale, rental, or stealing of public land to build personal residences. During this initial stage, public land and funds became the first objects of plunder by the rural cadres and party members because they were the most readily accessible items. Such behavior benefited not only the party members and cadres but also friends and relatives.[92]

Advanced Forms of Misconduct

As the scope of rural reforms broadened, and as new economic opportunities emerged, rural cadres and party members also developed more sophisticated schemes of economic crimes. Since many had no productive skills or market knowledge to generate incomes, they naturally exploited their administrative powers to achieve wealth. Many government services still were needed by the peasants, and most of them carried an illegal service charge.[93] In other words, every time the peasants' needs were processed through the hands of the cadres, they created opportunities for the latter to indulge in corruption.

The policy to allow Chinese peasants to form their own private enterprises also came as a bonanza for the rural bosses. Some immediately diverted public funds to form their own private enterprises. Others blackmailed peasants into giving them free shares in private enterprises. Once cadres and party members started their own enterprises, they were able to use their power to obtain scarce materials, win lucrative contracts, or assign profitable distribution routes to their own enterprises.[94]

The decline of party discipline in the countryside took on new dimensions in the 1980s. In many instances, party cadres and members acquiesced or actively participated in such practices as arranged and compulsory marriages, the abuse of women, sale of children, and medical quackery, in direct contravention to the party's sociocultural policies and its avowed revolutionary stand.[95] Equally noteworthy were the negative examples they set in violating the official one-child family policy. Many defied the government's ban against multiple pregnancies until they obtained a son. They proudly paid the fines for violating the one-child family policy, and even held banquets to celebrate the birth of a son. Such blatant behavior was a major reason why it was much harder for the policy to be enforced on the rest of the rural population after the mid-1980s.[96]

Therefore, whereas public attention in the urban areas was focused on the misconduct by top leaders and their children, China's peasants were much more angered by the misconduct of party cadres and members on the village level, because it is on these levels that the rural masses must bear the burden of poor party discipline. The decline of discipline on these levels greatly undermined the party's prestige in the minds of the peasants.

Rural Rectification

Even though the party's rectification campaign had been in operation in the urban areas since 1983, its relevance to the rural areas was still being widely doubted among rural party members when the rectification actually began in the countryside. In 1985, the mood of rural members toward rectification was one of anxiety, apprehension, and opposition. Many people believed that rectification should be confined to the urban-based leading organs where the top cadres had been the culprits. If these problems could be resolved, the lower levels would follow their example. Others were worried that a rectification campaign might revive the harsh methods of struggle and threaten the burgeoning vitality of the new rural economy, or even undo the economic gains of the past several years. Thus, many party cadres and members had already made up their minds to sit out the campaign and stay uninvolved.[97]

Between 1983 and 1985, rural disciplinary problems had actually gone from bad to worse as many rural party cadres and members realized that they had two more years to enrich themselves before rectification would arrive. When they witnessed how ineffectively the campaign was being conducted in the urban areas, many also felt assured that they could evade the party's disciplinary actions. Therefore, the decision to conduct the rectification campaign by stages not only did not enable the vast rural areas to better prepare for it, but ironically caused the conditions of misconduct to deteriorate to extremely grave proportions.

The Party's Strategies

In November 1985, the party announced that rural basic-level party rectification would begin shortly and last until the spring of 1987, during which rectification would be conducted consecutively on the *qu, xiang*, and village levels, each for about three or four months.[98] Whereas the party had granted party organs in the urban phase much leeway to conduct their rectification, it issued detailed instructions on how the rectification should be conducted in the rural areas, because it was afraid that rural organs might conduct the campaign too violently. In particular, the party warned against the possibility of committing excesses and producing a detrimental economic impact.

The PRC's history provided ample illustration of how, with rare exceptions, political campaigns in the countryside were nearly always conducted more mechanically, ruthlessly, and excessively, and produced far bloodier results than their urban counterparts. To prevent a recurrence of this outcome, the party instructed that rural rectification should put emphasis on "positive education" to raise members' ideological consciousness. As the party stated,

> Our party must take seriously the historical lesson of our past when, on a number of occasions, our rural work had come under the sway of leftist tendencies. In conducting rectification, rural party organizations shall not be allowed to extract confessions by coercion, shall not be allowed to hold struggle meetings, shall not be allowed to trace or expand a problem to absurd extremes. . . . They must forbid beating, scolding, and other forms of personal attacks. They must forbid people to seize rectification as a pretext to launch personal vendettas and retaliation. They must prevent the clan organizations from interfering with rectification work.[99]

On the issue of avoiding economic damage, the party was equally explicit:

> It must be pointed out emphatically: rural rectification must firmly serve the purpose of promoting reform and economic development, and implementing the party's rural policies. . . . [Therefore,] whenever major policies are at issue, lower-level party organizations must handle them with extreme care, promptly seek guidance from above, and refrain from taking action until approval is granted.[100]

The party pointed out that it was imperative for rectification not to interfere with production, and that it be conducted only during off seasons and holidays.[101]

Although the rural rectification was only a continuation of the party's overall rectification, it was clear from the beginning of the rural phase that the party's objectives had been sharply reduced. For one thing, the party announced that rural rectification did not need to address the issue of the "three types." In March 1986, Hu Yaobang instructed that rural rectification should focus primarily on two issues affecting the basic-level party cadres and members: the existence of "abuse of privileges for personal gains," and "illegal and undisciplined conduct." Subsequently, these issues were referred to as the "two serious [offenses]," the elimination of which became the focal point of the rural rectification.[102]

But the path of implementation in the rural areas was as rocky as in the urban areas. Not only were many of the factors impeding the urban phase of rectification present in the rural phase, but the rural areas had their own peculiar handicaps. Since a large number of rural cadres and members of the party's disciplinary structure had committed the "two serious offenses," they obviously could not be expected to expose their own misconduct. Consequently, they tried to divert the attention of the campaign by contending that rectification should provide "positive education" and not extract confessions through ugly confrontations. Others sought to deflect criticisms by arguing that the main focus of rectification was to acquaint party members with the concepts of commodity economy.[103]

If these rural party leaders could not be relied on to conduct rectification seriously, it was equally unrealistic to expect the rural party members to expose their leaders' wrongdoing. Rural members lived in very close physical proximity, sometimes for generations, and therefore were even more reluctant to antagonize their colleagues and neighbors. They also knew from past experience that the cost of reprisals from these local tyrants could be terribly high.

The party had probably anticipated such difficulties and decided that the rural rectification must be conducted differently from the urban rectification in one important aspect. During the urban phase, the party had specifically eschewed the use of "work teams," because such teams had often been associated with many excesses in earlier political campaigns. But in late 1985, the party required all provincial, district, county, and *xiang* party organizations to dispatch work teams (sometimes also called "teams of liaison-personnel") to participate in village-level rectification as propagandists, liaison agents, and supervisors. By late October 1986, nearly 550,000 cadres had been sent to the villages to help conduct rectification.[104] In provinces with fewer party members, such as Shaanxi, several thousand cadres were selected and sent downward. In provinces with larger party memberships, such as Hebei or Hubei, the number often reached 50,000 or more.[105]

Factors Affecting Implementation

Impressive as these numerical claims may be, their contribution to rural rectification is suspect. By early 1986, many county-level party secretaries had already become so disinterested in the whole campaign that they simply dreaded the prospects of having to go through an additional rural stage of rectification on the *xiang* and village levels.[106] They were in no mood to carry out the task of finding so many qualified cadres and sending them down to the villages.

Even when cadres were actually sent downward, they often felt unwelcome by the party members in the villages, who were required to house and feed them.[107] Their contribution to the local rectification process was severely constrained by their short stay in the villages as well as by their total unfamiliarity with the intricacies of local politics and personages. The peasants' highly dispersed residential pattern, their new physical mobility, and their preoccupation with their productive work only compounded the difficulties. Most work-team members were equally anxious to bring the rectification process to an end so that they could go home. By this time, the poor performance of the urban phase of rectification had become so apparent and the political atmosphere in the countryside had changed so drastically that even these work teams from above could not reverse the situation.

The three to four months allotted to party organs on each rural level to conduct their rectification were woefully inadequate to do a meaningful job. Yet many places even tried to shorten this length by omitting key aspects of the prescribed work. In some cases, the timetable was so compressed and the pressure to finish rectification work was so great that the entire process was pushed through the villages in less than one month.[108] In some places, a sizable portion of the village party branch and members never participated in the rectification process at all.[109] This explains why many provinces (e.g., Hebei and Guizhou) reported that they had already completed their rural rectification before October 1986, when most provinces had barely begun their village-level rectification.[110] There was nearly universal desire among rural party organs to rush through the rectification process to allow all party members to register indiscriminately and return to normal life.[111] As one Beijing-based party journal admitted in 1987, many leading party cadres in the rural areas obviously could not wait for the village rectification to be brought to an end, "so that they could focus attention on economic issues."[112]

Indeed, just like during the urban rectification, the tension between conducting a meaningful rectification and pursuing economic development was acutely felt in the rural areas. In late 1986, the party found that many rural leaders equated rectification with promoting new economic concepts and developing commodities and marketing techniques. Rural leaders defended such practices as constituting a "new-style party rectification" and contended that party members should be considered to have been sufficiently rectified and transformed if they could master these new economic concepts and techniques. On the other hand, they dismissed the "two serious offenses" as only marginal issues. Even though the party repeatedly criticized these local misinterpretations, it was unable to change rural party leaders' propensity to place economic interests above rectification needs.[113]

Just like their urban counterparts, rural leaders did not want to enforce discipline because they were reluctant to harm personal relations. Furthermore, since the rural party had traditionally encountered difficulty in attracting capable cadres to serve in the rural areas, its leaders were reluctant to prosecute incumbent cadres too earnestly for fear of scaring away future prospects.[114]

But another major factor behind their inaction was their fear of being accused of committing leftist errors. This fear was quite understandable in view of the party's ambiguous instructions. For instance, although numerous party members had compromised themselves in many economic activities since reform was launched, the party's guideline stated that "In all cases where the nature of such activities is ambiguous or hard to define . . . they do not need to be dealt with during this rectification." Instead, the party said that it would look for ways to solve these problems at an unspecified future date.[115]

Likewise, although the party wanted the rural rectification to correct cadres' misuse of privileges for self-enrichment, it provided a big loophole when it said, "but if the conditions for dealing with these cases are not present, then it is permissible to solve them after the conclusion of the present rectification campaign." Finally, with respect to those who had committed serious errors of coercion and commandism, the party's instruction was that they should be educated rather than disciplined as long as these acts were committed because the cadres were under the pressure of time, heavy workload, or emotional stress.[116]

Thus, on the one hand, all rural-level party organizations were told to resolutely correct serious misconduct, but on the other hand, they were given opportunities to evade these responsibilities. Taking a cue from the national party, the Sichuan provincial party specifically cautioned lower-level organs not to "expel people from the party lightly."[117] Indeed, the national leaders were genuinely eager to insulate the rural areas from further political instability in order to protect their economic accomplishments.

In this sense, the outbreak of urban unrest in the winter of 1986 and the subsequent high-level power struggle that led to the downfall of General Secretary Hu Yaobang assumed special importance. The timing could not have been worse, as this series of events occurred when the rural rectification was entering its final and presumably most critical stage. The entire party's attention was so riveted to the power struggle in Beijing that rural rectification work virtually came to a dead stop. Equally important was Acting General Secretary Zhao Ziyang's first important political message in which he announced that the rural areas would be exempt from the new anti–bourgeois liberalization campaign. His words virtually assured rural party cadres and members that they had no need to fear a renewed tightening of party discipline in the countryside. After these new developments, it became impossible for rural rectification to regain any momentum.

In April 1987, the village-level party rectification was finally brought to its conclusion. As usual, the party claimed many accomplishments: nearly all of the twenty million party members in some one million party branches participated in rural rectification. The financial mess in many villages had been cleared up, and the bulk of the monies taken out by cadres as personal loans had been returned to the public coffers. Most predictably, only "5 percent" of village-level party units had not successfully implemented the campaign.[118]

The available evidence makes it impossible to accept the veracity of the party's statement. In many places, party leaders' disinterest in rectification remained to the very end of rural rectification. They either tried to minimize their disciplinary problems or refused to investigate or punish known criminals.[119] The problem of party style was not improved, and party members failed, sometimes disastrously, to present themselves as models and vanguards to the masses. On the contrary, unqualified members were allowed to register and keep their party membership.[120] The "two serious offenses" had only worsened, and mass discontent increased sharply. Overall, the rural rectification campaign represented wasted energy and accomplished little insofar as discipline was concerned. This was hardly surprising when one remembers what had happened during the earlier, urban phase of rectification.

The Party's Changing Role in the Rural Areas

Since Liberation, China's rural power structure had undergone several changes. In the early 1950s, power was divided among the administrative heads of *xiang* and *qu*, the economic managers of cooperatives or production teams, and the public security and court personnel. But after the creation of people's communes in 1958, all powers (governmental, economic, and public security) were concentrated in the hands of a small number of people, particularly party secretaries. They became the local tyrants because they personified the party and the state, enjoyed nearly complete control over people's livelihood from cradle to grave, and often exercised their powers autocratically, against which the average peasants were virtually defenseless. Basically, their style of work was mechanical and coercive and relied heavily on simplistic and commandistic methods to carry out orders from above.[121] It was the peasants' lot to endure their leaders for as long as the party had absolute domination over the countryside.

But the rapid changes in the post-Mao era generated a basic transformation in the relationship between the rural party and the peasant masses that was manifested in two critical areas. First, the age and educational differences between them began to show their importance. Second, the expansion of economic opportunities began to undercut the rural party's centrality.

Age and Educational Gaps

The dynamics of China's demographic development created a trend that the population was getting younger with time. By the late 1970s, peasants above 50

Table 10

Literacy Rates of Chinese People by Age Group, 1987

Age	Percent literate
12–14	93
15–19	92
20–24	91
25–29	87
30–34	80
35–39	75
40–44	72
45–49	61
50–54	47
55–59	38
60–64	32
65 and over	21

Source: *Zhongguo 1987 nian 1% renkou chouyang diaocha ziliao* (Beijing: Chinese Statistical Press, 1988), tables 5–9.

years of age constituted only about 20 percent of the total rural work force, while those between 16 and 30 constituted over half of the rural working population, with those between 30 and 50 making up the balance. In other words, young and middle-aged peasants accounted for over 80 percent of the rural working population.[122] In addition, the national trend is that younger Chinese, both rural and urban, are likely to be much better educated than their elders (see table 10). In contrast, the rural party membership and particularly the rural cadre corps were plagued by the problem of the long-term aging process, as previously discussed. In addition, those in their thirties and forties contained many leftists and people of dubious moral character who had joined the party during the Cultural Revolution when party admissions were conducted indiscriminately. In some localities, such members accounted for over 40 percent of the total membership.[123]

Rural party leaders and cadres were even older than the rank and file, and extremely few people below 25 years of age were appointed as party branch leaders, the lowest party organs in the rural areas.[124] This is hardly surprising if one examines the origins of China's rural leadership. Those who rose within the rural areas were the poorer peasants who joined the party as youths during the revolutionary war or the land reforms of the early 1950s, who were promoted to cadre positions on account of their political activism. Thereafter, they stayed in these positions for the ensuing decades.

Another source of rural leadership was demobilized veterans from the PLA. The overwhelming majority of PLA soldiers since Liberation had been recruited from the countryside. Because the PRC had for many years followed the practice of sending demobilized soldiers back to their native places, soldiers from the urban and rural areas usually displayed different propensities. Most urban soldiers preferred to learn a trade or skill in the army that would enable them to get a better job in the urban areas after returning to civilian life. They were less interested in a lifetime career in the military.

Rural soldiers, on the other hand, were usually unenthused by the prospects of returning to the drudgery of farming life. Therefore, many wanted to stay in the army as professional soldiers. While some succeeded in doing so, the overwhelming majority of farm youths still had to be demobilized and returned to their villages. This latter group wanted to do everything possible to use their military service as a stepping stone to gain admission into the party and the rural cadre corps to avoid the life of plain peasants upon demobilization. This resulted in a large number of demobilized PLA soldiers among rural cadres.

In the late 1970s and 1980s, China's countryside was still overshadowed by a party structure very much in the hands of these two types of cadres. Both groups gained their positions through loyalty, class background, and political skills and performance.[125] Both groups were equally poorly educated: many were illiterate and possessed limited and simplistic comprehension of the ideology. But their allegiance to the party was strong and their leadership style was autocratic, haughty, and sometimes downright barbaric. In some places, rural cadres habitually used beating and cursing in dealing with the masses.[126] In contrast to their leaders, the younger Chinese peasants were more resourceful, more receptive to change, and much more aggressive in exploiting the new economic opportunities of the 1980s. They were prone to be discontent with the status quo, more materialistic, and less committed to traditional values. The Cultural Revolution also taught them invaluable lessons and made them much wiser and more cynical about politics.

What this meant was the emergence of a serious gulf between the rural leadership and masses when the objective conditions made such a situation possible. Survey data from many localities indicated the existence of serious mental and behavioral antagonism between the older rural cadres and the younger elements of the peasant masses. Many older cadres found it difficult to communicate with the younger peasants and regarded the latter as "crooked," "conceited," "contentious," or "undisciplined," having "low political consciousness." They were resentful and contemptuous of the younger peasants and would refuse, or did not know how, to deal with them. Consequently, not only was the party's recruitment work neglected, its political work was discarded because the cadres simply did not know how to conduct political work among the younger people.[127] The stagnation of the party's membership in the 1980s stood in sharp contrast to the dynamism in the rest of the rural society. The danger of the party's isolation from the masses had become serious indeed.

Declining Cadre Functions

For many years, party members below the county level occupied a huge number of administrative and managerial positions in the communes, brigades, and so forth. As such, the people were typically exempt from actual productive work or were only part-time peasants. In other words, the rural cadres' main functions previously had been political control, mobilization, and class struggle, and only marginally economic management and guidance. The majority wholeheartedly embraced the traditional economic views that held commercial activities in contempt and glorified the virtues of farming and self-sufficiency. Most were also ignorant about modern agricultural science.[128] Their livelihood was guaranteed by the existence of this sprawling rural administrative system.

This situation began to change after Mao's death. The basic-level rural cadres and party members' authority was severely challenged after the late 1970s; they felt confounded and did not know what to do. One thing, however, was clear. In this rapidly changing rural setting, cadres and members were no longer able to treat people as commandistically as before. The ordinary peasants now set their own work schedules and made major economic decisions without seeking permission from the party.

But even after the party had legitimized the rural reforms, it was for some time undecided on whether the reform measures should apply only to the ordinary peasants or also to party members and cadres. Thus from the late 1970s through the early 1980s, China's basic-level rural cadres and party members did not know whether they should participate in economically profitable activities. Only gradually did the party reach the decision that it was permissible for them to participate in the new economic activities, and many localities began actively to encourage party members to become keypoint families or specialized families. Yet even then, the party's message was ambiguous. For it said in effect that the only legitimate reason for cadres and members to participate in such economic activities was to demonstrate to the average peasants how to acquire wealth effectively, but that they should not go after wealth for its own sake.[129]

While the new line undoubtedly enabled many eager party members to join the bandwagon to strike it rich, it did little to remove the cognitive dissonance from the minds of many more cadres and members, who thought it best to play it safe and to allow the ordinary peasants to run their own affairs. What this means was that during a period of about five to seven years, much of the initiative for making changes in the rural areas was seized by the peasant masses without deference to the rural party. The paralysis of rural party cadres and members encouraged the peasant masses to go their own way, which further undercut the party's leadership position in the countryside.

Even after the party gave the green light for rural cadres and members to engage in economically profitable activities, only a few of them were actually capable of doing so, while many more simply lacked the necessary economic sense or ability. To maintain leadership positions in the new context, they needed not only to relearn their long-forgotten farming skills, but also to acquire new skills. Yet party members' low educational qualifications and cultural level prevented many from achieving this transformation.

The traditional policy of emphasizing political mobilization and class struggle rather than scientific and technological improvement in agriculture resulted in a severe shortage of agricultural expertise even though nearly 80 percent of Chinese lived in the rural areas and depended on agriculture for their living. In the late 1970s and early 1980s, the party simply did not have a large enough body of competent agricultural experts to help it fulfill its leadership functions in the countryside to meet the rising technical needs of the peasant masses at a time of rapid rural reforms.[130]

Although the party and state started to conduct training programs for cadres in the 1980s, the pace of upgrading their agricultural skills was very slow, and many such programs were extended only to high-level cadres and not basic-level cadres.[131] The party training schools or programs in many provinces specifically excluded rural basic-level party members because they did not regard this as their assignment, nor did they have the resources to do so. In Hebei Province, for instance, although rural members constituted 57 percent of the total party membership, no training program for them was offered up to 1986.[132]

Hence, the very people the party had counted on to promote its new policies and to serve as models of success had trouble correctly understanding these policies, lacked the technological know-how to lead the masses to implement the new policies, and were even incapable of improving their own livelihood.[133] In this respect, the case of Fujian was illuminating as it seemed to reflect a fairly widespread phenomenon. A survey in mid-1986 revealed that there were more "poor" party members in Fujian's total rural party membership proportionately than there were "poor" peasant households in the province's total peasant households.[134] Not surprisingly, the poorer peasants who had been given political advantages to join the party before now found it difficult to meet the new requirements for economic success.

Even when the more enterprising party members did well economically, they usually did not contribute to the party's cause. They often became engrossed in their own interests, lost interest in party work, or abused their privileges to get rich at the expense of the masses rather than helping the latter to get rich. The rural economic reforms reduced the centrality of both the party and its members in the rural areas and caused many formerly privileged people to suffer a relative deprivation in their economic well-being. In many places, party cadres and members only succeeded in assuming leadership in a small portion of the large number of new economic enterprises that sprang into existence in the countryside, a far cry from the old days when party members controlled practically all rural economic activities.[135] While some party cadres and members were invited by the peasants to play leading roles in these enterprises because of their organizational ability and better understanding of party policies, many others got their positions because of their extensive personal connections in the party and the government, which could open more doors and obtain more administrative advantages for their enterprises, mostly in an illegal way.[136]

In this new setting, the party's erstwhile strongholds in the countryside tended to feel particularly out of sync with the major socioeconomic value transformation that was sweeping through the rest of the society. These bastions of party support tended to become isolated pockets of backwardness. Faced with such threat of loss of power and relevance, it is not surprising that many old cadres and party members experienced severe disillusionment, bitterness, and demoralization and became fierce opponents of the economic and political reforms.

The separation of government from the commune, which occurred in the 1980s, only heightened the tension between the old rural elite and the new breed of Chinese peasants. The old cadres continued to barricade themselves in their party offices and clung to their residual administrative power for as long as they could, while the younger and better-educated peasants were busy expanding their activities through rural enterprises. The old cadres were not interested in recruiting younger people into the party, but they had neither a strategy to strengthen the rural party structure nor a plan to develop the rural economy.[137]

As the old rural elite's roles declined, the frequency of conflict between these two rural groups over personal interests increased. Numerous quarrels occurred between party members and ordinary people over capital, land, resources, and projects. The old elite tended to hang onto the old administrative practices. But the rural masses wanted less interference, more relaxation, and a broader scope of economic reforms. Under these circumstances, the party's relationship with the masses was significantly altered. The party no longer was regarded as the sole legitimate authority to set the terms of rural economic activities, and party cadres and members were no longer accepted as the vanguard in the rural society. On the contrary, many among the rural masses now regarded the party as a hindrance to their economic development that must be bypassed, and viewed party members as incompetent but unfair competitors in the new economic game.

10

Conclusion

THE EARLIER chapters of this work indicated that Deng Xiaoping's agenda upon resuming power in 1978 was to resuscitate the party quickly so that the country could march toward the goal of achieving the four modernizations. There is no doubt that the country was in deep economic trouble when Deng took over. The years of poor planning, mismanagement, and incessant campaigns had pushed the Chinese economy to the brink of bankruptcy.[1] What Deng wanted most urgently was to remove the impediments for the pursuit of rational economic policies by changing from the Maoist legacy, deradicalizing the ideology, downplaying the theme of class struggle and abandoning the "storming approach" of conducting political campaigns, and driving the remnants of the Gang of Four out of power. Deng's ultimate goal was to persuade the Chinese people to bury their memories of past sufferings and to "look forward" and work hard to achieve a greatly improved material life by the end of the century. The centerpiece of Deng's agenda since 1978 has been to build up the economy, because he strongly believed that the Chinese people's acceptance of party control could be assured if only the CCP could improve their economic conditions.

Deng further concluded that economic growth could be obtained only under conditions of unity and stability. As he said, "Before and above everything else, China needs stability. Without a stable environment, all other efforts will be in vain, and we will lose the gains we have already made. We need reforms, but we need stability before we can mount reforms. We will not be able to accomplish anything if we deviate from this point."[2]

How were these conditions to be achieved? Deng's stock answer was that unity must be maintained on the leadership level, and stability must be maintained through insistence on the absolute authority of the CCP over the state and society. His approach toward the party and Chinese politics was undoubtedly strongly influenced by his earlier career experience. It should be remembered that Deng was the general secretary of the party when the latter was at the peak of its power in the 1950s. Deng blamed the Cultural Revolution for having pushed Mao's cult of personality to extreme heights and undermined the party's domination over the masses. All along, Deng never regarded the CCP as the cause of the turmoil in the Cultural Revolution but only as its victim. To Deng, the rejection of the Cultural Revolution approach would be sufficient to restore the party to its previous status of predominance in the Chinese polity.

In this sense, it was hardly surprising that Deng was most emphatic among party leaders in espousing the four cardinal principles in the 1980s. Deng's actual views on three of these principles—Marxism, socialism, and proletarian dictatorship—were far less dogmatic, however, than his insistence on the fourth principle—the leadership of the Communist Party. Contrary to widespread expectations among the people, Deng never had serious democratic inclinations with regard to political issues even though he was ready to be pragmatic in economic policies. This was obvious as early as 1979 with his ruthless suppression of the Democracy Movement. His subsequent denunciations of "bourgeois liberalization" were only logical extensions of his strong stand on this point. In other words, even though Deng made tactical concessions to realities from time to time, he never wavered from his fundamentalist conviction in the need of maintaining the supremacy of the CCP in Chinese politics. Nor did he ever acknowledge any need to overhaul thoroughly the party itself. His goal was not a *transformation* of the party, but the *restoration* of the authority it enjoyed during the 1950s. Basically, Deng's views about the relationship among leadership unity, party dominance, and economic goals had not changed since his return to power in late 1978, and possibly had not changed since Liberation.

Given such vociferous insistence on the dominance of the Communist Party in Chinese politics, the intriguing question is how something like the Tiananmen Square incident of April–June 1989 could have happened. Why were the demonstrations in Beijing and other major cities able to draw such huge crowds? What factors sustained the emotional intensity of the demonstrations, and what did the demonstrators really want?

The party leaders, of course, had a ready answer to these questions. To Deng and his associates, the crisis resembled a turbulence and was caused by the interaction of two "climatic systems." As Deng contended on June 9, 1989, "This storm was bound to occur sooner or later. It was shaped by a major climate in the world and a minor climate inside China. It had to come, and it could not have been affected by people's subjective wills. The only question was when it would come, and how large its scale was going to be."[3]

According to the party's explanation, the "major climate" was caused by foreign enemies whose abiding goal was to bring about the transformation of China through peaceful means.[4] The eventual objective of these hostile and reactionary international forces was to make China abandon its socialist road and come under the domination of international monopolistic capital.[5]

The "minor climate," on the other hand, was caused by a small group of conspirators within China who favored bourgeois liberalization and schemed to overthrow the leadership of the CCP.[6] They advocated the total rejection of socialism in favor of wholesale adoption of Western ideas and institutions. The ringleaders of the "minor climate" were a few disgruntled intellectuals and ambitious and unscrupulous people, but they succeeded in misleading a lot of gullible students to perpetrate their political crimes. Therefore, the Tiananmen Square incident, in the words of the new general secretary, Jiang Zemin, was not "a tragedy" but "a counterrevolutionary riot to oppose the leadership of the CCP and to overthrow our socialist system."[7]

Insofar as the party's own responsibility for the incident was concerned, the leaders placed the major blame on the two previous general secretaries for not having been resolute enough in opposing bourgeois liberalization.[8] Corruption and poor discipline were mentioned as issues of complaint by the people, but they were by no means critical factors in precipitating the crisis.

The CCP's Crises in the 1980s

This explanation runs counter to the evidence assembled in this volume. While no one could have foreseen the actual events at Tiananmen Square, the discussions in the preceding chapters indicate that the crisis should have come as no surprise. The Tiananmen Square incident was but the flash point of the people's moral outrage and frustration with the quality of political life under the party's rule. The most serious danger to Chinese politics came from the CCP's own decaying process. By the early 1980s, the party had virtually lost its sense of mission and its reason for existence. Its organizational sinews had atrophied, its style of work had degenerated dangerously, and its prestige had plummeted. Although the party launched a rectification campaign, the unimaginative and perfunctory measures it took to correct its multiple problems had run out of steam by the mid-1980s. While the party could congratulate itself for having driven the "three types" out of office, it had little else to show as accomplishments.

To be sure, the party's decline coincided with the erosion of the Marxist-Leninist and Maoist ideology, but ideological erosion could hardly be blamed as the main factor for the decline. For one thing, the number of Chinese citizens or even CCP members who were conversant with the nuances of ideology was quite limited. Second, the party had gone through so many ideological twists and turns that most people had become accustomed to swallowing the current authoritative interpretation rather than scrutinizing the discrepancy between theory and realities. Third, during the decade of 1978–1988, the CCP's ideologues made several valiant efforts to reduce cognitive dissonance by adjusting their ideological stance to accommodate current policy needs. Deng's personal contribution to this effort was exemplified by his famous dictum, "White cat or black cat, the cat that catches mice is the good cat." In the early 1980s, the party admitted that the Marxist ideology needed "first to be upheld, and second to be developed."

The upshot of this new flexibility was the thesis of "socialism at its beginning stage" endorsed by the Thirteenth Party Congress in 1987, which provided an ingenious theoretical justification for the adoption of a wide range of capitalist practices.

Therefore, the root cause of the political crisis in the PRC was not that the people had lost faith in the ideology as such, but that the party under Deng was plagued by serious problems in at least three major areas: discipline, leadership, and relations with intellectuals.

Of these three problems, the party's difficult relations with the intellectuals has the longest history. In spite of the CCP's repeated avowals to respect the educated people and win them over, its relations with them ran into trouble almost from the very beginning of Deng's political return. In the ensuing years, the relationship has become more and more estranged.

It is recalled that the so-called crisis of trust and crisis of faith that marked the beginning of the deepening sense of alienation by China's educated people began with the Democracy Wall movement and underground organizations and publications of 1978–79. By 1980, a significant cultural change began to manifest itself on college campuses. Complaints were heard more frequently about how the paths of life under Communist rule had become progressively narrower. Toward the end of the year, college students began to agitate for the right to have free elections on campuses.

The anti–spiritual pollution campaign of 1982–83 did little to intimidate the college students. Unrest on individual campuses increased in both scale and frequency. On September 18, 1985, students combined their personal grievances and intellectual discontent with patriotic sentiments and successfully aroused a sizable following of nonstudents in public demonstrations. In 1986, college students were disappointed by the lack of progress in the promised political reforms and went into the streets again. Student demonstrations spread to many major cities during the fall of 1986 and the spring of 1987. But their demands were met with a crackdown. Deng reaffirmed his support for the four cardinal principles and denounced the student activities as manifestations of "bourgeois liberalization." After a brief hiatus, student unrest regained its momentum in 1988. In April, when the National People's Congress was in session, the college students demonstrated to demand redress for China's educational backwardness and for better treatment of intellectuals.[9]

Even when students showed no outward signs of unrest during these years, their mentality continued to undergo profound changes. Their confidence in the party and ideology slid even further.[10] Many college students became intensely interested in the political reforms of the USSR and Eastern Europe, as well as a harsh reevaluation of China's own culture.[11] Student-organized political activities, such as discussion groups and "democracy salons," mushroomed. Many well-known advocates of liberal ideas made public speeches on campuses in favor of private ownership, political pluralism, and leadership reforms.

After the second half of 1988, if not earlier, many educated people in China were anticipating major disturbances during the forthcoming anniversary of May Fourth in 1989. While they wanted to use the commemoration as a vehicle to express their discontent against the party and the government, the CCP tried desperately to mobilize the CYL, education departments, and government organs to contain it as a purely patriotic historical event without contemporary overtones. During the fall of 1988 and spring of 1989, students and intellectuals of all age groups became bolder by the day. They made open criticisms against public policies and party leaders, signed petitions for the release of political prisoners, and issued public demands for the redress of the party's past mistakes. But before May 4 arrived, former general secretary Hu Yaobang's death occurred in mid-April. This introduced an additional emotional dimension to the escalating confrontation between the party and the intellectuals and forced all events to be moved ahead of their original schedules.

In a nutshell, then, the party under Deng has never had good relations with China's intellectuals. On the contrary, that relationship deteriorated inexorably during the decade, and the party succeeded in alienating virtually all important groups of China's educated population. When the Democracy Wall movement began in the late 1970s, its followers consisted primarily of urban educated youths who were embittered by their experience during the Cultural Revolution. But their bold tactics and radical messages actually shocked and scared the mainstream intellectuals: the latter still wished to cooperate with the party and hoped that the rehabilitated leaders would give them the chance to do so. Many of them regarded the Democracy Wall protesters as "troublemakers" and were not sorry to see them imprisoned.

But it did not take long for the majority of these intellectuals to lose hope in the party's reforms. Meanwhile, the younger educated youths had gone through their own intellectual transformation on the college campuses. By the mid-1980s, desertions by intellectuals had reached uncontainable proportions.

Yet, however deep and palpable the educated people's grievances against the party and the regime were, they alone could not have posed a threat to the party's dominant role in Chinese society. After all, the CCP had oppressed intellectuals and denigrated education and knowledge for over three decades without endangering its own rule. The average Chinese was not inspired by ideas of Jeffersonian democracy, nor did he care much about the principle of separation of powers. The party's failure to enlist the support of the educated people could create serious difficulties in its ability efficiently to manage and develop the Chinese society and economy, but would not threaten the party's control over either. Even the occasional outbursts of educated people in favor of educational reforms were not enough to galvanize the general population to join forces with them. The relative ineffectiveness of student demonstrations and related activities by people in the fields of arts and literature before 1989 attested to the validity of this point; their slogans were too intellectualized to strike a responsive chord among the masses. The demonstrations of April–June 1989, however, were different precisely because the students, while continuing to press for democracy and freedom, were able for the first time to relate these concepts to concrete conditions of life that ordinary Chinese had to endure in their daily existence, and to arouse their indignation.

The key reason the students could swell the ranks of protesters from a few thousand in previous years to a million in Beijing alone and spread the demonstrations to many other cities throughout China in 1989 was that they were able to articulate the strongly felt grievances of Chinese from all walks of life. After the mid-1980s, the Chinese people had become increasingly disgusted with the corruption and abusive conduct of the cadres, the dishonesty and incompetence of the party and government, and the continued domination of the party elders over Chinese life. In short, the conduct of party members and leaders violated even the most rudimentary standards of fairness and justice and minimal political decency. The repressed anger of the Chinese people only needed a trigger to erupt into open conflagration, and the death of Hu Yaobang was conveniently seized for that purpose. Thus, the demonstrations began with profuse eulogies to Hu but quickly turned into a massive display of banners denouncing corruption and abuse of privileges, and advocating the overthrow of senile leaders. As the data presented in this volume suggest, it was the shared resentment against many manifestations of Chinese politics under the party's leadership that enabled the educated people to forge a solidarity in the spring of 1989 with the industrial workers, older intellectuals, ordinary urban residents, and even members of the party and state organs.

Poor discipline of party members had become a particularly onerous liability for the party in the 1980s. Even though the popular beliefs about the rectitude and honesty of the CCP's style of work in earlier decades had always been more myth than reality, it is nevertheless true that party members were never as corrupt and dishonest as they have been under Deng's leadership. There is no doubt that the Cultural Revolution took a heavy toll on the party's moral fiber from top to bottom. As party members witnessed the ruthlessness, arbitrariness, and fickleness of political power, they concluded that they should grab power aggressively and exploit it to the hilt while they could. In the late 1970s, the rehabilitated cadres set new examples of unscrupulous self-seeking and self-aggrandizing conduct that surpassed anything that had ever existed in the party's history. But since Deng needed the support of these people for his fledgling coalition at this time, the task of restoring the party's organizational vitality or reinjecting a sense of purpose and spirit of dedication among its rank and file was put off until the early 1980s. As documented in chapters 6 and 7, by then the magnitude of corruption and misconduct had already gotten out of control, and the problems only became worse with each passing year throughout the 1980s.

Meanwhile, the party's policies of mandatory retirement and orderly succession were seriously compromised by two adverse side-effects. One was the manner in which the retirement system was implemented. In effect, the party ended up paying large sums of ransom to send senior leaders into retirement, which could not but further undermine the standards of morality within the party. The other side-effect was the packing of the third echelon with the cronies and children of cadres on all levels. On top of these problems, it was also clear that the old leaders really did not want to retire completely. The Chinese Communist Party claimed to want youthfulness and vitality but remained a gerontocracy. And the moral quality of leadership it provided was clearly the worst since Liberation, and possibly as bad as any other in this century.

The Party's Failure to Resolve Its Crises

The history of the party's difficulties during the 1980s suggests that the three issues of its leadership, discipline, and relations with the educated people have been intimately related. This point can best be demonstrated by comparing the difficulties the CCP encountered in keeping its two previous general secretaries in office. Each of these two men in his own way failed to maintain the proper balance in his effort to resolve the party's three major problems.

In the early 1980s, Deng concluded that his leadership had been consolidated with the appointment of Hu Yaobang as general secretary and Zhao Ziyang as the prime minister. There is no doubt that Hu fully shared Deng's vision for achieving rapid economic progress, as evidenced by his frequent reference to the "takeoff" concept. But, on the other hand, Hu was also genuinely concerned with the health of the party and was particularly disturbed by the party's discipline problem and the retirement of the old guard.

On the question of discipline, Hu seemed genuinely repulsed by the widespread corruption and abuse of privileges. His own life-style was simple and frugal, and he was very sympathetic to the hardship of life on the basic level. During his tenure as general secretary, Hu made more personal inspection tours around the country than any other senior leader. He personally read many letters of complaint from the common people and attended to the correction of many cases where injustice had been done. From these contacts, Hu undoubtedly acquired an intimate appreciation of the magnitude of corruption and became more determined to eradicate it. This can be seen by his effort to give a new twist to the old distinction between antagonistic and nonantagonistic contradictions. Hu contended that the corruption of unscrupulous cadres should be classified as an antagonistic contradiction and should be punished without mercy. By late 1985, Hu had become so impatient with the lack of progress of the rectification campaign that he resorted to the dramatic step of assembling 8,000 cadres in early 1986, to issue them a stern warning against misconduct. Hu made a valiant but futile effort to take personal charge over the party's rectification campaign and threatened to punish high-ranking offenders.

On the question of retirement, Hu was equally committed and believed that the faithful implementation of this system was essential to the task of rebuilding the party. He was not only eager to force other old leaders into retirement, but he might even have urged Deng to do the same.[12]

But on the question of the party's relations with the intellectuals, Hu's attitude was far more relaxed. He enjoyed a good reputation among intellectuals, many of whom trusted his sincerity and goodwill toward them. It was during Hu's tenure that the party experimented with the practice of inviting prominent scholars to present seminars to party and government leaders inside the Zhongnanhai compound. In contrast to his harsh denunciation of party members' misconduct, Hu characterized the criticisms and liberal ideas espoused by intellectuals as nonantagonistic contradictions, because they were meant to help the party and therefore should be respected or at least tolerated.

Hu's downfall can be explained in terms of his tactical mistakes in handling the party's three related problems. His strong effort to cleanse the party of corruption, coupled with his unconcealed enthusiasm for the real retirement of senior leaders, constituted both an affront to their sense of self-importance and a threat to their political and material interests. On the other hand, his sympathy for the plight of the intellectuals and his unwillingness to take repressive measures against outspoken intellectuals alarmed those leaders who held fast to the belief that the party's authority should never be allowed to be questioned. In this sense, Hu made the worst possible enemies by driving the self-seekers and the ideological diehards into a coalition against him.

When Zhao Ziyang became acting general secretary upon Hu's demise in January 1987, he brought significantly different views into the office. While Hu was basically an organization man with the conventional respect for party predominance and an ardent desire to make the party good enough to deserve popular support, Zhao was basically a technocrat with a life-long career in economic affairs. His earlier careers in the provinces (Guangdong and Sichuan) and his elevation to the central government after 1978 had all been predicated on his reputation as an able manager of economic affairs. Therefore, he found it easy to share Deng's goal of economic growth and proceeded to prove how innovative he could be about it.

But Zhao never had much experience or interest in party work and probably often regarded it as an unwelcome interference with economic rationality. Zhao never expressed any strong commitment to build up the party. When Hu fell suddenly from power, Zhao was drafted to serve as acting general secretary against his own inclination. Almost the first act that he took in his new capacity was to minimize any backlash of Hu's downfall by announcing that the anti–bourgeois liberalization campaign would be limited in scope and would not interfere with the normal economic policies, nor would it affect the rural areas. Even when Zhao's post as general secretary was made official at the Thirteenth Party Congress, he still maintained that he would rather be prime minister.[13]

Zhao's approach in handling the three thorny issues discussed above also differed from his predecessor. First, Zhao never betrayed any sign of impatience with the aging leaders' continued meddling in party affairs but tried to keep them out of the economic realm as much as possible. Thus, instead of urging Deng's prompt retirement, Zhao actually supported the highly irregular secret arrangement to give Deng virtual veto power over the Politburo's major decisions shortly after the Thirteenth Party Congress. Nor was Zhao known to have pushed aggressively for other senior leaders' complete withdrawal from politics. Thus, for instance, Yang Shangkun was actually older than Li Xiannian but succeeded the latter as the president of the PRC, while Wang Zhen, another octogenarian, was made vice-president. Second, while Zhao paid lip service to the need to tighten party discipline, he never showed genuine indignation at such misdeeds. His own life-style was flashy by Chinese standards, and his sons were widely rumored to have profited from illegal commercial activities. Zhao might have indeed been sympathetic to the view that a certain amount of corruption was inevitable under the conditions of reform and rapid economic progress.[14] Therefore, in these two areas, Zhao blended in easily with the prevailing attitudes among party leaders and was probably regarded as a safe person in the top post. Predictably, once the rectification campaign was concluded, he was content to return to the normal state of affairs while in fact he presided over a period of even steeper decline of the party's discipline.

On the question of the party's relations with the intellectuals, however, Zhao's position deviated from the elders' norms. His preoccupation with economic development probably made him more appreciative of the value of intellectuals and more tolerant of different opinions. He was the first Chinese leader to have successfully utilized the "think-tank" format by enlisting the services of a number of bright young people as advisers.[15] He was also quite open-minded toward Western economic theories and often invited both overseas Chinese scholars and Western economists to suggest ways to accelerate China's economic growth rates.

Being uninterested in the task of party building, Zhao probably was not loathe to let the party take a backseat and allow the technocrats to run China's economy. In this connection, he might indeed have been influenced by an elitist view toward politics, which raised doubt about his commitment to uphold the critical political importance of the party or his adherence to the four cardinal principles.[16] It is not accidental that the concepts of the separation of the party and state and the adoption of objective criteria to manage the civil-service system both received extensive publicity under Zhao's leadership.

In spite of the party's warning against bourgeois liberalization at the time of Hu Yaobang' dismissal, the trend actually accelerated during Zhao's stewardship over the party. Dissident views had no trouble finding their way into print. People like Fang Lizhi got away with increasingly sharp attacks against the party, the ideology, the political system, and even individual leaders. Starting in late 1988, many more Chinese intellectuals threw caution to the wind and signed public letters taking positions on one issue or another in clear contravention of the party's policies. Long before the spring of 1989, several movements had been underway to turn the commemoration of the forthcoming seventieth anniversary of the May Fourth Movement into a political indictment of the present regime and to seek a complete rejection of the party's verdict on the antirightist campaign of 1957.

These trends were indeed alarming from the senior leaders' perspective because they fundamentally threatened the four cardinal principles and Deng's personal stature. Deng had been deeply involved in persecuting the intellectuals during the antirightist campaign. In the eyes of the senior leaders, Zhao could not escape his responsibility for being "ineffectual and indecisive" in arresting these dangerous trends. Indeed, as the subsequent accusations put it, Zhao might have actually acted as "the biggest protective umbrella of bourgeois liberal tendencies in the field of arts and literature."[17]

In the midst of these problems, the Chinese economy also had begun to show signs of serious trouble. The inflation rate had reached 30 percent or more in some major cities, and probably 20 percent throughout the entire country. A difference over economic policies began to develop between Zhao Ziyang, who favored the continuation of bold reforms, and Premier Li Peng and Deputy Premier Yao Yilin, who preferred to follow Chen Yun's advice to retrench and reimpose centralized control over certain key sectors. This economic debate inevitably also poisoned Zhao's relationship with some elder leaders of the party.

When the unrest began in the spring of 1989, Zhao perceived it as a threat to his economic program while the old guard perceived it as a challenge to the four cardinal principles and their right to rule. Zhao downplayed the points of confrontation between the demonstrators and the party in the hope that some gestures of conciliation from the party could placate the former and return the situation to normal as quickly as possible. But the senior leaders were gripped with the fear of a disastrous loss of face if the party should ever give in to popular pressure and chose instead to handle it as a last-ditch defense of the party and socialism. This fundamental difference in their perceptions of the nature and danger of student movements in 1989 eventually produced a break in the ranks of the Politburo.

There is no doubt that the two major personnel crises that the party encountered in less than three years (1987–89) both had their causes in the party's development under Deng. Although these crises occurred at the highest level of leadership, they were direct reflections of the party's deeper problems in the areas of discipline, leadership, and relations with the educated people. Both general secretaries found themselves in untenable situations. If they tried to enforce discipline and improve the quality of leadership, they would please the Chinese people and strengthen the party's legitimacy at the same time, but they would also endanger the self-interest of the power holders and provoke their retaliation. On the other hand, if they adopted a position of benign neglect of these issues, they would run the risk of further weakening the party's legitimacy to rule but would pacify the power holders within the party. By the same token, if they continued to oppress the intellectuals, they ran the risk of seeing their economic objectives go down the drain. But if they were conciliatory toward them, they might accelerate the pace of "bourgeois liberalization" and undermine the four cardinal principles, which Deng and many other senior leaders were determined to defend. The tensions between these demands grew with time, and the Tiananmen demonstrations showed that they finally were too strong to be contained.

Responses to the Tiananmen Crisis

Has the party learned any useful lessons from the terrible tragedy of the spring of 1989? What measures has it taken to remedy the problems? How effective will these measures be? These are all questions of momentous importance for China's future.

Party Leadership

The party's first order of business was to restore unity among the leadership. Even in the midst of the Tiananmen crisis, Deng tried to contain the damage of the schism within the top leadership by removing Zhao Ziyang and named Jiang Zemin as the new general secretary and the head of a "third generation" of leaders. Speaking to the members of the reconstituted Standing Committee of the Politburo on June 16, 1989, Deng said, "Since 1978 I have tried to groom successors, but unfortunately both Hu Yaobang and Zhao Ziyang were unable to stand on their own. Now we have created a third generation of leaders headed by Jiang Zemin. You all must support him and uphold the unity of the leadership core." Deng also warned the new leaders not to engage in quarrels or factional activities.[18]

Although Deng had personally anointed Jiang Zemin as the center of the new party leadership, it is too early to tell whether this leadership can avoid the pitfalls that have bedeviled the party's succession process since Liberation. It is recalled that Hua Guofeng built his legitimacy on the claim of being Mao's designated successor and tried to consolidate power by occupying the top party, army, and government posts simultaneously. Yet in less than three years was driven out of power. Both Hu and Zhao, as Deng's designated successors, fell by the wayside while Deng was alive. Both also had very strong personal credentials. Hu's career began during the Yan'an era, and he spent long years in charge of the CYL. Zhao's prestige as a capable economic expert was nationally respected. In addition to their strong personal stature, each also commanded a sizable bureaucratic following. In contrast, Jiang Zemin had little experience in party work and absolutely no military experience. Nor had he been prominently involved in national politics. If the two previous leaders could not escape failure, can Jiang survive, especially if Deng is gone?

The issue here is really much broader than which specific individuals can stay in power. It concerns whether the retirement system and the "third echelon" strategy will remain operative in the future. The party's original plan was to identify and groom worthy candidates for succession, install them in office under the stewardship of current leaders, and rely on this leadership core to stabilize power for the next twenty to thirty years. Yet within a decade, two sets of leaders had to be discarded, and a third set was installed with more haste and even less popular support. Such a track record inevitably calls into question the efficacy of the third-echelon approach to succession.

Closely related to the viability of the third-echelon strategy is the reliability of the system of compulsory retirement in the future. As chapter 3 demonstrates, the party in the early 1980s expended enormous amounts of energy and financial resources virtually to bribe a generation of old leaders to leave office. But obviously, the effort has not been completely successful. On both occasions of leadership changes of 1987 and 1989, the old retired and semiretired leaders played a heavy hand.

Although gerontocracy was a major point of complaint during the Tiananmen Square demonstrations, old leaders have shown increased zest for active political life in the months following the incident. Any hope raised by Deng's repeated promises that he and his fellow octogenarians will soon retire has been dampened by the other leaders' response of silence, and by Deng's own offer to give advice whenever the new leaders solicit it. This implies that even if they eventually retire from all official posts, they may not exit entirely from politics.

There is also no convincing reason to assume that the difficulty of enforcing retirement will disappear with the natural attrition of leaders in Deng's generation. In fact, the Thirteenth Party Congress set a dangerous precedent by giving Deng the ultimate authority to make important decisions. Mao Zedong never relinquished the chairmanship of the party during his lifetime; therefore, at the very least, he could claim to exercise authority in his institutional capacity as the head of the party. But in 1987, Deng actually abdicated his seat in the party's Central Committee and Politburo even though he retained ultimate power over the party. If Deng could do this, there is no reason why the next strongman cannot aspire to do likewise. The events during 1987–89 may have encouraged other elders to view themselves as serious contenders for the top power and may have inspired them to entertain more innovative schemes of exercising power even after their official retirement. In this respect, Deng may have done a great disservice to his own political reform and planted the seeds of future leadership instability. The eager manner with which a number of retired leaders (Chen Yun, Bo Yibo, Hu Qiaomu) and semiretired leaders (Yang Shangkun, Wang Zhen) sprang back to active political life after the Tiananmen Square incident provides some alarming signs of what may happen in the future.

Insofar as the mid- and lower-level leaders are concerned, the Tiananmen Square incident does not seem to have made much impact. The poor moral and professional qualities of some who obtained their positions by way of the third echelon are already part of China's political reality. In all likelihood, these leaders will stay in power for the next decade or two and can become a substantial handicap to the CCP's ambition to achieve modernization objectives quickly. There is no indication that the party can do much to improve this situation.

Party Discipline

The restoration of party discipline is an infinitely complicated problem. The centrality of the party's discipline to its political survival was graphically demonstrated during the Tiananmen Square crisis. The crisis revealed not only the dangerous loss of the party's moral credentials in the eyes of the Chinese masses, but also of the party's organizational control over its own members. For as Song Ping, the director of the party's Central Organization Department, admitted, many of the leading instigators and organizers of the demonstrations were CCP members. Party members and sometimes even entire party organs took the lead in writing and distributing leaflets critical of their leaders. Many party members also renounced their party membership during the crisis to show their disgust with the party.[19]

When confronted with such defiance, the party had virtually no organizational resources left with which to fight back. The city of Beijing had the highest concentration of party members in relation to its general population, but during the entire crisis the party was utterly unable to use regular organizational channels to defuse the situation or organize a counterdemonstration to show support for the party. Ultimately, the party leaders were driven to rely on guns to crush their own followers.

In the aftermath of the Tiananmen Square crisis, the party has taken several remedial steps. While insisting that the crisis was primarily engineered and executed by subversive and counterrevolutionary elements, the party did concede that poor discipline was a contributing factor. Deng's answer was to "do a few good things to make the people feel satisfied and encouraged."[20] Accordingly, the Politburo decided in late June to take seven specific actions to eliminate privileges and stop corruption.[21] This approach is quite reminiscent of the campaign to smash economic crimes of the early 1980s. In spite of the predictable claims of quick success,[22] one has yet to see a penalty imposed on anyone with known connections to high cadre families.[23] The whole operation may turn out to be yet another case of "smashing the flies, but not the tigers." Even if the campaign to smash economic crimes eventually implicates children of high cadres, it is likely that it will punish only those children whose parents have already fallen from political grace. Should this ever happen, the party will hardly bolster its image; instead, it will only confirm the Chinese masses' cynical view that "power holders can do no wrong." It remains to be seen whether the party is really able this time to find new mechanisms to extract compliance from its members.

The party's threat to prosecute corruption and abuses of privileges was accompanied by its renewed emphasis on political education to rid itself of undesirable elements. But the measures taken in the months immediately after the Tiananmen Square tragedy offered few signs of change from the same old tired formulas of exhortation, criticism, self-criticism, intensified political indoctrination, and wholesale reregistration, which constituted the party's conventional repertoire in handling intraparty disciplinary problems. But as the previous chapters on rectification in the 1980s conclusively show, the efficacy of such measures had been thoroughly refuted under the conditions of the 1980s. To be successful this time, the party needs to show that it has the capacity to do things differently.

Conceptually, the party has at least three broadly defined options to achieve good results in disciplinary matters. One is to restore the party's purity through intraparty organizational measures to enforce exacting standards of conduct on membership. This option may necessitate two things. First, the party must devise innovative methods to revitalize its own organizational control; second, it must have the determination to expel all unqualified members, whose numbers could potentially run into millions. Will the party be willing to take the political risk of alienating so many of its own people? Will it be afraid that the massive expulsion may actually be perceived by the Chinese people as a confirmation of how much the party has degenerated?

A second option is to forego any effort by the party to clean its own house but to yield the power to enforce discipline to the court system. If the courts could operate with complete independence and full integrity, the problems of corruption will be significantly reduced in due course. But of course this approach will entail the party's concession to the principle of separation of powers, which has been an anathema. Is the party willing to pay the price of abdicating from an important functional area of the government? What will the party become if it can no longer control the judiciary?

A final option for the party to restore its moral standards is to allow the citizenry to exercise censorial power over party members' conduct and to allow public opinion to serve as a check over misconduct. In theory, the CCP has no trouble accepting this approach, as it has always professed support for the mass line and has maintained that party members must enjoy the support of the people. But to allow the masses actually to exercise such democratic control over the party is an entirely different matter because it may ultimately threaten the principle of the supremacy of the party over the Chinese polity. The ramifications of this option for the future of the CCP in Chinese politics can be even more radical and unpredictable than the previous two approaches.

To put the possible consequences of these three options of party rectification in such stark terms is only to highlight the dilemma confronting the party. But the party's malaise has developed to such alarming proportions that nothing short of drastic measures could possibly accomplish the desired ends. Nonetheless, it is entirely conceivable for the party to eschew all these approaches and decide to do more of the same, as in the last decade. In such a case, the party may have to prepare itself to face a prolonged period of instability. A party incapable of correcting the problems of corruption and massive abuses of privileges and of improving its style of work will definitely remain a key factor of political turmoil in Chinese politics. If the party's organization cannot even serve as an instrument of effective control over the masses, as was the case during the Tiananmen Square crisis, then eruptions of public anger will occur periodically, and the party may have to rely increasingly on brute force to keep itself in power. How the CCP manages to avert this possibility will be a major challenge to the post-Tiananmen leaders in the coming years.

The Party and Intellectuals

The damage to the party's relations with educated people may be the most difficult to repair. The CCP's relationship with intellectuals suffered a serious rupture during the spring of 1989. Not only had the non-CCP intellectuals become thoroughly alienated by the party's behavior, even many of the party's own intellectuals had turned against it. It is significant that the faculty and students of People's University, the party's own ideological stalwart, actually played a leading role in the demonstrations. Furthermore, since 1978, the party had acquired a new group of younger, more flexible theorists who valiantly tried to adapt its ideology to the changing reality. These people were attached to the Institute of Economic Reform under the State Council, or the Chinese Academy of Social Sciences, and were scattered throughout the central ministries. But their attempts at peaceful change were branded as counterrevolutionary activities. Thus, in one blow, the post-Tiananmen leaders decimated the most innovative generation of party theorists by dismissal, exile, or imprisonment.

The party's handling of the Tiananmen Square crisis served as a powerful reminder that its basic mentality toward educated people had remained essentially the same since the antirightist campaign of 1957. Even though the party pledged in the midst of the crisis that it would not "settle the score," in fact it resorted to massive arrests and torture of people suspected of having participated in the demonstrations. Many intellectuals had to escape to foreign countries to avoid persecution and have since organized themselves into open opposition against the party. Those who stayed behind had to endure more humiliation and intimidation in silence, but they had definitely become even more embittered toward the party than ever before.

It may take many more years for the party to erase this record of bad faith and oppression and heal the wounds of the Tiananmen Square massacre, even if it tries. But at the time of this writing, the party is still busy carrying out punitive actions against the students and educated people.[24]

The party's policy toward intellectuals is inevitably complicated by its strong stand against "bourgeois liberalization." Since bourgeois liberalization was perceived as being opposed to socialism and the leadership of the CCP, the party was determined to expose all "bad elements" and "counterrevolutionaries" without mercy.[25] According to the party's thinking, one major component of bourgeois liberal thoughts that foreign enemies employed to realize their goal of the "peaceful transformation" of China was to utilize "pornography, drugs, and gambling" to dope the Chinese people.[26] Consequently, the party began a series of antiblack (counterrevolutionaries) and antiyellow (pornography) actions in late August 1989. Newly promoted Politburo Standing Committee member Li Ruihuan was dispatched to four southern provinces to combat these foreign-inspired activities. As Li reported, the antipornography campaign constituted "an important segment of the current struggle against bourgeois liberalization and had the strong support of Deng Xiaoping, Chen Yun, and Li Xiannian."[27] Since the concepts of "black" and "yellow" were far from precise, the campaign became an effective weapon to intimidate the intellectuals by closing down legitimate publications and silencing different opinions.

It is still unclear as to when the party plans to halt these punitive actions and start to repair the damage in its relations with educated people. One thing is clear, however: the CCP's chances of serving as an effective modernizing agent will be seriously jeopardized for as long as its relations with educated people remain estranged.

Other Major Developments

It is interesting to note that the Tiananmen Square tragedy has so far failed to stimulate the party leaders to search for bold new approaches to solve the party's long-standing problems. Instead, Tiananmen seems to have the effect of driving the party leaders back to their old ideological stance and policy line. The most noticeable sign of this mentality is Deng's pledge that the party would not change the general line or policies formulated at the Third Plenum of the Eleventh Party Congress, "not even a single word."[28]

Predictably, economic issues continued as the new leaders' top priority. Shortly after the Tiananmen Square incident, Deng decreed that the most important thing was not to allow the economy to slide downward. He cautioned the new leaders not to reopen the debate about the relative merits of a market economy versus a planned economy. Instead, he urged them to concentrate on maintaining a good rate of economic growth. Deng confidently estimated that the CCP would win wide support from the people if it could maintain a 6–7 percent growth rate per annum for the remainder of the twentieth century.[29] This view was quickly echoed in the official press. In an editorial on October 10, 1989, the

People's Daily announced that "Economic work will remain the central work for the CCP. We must guarantee that the economy will not slide downward, but will maintain a sustained, stable, and balanced growth trend."[30] The thesis of "one center and two basic points" was given prominent play in the mass media.[31] Finally, General Secretary Jiang Zemin revealed during his first major press conference that the main item on the party's agenda for the next two to three years would be economic development.[32]

The Tiananmen Square crisis also led the leaders to defend the four cardinal principles more vociferously. As Deng said after the crisis, "We must never give up the stand to oppose bourgeois liberalization, and to uphold the four cardinal principles. I have never made concessions on this issue at any time. What will China become without the four cardinal principles? Can we afford not to follow the system of proletarian dictatorship? Whether we insist on Marxism and socialism or not is a fundamental issue."[33]

This determination to uphold the party's supremacy over the state and society may have led it to back away from two reforms it introduced only two years before. At the Thirteenth Congress in 1987, the party unveiled a plan to implement the policy of the "separation of party and state." The intent of this policy, promoted energetically by Zhao Ziyang, was ostensibly to free the party from the chores of supervising the routine operations of state bureaucracy and economic enterprises so that it could concentrate its attention on managing its own affairs and formulating long-terms plans. But this policy also had the potential of taking the actual governing power out of the party's hands and shifting it to the technocrats and professionals. An important step to accomplish this goal was the introduction of a new classification system of the cadres into "political" and "professional" cadres. While the political cadres would presumably be appointed and controlled by the party, the professional cadres would be selected by objective criteria and would be regarded as nonpoliticized civil servants whose party affiliation would be less important than their technical expertise.

For the next year and half, the party had mobilized its propaganda machine to tout the virtues of the new principle of separation of party and state. It stated that under the new principle the party would exercise "political leadership" over the state organs but would abdicate "organizational" or "operational" leadership. But no sooner had this principle been adopted than opposition emerged. Many in the party argued that the separation of party and state would reduce the party's power. Cadres who specialized in political work were particularly worried that the party's functions would be greatly reduced after the separation of party and state, and that nobody would want to do party work.[34] Others argued that the civil-service reforms would spell the end of party leadership and threaten incumbent administrative cadres' jobs.[35]

The Tiananmen Square incident may have provided an impetus for the new leaders to reverse the party's previous thinking on this issue. Speaking on behalf of his Politburo colleagues, Jiang Zemin contended, "It is not enough to say that the party's leadership function is limited to political leadership; the party must also exercise ideological leadership and organizational leadership," for "the principle of political leadership is empty if it is divorced from organizational leadership and ideological leadership. This point must be made very clearly."[36] Similar assertions of the party's dominant role began to appear frequently in the official press.[37] All these signs suggest that both reforms may have been either abandoned or indefinitely postponed.

An equally noteworthy development was the reappearance of the theme of class struggle, which had not been mentioned in the official press for nearly a decade. After June 1989, however, leaders ominously warned that it would be a mistake to dismiss the current relevance of class struggle. They pointed out that as long as the party was the proletariat's vanguard, it should never abandon the method of using "class struggle" to analyze the world even though it should avoid the excess of "using class struggle to explain everything." The Tiananmen Square incident was presented as evidence of how pertinent class struggle analysis still was.[38]

What is probably most revealing in these developments is the incapacity of the CCP leaders to understand that the party itself constituted the major reason for the fundamental malaise in Chinese politics. Instead, in July, a confident Deng estimated that the CCP would need only three to six months of good, hard work to restore its image and win back popular support.[39] It is nothing short of amazing that, after suffering a decade of demonstrable failures, and especially after being buffeted by a major crisis that resulted in enormous bloodshed, the party's leaders still could not see the handwriting on the wall.

Prospects for the Future

Deng was correct in attributing the Tiananmen Square crisis to the convergence of both internal and external factors, but he completely misidentified these factors. Deng's thesis that a small group of unorganized intellectuals could have persuaded millions of people to go into the streets throughout China is as unconvincing as the government's other thesis that Nationalist spies from Taiwan incited these uprisings. The most critical factor contributing to the formation of the "minor climate" inside China was none other than the party, which succeeded in offending the majority of the Chinese people through its repugnant style of work and incompetent leadership. It was the party's violation of popular Chinese senses of justice, honesty, and decency, and not the Western concepts of individualism, democracy, and inalienable rights, that provoked the average citizens to take to the streets to express their anger. The responsibility for creating the minor climate must rest squarely on the CCP's own shoulders.

On the other hand, the critical factor contributing to the formation of the "major climate" was not the Western countries' concerted conspiracy to subvert socialism in China. Instead, it consisted of three major elements. First, Western democratic theories definitely have won a tiny number of converts among the highly educated circles. Second, the reforms in other socialist countries such as the Soviet Union and Poland probably inspired more people, especially students and party members, because of the similarities between their systems and China's. Third, an equally and possibly more important element is the widespread awareness among ordinary Chinese in all walks of life and geographical areas of the impressive progress made by neighboring East Asian societies such as Japan, South Korea, Taiwan, Hong Kong, and Singapore. To the overwhelming majority of common people in China, it may overstretch their imagination to compare China with the United States or even the Soviet Union, but it is entirely sensible to compare China with other Asian peoples. It was this comparison that sharpened their sense of relative deprivation. When Chinese saw other Asian peoples' quality of political and economic life outstripping theirs by ever-widening margins, they inevitably concluded that they had been shortchanged by their own system.[40]

Since the Tiananmen Square tragedy, the major climate in the contemporary world has become even more disturbing for the Chinese Communists for two additional reasons. First, the political agitation in Eastern European socialist countries directly contradicts the validity of Deng's assumption that the Chinese people will support the CCP if the latter is able to provide better economic conditions in China. For one thing, the economic conditions in most of these Eastern European countries are far better than those in the PRC, but this has not spared these countries from serious political challenges. For another thing, the Tiananmen Square crisis occurred after a decade of sustained high growth of the Chinese economy. If the party could not defuse public discontent after a decade of economic growth rates in excess of 10 percent, it is unclear how the party could expect to placate the people with a 6–7 percent growth rate per annum projected for the 1990s.

Second, most ruling Communist parties in Eastern Europe have accepted plans to share power with non-Communist groups. In the face of this broad trend of reform and democratization throughout the Communist bloc, it is difficult to imagine how the CCP will be able to insulate itself and maintain an oppressive regime indefinitely. It is entirely possible that these Eastern European Communist leaders learned a valuable lesson from China's disastrous handling of its political problems and concluded that conciliation was preferable to confrontation and bloodshed. But do the Chinese leaders have the same capacity to learn a lesson from their Eastern European comrades as well? For many decades, the CCP has stoutly maintained that "only socialism can save China." But, after witnessing the rapid crumbling of socialism in the USSR and Eastern Europe, the Chinese people have begun to joke that now "only China can save socialism." But can China really save socialism? Can the Chinese Communist Party save itself?

The data presented in this volume suggest that the CCP's own viability as well as its role in China's political future will hinge on its ability to meet several major challenges ahead. First, will the party be able to regain its moral strength and restore its legitimacy in the eyes of the people? Second, can it reinvigorate its organizational sinews to carry out the normal functions of control over the state and society? Finally, does it have the ability to improve the educational and professional qualifications of its members and leaders to play a central role in fulfilling China's objectives for political and economic modernization? Only time will tell if the CCP has the ability to meet these challenges.

Notes

Preface

1. *Renmin ribao* (*RMRB*), overseas edition, October 17, 1989, p. 1.
2. According to the 1982 census, there were 510 million Chinese between ages 15 and 64 who were employed. Party members constituted 8 percent of this group, with one party member for every twelve to thirteen employed Chinese. Zhao Shuhai, "Tantan tigao gongchandangyuan di zhiliang wenti," in *Kexue shehui zhuyi* [Beijing], 1987, no. 4, pp. 33–38.
3. As the literature on Chinese politics has become quite extensive, I will not cite specific illustrations here. For references, interested readers are urged to consult the bibliography in any standard text on Chinese politics.

Chapter 1

1. Jurgen Domes, *The Government and Politics of the PRC: A Time of Transition*, pp. 140–42.
2. A corollary of Hua's policy was the dogma that "one sentence uttered by Chairman Mao exceeded the wisdom of ten thousand sentences by other people."
3. According to Domes, in the State Council, two vice-premiers and four ministers were purged during late 1976. Of the ten new ministers appointed, seven had been purged during the Cultural Revolution. Between October 1976 and July 1977, thirteen of the twenty-nine provincial units received new party first secretaries. Of these, nine had been purged during the Cultural Revolution but recently rehabilitated, and four had survived the Cultural Revolution in office. See Domes, *Government and Politics*, pp. 140–42.
4. The process began on February 1, 1977, when two Politburo members (Xu Shiyou and Wei Guoqing, both from the Guangdong Military Region) wrote Hua Guofeng a letter demanding Deng's rehabilitation. Soon their cause was joined by many other provincial leaders. At the March 10–23 enlarged Politburo meeting, the pressure became so strong that Hua finally agreed to rehabilitate Deng. See ibid., pp. 146–47.
5. Deng made this observation in his conversation with Wang Zhen and Deng Liqun in May 1977. *Deng Xiaoping wenxuan: 1975–1982* (*DXPWX*), pp. 35–36.
6. *Guangming ribao* (*GMRB*), May 11, 1978, p. 1.
7. Deng's speech of December 13, 1978, in *DXPWX*, p. 133.
8. "Zhongguo gongchandang di shiyijie zhongyang weiyuanhui disanze quanti huiyi gongbao," December 22, 1978, in *Shiyijie sanzhong quanhui yilai zhongyao wenxian xuandu* (hereafter *Major Documents*), pp. 1–14.
9. Ibid. Domes estimates that among the twenty-seven Politburo members, Deng now

controlled at least twelve, while Hua controlled only seven. Domes, *Government and Politics*, pp. 162–63.

10. Qixin, "Zhonggong wanchenglian jizhuangwan," *The Seventies*, 1979, no. 2, pp. 7–17.

11. Domes argues that after the fourth plenum convened September 25–28, 1979, the new Politburo line-up included thirteen to fourteen Deng supporters, seven Hua supporters, and seven or eight members falling in a middle group. Domes, *Government and Politics*, p. 169.

12. *Wenhuibao*, July 4, 1983, p. 3.

13. Domes suggests that Deng now had four votes in the Standing Committee, Hua had only one vote, and the middle group had two votes. Among the twenty-four Politburo members, Deng's backers comprised thirteen or fourteen members; Hua's, three; and Ye-Li's, seven or eight. Domes, *Government and Politics*, pp. 170–71.

14. Of the ten secretaries, Deng had seven, Ye-Li had three, and Hua had none. Ibid.

15. These changes were only officially announced in June 1981.

16. To earn the trust of Hua and other Maoist leaders immediately after his rehabilitation, Deng volunteered to assume responsibility over the development of science and education, which were regarded as two relatively innocuous policy areas at the time. *RMRB*, July 1, 1983, p. 3.

17. *GMRB*, November 16, 1978, p. 1. The official action was taken on November 15, 1978 and was followed by a spate of exonerations, including the case of the play, "The Dismissal of Hairui."

18. The most important publications included *Beijing zhiqun* (Beijing spring), *Qunzhong cankao xiaoxi* (Masses' reference work), *Renmin zhisheng* (People's voice), *Siwu luntan* (April 5 tribune), *Tangsuo* (Exploration), and *Zhongguo renquan* (Chinese human rights). A large number of books contain accounts of this movement. See Fox Butterfield, *China: Alive in the Bitter Sea* (New York: Times Books, 1982), pp. 406–34; John Fraser, *The Chinese: Portrait of a People* (New York: Summit Books, 1980), pp. 199–271; David S. G. Goodman, *Beijing Street Voices; The Poetry and Politics of China's Democracy Movement* (London: Marion Boyars, 1981); Lin Yitang, ed., *What They Say: A Collection of Current Chinese Underground Publications* (Taipei: Institute of Current China Studies, 1980); and James D. Seymour, ed., *The Fifth Modernization: China's Human Rights Movement, 1978–79* (Stanfordville, NY: Coleman, 1980). For a collection of publications during this movement, see Institute of the Study of Chinese Communist Problems, Taipei, ed., *Dalu dixia kanwu huibian* (Collection of mainland underground publications) (Taipei, 1980–).

19. Deng's speech, "Jiefang sixiang, shihshih qiushi, tuanjie yizhi xiangqiankan," in *Major Documents*, pp. 18–33.

20. Qixin, "Zhonggong hui xuanqi pi Mao yundong ma?" *The Seventies*, 1979, no. 1, pp. 67–71.

21. Deng's speech, "Shixian sige xiandaihua bixu jianchi sixiang jiben yuanze," March 30, 1979, in *Major Documents*, pp. 44–61. In early January 1979, Fu Yuehua led ten thousand peasants from four provinces in street demonstrations in Beijing, to demand better living conditions and work permits. On February 5 and 6, about twenty-five thousand people demonstrated in Shanghai, occupying the railway station and blocking traffic. Domes, *Government and Politics*, p. 160.

22. Deng's speech, "Shixian sige xiandaihua bixu jianchi sixiang jiben yuanze," March 30, 1979, in *Major Documents*, pp. 44–61.

23. They referred to big blooming, big contending, big debate, and big-character posters.

24. Qixin, "Zhonggong wanchenglian jizhuangwan," *The Seventies*, 1979, no. 2, pp. 7–17.

25. *Jilin ribao*, March 31, 1983, p. 1.

26. Deng's speech on January 16, 1980, "Muqian de xinshi he renwu," in *Major Documents*, pp. 125–62.

27. One example was the PLA's role in implementing certain of Mao's instructions, such as the "three supports and two militarys."

28. Qixin, "Liuzhongquanhui yiho yanhuan?" *The Seventies*, 1981, no. 5, pp. 61–64.

29. The Chinese called these the *yuan, jia, cuo* cases.

30. For example, in Shaanxi Province alone, hundreds of thousands of cadres and ordinary people had been abused, and more than 2,000 cadres were beaten to death during the Cultural Revolution. There were 2,300 major cases of political persecution, each case implicating a large number of people. *Shaanxi ribao*, April 19, 1983, p. 1.

31. Qixin, "Zhonggong wanchenglian jizhuangwan," *The Seventies*, 1979, no. 2, pp. 7–17.

32. *Jiefangjun bao*, February 20, 1979, p. 1.

33. Qixin, "Kan Zhonggong ruho qianghua zuzhi," *The Seventies*, 1980, no. 4, pp. 55–60.

34. *RMRB*, July 22, 1983, p. 1.

35. *Qinghai ribao*, April 13, 1983, p. 1.

36. Reprinted in "Hu Yaobang tan Zhonggong guoneiwai zhengce dongxiang," *The Seventies*, 1980, no. 8, pp. 21–22.

37. For instance, before 1983, Shaanxi Province exonerated some 190,000 people wrongly accused during the Cultural Revolution, and another 185,000 people who had been mistreated before. *Shaanxi ribao*, April 19, 1983, p. 1. A sparsely populated province like Ningxia Autonomous Region had reviewed and settled about 90,000 people's political cases before 1983. *Ningxia ribao*, July 29, 1983, p. 1.

38. In 1979 alone, these offices received over a million such letters. *Liaowang*, 1983, no. 4, pp. 2–4.

39. At the peak of this phenomenon in August and September 1979, over seven hundred people arrived in Beijing from the provinces each day. For a description of the so-called visit upward (*shangfang*) phenomenon, see ibid.

40. One direct cause of this decline was the beginning of the individual responsibility system in rural areas. When the peasants no longer were subject to oppressive and coercive domination by cadres, the masses' complaints also declined. Ibid.

41. "Zhongguo gongchandang di shiyijie zhongyang weiyuanhui disanze quanti huiyi gongbao," December 22, 1978, in *Major Documents*, pp. 1–14. In a speech made on December 13, 1978, Deng acknowledged the existence of widespread domestic and international interest in assessing Mao and the Cultural Revolution. He noted that Mao had made great contributions to revolution, and that his Thought was a great treasure for the party. Deng said, "Of course, Comrade Mao Zedong was not without defects or mistakes. It would be un-Marxist to demand that a revolutionary leader have no defect or make no mistake." But he quickly skirted the question and said that the party must "scientifically and historically" study Mao's greatness. Likewise, the Cultural Revolution must be viewed "scientifically and historically" and there was no rush to arrive at any judgment at this point. See Deng's speech of December 13, 1978, "Jiefang sixiang, shihshih qiushi, tuanjie yizhi xiangqiankan," in ibid., pp. 18–33.

42. Qixin, "Zhonggong de fei Mao hua yundong," *The Seventies*, 1979, no. 4, pp. 15–18.

43. New China News Agency, September 30, 1979.

44. For the full text of the resolution passed by the Fifth Plenum of the Eleventy Party Congress and published on February 29, 1980, see *Major Documents*, pp. 185–92.

45. *Jiefangjun bao*, April 10, 1980, p. 1.

46. Deng's interview with the publisher of *Ming bao* on July 18, 1981. See "Zhonggong

zhongyang fuzhuxi Deng Xiaoping de tanhua jilu," *Ming bao* (September 1981), p. 3; Qixin, "Liuzhongquanhui yiho yanhuan?" *The Seventies*, 1981, no. 5, pp. 61–64.

47. "Zhongguo gongchandang di shiyijie zhongyang weiyuanhui disanze quanti huiyi gongbao," December 22, 1978, in *Major Documents*, pp. 1–14.

48. For full text of Ye's speech on September 29, 1979, commemorating the thirtieth anniversary of the founding of the People's Republic, "Xiangche sige xiandaihua de hongwei mubiao qianjin," see ibid., pp. 79–94. Quotation is on page 81.

49. "Zhongguo gongchandang di shiyijie zhongyang weiyuanhui disanze quanti huiyi gongbao," December 22, 1978, in ibid., pp. 1–14.

50. Ibid.

51. Deng's speech, "Jiefang sixiang, shihshih qiushi, tuanjie yizhi xiangqiankan," December 13, 1978, in ibid., pp. 18–33.

52. "Zhongguo gongchandang di shiyijie zhongyang weiyuanhui disanze quanti huiyi gongbao," December 22, 1978, in ibid., pp. 1–14.

53. Deng said that among the four cardinal principles, "the most important principle is the leadership by the Chinese Communist Party." The CCP must not only insist on providing leadership, but also try to provide good leadership. "Zhonggong zhongyang fuzhuxi Deng Xiaoping de tanhua jilu," *Ming bao* (September 1981), p. 5.

54. Deng said that the insistence on socialism, proletarian dictatorship, leadership by the Communist Party, and Marxism/Mao Zedong Thought were the preconditions of implementing four modernizations. See Deng's speech, "Shixian sige xiandaihua bixu jianchi sixiang jiben yuanze," March 30, 1979, in *Major Documents*, pp. 44–61.

55. Chen's speech at the Central Work Conference on November 12, 1978. *Chen Yun wenxuan (1956–1985)*, *CYWX*, p. 208.

56. "Zai zhongyang gongzuo huiyishang de jianghua," April 5, 1979, in *Major Documents*, pp. 62–78.

57. Li Xiannian's speech to the Central Work Conference, "Zai zhongyang gongzuo huiyishang de jianghua," April 5, 1979, in ibid.

58. They were called, respectively, the three-year, eight-year, and twenty-three–year plans. Chen's primary attention was on issues of economic readjustment during March 1979 and November 1980. For his ideas, see *CYWX*, pp. 220–44.

59. For full text of Deng's speech, see *Major Documents*, pp. 125–62.

60. Deng's speech, "Guanche tiaozheng fangzheng, baozheng anding tuanjie," December 25, 1980, in ibid., pp. 242–63.

61. Ibid.

62. "Guanyu jiji fazhan nongcun dozhong jinying de baogao," March 31, 1981. For texts, see ibid., pp. 269–87.

63. Zhao's speech, November 30 and December 1, 1981, "Jinghou jingji jianshe de fangzheng," in ibid., pp. 361–93.

64. Deng's speech, "Shixian sige xiandaihua bixu jianchi sixiang jiben yuanze," March 30, 1979, in ibid., pp. 44–61.

65. Zhao's speech, November 30 and December 1, 1981, "Jinghou jingji jianshe de fangzheng," in ibid., pp. 361–93.

66. For texts, see *Major Documents*, pp. 398–410.

67. Mufu, "Jixu fei Mao hua de wushi dahui," *The Seventies*, 1982, no. 10, pp. 14–15.

68. Ibid.

Chapter 2

1. For example, many *zhibu* held zhibu committee meetings once a month, zhibu general membership meetings once every two months, and internal party democratic life

meetings once every quarter. *RMRB*, July 22, 1986, p. 5.

2. A "democratic life meeting" usually had an agenda to focus on one or two problems, such as the abuse of power by children of leading cadres. See *RMRB*, January 28, 1983, p. 4.

3. Ibid.

4. Ibid.

5. *RMRB*, June 7, 1982, p. 2.

6. *RMRB*, June 28, 1982, p. 3.

7. *Beijing ribao* (*BJRB*), May 14, 1980, p. 2; *RMRB*, June 11, 1982, p. 3.

8. *BJRB*, December 8, 1979, p. 1.

9. *RMRB*, June 30, 1980, p. 1. Zhou Enlai and his wife Deng Yingchao were frequently cited as the models of protecting party secrets. Deng supposedly never asked her husband about his work, and Zhou never volunteered any information that she was not supposed to know. See *RMRB*, July 24, 1982, p. 1.

10. *BJRB*, April 11, 1980, p. 1.

11. For example, when the author was in Beijing in 1983, the public circulated the story that some children of high officials had learned about the government's secret decision to raise the prices of certain commodities. They quickly hoarded the items and reaped a windfall profit.

12. *BJRB*, March 5, 1980, p. 3.

13. *BJRB*, April 23, 1980, p. 3; May 14, 1980, p. 2.

14. Ximenghui, "Tequan jieji zai Zhongguo," *The Seventies*, 1979, no. 9, pp. 11–12. In 1978–79, some national leaders were alleged to have spent huge sums of public funds to refurbish their residences lavishly. Wang Dongxing's extravagance, for example, provoked the poet Ye Wenfu to write a poem of protest entitled "General, You Must Not Do This!" in 1979.

15. *GMRB*, September 28, 1979, p. 1.

16. *RMRB*, May 28, 1981, p. 4; July 12, 1981, p. 5.

17. The owners helped themselves with the gasoline allocation of their work units. According to one estimate made by the Beijing municipal police bureau, 98.2 percent of the gasoline consumed by the twelve thousand privately owned motorcycles in 1980–81 was purloined from work units. *RMRB*, May 9, 1981, p. 2; June 5, 1981, p. 3.

18. *RMRB*, April 10, 1984, p. 5.

19. *BJRB*, December 30, 1979, p. 1.

20. The most notorious example of this kind of behavior was the so-called Friendship Boat that visited Japan under the leadership of Liao Chengzhi in May 1979. The delegation consisted of about six hundred people, about two-thirds of whom were the spouses or children of high-ranking figures, and came back with a full load of gifts and purchases from Japan. It was a shopping spree dressed up as a diplomatic mission. Ximenghui, "Tequan jieji zai Zhongguo," *The Seventies*, 1979, no. 9, pp. 11–12.

21. *GMRB*, September 28, 1979, p. 1.

22. In one case, at a county-level conference of cadres in Yueyang County, Hubei Province, in 1981, the fifty attendees consumed four cows, eight hogs, and eighty catties of liquor in five days, all courtesy of their work units. *RMRB*, June 29, 1980, p. 1; May 28, 1981, p. 4; June 21, 1981, p. 3.

23. *BJRB*, November 22, 1979, p. 1.

24. *BJRB*, December 30, 1979, p. 1. A couple of gifts could easily wipe out the entire monthly pay of an average basic-level cadre, thus representing a heavy financial burden. In the single month of December 1979 in Shanxi, a dozen county-level cadres all threw separate parties to celebrate their children's weddings. Each of these parties was attended by more than four hundred guests, and three county party secretaries each collected more

than RMB $1,500 in gifts. *GMRB*, April 2, 1980, p. 1; *RMRB*, July 22, 1981, p. 4.

25. *GMRB*, April 2, 1980, p. 1.

26. For example, for four months in the winter of 1981, the best cigarettes produced in China (from Yunnan Province) suddenly disappeared entirely from the market and caused a national scandal. This shortage occurred because the entire stock had been preempted by *guanxihu* who in one way or another had a stranglehold over the tobacco factories. One single cigarette factory had to set aside 580,000 cartons to meet its social obligations. As the Central Discipline Committee admitted, even a case of this magnitude was not uncommon. *RMRB*, June 13, 1981, p. 1.

27. The most celebrated case involved national Minister of Commerce Wang Lei, who made a practice of paying a nominal fee for expensive banquets at a Beijing restaurant. His case was exposed by a young chef in October 1980 and caused the CCP Central Disciplinary Committee to issue a notice to the entire country. *BJRB*, October 17, 1980, p. 1.

28. This explains why, for some time, the workers of electricity stations could inspire such terror among their users and generally got whatever they wanted: their means of retaliation was most decisive and effective. They would simply cut the electric supply and force their victims' work to cease. *RMRB*, May 14, 1982, p. 2; June 19, 1982, p. 5.

29. *RMRB*, July 23, 1981, p. 4.

30. *RMRB*, May 24, 1982, p. 4.

31. These activities now covered the full range of illegal trading, black-marketeering, hoarding, theft of large quantities of public properties, evasion of taxes, fabrication or falsification of accounts, and smuggling of contraband along the coast. For instance, an "auto dealer" from Henan Province was able to use bribery and false records to acquire and sell 1,300 cars, 72 motorcycles, and 29 tractors and made a profit of $1.3 million yuan. His activities were carried out in fifteen provinces with the help of ninety-five state cadres and seventy-five CCP members. *RMRB*, March 2, 1982, p. 4. In another case in Guangdong Province, seventy-one members of the Coast Guard, including thirty-two CCP members, sold the contraband they captured from smugglers and made a profit of $670,000 yuan in just over one year. *RMRB*, February 20, 1982, p. 2.

32. *RMRB*, October 6, 1982, p. 3.

33. *RMRB*, August 7, 1981, p. 1.

34. Qixin, "Zhonggong hui xuanqi pi Mao yundong ma?" *The Seventies*, 1979, no. 1, pp. 67–71; Yu Congzhe, "Wusi yu Zhongguo," *The Seventies*, 1979, no. 5, pp. 76–79.

35. Wei Jingsheng, "Yao minzhu haishiyao xinde ducai," reprinted in *Ming bao* (January 1980), pp. 29–30.

36. Deng's speech, "Shixian sige xiandaihua bixu jianchi sixiang jiben yuanze," March 30, 1979, in *Major Documents*, pp. 44–61.

37. *RMRB*, November 30, 1983, p. 1.

38. Deng's speech, "Shixian sige xiandaihua bixu jianchi sixiang jiben yuanze," March 30, 1979, in *Major Documents*, pp. 44–61.

39. Ibid. See also Niming, "Wei Jingsheng an pingyi," *The Seventies*, 1979, no. 12, pp. 72–75; Qixin, "Zhonggong jianguo sanshinian de huigu," *The Seventies*, 1979, no. 10, p. 21.

40. Deng's speech, "Shixian sige xiandaihua bixu jianchi sixiang jiben yuanze," March 30, 1979, in *Major Documents*, pp. 44–61.

41. Ibid. See also Niming, "Wei Jingsheng an pingyi," *The Seventies*, 1979, no. 12, pp. 72–75.

42. Qixin, "Liuzhongquanhui yiho yanhuan?" *The Seventies*, 1981, no. 5, pp. 61–64.

43. Yu Congzhe, "Zhonggong de wenyi luxiang," *The Seventies*, 1979, no. 12, pp. 15–19. For a reprint of Liu Binyan's work, see ibid., pp. 22–38.

44. The leading works of the new socialist realism included Ye Wenfu's "General, You

Must Not Do This!'' (August 1979), Liu Binyan's ''Between Human and Demon'' (September 1979), Sha Yexin's ''If I Was Real'' (August 1979), Wang Jing's ''In the File of the Society'' (October 1979) and ''Manager Qiao Arrives at the Factory'' (September 1979), Shen Rong's ''At Middle Age'' (January 1980), and Bai Hua's ''The Story of 'Looking Forward' '' and ''A Bundle of Letters'' (January 1980). See *The Seventies*, 1980, no. 1; Li Yi, ''Zhongguo xin xieshizhuyi wenyi de xinqi,'' *The Seventies*, 1980, no. 5, pp. 21–27.

45. They included a general in Ye Wenfu's ''General, You Must Not Do This!,'' a national military leader in ''In the File of the Society,'' and a political commissar in ''Flying toward the Sky.''

46. Chen Ruoxi, ''Chikai de xieshizhuyi huado,'' *Ming bao* (July 1980), pp. 94–97.

47. One good specimen of new socialist realism writing was Bai Hua's ''A Bundle Of Letters,'' which satirized old revolutionaries who had abandoned their idealism and abused their privileges to secure preferential treatment for their children. The story also depicted the decadent lifestyles of children of influential people. *Renmin wenxue*, 1980, no. 1; reprinted in *The Seventies*, 1980, no. 3, pp. 98–108. For a general discussion of the school, see Li Yi, ''Wenyi xinxuo zhong so fanyin de Zhongguo xianshi,'' *The Seventies*, 1980, no. 6, pp. 28–33.

48. *RMRB*, April 1, 2, 5, 7, and 11, 1979; *GMRB*, April 1, 6, 10, and 13, 1979.

49. Shihong, ''Renquan buko fouding,'' *The Seventies*, 1979, no. 6, pp. 49–50.

50. Jizhi, '' 'Qingnian minzhupai' jingnian huodong dashi jiyao,'' *The Seventies*, 1981, no. 6, pp. 15–17; Qixin, ''Liuzhongquanhui yiho yanhuan?'' *The Seventies*, 1981, no. 5, pp. 61–64.

51. See editorials of the *Jiefangjun bao*, January 4, February 22 and 24, March 4, April 17 and 26, 1981.

52. They included Patriotism, Learn from Lei Feng, and ''Five Emphases, Four Beauties'' (civilized, courteous, hygenic, orderly, moral; beautiful spirit, beautiful language, beautiful behavior, and beautiful environment).

53. See, for example, Li Honglin's article ''Women jianchi shenmoyang de shehuizhuyi?'' (What kind of socialism do we uphold?), in *RMRB*, May 9, 1979, p. 1.

54. *Hongqi*, 1980, no. 24, pp. 13–16.

55. *CYWX*, p. 207.

56. *RMRB*, July 1, 1983, p. 3.

57. ''Zhongguo gongchandang di shiyijie zhongyang weiyuanhui disanze quanti huiyi gongbao,'' December 22, 1978, in *Major Documents*, pp. 1–14.

58. *Xinhua yuebao, Wenxianban* (hereafter *Xinhua Documents*) (January 1979), p. 20

59. Ibid.

60. Chen's inaugural speech to the Discipline Committee on January 4, 1979, in *CYWX*, pp. 215–19.

61. *RMRB*, July 31, 1979, p. 1.

62. *Xinhua Documents* (January 1979), pp. 20–21.

63. Special Commentator, *BJRB*, July 21, 1979, p. 1.

64. *Xinhua Documents* (January 1979), pp. 20–21; *RMRB*, editorial, June 30, 1979, p. 1; July 31, 1979, p. 1.

65. *Xinhua Documents* (March 1979), pp. 1–4.

66. Deng's speech on March 30, 1979, ''Shixian sige xiandaihua bixu jianchi sixiang jiben yuance,'' in *Major Documents*, pp. 44–61.

67. Special Commentator, *RMRB*, July 1, 1979, p. 1.

68. See, for example, *Xinhua Documents* (July 1979), pp. 1–6.

69. See editorial in *RMRB*, June 30, 1979, p. 1; Special Commentator, *RMRB*, July 1, 1979, p. 1.

70. For Hu Yaobang's remarks, see *RMRB*, July 31, 1979, p. 1; for similar views, see Special Commentator, *BJRB*, July 21, 1979, p. 1.

71. *RMRB*, July 1, 1983, p. 3.

72. For full text see *Beijing Review*, 1980, no. 14, pp. 11–19.

73. By the summer of 1979, the Central Discipline Inspection Committee reported that the work of correcting past cases of miscarriage of justice had been essentially completed. Therefore, its mission was shifted to solving current disciplinary problems. Up to the summer of 1979, the committee received and processed hundreds of thousands of complaints from citizens and brought 34,400 cases under investigation. In the provinces, discipline committees dispatched investigative teams to local levels to gather firsthand information on misconduct and to employ "education" to reform the errant members. See *GMRB*, August 23, 1979, p. 1.

74. *BJRB*, December 30, 1979, p. 1.

75. *GMRB*, September 28, 1979, p. 1. The most celebrated case during this time was the death sentence imposed on Wang Shouxin in the spring of 1980. Wang, who was the party secretary and manager of a county fuel company in Heilongjiang Province, was convicted of embezzling about half a million yuan. Even in this case, Wang's criminal activities had spanned nearly a decade before she was exposed. *BJRB*, February 29, 1980, p. 1.

76. For example, the reprinting of Zhang Wentian's articles of many years ago on this point. See *Xinhua Documents* (July 1979), pp. 1–6.

77. Special Commentator, "Dui ganbu de chuli yao zhao yan yu jiaoyu," *Jiefangjun bao*, May 8, 1979, p. 1,

78. Deng's speech on January 16, 1980, in *Major Documents*, pp. 125–62.

79. Ma was a county-level party secretary in the Tianjin district. He mobilized his own organizational support to refuse to resolve certain cases of political oppression in which he was personally implicated, in spite of repeated and explicit orders from the Tianjin party and the national party. *BJRB*, April 25, 1980, p. 1.

80. According to an official bill of complaints, they showed the preference for doing factional work, gave their allegiance not to their superiors but to their old cronies, and went out of the organizational framework to advance their collective interests. This preference for their cronies was shown in a myriad of ways when distributing rewards (e.g., recruitment into the party, promotion, salary increase, housing assignment, job evaluation). *BJRB*, May 14, 1980, p. 1.

81. *RMRB*, July 1, 1983, p. 3.

82. *CYWX*, p. 245.

83. *DXPWX*, p. 336.

84. One such example was using public funds to pay bonuses, or giving public properties to the workers. *RMRB*, April 20, 1982, p. 1.

85. *Minzhu yu fazhi* (Democracy and legal system), 1982, no. 6, pp. 11–12.

86. *CYWX*, pp. 245–46.

87. For the text of the Resolution by the National People's Congress passed on March 8, 1982, entitled, "Guanyu yanchen yanzchong pohuai jingji de zuifan de jueding," see *Major Documents*, pp. 422–29.

88. Deng's speech, "Jianjue daji jingji fanzui huodong" (Resolutely smash economic criminal activities), April 10, 1982, in *DXPWX*, pp. 357–59.

89. The propaganda vowed that the campaign would not simply swat the "flies" but would kill the "tigers." See *Minzhu yu fazhi*, 1982, no. 3, pp. 2–3, 14–16; *RMRB*, June 9, 1982, p. 3.

90. The *People's Daily* exposed a large number of cadres' economic crimes between February and March 1982, but all were flies, not tigers. *RMRB*, February–March 1982.

91. *Minzhu yu fazhi*, 1982, no. 5, pp. 15–16.

92. *RMRB*, September 28, 1982, p. 5.

93. In the summer of 1982, for example, the Central Discipline Committee had to send 154 investigators directly from the capital to various localities to ensure that prosecution of major cases of economic crimes would be conducted vigorously. *RMRB*, May 24, 1982, p. 4; July 23, 1982, p. 1.

94. *RMRB*, September 5, 1983, p. 1.

95. Deng's speech, ''Dang he guojia lingdao zhidu de gaige,'' August 18, 1980, in *Major Documents*, pp. 204–28.

96. For example, in the Xuancheng region of Anhui, which consisted of five counties, the number of cadres above the rank of deputy county magistrate increased from 227 before retrenchment to 292 after retrenchment. *RMRB*, August 28, 1984, p. 5.

97. For cases in mid-1983, see *RMRB*, May 11, 1983, p. 8.

98. *DXPWX*, p. 336. In July 1977, Deng said, ''It is quite necessary to rectify the party and rectify the style.''

Chapter 3

1. Deng's speech of December 13, 1978, in *DXPWX*, pp. 130–43.

2. Ibid.

3. *DXPWX*, p. 197.

4. Deng's speech of June 2, 1978, in *DXPWX*, pp. 117–18.

5. *DXPWX*, pp. 144–45.

6. *Guangxi ribao*, June 20, 1983, p. 1.

7. *Xinhua Documents*, 1979, no. 7, pp. 31–36.

8. Deng's speech of July 29, 1979, in *DXPWX*, pp. 175–78.

9. Deng's speeches of January 16 and August 28, 1980, in *DXPWX*, pp. 232, 283. Also *Xuexi yu yanjiu* [Beijing], 1984, no. 10, p. 23.

10. Deng's speech, ''Guanche tiaozheng fangzheng, baozheng anding tuanjie,'' December 25, 1980, in *Major Documents*, pp. 242–63.

11. Deng's speech of December 25, 1980, in *DXPWX*, p. 329.

12. *RMRB*, February 14, 1984, p. 1.

13. *Lanzhou xuekan*, 1984, no. 1, pp. 11–17.

14. *RMRB*, December 17, 1983, p. 5.

15. *Guangxi ribao*, June 20, 1983, p. 1.

16. *Lanzhou xuekan*, 1984, no. 1, pp. 11–17.

17. *RMRB*, editorial, March 15, 1984, p. 1.

18. *RMRB*, Commentator, August 4, 1984, p. 1.

19. *RMRB*, editorial, October 14, 1983, p. 1.

20. ''Resolution on Party Rectification'' passed on October 11, 1983, full text printed in *Hongqi*, 1983, no. 20, pp. 2–11.

21. *CYWX*, pp. 281–84.

22. Bo Yibo's speech of December 21, 1984, in *Zheng dang yinian* (Beijing: Renmin ribao chubanshe, 1985), pp. 36–38.

23. *Sichuan ribao*, January 8, 1984, p. 1.

24. *Xuexi yu yanjiu*, 1984, no. 10, p. 23.

25. *BJRB*, July 4, 1984, p. 1.

26. *CYWX* , pp. 293–94.

27. *Xuexi yu shijian* [Wuhan], 1985, no. 2, pp. 8–11; *RMRB*, November 13, 1984, p. 5.

28. *RMRB*, December 17, 1983, p. 5.

29. For instance, the party acknowledged that many people had engaged in beating,

smashing, and looting, but only those who had exploited and personally gained through such activities would be the targets. Likewise, many people had participated in factional activities, but only those who showed "serious factional thoughts" would be the targets. Finally, many had participated in rebellious acts, but only those who built a career on rebellious acts would be the targets. See *Xuexi yu yanjiu*, 1984, no. 10, p. 23.

30. *BJRB*, July 4, 1984, p. 1.

31. *Yangcheng wanbao* [Guangzhou], January 25, 1984, p. 2.

32. *RMRB*, December 21, 1983, p. 1.

33. For example, for Fujian see *Xuexi yuekan* [Fuzhou], 1985, no. 2, pp. 16–17.

34. *Hongqi*, 1984, no. 21, p. 13; *RMRB*, November 27, 1984, p. 1.

35. *Zheng dang yinian*, p. 39; *Liaowang*, 1986, no. 15, pp. 14–15.

36. *RMRB*, December 23, 1984, p. 1. Also *Zheng dang yinian*, pp. 38, 39.

37. *RMRB*, December 23, 1984, p. 1.

38. *RMRB*, July 15, 1985, p. 1. For other examples, see *Sixiang zhengzhi gongzuo yanjiu* [Beijing], 1984, no. 6, p. 12; *Jiefang ribao* [Shanghai], January 8, 1985, p. 1.

39. For a report on Shandong, see *Dazhong ribao* [Jinan], September 27, 1984, p. 1. For Jiangxi, see *Qiushi* [Nanchang], 1985, no. 1, p. 47.

40. For Beijing, see *BJRB*, January 25, 1985, p. 1. For Jiangsu, see *Qunzhong* [Nanjing], 1985, no. 1, p. 13. For Jiangxi, see *Qiushi* [Nanchang], 1985, no. 1, p. 47.

41. For Fujian, see *Xuexi yuekan* [Fuzhou], 1985, no. 2, pp. 16–17. For Jiangxi, see *Qiushi*, 1985, no. 1, p. 47. For Hubei, see *Xuexi yu shijian* [Wuhan], 1985, no. 2, pp. 8–11. For Inner Mongolia, see *Shijian* [Huhehot], 1985, no. 4, pp. 9–10.

42. *Hongqi*, 1985, no. 20, p. 5.

43. *RMRB*, May 31, 1987, p. 1.

44. *Yangcheng wanbao* [Guangzhou], January 25, 1984, p. 2.

45. Deng's speech of November 2, 1979, in *DXPWX*, p. 198.

46. Chen Yun's speech of May 8, 1981, in *CYWX*, pp. 262–66.

47. *Shijian*, 1983, no. 18, p. 20.

48. Domes, *Government and Politics*, pp. 187–88.

49. *BJRB*, June 27, 1981, p. 1; Chen Yun's speech of May 8, 1981, in *CYWX*, p. 262.

50. *DXPWX*, p. 193.

51. *CYWX*, pp. 232–34.

52. Chen Yun's speech of May 8, 1981, in *CYWX*, pp. 262–67.

53. *BJRB*, June 27, 1981, p. 1.

54. *DXPWX*, pp. 193–95.

55. Ibid.

56. *Dangshi yanjiu*, 1983, no. 5, p. 13.

57. *CYWX*, pp. 233–34.

58. *DXPWX*, p. 176.

59. *Dang shi yanjiu yu jiaoxue* [Fuzhou], 1988, no. 2, pp. 1–9.

60. *RMRB*, April 2, 1982, p. 3.

61. *CYWX*, pp. 263, 267.

62. Ibid., pp. 271–72.

63. Ibid., pp. 262, 267, 374.

64. For the full text of the resolution, see *Major Documents*, pp. 411–21.

65. *RMRB*, May 16, 1983, p. 5; *Qinghai ribao*, October 3, 1983, p. 3.

66. *CYWX*, p. 263.

67. *RMRB*, May 17, 1982, p. 3; August 28, 1985, p. 4.

68. *RMRB*, April 15, 1982, p. 5.

69. *RMRB*, July 20, 1983, p. 4. These sentiments were generally referred to by the saying, "After the guest has departed, the tea will turn cold."

70. *RMRB*, July 11, 1983, p. 3.

71. Ibid.

72. For example, see *RMRB*, February 6, 1983, p. 1.

73. *RMRB*, June 26, 1981, p. 1; July 6, 1983, p. 4.

74. *RMRB*, December 7, 1984, p. 4.

75. *RMRB*, July 7, 1983, p. 4.

76. *RMRB*, January 3, 1982, p. 4.

77. *RMRB*, February 22, 1982, p. 3; April 15, 1982, p. 5; June 21, 1982, p. 3; August 1, 1983, p. 3.

78. *RMRB*, May 17, 1982, p. 3; August 28, 1985, p. 4.

79. *RMRB*, January 3, 1982, p. 4.

80. *RMRB*, April 30, 1983, p. 4; November 9, 1984, p. 4.

81. *RMRB*, November 9, 1984, p. 4.

82. *RMRB*, March 22, 1983, p. 2; October 11, 1983, p. 5.

83. *RMRB*, November 9, 1984, p. 4.

84. *RMRB*, April 18, 1982, p. 4.

85. *RMRB*, November 9, 1984, p. 4.

86. *Dangde zuzhi gongzuo cidian* [Beijing, 1987], pp. 94–95.

87. Deng's speech of August 18, 1980, in *DXPWX*, p. 299. Deng first proposed using the advisory system to ease aging cadres out of active service in 1975, before Mao's death. See *DXPWX*, p. 23. Little progress was made in the next several years as Deng himself fell from power. In late 1979, Deng stated that he now believed that the establishment of a rational retirement system was more fundamental than the advisory system, and he urged party leaders to give retirement policy serious thought. See Deng's speech of November 2, 1979, in *DXPWX*, p. 198.

88. Interview with Bo Yibo, in *Liaowang*, 1983, no. 10, pp. 2–4.

89. Ibid.

90. Ibid.

91. *CYWX*, p. 282.

92. *RMRB*, January 24, 1984, p. 1.

93. Deng's statement to the party's Central Military Affairs Commission, July 4, 1982, *DXPWX*, p. 366.

94. *Hongqi*, 1983, no. 16, pp. 2–6.

95. *RMRB*, June 26, 1981, p. 1.

96. *RMRB*, May 11, 1982, p. 4.

97. *RMRB*, July 20, 1983, p. 4.

98. *RMRB*, September 9, 1983, p. 3; September 26, 1983, p. 1.

99. *Hongqi*, 1986, no. 15, pp. 4–5.

100. *RMRB*, July 6, 1983, p. 4.

101. *RMRB*, January 24, 1984, p. 1.

102. *RMRB*, November 9, 1984, p. 4.

103. *Lilun yuekan* [Beijing], 1985, no. 2, p. 8.

104. *RMRB*, November 9, 1984, p. 4.

105. In February 1985, about 900,000 old comrades had taken the lead to retire to second and third lines, a reference to *lixiu*. See *RMRB*, February 11, 1985, p. 1.

106. *RMRB*, February 11, 1985, p. 1.

107. *RMRB*, April 10, 1985, p. 1.

108. See Hu's opening speech to the Fourth Plenum of the Twelfth Party Congress, in *Hongqi*, 1985, no. 19, p. 8.

109. Lin Wei, "Cong renshi quliu kan Zhonggong dongxiang," *The Nineties*, 1985, no. 10, pp. 17–19.

110. *RMRB*, January 24, 1984, p. 1; *Xuexi yu yanjiu* [Beijing], 1984, no. 3, p. 4.

111. *Xuexi yu yanjiu*, 1984, no. 3, p. 4.

112. They included sixty-four members of the Central Committee, thirty-seven members of the Central Advisory Committee, and thirty members of Central Discipline Committee. See *RMRB*, September 17, 1985, p. 1. For the three complete lists, see *Hongqi*, 1985, no. 19, pp. 3–5.

113. *RMRB*, September 24, 1985, p. 1.

114. *Hongqi*, 1985, no. 19, p. 8.

115. *RMRB*, August 28, 1985, p. 4.

116. Ibid.

117. *Hongqi*, 1986, no. 12, p. 2.

118. Bo Yibo's estimate as quoted in *RMRB*, January 26, 1984, p. 1.

119. *RMRB*, July 6, 1986, p. 1.

120. The party scoffed at this criticism in 1982 and asserted that the retirement system was but another manifestation of the superiority of the socialist system, as well as of its high moral standards. See *RMRB*, March 1, 1982, p. 3.

121. According to an interview with WQL, a section chief in the Liaoning provincial government, even in December 1987 there were still a number of quite old leading provincial cadres in Liaoning. The same situation existed in Shandong, according to members of the visiting delegation from Zouping County in early 1987.

122. Chapter 6 of "Zhongguo gongchandang zhangcheng," September 6, 1982, is devoted specially to cadres. For the full text, see *Major Documents*, pp. 526–54.

123. For example, shortly after Liberation, the criteria for party cadre selection and promotion were "virtue, talent, and seniority" (*de, cai, zi*). During the early phase of the Cultural Revolution, the criteria were "combination of virtue and talent," but "virtue" was interpreted to mean those cadres who dared to rebel against tradition and carry out a leftist line. During the later phase of the Cultural Revolution, cadre policy was guided by the concept of the combination of old, middle-aged, and youthful cadres, which forced many veteran cadres to the sideline. The new criteria for cadres in the 1980s were that they should be "revolutionary, intellectual, young, and professional." See *Yangcheng wanbao*, September 18, 1985, p. 2.

124. *Anqing shiyuan xuebao, shekeban* [Anhui], 1987, no. 1, p. 31.

125. *RMRB*, May 3, 1984, p. 1.

126. For a general evaluation of the PRC cadre system, see *Jianghuai luntan* [Hefei], 1986, no. 6, pp. 35–36.

127. Qixin, "Zai Beijing, minzhu shi zhongxin huati," *The Seventies*, 1979, no. 6, pp. 46–47.

128. Deng's speech of July 29, 1979, in *DXPWX*, pp. 175–78.

129. Deng's speech of November 2, 1979, in *DXPWX*, p. 194.

130. Deng's speech of July 29, 1979, in *DXPWX*, pp. 175–78.

131. Ibid. Ye Jianying in late 1979 only recommended that some young and middle-aged cadres be promoted to the leadership core to share the burden of the older leaders under the latter's continued guidance and assistance. He said nothing about promoting the younger ones to "replace" the older leaders. See Ye Jianying's speech of September 29, 1979, in *Zhishi fenzi wenti wenxian xuanbian* (hereafter *Documents on Intellectuals*), pp. 67–70.

132. Deng's speech of November 2, 1979, in *DXPWX*, pp. 192–93, 197.

133. Ibid., pp. 195–96.

134. *RMRB*, July 2, 1983, p. 1.

135. *DXPWX*, pp. 192–93, 195–96. Chen Yun's speech of May 8, 1981, in *CYWX*, pp. 262–66. For an illustration of the difficulties encountered by the municipal party and

government of Beijing, where the greatest progress should have taken place, see *RMRB*, June 27, 1981, p. 1.

136. Chen Yun cited the example of Li Peng's promotion to be the minister of electric power at the age of fifty-two, which was made possible only after direct intervention by many senior leaders, including Chen himself. See Chen Yun's speech of July 2, 1981, in *CYWX*, pp. 268–69.

137. Chen Yun's speech of May 8, 1981, in *CYWX*, pp. 262–66.

138. Chen Yun's speech of July 2, 1981, in *CYWX*, pp. 267–68.

139. Ibid., pp. 270–71, and *RMRB*, July 2, 1983, p. 1.

140. See, for example, Ye Jianying's speech in late 1979 in *Documents on Intellectuals*, pp. 67–70. Ye's three requirements were endorsed by Deng shortly afterward. See *DXPWX*, p. 194.

141. For instance, Deng proposed in August 1980 that the candidates must be workers committed to socialist modernization who were relatively young, and who possessed professional knowledge. Chen Yun also proposed that cadres must possess both virtue and talent. While virtue was measured by the cadres' loyalty to socialism and the party's leadership, talent was measured by their youth, education (or knowledge), and professional expertise. *RMRB*, July 2, 1983, p. 1.

142. *RMRB*, June 26, 1981, p. 1.

143. Ibid.; Chen Yun's speech of May 8, 1981, in *CYWX*, pp. 262–66.

144. Chen Yun's speech of July 2, 1981, in *CYWX*, pp. 269–70.

145. Chen Yun's speech of May 8, 1981, in *CYWX*, pp. 262–66, 270. Chen Yun basically favored the method of promoting the majority of cadres one grade at a time, while allowing a few to move up by skipping several grades at a time. On the other hand, Deng did not take a strong position in favor of either orderly or accelerated promotion process. While he certainly objected to promoting cadres "by elevators" as practiced during the Cultural Revolution, he also said that it might be necessary to avoid a mechanical orderly promotion process to give the real talents a chance to reach the top. *RMRB*, July 2, 1983, p. 1.

146. Hu Yaobang's interview with a Japanese journalist, *RMRB*, October 10, 1983, p. 4.

147. *RMRB*, July 22, 1983, p. 1.

148. Zhang Guangxin, "Disan tidui yu dang de zuzhi jianshe," in *Mao Zedong sixiang yanjiu* [Chengdu], 1985, no. 3, pp. 64–68.

149. Deng's interview with a Japanese visitor in July 1985 as reported in *RMRB*, July 22, 1985, p. 1.

150. *RMRB*, October 21, 1984, p. 1.

151. *Liaowang*, 1983, no. 10, p. 8.

152. Ibid., no. 2, p. 12.

153. *BJRB*, August 31, 1983, p. 1.

154. *BJRB*, Commentator, August 31, 1983, p. 1; also *RMRB*, September 1, 1983, p. 1.

155. *RMRB*, May 4, 1982, p. 5; March 28, 1983, p. 3. Indeed, not infrequently, young cadres who had been promoted to leadership position found it difficult to be accepted by their subordinates and colleagues with respect. This was a continuous manifestation of the bias in Chinese political culture that puts inordinate emphasis on age and seniority.

156. As the *Beijing ribao*'s editorial pointed out on August 31, 1983, many of the recently installed leaders lacked the professional qualifications to meet the needs of the four modernizations and about 30 percent of them were so old that they would have to retire by 1985. *BJRB*, Commentator, August 31, 1983, p. 1; *RMRB*, September 1, 1983, p. 1.

157. *BJRB*, Commentator, August 31, 1983, p. 1; *RMRB*, September 1, 1983, p. 1.

158. *RMRB*, editorial, January 24, 1984, p. 1.

159. *RMRB*, April 20, 1984, p. 1.

160. *Xuexi yu yanjiu*, 1984, no. 3, p. 6.

161. *RMRB*, April 28, 1985, p. 1.

162. *Zheng dang yinian*, p. 37

163. *RMRB*, October 24, 1984, p. 1.

164. *Zheng dang yinian*, p. 37

165. *RMRB*, April 10, 1985, p. 1.

166. *Liaowang*, 1985, no. 2, p. 12.

167. Ibid.

168. They included nine persons from the national party and the State Council, eighteen from provincial party and government organs, and eight from various branches of the People's Liberation Army. See *Xuanchuan shouce*, [Beijing], 1985, no. 21, p. 4.

169. *RMRB*, October 11, 1985, p. 1.

170. Many provincial party standing committees had reduced their membership from twenty to only ten, and reduced the number of secretaries from fourteen or fifteen to only five. Altogether, some two hundred members of standing committees as well as about one hundred secretaries of the twenty-nine provincial party units were abolished in 1983. See *Banyuetan*, 1983, no. 8, pp. 9–11; *Liaowang*, 1983, no. 10, p. 8.

171. *BJRB*, October 18, 1984, p. 4; *Wenhuibao*, October 31, 1985, p. 3; *RMRB*, September 9, 1985, p. 1.

172. In minority areas (such as Tibet, Inner Mongolia, and Xinjiang), members of minorities constituted over half of the standing committee members and two-thirds of the party secretaries. See *Banyuetan*, 1983, no. 8, pp. 9–11.

173. *Wenhuibao*, October 31, 1985, p. 3; *RMRB*, September 9, 1985, p. 1.

174. *Liaowang*, 1985, no. 2, p. 12.

175. *RMRB*, October 5, 1984, p. 1; *BJRB*, October 18, 1984, p. 4; *Wenhuibao*, October 31, 1985, p. 3; *RMRB*, September 9, 1985, p. 1; *Liaowang*, 1985, no. 2, p. 12.

176. Thus, for example, one oft-cited figure was that more than eighty thousand younger cadres had been promoted to "leadership positions" above the county level by early 1985. *Liaowang*, 1985, no. 2, p. 12; *BJRB*, October 18, 1984, p. 4; *Wenhuibao*, October 31, 1985, p. 3; *RMRB*, September 9, 1985, p. 1.

177. *RMRB*, June 29, 1986, p. 1; *Hongqi*, 1986, no. 12, p. 2.

178. Some 1,268,000 old cadres had been retired from February 1982 to December 1985. *RMRB*, June 29, 1986, p. 1.

179. For example, according to the party's Central Organization Department, by December 1984, of the total number of cadres recently promoted to leadership positions above the county level for the entire country, more than 60 percent had a college education. Of this same group, those under 50 years of age (numbering some 150,000) seemed to have the highest concentration of college education, for 113,000 had formal college education and more than 7,000 others had acquired an equivalent of college education through self-study. *RMRB*, January 3, 1986, p. 1.

180. *Hongqi*, 1985, no. 19, p. 35. For a similar expression of confidence, see *RMRB*, September 9, 1985, p. 1.

181. *RMRB*, September 27, 1985, p. 1.

Chapter 4

1. *RMRB*, March 18, 1982, p. 1; *Liaowang*, 1983, no. 10, p. 10.

2. *RMRB*, June 26, 1981, p. 1.

3. *Liaowang*, 1983, no. 10, p. 10.

4. Hu Qili, "Zai zhongguo gongchang zhuyi qingniantuan di shiyici quanguo daibiao

dahui shang de zhuci," in *Zhongguo gongchan zhuyi qingniantuan di shiyici quanguo daibiao dahui wenjian huibian* (hereafter *CYL Documents*) [Beijing], 1983, pp. 1–6.

5. *Yangcheng wanbao*, September 18, 1985, p. 2.

6. In November 1984, Li Rui made a speech in which he listed the defects in the working styles of the organization departments on various levels and warned that they should be changed promptly. See Li Rui's speech, "Xinxingshi yu ganbu gongzuo" (The new situation and cadre work), in *Lilun yuekan* [Beijing], 1985, no. 2, pp. 8–9.

7. *Fendou* [Haerbin], 1984, no. 11–12, p. 3.

8. Ibid.

9. *Dongyue luncong* [Jinan, Shandong], January 1986, pp. 11–15.

10. For expressions of the above criticisms, see *RMRB*, September 4, 1984, p. 5.

11. *Lilun xuekan* [Jinan, Shandong], February 1986, pp. 31–33; for the many complaints about the selection process made in December 1984, see *RMRB*, December 5, 1984, p. 8.

12. *Lilun xuekan*, February 1986, pp. 31–33.

13. See *RMRB*, December 5, 1984, p. 1, for complaints about the selection process made in December 1984.

14. *Jiefang ribao*, December 17, 1985, p. 4.

15. *RMRB*, December 5, 1984, p. 1. These complaints about the selection process were made in December 1984.

16. *BJRB*, January 25, 1985, p. 1.

17. *Xueshu luntan*, 1986, no. 4, pp. 13–14.

18. *BJRB*, January 25, 1985, p. 1. For another example from Shenyang, see an article written by a party secretary of Shenyang City, who was also municipal minister of economic affairs, see *Xiandai qiyejia* [Shenyang], March 1986, pp. 3–6.

19. *Jiefang ribao*, December 17, 1985, p. 4.

20. Ibid.

21. *RMRB*, January 3, 1986, p. 1.

22. For Hu Yaobang's criticism in 1985 that lower-level leaders should not be so rigid, see *Jiefang ribao*, December 17, 1985, p. 4.

23. Ibid.

24. For provincial cases, see Hu Qili, in *CYL Documents*, pp. 1–6. For county cases, see *Lilun yuekan*, 1986, no. 3, pp. 33–36.

25. *RMRB*, August 11, 1983, p. 8.

26. *Qunzhong*, 1985, no. 2, pp. 31–33; *Hebei ribao*, January 9, 1985, p. 4.

27. Chen Yun, for instance, had criticized the tendency of the old cadres to dismiss younger ones as "inexperienced" because he contended that young people must be given a chance to gain experience from service. See Chen Yun's speech of May 8, 1981, in *CYWX*, pp. 262–66.

28. Ibid.

29. *RMRB*, August 24, 1984, p. 1.

30. *Qunzhong*, 1985, no. 2, pp. 31–33; *Hebei ribao*, January 9, 1985, p. 4. Also *RMRB*, September 1, 1983, p. 8.

31. As the first provincial party secretary of Henan Province pointed out in 1983, an alarming 60–70 percent of promising middle-aged and young cadres were given this particular criticism when their qualifications to be promoted as successors were evaluated. See *RMRB*, August 12, 1983, p. 8.

32. *Qunzhong*, 1985, no. 2, pp. 31–33; *Hebei ribao*, January 9, 1985, p. 4; *RMRB*, October 30, 1984, p. 5, contained many criticisms made by Heilongjiang Party Secretary Li Li'an, in October 1984. Also see *RMRB*, August 24, 1984, p. 1.

33. Hu Qili, in *CYL Documents*, pp. 1–6.

34. *Lilun yu shijian*, 1984, no. 11, pp. 25–27.

35. *Qunzhong*, 1985, no. 2, pp. 31–33; *Hebei ribao*, January 9, 1985, p. 4.

36. *RMRB*, August 11, 1983, p. 8; September 1, 1983, p. 8.

37. *Lilun xuekan*, 1986, no. 2, pp. 31–33.

38. Criticisms made by Heilongjiang Party Secretary Li Li'an in October 1984. See *RMRB*, August 24, 1984, p. 1; October 30, 1984, p. 5.

39. *Jiefang ribao*, December 17, 1985, p. 4.

40. Li Rui's speech of November 1984 in which he listed the defects in the working styles of organization department personnel on various levels that needed to be changed promptly. See Li Rui's speech, "Xinxingshi yu ganbu gongzuo," in *Lilun yuekan*, 1985, no. 2, pp. 8–9.

41. *Lilun yuekan*, 1986, no. 3, pp. 33–36.

42. These included the three types, the people who had opposed the party since the Third Plenum, and all kinds of criminals.

43. Many leading cadres accepted the conventional wisdom that people's political interests were best served when they were "backed by a patron in the court and surrounded by protégés underneath." See *RMRB*, March 21, 1983, p. 3.

44. The situation became so bad in 1984 that the official press made appeals to suggest that old cadres should learn that they could do more by doing less to interfere. See *RMRB*, April 27, 1983, p. 2; September 1, 1984, p. 1.

45. *Lilun yuekan*, 1986, no. 3, pp. 33–36.

46. *RMRB*, March 21, 1983, p. 3.

47. *RMRB*, overseas edition, September 27, 1986, p. 2.

48. *Lilun yuekan*, 1986, no. 3, pp. 33–36.

49. *Shehui kexue pinglun* [Xi'an], 1985, no. 9, pp. 35–36.

50. *RMRB*, January 5, 1987, p. 1.

51. Hu Qili, in *CYL Documents*, pp. 1–6.

52. Chen Boda, *Zhongguo sida jiazu* (N.p., 1946).

53. Moming, "Congjun—shangxue—chuguo: ganbu zinu shinian daolu," *The Seventies*, 1979, no. 12, pp. 8–9.

54. Ibid.

55. For instance, many of the children of high-ranking party and military leaders of Sichuan were sent to Shaanxi Province to work on farms. Some fell in love and got married later. Interview with RXP, July 10, 1987. For other examples, see "Zhongguo tequan jieceng goutu," in *The Seventies*, 1983, nos. 8, 9, 10. According to this report, Yu Qiuli seemed to be the best-connected family. One of his daughters married the son of Huang Hua, another daughter married the son of Lin Hujia, and his son married the daughter of General Xu Shiyu.

56. For some cases of children of county officials who were workers but were promoted to county leaders, see *Lilun yu shijian* [Shenyang], 1986, no. 6, pp. 8–10.

57. *Anqing shiyuan xuebao, shekeban* [Anhui], 1987, no. 1, p. 31.

58. *Lilun yu shijian*, 1986, no. 6, pp. 8–10.

59. *Anqing shiyuan xuebao, shekeban*, 1987, no. 1, p. 31.

60. "Guanyu dangnei zhengzhi shenghuo de rogan zhunce" (Guidelines on internal party life), issued by the Fifth Plenum of the Eleventh Party Congress in March 1980. For text, see *GMRB*, March 15, 1980, pp. 1–2.

61. *RMRB*, February 2, 1986. p.1.

62. *RMRB*, March 18, 1982, p. 1.

63. *Lilun yuekan*, 1984, no. 5, p. 1.

64. *BJRB*, November 11, 1979, p. 1.

65. *BJRB*, February 21, 1980, p. 1.

66. *GMRB*, March 11, 1980, p. 1.

67. *BJRB*, November 11, 1979, p. 1.

68. *RMRB*, April 25, 1987, p. 4. The figures in various official reports are not always identical. Cf. July 1983 report by the party's Organization Department, in *RMRB*, July 22, 1983, p. 1; also October 2, 1982, p. 2.

69. In 1982–83, the number of cadres was around twenty-one million. *RMRB*, July 22, 1983, p. 1.

70. *RMRB*, May 14, 1982, p. 1.

71. *RMRB*, October 26, 1984, p. 2.

72. Ibid.

73. In Fangshan County (Hebei Province), cadres working in the fields of finance and commerce who had college education constituted 1.6 percent, and cadres who had senior high school education constituted another 10.5 percent of total personnel, while the rest (87.9 percent) had junior high school education or less. See *RMRB*, October 26, 1984, p. 2. South China's famous scenic city, Wuxi, was one of the most modernized cities in Jiangsu Province, yet 90 percent of the entire municipal work force were classified as having no technical knowledge at all. Furthermore, 96 percent of the workers in the municipal industries, and 99 percent of the cadres in economic management, had no expertise. In the neighboring county of Shachou, only 1.63 percent of the county's work force had any expertise, and only 0.0083 percent of the *xiang* and *zhen* enterprises' work force had any professional knowledge. See *RMRB*, November 11, 1984, p. 5.

74. *BJRB*, November 11, 1979, p. 1.

75. *RMRB*, March 15, 1983, p. 4.

76. *Xin changzheng*, 1983, no. 5, p. 42.

77. *RMRB*, July 1, 1982, p. 3; October 14, 1982, p. 1.

78. *RMRB*, May 20, 1983, p. 1.

79. *Funu shenghuo*, 1983, no. 6, p. 41.

80. *Banyuetan* [Beijing], 1984, no. 3, pp. 9–11.

81. *Liaowang*, 1983, no. 3, pp. 9–11.

82. See *Hebei xuekan* [Shijiazhuang], 1984, no. 5, p. 51.

83. *RMRB*, May 20, 1983, p. 1.

84. *RMRB*, October 14, 1982, p. 1.

85. Ibid.; and March 4, 1983, p. 1.

86. *RMRB*, July 22, 1983, p. 1.

87. *Liaowang*, 1983, no. 3, pp. 9–11.

88. They were supposed to be young, educated, revolutionized, and professionalized. See *RMRB*, July 22, 1983, p. 1.

89. *Hebei xuekan*, 1984, no. 5, p. 51.

90. For a description of the party's new rules on training, see *RMRB*, October 14, 1982, p. 1.

91. *Lilun yu shijian* [Shenyang], 1985, no. 12, p. 4.

92. *Lilun yuekan*, 1984, no. 5, p. 2.

93. *Guangxi dangxiao xuebao* [Nanning], 1987, no. 1, pp. 18–19; also *Shaanxi ribao*, December 16, 1984, p. 2.

94. *Lilun xuekan*, 1985, no. 1, pp. 2–7; also *RMRB*, June 13, 1983, p. 4.

95. There was a conspicuous and widespread tendency among many oganizations to give prominence to their reduction of age and increase of education as proof of their faithful implementation of the party's cadre policy. Between 1983 and the end of 1985, many provinces made two major readjustments of leading cadres.They usually reported their progress by year, sometimes citing percentages of decrease of age and increase of

educational qualifications with great precision down to one place after the decimal point, and also by detailed categories of leading cadres. See *RMRB*, February 22, 1984, p. 1; May 3, 1984, p. 1; February 2, 1983, p. 3; June 6, 1983, p. 3; *Qunzhong*, 1985, no. 11, p. 2. For Jiangsu Province, see *Xinhuabao* [Nanjing], December 22, 1984, p. 1; *Qunzhong*, 1985, no. 1, pp. 3–4. For Zhejiang Province in late 1983, see *Zhejiang ribao*, November 25, 1983, p. 1. For Liaoning Province, see *Lilun yu shijian*, 1983, no. 10, pp. 18–20. For the autonomous region of Ningxia in mid-1983, see *Ningxia ribao*, July 29, 1983, p. 1. For data on Henan, see *RMRB*, March 18, 1982, p. 1; August 24, 1984, p. 1. For Shanxi Province, see *Hongqi*, 1985, no. 3, p. 26.

96. They included "party schools," which usually existed only above the *xian* level; "cadre schools"; and "cadre management academies." See *RMRB*, overseas edition, April 22, 1987, p. 1. By 1984, when the training program reached full growth, there were about 55,000 people listed as teachers in the program for the entire country. See *Lilun yuekan*, 1984, no. 5, p. 2; *RMRB*, February 23, 1983, p. 1.

97. *RMRB*, April 25, 1987, p. 4.

98. *RMRB*, February 5, 1983, p. 1.

99. According to a report in early 1987, there were only some 800 full-time instructors for all these schools. *RMRB*, overseas edition, April 22, 1987, p. 1.

100. *GMRB*, November 10, 1984, p. 3.

101. Colleges and universities under the jurisdiction of certain national ministries or provincial governments were sometimes obligated to train cadres in their respective fields by orders from above. A good example was the Ministry of Agriculture, Animal Husbandry, and Fishery, which ordered the agricultural colleges under its administrative control to provide training on the science and economics of agriculture to the leading cadres of county level and above. By 1984, it was reported that more than 90 percent of counties in China had at least one leading cadre who had received such training. See *Lilun yuekan*, 1984, no. 5, p. 2. When work units did not possess their own institutions of higher learning, they had to contract other regular colleges and universities to train cadres for them.

102. In 1981–82, only about 7,000 cadres had been trained at these colleges annually. See *RMRB*, August 21, 1982, p. 3. By 1984, about 200 colleges and universities had participated in the program of offering two-year training to cadres and had enrolled only 46,000 cadres throughout the country up to that time. See *Lilun yuekan*, 1984, no. 5, p. 2. In the spring of 1987, the party's Central Organization Department claimed that some 1,500 nonparty colleges and universities also helped the party train its personnel. See *RMRB*, overseas edition, April 22, 1987, p. 1.

103. *Guangxi dangxiao xuebao* [Nanning], 1987, no. 1, pp. 18–19.

104. *Lilun yuekan*, 1986, no. 5, pp. 46–49.

105. *Guangxi dangxiao xuebao*, 1987, no. 1, pp. 18–19. Also *GMRB*, November 10, 1984, p. 3.

106. Jiang Nanxiang, vice-president of the Central Party School, complained of this problem in early 1985. See *Lilun yuekan*, 1985, no. 4, p. 4.

107. They ranged from several hundred to a few thousand cadres a year for each school. For some enrollment figures of the Central Party School, see *Liaowang*, 1983, no. 3, pp. 9–11. For a review of the party school in Fujian, see *Xuexi yuekan* [Fuzhou], 1985, no. 8, p. 2. In 1983, the Jiangxi provincial party school only admitted 173 cadres for a two-year program. See *Qiushi* [Nanchang], 1985, no. 4, p. 6.

108. *Lilun xuekan* [Xi'an], 1985, no. 1, pp. 2–7.

109. *RMRB*, October 14, 1982, p. 1.

110. *Shaanxi ribao*, December 16, 1984, p. 2.

111. The ratio was often four to one. See *Lilun xuekan*, 1985, no. 6, p. 3.

112. Ibid.

113. *GMRB*, November 10, 1984, p. 3.

114. *RMRB*, October 14, 1982, p. 1.

115. *GMRB*, November 10, 1984, p. 3.

116. *RMRB*, July 10, 1983, p. 1; July 13, 1983, p. 8; September 5, 1983, p. 5.

117. *Lilun yuekan*, 1984, no. 5, p. 3.

118. *Lilun xuekan*, 1984, no. 6, p. 3

119. Ibid., 1985, no. 10, pp. 1–2.

120. *Lilun yuekan*, 1984, no. 5, p. 3.

121. Ibid.; also see *Guangxi dangxiao xuebao*, 1987, no. 1, pp. 18–19. During 1980–85, for instance, of the 5.5 million cadres trained, half of them earned either a diploma or a certificate. Over one-third of those who earned diploma earned a "college diploma." See *RMRB*, April 25, 1987, p. 4.

122. *Banyuetan* [Beijing], 1984, no. 3, pp. 9–11.

123. Statistics from some provinces showed that actually less than 20 percent of the attendees of cadre/party schools would ever receive new assignments. This put a serious damper on the willingness of cadres to participate in training. See *Lilun yuekan*, 1986, no. 8, p. 58.

124. *RMRB*, May 14, 1982, p. 1; February 5, 1983, p. 1.

125. The party's own statements sometimes added fuel to the cadres' speculation and anxiety. In 1983, for example, the party advised lower units to take advantage of the bureaucratic contraction to relieve "a large number of cadres" from their work and to send them into training for "two or three years." *RMRB*, February 5, 1983, p. 1.

126. For instance, fewer than 7 percent of the sixteen thousand cadres on the county level and above in Shaanxi Province had gone through a one-year training at the provincial party school. The number of cadres who had gone through training on the local level was insignificant. See *Lilun yuekan*, 1986, no. 8, p. 58.

127. For examples, see *RMRB*, March 18, 1982, p. 1.

128. See Zhang Yupu, "Dangzheng lingdao ganbu zai zhuanye zhishi jiegou fangmian di wenti jidai jiejue," in *Lilun yu shijian* [Shengyang], 1987, no. 12, pp. 24–25.

129. *RMRB*, August 20, 1982, p. 3. The above criticisms were made by the first provincial party secretary of Henan, Liu Jie.

130. Commentator, "Xinshanglai de ganbu yeyao nengshang nengxia" (The newly promoted cadres must also be able to move both upward and downward), *Hongqi*, 1986, no. 14, p. 3.

131. Notice issued by the Central Organization Department, "Guanyu tiaozheng bushenren xianzhi lingdao ganbu zhiwu jige wenti de tongzhi."

132. Commentator, "Xinshanglai de ganbu," *Hongqi*, 1986, no. 14, p. 3. For a sample of instructions issued by the Central Organization Department, see *RMRB*, January 5, 1987, p. 1.

133. *Xuexi yu shijian* [Wuhan], July 1986, pp. 29–31.

134. *RMRB*, overseas edition, July 30, 1987, p. 2.

135. *RMRB*, January 5, 1987, p. 1.

136. *BJRB*, April 15, 1987, p. 3.

137. *RMRB*, May 31, 1987, p. 1.

138. *Xueshu luntan* [Nanning], 1986, no. 4, pp. 13–14.

139. *Lilun xuekan*, 1985, no. 10, p. 1.

140. *Hongqi*, 1985, no. 7, p. 18.

141. In Liaoning Province, a provincial survey indicated that of the 329 college graduates currently serving as county-level leading cadres, 110 had graduated twenty years ago, 170 graduated ten years ago, and 19 graduated five years ago. Zhang Yupu, "Dangzheng

lingdao ganbu zai zhuanye zhishi jiegou fangmian di wenti jidai jiejue," in *Lilun yu shijian* [Shengyang], 1987, no. 12, pp. 24–25.

142. *Hongqi*, 1985, no. 7, p. 18.

143. From 1950 to 1980, the entire Chinese educational system produced about 100,000 college and professional high-school students with specialization in finance and fiscal issues. This constituted only about 3 percent of the total number of college and professional school graduates. These disciplines were suspended during the entire Cultural Revolution era and were revived only in the 1980s. See *Lilun yuekan* [Beijing], 1985, no. 2, p. 9.

144. *Xuexi yu yanjiu*, 1985, no. 6, p. 25.

145. *Lilun yuekan*, 1984, no. 5, p. 3.

146. *RMRB*, April 25, 1987, p. 4.

147. Yang Manke, "Deng Xiaoping de tupo yu juxian," *China Spring* (May 1986), p. 29.

148. *Xuexi yu yanjiu*, 1984, no. 3, p. 4.

149. *Lilun yuekan*, 1986, no. 6, p. 64.

150. *Jingji ribao*, October 7, 1985, p. 3.

151. *RMRB*, September 4, 1984, p. 5. These criticisms were made in September 1984.

152. *RMRB*, September 5, 1983, p. 5; March 18, 1982, p. 1. In some extreme cases, newly promoted cadres were actually even framed in criminal charges by the veterans. *RMRB*, August 24, 1984, p. 1.

153. *Dangde jianshe* [Chengdu] (January 1986), pp. 21–23.

154. *Jiangxi shehui kexue* [Nanchang] (January 1986), pp. 109–11, 58.

155. *Lilun yuekan*, 1986, no. 3, pp. 33–36.

156. Hu Qili, in *CYL Documents*, pp. 1–6.

157. The adversarial relationship between the masses and the party leaders is graphically demonstrated in a popular saying of the mid-1980s, "900 million of the 1 billion Chinese people are preoccupied with making money, and they are also united in their common effort to deceive the party center."

158. Yang Manke, "Deng Xiaoping de tupo yu juxian," *China Spring* (May 1986), p. 29.

159. For example, in the spring of 1985, Hu Yaobang indicated that it was not only necessary to cultivate a third echelon at the present, but to do the same for many generations to come. Hu said that this system of having the old revolutionaries of the first echelon watching and helping from the sideline and the second and third echelon actually doing the work should be conducted "for several hundred years," and he proposed that "the first step is to conduct it for one hundred years." See *Liaowang*, 1985, no. 7, p. 11.

160. Ibid., no. 49, p. 8.

161. *RMRB*, July 2, 1983, p. 1.

162. Hu Qili, in *CYL Documents*, pp. 1–6.

163. Some changes were proposed by Hua Guofeng in his political report to the Second Meeting of the Fifth National People's Congress.

164. *Anqing shiyuan xuebao, shekeban* [Anhui], 1987, no. 1, p. 31. For another example, see *Lilun yuekan*, 1986, no. 6, p. 65.

165. *Zhongguo nianjian: 1988* (People's Republic of China yearbook, 1988) (Beijing: Xinhua chubanshe, 1989), p. 66.

166. Interview with YBH, who participated in this project, June 29, 1989.

167. *Lilun yuekan*, 1986, no. 6, p. 65.

Chapter 5

1. Ding Mao, "Zenyang kandai jianguo yilai di fazhan dangyuan gongzuo," *Dangjian wenhui* [Shenyang], 1988, no. 1, pp. 27–29.

2. "Daliang xishou zhishi fenzi," in *Mao Zedong xuanji* (Beijing, 1964), pp. 611–13.

3. *Chen Yun wenxuan (1926–1949)* (Beijing: Renmin chubanshe, 1983), p. 147.

4. Ibid., p. 145.

5. *Tudi gaige zhongyao wenxian huibian* (Beijing: Renmin chubanshe, 1951), p. 51.

6. *Chongqing shehui kexue* [Chongqing], 1985, no. 3, p. 42.

7. "Guanyu zhishi fengzi wenti de baogao," speech delivered by Zhou Enlai in Guangzhou on March 2, 1962, in *Zhou Enlai lun wenyi* (Beijing: Renmin wenxue chubanshe, 1979), p. 131.

8. *Fuyang shifan xueyuan xuebao: shekeban* [Anhui], 1984, no. 4, pp. 32–41.

9. Ibid.

10. Deng's speech of May 24, 1977, in *DXPWX*, pp. 38, 45–55.

11. *DXPWX*, p. 64.

12. Ibid., pp. 82–97. Quotation is on page 86.

13. *Documents on Intellectuals*, p. 53.

14. *RMRB*, October 5, 1982, p. 3.

15. *Documents on Intellectuals*, pp. 247–49.

16. *DXPWX*, p. 85.

17. *Documents on Intellectuals*, p. 12.

18. Ibid., p. 3.

19. By the end of 1978, the Central Organization Department claimed that 60 percent of the cases affecting intellectuals had been reviewed and the erroneous verdicts overturned. Ibid., p. 54.

20. *RMRB*, January 27, 1983, p. 3.

21. *RMRB*, April 4, 1984, p. 3.

22. *Documents on Intellectuals*, pp. 45–50, 53.

23. *Fuyang shifan xueyuan xuebao: shekeban*, 1984, no. 4, pp. 32–41; *Fuzhou shizhuan xuebao* [Jiangxi], 1985, no. 1, p. 16.

24. *Jingji yanjiu cankao ziliao*, 1983, no. 95.

25. These four groups roughly corresponded to four age brackets when the 1982 national population census was taken: above 55 years, between 40 and 54, between 25 and 39, and below 24 years.

26. These models included the Chinese Academy of Sciences, the Anshan Steel Corporation, some central ministries, and the cities of Beijing, Shanghai, Guangzhou, Dalian, and Shenyang. See *BJRB*, February 16, 1980, p. 1; June 27, 1981, p. 1. RMRB, July 19, 1981, p. 3; April 5, 1982, p. 4.

27. For example, it was reported that 43.5 percent of the 1980 recruits and 52 percent of the 1981 recruits for the central government ministries were intellectuals, whereas 63 percent of the party recruits during 1977–1981 for the Chinese Academy of Sciences were intellectuals. *RMRB*, April 20, 1982, p. 4.

28. *RMRB*, February 27, 1984, p. 1.

29. *Documents on Intellectuals*, pp. 188–91.

30. *RMRB*, July 4, 1983, p. 1; July 22, 1983, p. 1; *Qiushi*, 1985, no. 2, p. 32. Such attitudes were typified by a statement made by a leading cadre of an enterprise in Tianjin in 1983: "Machines would continue to run even without the intellectuals." *RMRB*, May 23, 1983, p. 3.

31. *Dazhong ribao* [Jinan], January 17, 1985, p. 4; *BJRB*, January 25, 1985, p. 1.

32. *RMRB*, July 4, 1983, p. 1; October 5, 1982, p. 3; November 3, 1984, p. 3; February 24, 1983, p. 1; *Qiushi* [Nanchang], p. 32.

33. *Qiushi*, 1985, no. 2, p. 32; *GMRB*, November 20, 1984, p. 1; *RMRB*, November 21, 1984, p. 1; *Fuyang shifan xueyuan xuebao: shekeban*, 1984, no. 4, pp. 32–41.

34. Report from Jiangxi Province in 1985. *Fuzhou shizhuan xuebao* [Jiangxi], 1985, no. 1, p. 17.

35. *Wuhan daxue xuebao: shekeban*, 1985, no. 3, p. 66; *Qiye yanjiu* [Changchun], 1986, no. 4, p. 43; *Fuzhou shizhuan xuebao*, 1985, no. 1, pp. 18–19.

36. *RMRB*, January 24, 1983, p. 5; May 23, 1983, p. 3; October 19, 1982, p. 3; February 4, 1983, p. 1; April 22, 1983, p. 5; December 1, 1984, p. 3; November 21, 1984, p. 8.

37. *Dazhong ribao* [Jinan], January 17, 1985, p. 4; *BJRB*, January 25, 1985, p. 1; *Qiye yanjiu* [Changchun], 1986, no. 4, p. 43.

38. *RMRB*, May 7, 1984, p. 3; July 4, 1983, p. 1; July 2, 1983, p. 4.

39. *RMRB*, March 1, 1983, p. 3; August 28, 1984, p. 5.

40. *RMRB*, July 22, 1983, p. 1.

41. This fear was summed up succinctly in a popular saying, "We conquered the country, but the intellectuals took it away from us." *RMRB*, February 6, 1983, p. 1; May 23, 1983, p. 3.

42. *RMRB*, January 27, 1983, p. 3.

43. Ibid.

44. *RMRB*, July 4, 1983, p. 1.

45. *Renmin zhengxie bao* [Beijing], March 21, 1986, p. 3; *Qiushi*, 1985, no. 2, p. 32; *RMRB*, February 5, 1983, p. 1.

46. *RMRB*, February 17, 1984, p. 3; December 8, 1984, p. 5.

47. *GMRB*, November 20, 1984, p. 1; *RMRB*, February 6, 1983, p. 3; November 21, 1984, p. 1; December 1, 1984, p. 3.

48. *GMRB*, November 20, 1984, p. 1.

49. *RMRB*, December 8, 1984, p. 5.

50. *Hongqi*, 1984, no. 23, p. 16; *RMRB*, June 27, 1983. p. 3.

51. *RMRB*, June 27, 1983. p. 3. A successful case seems to be the city of Sipingshi in Manchuria. Here from 1980 to 1983, intellectuals constituted 51 percent of the cadres promoted to leadership positions, and 52.3 percent of newly recruited members into the party. See *RMRB*, April 21, 1983, p. 3. Another successful case seems to be the province of Kiangsu. *RMRB*, May 6, 1983, p. 3.

52. For testimonies by the provincial party secretary of Jiangsu, see *RMRB*, May 6, 1983, p. 3; by the first party secretary of Beijing, *RMRB*, February 4, 1983, p. 1.

53. *RMRB*, February 2, 1983, p. 3; February 6, 1983, p. 3; June 30, 1983, p. 1; July 13, 1983, p. 5.

54. *Fuzhou shizhuan xuebao*, 1985, no. 1, p. 15.

55. *RMRB*, May 7, 1984, p. 3.

56. *RMRB*, April 22, 1983, p. 5; September 21, 1983, p. 3.

57. *RMRB*, July 7, 1983, p. 5.

58. *RMRB*, July 4, 1983, p. 1; *CYWX (1956–1985)*, pp. 265–66. In 1982–83, there were many more cases of intellectuals being granted party membership posthumously. *RMRB*, February 6, 1983, p. 3.

59. *RMRB*, February 24, 1983, p. 1.

60. *RMRB*, July 4, 1983, p. 1.

61. For 1983 cases, see *RMRB*, April 22, 1983, p. 5; September 21, 1983, p. 3. For 1984 cases, see *RMRB*, August 28, 1984, p. 5. For 1985 cases, see *Dazhong ribao* [Jinan], January 17, 1985, p. 4; *RMRB*, January 25, 1985, p. 1.

62. In September 1984, the Guangdong provincial party secretary demanded that lower levels treat intellectuals' recruitment as a key mission. Under this policy, the cities and counties in the province mounted a strong effort to recruit intellectuals. See *RMRB*, December 22, 1984, p. 1. The first party secretary of Hebei Province frankly admitted that the work on intellectuals was "behind schedule by a very wide margin" not only in his province but also in the rest of the country. See *RMRB*, May 28, 1984, p. 3.

63. *RMRB*, October 27, 1984, p. 1.

64. *RMRB*, October 27, 1984, p. 1.

65. *Hongqi*, 1984, no. 23, pp. 16–18.

66. *GMRB*, November 20, 1984, p. 1.

67. For instance, in 1984, the Shandong provincial party sent more than 10,000 party cadres down to the local basic levels and spent more than a month checking on the performance of basic-level party organization in recruiting intellectuals. *GMRB*, November 19, 1984, p. 1.

68. *GMRB*, November 20, 1984, p. 1.

69. *RMRB*, November 3, 1984, p. 3.

70. *RMRB*, November 15, 1984, p. 3; *GMRB*, November 20, 1984, p. 1.

71. *Qiushi*, 1985, no. 2, p. 32.

72. The party said that all remaining problems affecting intellectuals had to be resolved prior to the Thirteenth Party Congress. *RMRB*, July 18, 1985, p. 1.

73. *Renmin zhengxie bao* [Beijing], March 21, 1986, p. 3; *1982 Population Census of China*, table 47.

74. *RMRB*, January 25, 1984, p. 2; February 25, 1984, p. 3.

75. Interview with YBH, September 10, 1986.

76. *RMRB*, November 3, 1984, p. 3; July 4, 1983, p. 1; October 11, 1983, p. 5.

77. Interview with YBH, September 10, 1986. Most alarming were indications that the mortality rate of middle-aged intellectuals had been consistently higher than the rest of the population by a wide margin.

78. *RMRB*, January 25, 1984, p. 2; February 25, 1984, p. 3. Even the city of Shanghai, which probably had the largest concentration of intellectuals, reported that it was only beginning to tackle the intellectuals' plight in the late spring of 1984. *RMRB*, April 7, 1984, p. 3.

79. The fate of Wu Zuguang and Fang Lizhi is quite revealing. Wu was asked to withdraw from the party, to which he gladly obliged, saying that he never felt much joy in joining, and felt no sense of loss on leaving. Fang's reputation also did not suffer. On the contrary, all these people seemed to have gained in personal stature because of their expulsion.

Chapter 6

1. *RMRB*, August 27, 1984, p. 1; Zhang Yun, "Quanmian tigao dangyuan suzhi shi dangfeng genben haozhuan de jianshi jicu," *Hongqi*, 1986, no. 10, pp. 3–14.

2. *GMRB*, January 17, 1984, p. 1. A different estimate was given by the *New York Times*: of the 1,280,000 college students on campus in 1982, only 3.8 percent (or 48,640 students) were members of the CCP. *New York Times*, September 5, 1982, E3.

3. *RMRB*, August 27, 1984, p. 1; Zhang Yun, *Hongqi*, 1986, no. 10, pp. 3–14.

4. Zhang Yun, *Hongqi*, 1986, no. 10, pp. 3–14.

5. In one extreme case in 1985, one district in Inner Mongolia had a population of 200,000 people, but young party members constituted only 0.06 percent of that district's party membership. *Shijian* [Huhehot], 1985, no. 7, pp. 22–23. In Shanghai, the 1983 figure for ages 25 and below was only 2.25 percent, and the 1984 figure was 2.2 percent of the Shanghai party membership. *RMRB*, August 27, 1984, p. 1. Even those 26–30 years of age constituted only 9.8 percent of Shanghai's total party membership in 1984. *Jiefang ribao* [Shanghai], November 2, 1984, p. 4.

6. During 1984–86, the party recruited nearly 2 million new members a year. This means that very few people of less than 25 years of age bothered to join in spite of the great relaxation of admissions standards. Kang Shijian, "Nuli jianshe yizhi jingdeqi

'liangge kaoyan' di dangyuan duiwu," in *Shishi qiushi* [Urumqi], 1988, no. 1, pp. 59–62.

7. Zhang Yun, *Hongqi*, 1986, no. 10, pp. 3–14.

8. *1982 Population Census of China*, pp. 272–73. Another measure of comparison is the population between 18 and 30 years of age: 18 was the minimum age admittable into the Communist Party. Chinese in this age bracket accounted for 22 percent of the total population.

9. *GMRB*, January 17, 1984, p. 1; *Hengyang sizhuan xuebao: shekeban* [Hunan], 1985, no. 3, p. 21; *Yichun Shizhuan xuebao zhesheban*, [Yichun], March–April, 1985, pp. 13–14, 25; *Hongqi*, 1984, no. 23, p. 17.

10. *GMRB*, March 24, 1985, p. 1.

11. *Liaowang* [Beijing], 1986, no. 26, p. 9.

12. *Hengyang sizhuan xuebao: shekeban* [Hunan], 1985, no. 3, p. 25.

13. The official claims of accomplishments of recruitment are confusing and inconsistent because they used such terms as "intellectuals," "technical personnel," "educated youths," and "experts" very loosely and interchangeably. The level of education of each kind of people was never spelled out explicitly. Therefore, official figures of this kind do not add much to our understanding of recruitment.

14. *GMRB*, March 24, 1985, p. 1.

15. *Xuanchuan shouce* [Beijing], 1985, no. 13, pp. 3–4.

16. *Xuexi yu yanjiu*, 1985, no. 2, pp. 30–31.

17. Colleges in Beijing admitted 3,200 such students in 1984. See *BJRB*, January 20, 1985, p. 1.

18. *GMRB*, March 24, 1985, p. 1.

19. Interview with ZZL, August 15, 1984.

20. *Yichun Shizhuan xuebao zhesheban*, March–April 1985, pp. 13–14, 25.

21. *Hengyang sizhuan xuebao: shekeban* [Hunan], 1985, no. 3, p. 21.

22. *RMRB*, March 15, 1985, p. 1.

23. *Xuexi yu yanjiu*, 1985, no. 2, pp. 35–36.

24. *Henan ribao*, February 1, 1985, p. 1.

25. The total increase was 5,170,000: from 35,780,000 in 1976, to 40,950,000 in 1983. See *RMRB*, August 27, 1984, p. 1. Another report indicated that from 1979 to mid-1983, the party recruited about 4 million new members, or an annual intake of about 888,000. *RMRB*, July 22, 1983, p. 1.

26. Multiplying 3.34 percent by 40,950,000 yields 1,368,000 party members below 25 in 1983.

27. *Jiefang ribao*, November 2, 1984, p. 4.

28. *RMRB*, August 27, 1984, p. 1.

29. "Zhongguo gongchan zhuyi qingniantuan zhangcheng," hereafter Communist Youth League Charter, in *CYL Documents*, p. 39.

30. "Gao Zhanxiang tongzhi da jiche wen," hereafter Gao Zhanxiang's press conference, in *CYL Documents*, pp. 181–82.

31. Wang Zhaoguo, "Zai zhongguo gongchan zhuyi qingniantuan ti shiyice quanguo daibiao dahui shang de gongzuo baogao," hereafter Wang Zhaoguo's work report, in *CYL Documents*, p. 13.

32. Ibid., p. 11.

33. *RMRB*, December 16, 1982, p. 1.

34. Zhang Yun, in *Hongqi*, 1986, no. 10, p. 12.

35. Wang Zhaoguo's work report, in *CYL Documents*, p. 11.

36. *RMRB*, August 27, 1984, p. 1.

37. Hu Qili, in *CYL Documents*, pp. 4–5.

38. Gao Zhanxiang's press conference, in *CYL Documents*, p. 184.

39. Hu Qili, in *CYL Documents*, pp. 4–5.

40. Wang Zhaoguo, "Zai gongqingtuan shiyijie yizhong quanhui shang de jianghua," hereafter Wang Zhaoguo's speech, in *CYL Documents*, pp. 68–69.

41. In the case of a teachers' college in Jiangxi, 86.8 percent of the 1,796 students were CYL members, but only 1.3 percent had joined the party itself. During the five years from 1978 to 1983, only six students were recruited into the party. *Yichun shizhuan xuebao zhesheban* [Yichun], March–April 1985, pp. 13–14, 25.

42. *Shijian* [Huhehot], 1985, no. 7, pp. 22–23.

43. Zhang Yun, in *Hongqi*, 1986, no. 10, p. 12.

44. *GMRB*, January 23, 1984, p. 2.

45. Wang Zhaoguo's work report, in *CYL Documents*, pp. 23, 34–35; 68.

46. Ibid., pp. 29–31.

47. See Education Minister He Dongchang's report in *RMRB*, October 3, 1982, p. 3.

48. *RMRB*, May 5, 1983, p. 3.

49. Working paper issued by State Commission of Higher Education, October 22, 1988.

50. Between 1978 and 1982, some 43,000 graduate students were admitted. *RMRB*, October 3, 1982, p. 3.

51. *RMRB*, August 29, 1982, p. 3.

52. The increase in 1981 was 36.7 percent. *RMRB*, May 5, 1983, p. 3. Graduate enrollment in 1985 increased by another 42 percent over 1984. *XNB*, Oct. 24, 1984, p. 17.

53. Working paper issued by State Commission of Higher Education, October 22, 1988.

54. *RMRB*, November 23, 1984, p. 1.

55. Ibid. The desire to study abroad was so pervasive among college students that when the government announced in 1985 the new regulation that no graduate students would be allowed to go abroad either during their enrollment in a Chinese graduate program or within two years after they had earned their graduate degrees in China, many Chinese universities suddenly developed difficulties in attracting the best minds to their graduate programs. Bright students would rather forgo a graduate education in China if it meant jeopardizing their prospects of studying abroad.

56. In July 1984, for instance, 1.6 million high school graduates competed for about 430,000 places in the freshman class for the nation's colleges and universities. *Beijing Review*, no. 31 (1984), p. 10.

57. *RMRB*, September 30, 1982, p. 5.

58. Most of the characterizations of Chinese college students' ideas are gleaned from a collection of essays written by students from some of the best-known colleges and universities in China in response to the invitation by *GMRB* in 1984 to comment on campus intellectual issues. *Daxuesheng tan zhongguo shehuizhuyi* (Jilin renmin chubanshe, 1984), pp. 68–69, hereafter given as page numbers in parentheses in the text.

59. *Hengyang sizhuan xuebao: shekeban* [Hunan], 1985, no. 3, pp. 23–24.

60. Ibid., pp. 21–22.

61. *Kexue, jingji, shehui* [Lanzhou], 1987, no. 2, p. 106. A survey of 150 high school graduates in Shanghai in 1982. See Su Haobin, "Yifen Zhongguo chengshi qingnian de sixiang zhuangkuang diaocha," *The Seventies*, 1982, no. 11, pp. 36–38.

62. Interview with WQL, December 10, 1987.

63. Interview with Prof. YJH of Shanghai University, February 25, 1989. For a discussion of this phenomenon in English, see Leo A. Orleans, "The Effects of China 'Business Fever' on Higher Education at Home and on Chinese Students in the U.S.," *China Exchange News* 17, 1 (March 1989), pp. 8–14.

64. A survey conducted at the Hengyang Normal College in Hunan province in 1985

showed that only about one-third of the student respondents expressed strong desire to join the party. Another one-third would like to join but would not dare to submit applications because of fear of peer disapproval. Another one-third were uninterested in politics or absorbed totally in academic work. *Hengyang sizhuan xuebao: shekeban,* 1985, no. 3, pp. 21–24.

65. Interview with WQL, December 10, 1987.

66. One informant who was a member of the CYL's national committee said that in the mid-1980s national CYL meetings were attended in large numbers by people who only had very short membership history. Once in, they were quickly promoted through the ranks. They got into the CCP easily, and their leadership position in the CYL could often earn them very good assignments in party and government. Some smart students saw this career path clearly and did not want to take the academic track. By my informant's estimate, if a young student took the political track through CYL and CCP, he could become a division chief in four to five years, taking advantage of forced retirement of older cadres and political apathy of most other people. Interview with RXP, August 15, 1986.

67. *RMRB,* July 18, 1985, p. 1; Xia Honggen, "Dui jianguo yilai dang guanyu zhishi fenzi wenti zhengce di tanxie," *Jiangxi shehuikexue* [Nanchang], 1987, no. 6, pp. 94–98.

68. Interview with Professor WWL of People's University, March 14, 1988.

69. *GMRB,* November 20, 1984, p. 1; *Xuexi yu yanjiu,* 1985, no. 2, p. 30; *RMRB,* June 27, 1983, p. 3.

70. *RMRB,* July 22, 1983, p. 1.

71. *Xuanchuan shouce* [Beijing], 1985, no. 13, pp. 3–4; *GMRB,* June 26, 1985, p. 1.

72. The figure for 1982 was about 40–50 percent of this. *RMRB,* June 27, 1983, p. 3.

73. *RMRB,* June 23, 1988, p. 1; May 22, 1983, p. 1; March 15, 1985, p. 1.

74. *Dangyuan de shenghuo* [Wuhan], 1986, no. 6, pp. 4–5.

75. In these two years, intellectuals constituted 41 percent of total new recruits in the province. *Gongchan dangyuan* [Shijiazhuang], 1986, no. 5, p. 15.

76. *Hebei ribao,* June 4, 1985, p. 2; Ding Mao, "Zenyang kandai jianguo yilai di fazhan dangyuan gongzuo," *Dangjian wenhui* [Shenyang], 1988, no. 1, pp. 27–29; *RMRB,* June 23, 1988, p. 1.

77. *RMRB,* overseas edition, October 17, 1989, p. 1.

78. Ding Mao, "Zenyang kandai jianguo yilai di fazhan dangyuan gongzuo," pp. 27–29.

79. *DXPWX,* p. 232. See also Zhao Shuhai, "Tantan tigao gongchandangyuan di zhiliang wenti," *Kexue shehui zhuyi* [Beijing], 1987, no. 4, pp. 33–38.

80. Ding Mao, "Zenyang kandai jianguo yilai di fazhan dangyuan gongzuo," pp. 27–29.

81. Wang Tianfu, "Fazhan dangyuan bixu baozhen zhiliang," *Dangjian* [Beijing], 1988, no. 3, pp. 28–29.

82. Hu Jianrong, "Shiyin gaige kaifang, jianchi congyan zhidang," *Shishi qiushi* [Urumqi], 1988, no. 2, pp. 49–51; *Gongren ribao* [Beijing], April 29, 1988, p. 3.

83. Wang Tianfu, "Fazhan dangyuan bixu baozhen zhiliang," pp. 28–29; Shi Changtu, "Quantui ho chumin shi baochi dang di huoli di zhongyao cuoshi," *Lilun tantao* [Haerbin], 1988, no. 3, pp. 62–64.

84. For some samples of such criticisms, see Guo Jingqing, "Xinshiqi nongmin xihuan shimoyang di dangyuan ganbu?" *Nongming ribao* [Beijing], February 2, 1988, p. 3; Fang Yuan, "Weishimo yu zhemodo dangyuan zuo weizheng?" *RMRB,* February 5, 1988, p. 4; Gu Changgen, "Zai gaige kaifang zhong tigao dangyuan suzhi," *Qunzhong* [Nanjing], 1988, no. 2, pp. 10–11; Liang Guanwen, "Qiantan zhongqingnian ganbu di dangxin duanlian," *Guangxi ribao,* February 25, 1988, p. 3; Wu Dongchang, "Congyan zhi dang, tigao dangyuan suzhi," *Gannan shifan xueyuan xuebao: chesheban* [Ganzhou], 1988, no. 1, pp. 5–6; Zhang Mulian, "Zai gaige shijianzhong tigao dangyuan suzhi,"

Fentou [Haerbin], 1988, no. 4, pp. 16–17; Lo Dewen, "Bixu zhaoyan yu tigao dang-yuan di suzhi," *Lingnan xuekan* [Guangzhou], 1988, no. 2, pp. 72–74; Shi Changtu, "Quantui ho chumin shi baochi dang di huoli di zhongyao cuoshi," *Lilun tantao* [Haerbin], 1988, no. 3, pp. 62–64; Cai Xi, "Qianyi jianchi gongchandangyuan bianzhun wenti," *Lilun tantao* [Haerbin], 1988, no. 3, pp. 58–61; Kang Shijian, "Nuli jianshe yizhi jingdeqi 'liangge kaoyan' di dangyuan duiwu," *Shishi qiushi* [Urumqi], 1988, no. 1, pp. 59–62.

85. Ding Mao, "Zenyang kandai jianguo yilai di fazhan dangyuan gongzuo," *Dang-jian wenhui* [Shenyang], 1988, no. 1, pp. 27–29; Kang Shijian, "Nuli jianshe yizhi jingdeqi 'liangge kaoyan' di dangyuan duiwu," *Shishi qiushi*, 1988, no. 1, pp. 59–62.

86. *RMRB*, December 18, 1986, p. 4.

87. Ibid.

88. *BJRB*, February 6, 1985, p. 3.

89. *RMRB*, December 18, 1986, p. 4.

90. Xiang Tang, "Chengshi gaige ceyin," *China Spring* (February 1985): 47–48.

91. *BJRB*, February 6, 1985, p. 3.

92. Kang Shijian, "Nuli jianshe yizhi jingdeqi 'liangge kaoyan' di dangyuan duiwu."

93. *RMRB*, overseas edition, October 17, 1989, p. 1.

94. *RMRB*, June 23, 1988, p. 1.

95. *GMRB*, November 20, 1984, p. 1.

96. *Lilun yuekan*, 1985, no. 3, p. 55; *RMRB*, March 15, 1985, p. 1.

97. Kang Shijian, "Nuli jianshe yizhi jingdeqi 'liangge kaoyan' di dangyuan duiwu."

98. *The World Journal*, October 16, 1989, p. 32.

99. *Kaituo* [Chengdu], 1987, no. 1, p. 56.

100. *RMRB*, June 29, 1983, p. 3.

101. *1982 Population Census*, table 47, p. 360.

102. Zhang Yun, *Hongqi*, 1986, no. 10, pp. 3–14.

103. *RMRB*, January 26, 1987, p. 4.

104. *Qiye yanjiu* [Changchun], 1986, no. 4, p. 43.

105. Ibid.

Chapter 7

1. *Shijian* [Huhehot], 1985, no. 4, p. 7.

2. Hu's speech, "Quanmian kaichuang shehui zhuyi xiandaihua jianshe de xinju-mian," September 1, 1982, in *Major Documents*, pp. 469–525.

3. *RMRB*, June 7, 1983, p. 1.

4. *RMRB*, March 26, 1983, p. 4.

5. *RMRB*, June 7, 1983, p. 1. For example, eighteen units in Shandong Province were picked as experiment points and completed their rectification by June 1983. Yet there were several common faults of rectification work. Primarily, the party secretaries paid little attention to rectification, were ignorant about real conditions under their juris-diction, had no faith in their work, and did not dare to handle tough cases. They did not want to offend their superiors if the latter abused power or held an erroneous political line.

6. *RMRB*, March 26, 1983, p. 4.

7. *RMRB*, Commentator, February 7, 1984, p. 1; "Resolution on Party Rectifica-tion," October 11, 1983, full text printed in *Hongqi*, 1983, no. 20, pp. 2–11; Bo Yibo's speech of December 21, 1984, in *Zhengdang yinian*, pp. 34–38.

8. Directive no. 6, dated January 1, 1984, in *Zhengdang yinian*, pp. 12–13. The misconduct that was said to have aroused the greatest resentment among the masses at this time was the leading cadres' attempt to use their own power to obtain good work assign-

ments for their children, relatives, and friends, to grab the bigger and newer housing for themselves, to accept bribes and gifts, and to cover up criminal conduct of their family members or friends and shield them from the law. These were the most outstanding examples of how cadres "use power to serve personal interest."

9. Ibid., p. 41.

10. *Shijian* [Huhehot], 1984, no. 1, p. 26. Some provinces also set a minimum amount of two hundred hours for study of these documents. *Lilun yu shijian* [Shenyang], 1984, no. 1, p. 8.

11. *Zhengdang yinian*, pp. 15–16, 23.

12. Ibid., pp. 27–28.

13. "Resolution on Party Rectification" passed on October 11, 1983, full text printed in *Hongqi*, 1983, no. 20, pp. 2–11.

14. *Zhengdang yinian*, pp. 5–6.

15. Article 3 stated: "Those party members whose revolutionary will has eroded, who fail to carry out their duties as party members, who do not meet the requirements as party members, and who have failed to rectify themselves after repeated efforts [by the party] to educate and assist them, shall be asked to leave the party and shall be denied registration." Article 4 stated that those who failed or refused to participate in the rectification process shall be removed from the membership roster. "Resolution on Party Rectification"; see also *RMRB*, November 29, 1984, p. 4.

16. These practices were so prevalent that together they were referred to by the official press as the "three recruitments and three status changes" (*sanzhao sanzhuan*). *Hongqi*, 1986, no. 3, pp. 5–7.

17. *Lilun yu shijian*, 1986, no. 6, pp. 8–10.

18. *Hongqi*, 1986, no. 3, pp. 5–7.

19. *Hongqi*, 1986, no. 5, pp. 8–10; 1985, no. 19, p. 40; *CYWX*, pp. 309–10. The figure of twenty thousand was definitely an underestimation that covered only twenty provinces. In Liaoning Province alone, some nine hundred commercial enterprises on or above the county level sprang into existence in the short period of August–November 1984. *RMRB*, January 26, 1985, p. 1.

20. For instance, some companies could obtain steel at the state-fixed price of RMB 600–700 a ton and resell it in the free market for three times the price. *Qiushi*, 1985, no. 3, pp. 6–8.

21. Gleaned from a list of criminal methods reported by the deputy secretary of the Gansu provincial party's disciplinary committee. *Dang de jianshe* [Lanzhou], 1986, no. 7, p. 20.

22. Notice issued by Central Discipline Committee on December 18, 1985. *RMRB*, January 15, 1986, p. 1.

23. *Xuexi yu yanjiu*, 1986, no. 4, p. 30.

24. They could be the housing bureau, bus company, electric station, grain storage, distribution outlet, tax bureau, police station, bank, or even public health agency. *Lilun yu shijian*, 1986, no. 6, pp. 8–10. Construction companies could hike their prices or demand a slice of land from a customer, or bid up the cost but then sell the right to build to another, smaller company and pocket the difference. Trade outlets would hoard goods in short supply for illegal prices, sell inferior goods for top prices, compel customers to buy a certain portion of inferior goods if they wanted to buy goods of superior quality, or demand kickbacks in transactions. The electric power company might demand extra cash, free goods, and materials from customers or their power supply would be cut off. Even railway stations assigned boxcars to the highest bidders. *RMRB*, May 29, 1986, p. 1.

25. One factory in Jiangsu Province arranged a bank loan to give every cadre and worker a 20-inch color TV worth more than RMB $2,000 each. The bank gladly granted

the loan in the interest of "stimulating consumption." *Qunzhong*, 1985, no. 5, pp. 23–25.

26. Ibid. On the payment of bonuses, in 1984, Jiangxi Province experienced a 36.5 percent increase of such payments over 1983, but the industrial and agricultural output increased only 13.3 percent, and the provincial fiscal income increased only 15.3 percent. *Qiushi*, 1985, no. 3, pp. 6–8.

27. *CYWX*, pp. 309–10; *Hongqi*, 1985, no. 19, p. 40.

28. Probably the most notorious case was the illegal sale of automobiles on Hainan Island, which lasted from January 1984 to March 1985 and was engineered by the majority of the party and government leadership of this administrative region. *CYWX*, pp. 310, 380.

29. Bo Yibo claimed in December 1984 that the cadres' practices of taking more housing for themselves and arranging better jobs for their children had already been effectively halted. *Zhengdang yinian*, pp. 38, 41.

30. A township in Liaoning budgeted five hundred yuan per cadre for sightseeing. See *Lilun yu shijian*, 1986, no. 6, pp. 8–10.

31. According to a report, an all-people factory with less than one thousand workers adopted an extremely penny-pinching approach and still used more than RMB $20,000 for entertaining and gift-giving in 1986. *RMRB*, April 7, 1987, p. 1.

32. For a detailed description of these "new erroneous styles," see *Hongqi*, 1985, no. 6, p. 23.

33. *RMRB*, April 10, 1987, p. 1. During this five-year period, the annual growth rate for administrative cost was 14 percent, while the GNP only grew at 12 percent per year, and the government's revenues only grew at 8.8 percent per year. According to one survey, some RMB $30 million were spent by public agencies for 150,000 feasts in the restaurants in Shanghai's Huangpu district in 1986 alone.

34. *Qunzhong*, 1985, no. 7, p. 13.

35. *RMRB*, May 29, 1986, p. 1.

36. *Dang de jianshe* [Lanzhou], 1986, no. 7, p. 20; *Hongqi*, 1986, no. 23, p. 16.

37. *Liaowang*, 1985, no. 6, p. 4; *Qiushi*, 1985, no. 3, pp. 6–8; *Hongqi*, 1986, no. 23, p. 16.

38. For a description of some of these tactics, see *Qiushi*, 1985, no. 3, pp. 6–8.

39. *Xuexi yu yanjiu*, 1986, no. 4, pp. 29–30.

40. See Hu Qili's report in *RMRB*, March 14, 1985, p. 1.

41. Hu said, "I am in favor of giving severe punishment to those who had seriously damaged the interest of the state and people for the sake of their personal and small group interests. We must expel some people from the party to serve warning. Otherwise, we will not be able to stem the tide of the erroneous style." *Liaowang*, 1985, no. 7, p. 12.

42. Document no. 57 released in November 1985 included the illegal importation of passenger cars for leading cadres' use, the use of excuses to send visitors abroad, the lavish expenditure of public funds for sightseeing, lavish entertainment and expensive gifts with public funds, the acceptance of bribes and other forms of exactions, and the use of official cover to engage in unauthorized commercial activities. *Zhibu shenghuo*, 1986, no. 4, pp. 2–3. A similar but more detailed list of the ten most prevalent misdeeds by cadres in the economic realm was provided in December 1985 by the deputy director of the PRC's State Economic Commission, Yuan Baohua. *RMRB*, December 15, 1985, p. 2.

43. Bo Yibo's speech, "Guanyu xinshiqi dang di jianshe di jige wenti," in *Hongqi*, 1986, no. 16, pp. 4–5.

44. *RMRB*, March 13, 1985, p. 1.

45. *RMRB*, February 6, 1986. p. 1.

46. The six major problems listed in the statement were the indiscriminate importation of automobiles, indiscriminate sending of personnel abroad, cadres spending public funds

for tours and feasting, cadres accepting illegal incomes, and cadres engaging in commercial activities. *RMRB*, December 12, 1985, p. 1.

47. The scope of this directive not only included the recently identified six major forms of corruption, but also liberalism, bureaucratism, and cadre abuse of privileges for personal gain. *RMRB*, December 31, 1985, p. 1.

48. *RMRB*, December 16, p. 1; December 21, p. 1; December 30, p. 1. The Beijing case implicated twenty-one municipal cadres involving about RMB $1.5 million. The Fushan case implicated eighty-eight bureaucratic units in seventeen provinces, involving some RMB $20 million. Finally, the Fuzhou case implicated countless people and involved a whopping RMB $240 million.

49. *Liaowang*, 1986, no. 14, pp. 11–12; also see Bo Yibo's speech in *Hongqi*, 1986, no. 16, pp. 4–5.

50. *Hongqi*, 1986, no. 5, pp. 8–10.

51. *RMRB*, January 11, 1986, p. 1.

52. The best-known among them included the Aerospace Ministry's importation of color TV sets; Zhou Erfu's expulsion from the party for damaging national pride; Ye Zhifeng (former naval commanding officer Ye Fei's daughter) taking bribes from foreign businessmen in exchange for state trade secrets; and Hu Xiaoyang (son of Hu Lijiao, retired municipal party leader of Shanghai) engaging in gang-raping. There was also a swindle case by Du Guozheng, and a case of an Agricultural Product Company engaged in illegal sale of foreign currency, automobiles, steel products, and color televisions.

53. The grapevine suggested that those high-ranking leaders whose children were implicated in questionable conduct included several members of the Politburo.

54. *RMRB*, May 28, 1987, p. 1.

55. Ibid.

56. *RMRB*, May 31, 1987, p. 1.

57. *RMRB*, February 7, 1986, p. 1.

58. *Liaowang*, 1986, no. 15, pp. 14–15.

59. For examples, see *RMRB*, February 4, 1986, p. 1.

60. *Kaituozhe* [Guangzhou], 1986, no. 5, p. 2.

61. *Hongqi*, 1986, no. 23, p. 18.

62. *GMRB*, May 10, 1987, p. 1.

63. *Qunzhong*, January 1986, pp. 11–12.

64. *RMRB*, December 4, 1986, p. 4.

65. *Hongqi*, 1987, no. 1, pp. 4–5.

66. *Xuexi yu yanjiu* [Beijing], February 1986, pp. 18–19.

67. *Hongqi*, 1987, no. 11, p. 16.

68. *Jingji ribao*, March 11, 1988, p. 1.

69. *RMRB*, November 27, 1984, p. 1. For example, Bo Yibo stated that from the winter of 1984 to the fall of 1985, the rectification campaign would be carried out on the two levels of region and county (including the major enterprises, colleges, research institutes), and from the winter of 1985 to the fall of 1986, the rectification would be completed for the levels below the county. See *Zhengdang yinian*, p. 46.

70. *Zhengdang yinian*, p. 34.

71. Directive no. 11, dated January 7, 1985. *RMRB*, January 9, 1985, p. 1. There also began quiet suggestions that a fundamental change of party style for the good might require an additional year (i.e., until 1987) to accomplish. *Shijian* [Huhehot], 1985, no. 4, p. 6.

72. *Zhengdang yinian*, p. 32.

73. Reported by the first party secretary of Guangdong, Ren Zhongyi, in September 1984. *Nanfang ribao* [Guangzhou], September 26, 1984, p. 1.

74. For full text of his speech, see *Hongqi*, 1985, no. 19, pp. 35, 40.

75. *RMRB*, March 13, 1985, p. 1.

76. *RMRB*, July 15, 1985, p. 1.

77. "Guanyu xinshiqi dang di jianshe di chige wenti," *Hongqi*, 1986, no. 16, p. 5.

78. Zhang Yun, in *Hongqi*, 1986, no. 10, p. 9.

79. *RMRB*, June 3, 1986, p. 5.

80. *Hongqi*, 1986, no. 5, p. 9.

Chapter 8

1. *Liaowang*, 1986, no. 15, pp. 14–15.

2. *Xuexi zazhi* [Chengdu], 1986, no. 4, p. 1; *Dang de jianshe* [Lanzhou], 1986, no. 7, p. 21.

3. *Fendou* [Haerbin], May 1986, p. 4–6.

4. *Qunzhong*, 1986, no. 1, pp. 11–12.

5. *Lilun yu shijian*, 1984, no. 1, pp. 4–8; *RMRB*, February 17, 1984, p. 5.

6. *Lilun yu shijian*, 1984, no. 1, pp. 4–8.

7. Bo Yibo reported that even in 1985 the party still lacked a consensus on the need to conduct a rectification campaign. *RMRB*, June 30, 1985, p. 1.

8. *Qiushi*, 1985, no. 1, p. 46.

9. The national organ was initially called the Central Discipline Investigation Committee or Zhongyang Jili Jianzha Weiyuanhui, later changed to the Central Censorial Committee or Zhongyang Jianca Weiyuanhui. *Lilun xuekan*, 1986, no. 11, p. 27.

10. Probably the most notorious examples of this approach were the "Workers' Propaganda Teams of Mao Zedong's Thought," employed extensively during the Cultural Revolution.

11. Each field consisted of a cluster of similar professions and was called a *kou*, which literally meant "mouth." *RMRB*, January 6, 1984, p. 1.

12. *Guanli shijie* [Beijing], 1987, no. 3, pp. 111–17.

13. Report by Zhou Hui, first party secretary of Inner Mongolia, *Shijian* [Huhehot], 1985, no. 4, p. 9.

14. Another method that would have imposed some measure of central control but was abandoned by the party was the sending of liaison teams (Directive no. 4, December 10, 1983) to the local work units to gather information, listen to progress reports, and make on-the-spot instructions on corrective measures. See *Zhengdang yinian*, pp. 7–9. During the first stage, the Central Guidance Committee dispatched forty-nine liaison teams and ten guidance teams to promote rectification work. *RMRB*, March 13, 1985, p. 1. But this practice was discontinued during the second stage. Instead, the party sent seven roving teams of inspectors, with the responsibilities to learn about conditions, discover problems, sum up experience, and make recommendations. But these roving teams were instructed to respect the leadership of the local party secretary in conducting rectification. *RMRB*, March 13, 1985, p. 1.

15. Thus, for example, only one-fourth of Guizhou Province's cadres serving in the discipline committees during 1981–86 had received any training related to their work. *RMRB*, July 1, 1986, p. 5.

16. *Jiangxi shehui kexue* [Nanchang], 1984, no. 5, pp. 90–93.

17. The superiors could defame them, isolate them, give them impossible assignments, discriminate against them in housing, salary, promotion, etc. In Chinese, these were called to "give them tight shoes to wear" (*chuanxiaoxie*). *RMRB*, July 4, 1983, p. 3.

18. *Dang de jianshe* [Lanzhou], 1986, no. 3, pp. 4–5.

19. *RMRB*, July 1, 1986, p. 5; *Hongqi*, 1986, no. 5, pp. 8–10.

20. This was the party's own survey, which covered nineteen provinces, autonomous regions, and municipalities. Zhang Yun, in *Hongqi*, 1986, no. 10, pp. 5–6.

21. Ibid., pp. 10–11.

22. *Shanxi ribao*, January 22, 1984, p. 1.

23. "Resolution on Party Rectification," October 11, 1983, full text printed in *Hongqi*, 1983, no. 20, pp. 2–11.

24. *Tansuo* [Chongqing], 1986, no. 3, pp. 60–62.

25. *RMRB*, July 4, 1983, p. 3.

26. Bao Zheng was a Song dynasty official famous for his rectitude and relentless and often ingenious investigation of criminal deeds.

27. *Liaowang*, 1986, no. 18, pp. 5–6.

28. One person who was perceived as a "Minister Bao" was the noted journalist Liu Binyan, who ended up offending too many leaders and was expelled from the party in 1987.

29. *Yiyang diwei dangxiao xuebao* [Hunan], 1987, no. 1, pp. 17–18.

30. For instance, a survey in the city of Yiyang showed that over 60 percent of neighborhood party members were above 56 years of age, and over 60 percent had only primary school education or were illiterate. Ibid.

31. *Zhengdang yinian*, pp. 15–16.

32. *RMRB*, February 7, 1984, p. 5.

33. Ibid.

34. *RMRB*, December 11, 1983, p. 1; editorial, March 25, 1984, p. 1.

35. *Banyuetan*, 1984, no. 2, pp. 44–46.

36. Ibid.

37. These were offered as a package and referred to as the policy of "four allows and four disallows." *Zhengdang yinian*, p. 40.

38. *Hongqi*, 1987, no. 1, p. 6; also see *RMRB*, December 3, 1986, p. 1. For a provincial report that described this problem in Jilin, see *Xinchangzheng* [Changchun], 1987, no. 8, pp. 23–24.

39. *Zhengzhou gongxueyuan xuebao: chesheban*, 1984, no. 3, pp. 104–6.

40. For one such complaint by Wang Zhaoguo, see *Hongqi*, 1987, no. 1, pp. 6–7.

41. For examples of such criticisms, see *Xinchangzheng* [Changchun], 1987, no. 8, pp. 23–24.

42. For Wang Zhaoguo's comments concerning this popular view, see *RMRB*, December 3, 1986, p. 1.

43. *Hongqi*, 1987, no. 1, pp. 6–7.

44. *RMRB*, editorial, March 25, 1984, p.1.

45. *Liaowang*, 1986, no. 26, p. 9.

46. *Zhengzhou gongxueyuan xuebao: chesheban*, 1984, no. 3, pp. 103–106.

47. *Hongqi*, 1984, no. 13, p. 13.

48. *Qiushi*, 1985, no. 1, pp. 48–49; *Xinchangzheng* [Changchun], 1987, no. 8, pp. 23–24.

49. *Qiushi*, 1985, no. 1, pp. 48–49; *Zhengzhou gongxueyuan xuebao: chesheban*, 1984, no. 3, pp. 103–6; *Xinchangzheng* [Changchun], 1987, no. 8, pp. 23–24; *Zhengdang yinian*, pp. 22–23.

50. *Zhengdang yinian*, p. 18; *RMRB*, March 24, 1986, p. 1.

51. *Hongqi*, 1987, no. 1, p. 10.

52. See *Renmin ribao*, December 11, 1983, p. 1.

53. *CYWX*, p. 246; *Fendou* [Harbin], May 1986, p. 4.

54. Prior to the campaign, many had been worried that it might commit many of the "leftist" excesses of previous political campaigns. See *Zhengdang yinian*, p. 44.

55. *Hebei xuekan* [Shijiazhuang], 1985, no. 4, pp. 9–10; *Shijian* [Huhehot], 1985, no. 4, pp. 9–10.

56. *Tansuo*, 1986, no. 3, pp. 60–62.

57. Ibid.

58. *Xuexi yu yanjiu*, 1986, no. 4, pp. 29–30.

59. *CYWX*, p. 294.

60. Lu Keng, *An Interview with Hu Yaobang* (New York: Sino Daily Express, 1985), p. 40.

61. *Zhongguo nianjian*, 1988, p. 70.

62. *The World Journal*, October 16, 1989, p. 32.

63. *Liaowang*, 1986, no. 18, pp. 5–6. The party's 1987 report also claimed that between February 1982 and July 1986, some 67,613 party members were given intraparty sanctions for their economic crimes, and 25,598 were expelled.

64. *Xuexi yu yanjiu*, 1986, no. 4, p. 29.

65. *Dang de jianshe*, 1986, no. 7, p. 21.

66. *Xuexi yu yanjiu*, 1986, no. 4, pp. 29–30.

67. *Lilun yuekan*, 1986, no. 3, pp. 33–36.

68. *Liaowang*, 1986, no. 15, pp. 14–15.

69. *Dang de jianshe*, 1986, no. 3, p. 4.

70. Zhang Yun, in *Hongqi*, 1986, no. 10, pp. 13–14.

71. *RMRB*, January 13, 1986, p. 1.

72. Zhang Yun, in *Hongqi*, 1986, no. 10, pp. 9, 14; *RMRB*, January 11, 1986, p. 1.

73. *RMRB*, January 13, 1986, p. 1.

74. The most important instruction contained six rules of conduct: the reception and farewell ceremonies for high-ranking leaders must be simplified; the number of people in the entourage of traveling leaders and their traveling accommodations must be reduced; their living arrangements during travel must be economized; lavish gifts to visiting leading cadres should be banned; briefings to visiting leaders should be fact-based; and publicity about visiting leading cadres should be downplayed. *RMRB*, January 11, 1986, p. 1; January 31, 1986, p. 1.

75. *RMRB*, February 3, 1986, p. 1.

76. One case was the execution of the son of a dead Shanghai party boss, Hu Lijiao. Another case was the imprisonment of the daughter of a naval commander, General Ye Fe.

77. In February 1986, the minister, deputy minister, and a host of key officials of the Aerospace Industries Ministry were implicated in an elaborate scheme of smuggling and speculative activities amounting to U.S. $41 million. But only five junior officials were dealt with by the courts, while the major figures all received only internal party sanctions. See *RMRB*, February 7, 1986, p. 1.

78. For the details of the case of governor Ni Xiance of Jiangxi, see *RMRB*, May 28, 1987, p. 1. Also for the case of Zhou Erfu for immoral conduct, see *RMRB*, March 4, 1986, p. 1.

79. According to the party's claim, its investigations resulted in punishment being given to 74 members on the provincial army level, and 635 members on the district division level during 1985 and 1986. See *Zhongguo nianjian*, 1988, p. 70.

80. Zhang Yun, in *Hongqi*, 1986, no. 10, pp. 3–14.

81. PRC policy for many years was to forbid rural people to move to urban areas, to become industrial workers, or to become students in urban schools.

82. *Shijian* [Huhehot], 1985, no. 4, p. 7.

83. An oft-cited example of this phenomenon was the Baoshan Steel Mill near Shanghai. Another example was the plan to establish a separate province to cover the Three

Gorges of the Yangzi River. Had it not been for vehement criticisms by overseas Chinese scientists, the project would probably have been implemented in 1986.

84. *Jingji cankao* [Beijing], August 5, 1987, p. 4.

85. *RMRB*, August 1, 1985, p. 1.

86. Hui Go, "Hainan de jintian jiushi Zongguo gaige de mingtian?" *China Spring* (January 1986), p. 57.

87. For example, many party members were puzzled as to why the principle of commodity exchange could be applicable to one area and not others. Others also raised the question of whether party members were entitled to do things that the party's new policy allowed other citizens to do. Thus, for instance, while nonparty people had the right to religious freedom and to engage in profitable personal economic ventures, party members at one point could do neither. Most were unhappy about such restrictions and thought that they had been discriminated against. They believed that as long as their behavior did not violate the party's explicit policy, then it was all right. *Qunzhong*, 1985, no. 5, pp. 19, 22.

88. The best example of the former was the actions taken by peasants to depart from the commune systems of production and ownership in favor of privatizing their economic activities. The best example of the latter was the bonus system. Soon after the government made bonuses legal, many enterprises issued them so indiscriminately and so lavishly that the government quickly put new restrictions on the granting of bonuses.

89. Two good illustrations of this pattern were the payment of bonuses and the sending of students to study abroad. When the bonus system was first introduced, many enterprises and even noneconomic work units resorted to indiscriminate payment of bonuses. When the government tightened control, they then resorted to bonuses in other guises, such as free distribution of products to workers or hiding bonuses in normal production costs. Likewise, the policy of sending students abroad saw numerous changes in the 1980s. Each time a new regulation was announced, it created a panic and led more students to leave the country because they expected the restriction to become worse later.

90. *RMRB*, January 26, 1985, p. 1.

91. *Lilun yu shijian*, 1985, no. 13, p. 10.

92. "Resolution on Party Rectification," October 11, 1983, full text printed in *Hongqi*, 1983, no. 20, pp. 2–11.

93. *Xuexi zazhi* [Chengdu], 1984, no. 7, p. 1; *RMRB*, October 22, 1984, p. 1.

94. His analysis was that China had experienced three takeoffs (*tengfei*) in the modern age. The first one was the 1911 Revolution, which overthrew the imperial system. The second was the New Democratic Revolution, which created socialist China. He stated that China was in the middle of the third takeoff, to achieve the quadrupling of the GNP by the end of the century. *Hubei ribao*, December 16, 1984, p. 1.

95. *RMRB*, October 24, 1984, p. 1.

96. Hu argued that this latest round of takeoff must depend on three preconditions: (1) to make correct policies to mobilize the progressivism of the entire population; (2) to have a healthy political life so that the twenty-one million cadres could fully utilize their talents; and (3) to pay particular attention to science, technology, and education, to discover and promote talents among the third echelon, which will become the main force to realize the third takeoff. The takeoffs in the next century will depend on the third echelons of the next century. *RMRB*, October 22, 1984, p. 1.

97. For a detailed analysis of the Seventh Five-Year Plan, see *Wenhuibao*, October 17, 1985, p. 3.

98. Resolution by the Third Plenum of the CCP's Twelfth Party Congress, October 20, 1984, "Zhonggong zhongyang guanyu jinji tizhi gaige de jueding." For the full text, see *Hongqi*, 1984, no. 20, pp. 2–13.

99. *RMRB*, March 13, 1985, p. 1.

100. *RMRB*, December 21, 1983, p. 1; *Zhengdang yinian*, p. 40.

101. *RMRB*, December 13, 1983, p. 1.

102. *Hebei xuekan*, 1985, no. 4, p. 12.

103. *RMRB*, December 23, 1984, p. 1.

104. *Xuexi zazhi* [Chengdu], 1984, no. 7, p. 1.

105. *Qiushi*, 1985, no. 4, p. 62.

106. *Hebei xuekan*, 1985, no. 4, p. 12.

107. *Zhibu shenhuo* [Fuzhou] (January 1986), pp. 3–4.

108. Directive no. 5, December 16, 1983. *Zhengdang yinian*, pp. 9–11.

109. *Hebei xuekan*, 1985, no. 4, p. 12.

110. *Zhibu shenhuo* (January 1986), pp. 3–4.

111. *Zhengdang yinian*, p. 50.

112. *Qunzhong*, 1985, no. 4, p. 20.

113. *Lilun yu shijian*, 1985, no. 24, pp. 4–5, 11; *Hongqi*, 1985, no. 14, pp. 3–4; *RMRB*, June 30, 1985, p. 1; *Qunzhong*, 1985, no. 7, p. 15.

114. For instance, Chen Yun said, "The issue of relaxation does not exist insofar as party principles and party discipline are concerned. Reform cannot be implemented without good party style of work." *Hongqi*, 1986, no. 16, p. 12.

115. This view was particularly popular in the six coastal areas of Tianjin, Shanghai, Jiangsu, Zhejiang, Fujian, and Guangdong. Not surprisingly, the central party rejected this rationale and said that even more stringent standards should be applied to the economically more advanced areas. *RMRB*, June 1, 1986, p. 1.

116. *Hongqi*, 1986, no. 16, p. 12.

117. *Hongqi*, 1985, no. 20, p. 7.

118. *Sixiang zhengzhi gongzuo yanjiu* [Beijing], 1985, no. 8, p. 4.

119. *RMRB*, January 17, 1987, p. 1.

120. Zhao Ziyang speech, *RMRB*, January 30, 1987, p. 1.

121. *RMRB*, May 28, 1987, p. 1.

122. As quoted in "Shisanda daibiao fengzu shenyi Zhao Ziyang di baogao di taolun," in *Jiangxi ribao*, 1987, October 30, p. 1.

123. Kang Shijian, "Nuli jianshe yizhi jingdeqi 'liangge kaoyan' di dangyuan duiwu," in *Shishi qiushi* [Urumchi], 1988, no. 1, pp. 59–62.

124. *RMRB*, 1988, June 26, p. 1. It was estimated that "unqualified" party members accounted for about 5–10 percent of current party members. See Ding Mao, "Zenyang kandai jianguo yilai di fazhan dangyuan gongzuo," in *Dangjian wenhui* [Shengyang], 1988, no. 1, pp. 27–29.

125. Lo Haigang, "Dang ne fubai xianxiang tanyuan," *Lilun yuekan*, 1988, no. 5, pp. 25–27.

Chapter 9

1. Such notions seldom went beyond class struggle, the need to overcome physical hardship to serve communistic ideals, and, above all, "the people's commune is the bridge leading to the communist heaven." Many party members did not even know when the party's birth date was. Zhao Shengron, "Ruhe gaohao xingshiqi de dangyuan jiaoyu," *Lilun jiaoyu* [Taiyuan], 1985, no. 11, pp. 8–11.

2. By the early 1980s, about 35–40 percent of rural members had joined the party during the Cultural Revolution. Ibid., p. 9.

3. Thus, in spite of the government's policy to allow individual households to specialize in businesses and to acquire larger pieces of responsibility land or develop

larger-scale enterprises, party cadres even in the mid-1980s sometimes forced the peasants to give up the land or reduce the size of their enterprises to fit socialiste standards. Ibid., p. 8.

4. Weizhong, "Nongcun zhengdang yao jianchi cujin, baozheng gaige he jingji fanzhan de fangzhen," *Lilun yu shijian*, 1986, no. 4, p. 16.

5. Zhao Shengron, in *Lilun jiaoyu*, pp. 8–11; *Lilun xuekan*, 1987, no. 5, p. 40.

6. Study sessions were poorly attended and became ineffective. *Fuzhou shehui kexue* [Jiangxi], 1985, no. 1, pp. 9–10.

7. "Zenyang gaohao nongcun zhengdang gongzuo," *Zhibu shenghuo* [Guangzhou], 1986, no. 3, p. 3.

8. Many party members took advantage of these reforms to become 10,000-yuan household while leaving fellow villagers way behind. In some cases, the few party members were the only people to get rich way out of proportion to the poverty in their villages. In one village in Hebei, the leading cadre's family income was 1,700 yuan per person while the other villagers were making 31 yuan per person. Zhao Shengron, in *Lilun jiaoyu* [Taiyuan], pp. 8–11.

9. Sometimes party cadres tried to levy compulsory collections from the villagers to enrich themselves. In one such case, the cadres from two *xiang* collected more than 20,000 yuan from the people, to be distributed among themselves as work bonuses. Ibid.

10. *Lanzhou xuekan* [Lanzhou], 1986, no. 5, p. 15.

11. *Lilun yu shijian* [Shenyang], 1986, no. 2, pp. 26–27.

12. *Chongqing shehui kexue* [Chongqing, Sichuan], 1986, no. 4, p. 45.

13. *Hebei xuekan* [Shijiazhuang], 1985, no. 1, p. 108.

14. *Lilun xuekan*, 1986, no. 4, pp. 44–46. For a portrait of the majority of the rural leaders in Hubei in 1984, see *Nongcun gongzuo tongxin* [Beijing], 1985, no. 11, p. 12.

15. On the leaders' lack of education, see *Lilun yu shijian*, 1986, no. 2, pp. 26–27; *Lilun xuekan*, 1986, no. 4, pp. 44–46. For an assessment by the Gansu provincial party in September 1985, see *Gansu ribao*, August 28, 1985, p. 1. In Jinxian, Liaoning, in 1984, the basic conditions were the same: 40 percent of the village *zhibu* secretaries were above 45; 53 percent had only primary school education or less. See *Liaoning ribao*, January 12, 1985, p. 2. In a rural district of Zhejiang Province in 1985, the rural leaders were not much better. Of the 179 *zhibu* leaders, 46.6 percent were above 46 years old, with 13.4 percent actually above 56 years old. Some 71.5 percent of these leaders had primary school education or less. In fact, 31.3 percent were illiterate or semiliterate. *Nongmin ribao* [Beijing], May 21, 1985, p. 3.

16. *Hebei xuekan*, 1985, no. 1, p. 108.

17. The Chinese press called the old-fashioned rural economy the "grain and cotton type" and the new rural economy the "trade and industry type." For a survey report of the common characteristics of rural cadres in Shandong Province, see *Nongcun gongzuo tongxun*, 1985, no. 10, p. 18.

18. *Liaoning ribao*, January 12, 1985, p. 2.

19. *Gongchan dangyuan* [Shijiazhuang], 1986, no. 5, p. 14; *Lilun yu shijian*, 1986, no. 2, pp. 26–27.

20. *Nongcun gongzuo tongxun* [Beijing], 1985, no. 10, p. 17; *Dang de jianshe* [Lanzhou], 1986, no. 5, pp. 5–6.

21. In Zhejiang, complaints were that *zhibu* leaders were too old, inadequately educated, their thoughts were too rigid and conservative, they showed organizational laxity, and they lacked combative spirit. Some had committed serious criminal acts and indulged in serious abuse of privileges. Some continue to commit new acts of wrongdoing as they pretended to rectify old ones. Such phenomena were reported to be common in the countryside. *Gongchan dangyuan* [Hangzhou], 1986, no. 11, p. 5. In Hunan Province, after repeated efforts of adjustment and replacement, the rural basic-level party leadership

continued to be plagued by the problems of advanced age, low educational qualifications, poor administrative skills, and "leftist" political orientation. Such leaders continued to follow an outmoded style of leadership. They tended to be mechanical and rigid, domineering, whimsical, and intolerant of different views. *Lingling shizhuan xuebao, zhesheban* [Hunan], 1987, no. 1, p. 2.

22. *RMRB*, April 18, 1987, p. 1.

23. *Gongchan dangyuan*, 1986, no. 11, p. 5; *Lilun yu shijian*, 1986, no. 2, pp. 26–27.

24. They were usually described as having "big bitterness and deep hatred toward the old society, correct root and red seed in their social and class background, and reliability and obedience in their personal conduct." *Nongcun gongzuo tongxun*, 1985, no. 10, p. 18.

25. Ibid.; *Liaoning ribao*, January 12, 1985, p. 2.

26. *Nongcun gongzuo tongxun*, 1985, no. 10, p. 17.

27. *Liaoning ribao*, January 12, 1985, p. 2.

28. For an example of progress in Hubei Province in 1984, see *Nongcun gongzuo tongxun*, 1985, no. 11, p. 12. But in mid-1985, the press still criticized the laxity and weakness of rural party leadership. Rural leaders' political thoughts, age, and culture were judged to be imcompatible with the requirements of economic reforms in the countryside. Ibid., no. 10, p. 17.

29. *Hubei ribao*, November 4, 1985, p. 2.

30. They included gaining entry into the party or army for their relatives, preferential access to scarce resources, better food and health care, and so forth. When they were promoted to higher-level organs, they also had the chance to leave the countryside. *Neimenggu ribao*, August 27, 1985, p. 4.

31. Ibid.; *Gongchan dangyuan*, 1986, no. 11, p. 5.

32. *Zhejiang ribao*, March 3, 1986, p. 1.

33. *Lilun yu shijian* [Shenyang], 1986, no. 2, pp. 26–27.

34. For instance, in Hebei Province, the reconstitution of rural leadership began in 1984, and by mid-1986 the provincial party still judged half of the reconstituted leadership as falling short of the standards. *Gongchan dangyuan*, 1986, no. 5, p. 14.

35. In early 1986, some 279 village-level party branch secretaries in a county in Zhejiang "resigned" from their posts. Resignation of this scale was quite unheard of in CCP history. See *RMRB*, May 20, 1986, p. 4.

36. *RMRB*, March 17, 1983, p. 1.

37. *Nongye jingji yu jishu* [Guiyang], 1987, no. 2, pp. 25–26.

38. *Zhibu shenghuo* [Fuzhou], August 1986, pp. 9–10. For the case of Hebei Province, see *Hongqi*, 1987, no. 2, p. 36.

39. For a complaint by the provincial deputy party secretary of Gansu, see *Gansu ribao*, August 28, 1985, p. 1.

40. *Nongmin ribao* [Beijing], March 4, 1987, p. 2.

41. *RMRB*, November 14, 1986, p. 4.

42. Zhao Shengron, in *Lilun jiaoyu*, pp. 8–11.

43. *Hongqi*, 1985, no. 5, p. 25. In this case, there were 9,000 rural party members, and 4,600 of them had left farming.

44. *Hongqi*, 1987, no. 2, p. 36.

45. For instance, in 1986, a survey of Handan City in Hebei showed that 1,200 party members from the villages had found temporary work there. *RMRB*, December 22, 1986, p. 4.

46. *BJRB*, October 30, 1985, p. 3.

47. *Chongqing shehui kexue* [Chongqing, Sichuan], 1986, no. 4, p. 47.

48. *Hongqi*, 1987, no. 2, p. 36; *Nongmin ribao*, March 21, 1985, p. 2; *RMRB*, December 22, 1986, p. 4. For a case study of Huaijen County of Shanxi in 1984, see Zhao

Shengron, in *Lilun jiaoyu*, pp. 8–11. In this county more than half of the peasants who traveled constantly to engage in trade away from home were party members. In some *xiang* and *zhen*, over 70 percent of party members were engaged in long-distance trading, sought employment away from home, or were in transit constantly.

49. *Nongmin ribao*, March 21, 1985, p. 2.

50. *BJRB*, October 30, 1985, p. 3.

51. *Nongmin ribao*, December 4, 1985, p. 1.

52. *BJRB*, October 30, 1985, p. 3; *Nongmin ribao*, March 21, 1985, p. 2; *Nongcun gongzuo tongxun*, 1985, no. 10, p. 20. In February 1986, the Organization Department issued a document entitled "Guanyu tiaozheng he gaijin nongcun zhung dang de jiceng cuzhi shezhi de yijian" (Views on rearranging and improving the party's basic organs in the villages) that contained many of these basic ideas. *RMRB*, October 21, 1986, p. 5. For reiterations and refinements of these same ideas in 1987, see *Hongqi*, 1987, no. 2, p. 36.

53. For details of these experimental models and general principles, see *Nongcun gongzuo tongxun*, 1985, no. 10, p. 20; *Hubei ribao*, December 2, 1985, p. 2. Some experimental models demanded so much time and energy on the part of party members that they probably never had a chance of succeeding. For an illustration of some of the regulations adopted by one particular model, see *BJRB*, October 30, 1985, p. 3.

54. *Hongqi*, 1987, no. 2, p. 36.

55. For instance, the party indicated that it was permissible for members with high geographical mobility to form "temporary" branches or cells, or to choose to belong only to the organs in their home villages, or even merely to conduct political study on their own without participating in party activities. *RMRB*, October 21, 1986, p. 5.

56. *Dang de shenghuo* [Harbin], 1986, no. 11, pp. 8–10.

57. *BJRB*, October 30, 1985, p. 3; *Nongmin ribao* [Beijing], March 21, 1985, p. 2.

58. *Dang de shenghuo*, 1986, No. 4, pp. 4–8.

59. Ibid.

60. *RMRB*, December 22, 1986, p. 4.

61. *Lingling shizhuan xuebao, zhesheban* [Hunan], 1987, no. 1, p. 2.

62. Zhao Shengron, in *Lilun jiaoyu*, pp. 8–11.

63. *RMRB*, overseas edition, August 16, 1988, p. 4.

64. Ibid., September 28, 1989, p. 4.

65. *Nongmin ribao*, April 9, 1985, p. 3.

66. It was believed that they not only had the correct social origins but also harbored "deep hatred and great bitterness" against the old society, and therefore could be relied on by the party.

67. *Hebei xuekan* [Shijiazhuang], 1986, no. 1, p. 108; *Liaoning ribao*, January 12, 1985, p. 2.

68. *Hongqi*, 1984, no. 23, p. 18; *Liaoning ribao*, January 12, 1985, p. 2.

69. *Nongmin ribao*, April 9, 1985, p. 3. A substantial number of village *zhibu* had not recruited anyone at all since 1980. For some case reports, see *Nongmin ribao*, May 21, 1985, p. 3; *Jilin ribao*, November 16, 1984, p. 3. In one of the worst cases, Conzizhou County in Shaanxi had a peasant population of over 200,000, yet in 1983–84 only about twenty-two new members were admitted each year. This meant that only one out of 10,000 peasants joined the party. *Lilun xuekan*, 1986, no. 4, pp. 44–46. A large-scale survey of the Chengde region in Hebei Province in 1984 showed that of the 290 *xiang* and *zhen* in this region, more than 50 (17 percent) did not recruit a single member for all of 1984. *Nongmin ribao*, January 23, 1985, p. 2.

70. In a survey conducted in three *xiang* in Jiangsu Province in 1985, there were 2,962 party members, but only 62 (or 2.1 percent) were below 25 years of age. *Nongcun gongzuo tongxing*, 1985, no. 7, p. 7. A survey of Nantong District in Chongqing showed

that only 11 percent of the new recruits of 1985 were rural youths. In Guanbei *xiang*, there had been only four rural youths during 1978–1985. Of the ten villages in this *xiang*, nine had no rural recruits during this period. *Chongqing shehui kexue*, 1986, no. 4, p. 49.

71. In Congzizhou County, Shaanxi, women constituted only 14 percent of the county's total party membership. See *Lilun xuekan*, 1986, no. 4, pp. 44–46.

72. *Nongcun gongzuo tongxing*, 1985, no. 7, pp. 7–8.

73. *Zhongguo nongminbao* [Beijing], November 23, 1984, p. 1; *Nongmin ribao*, January 23, 1985, p. 2; April 19, 1985, p. 3; *Zhibu jianshe* [Taiyuan], 1986, no. 4, p. 14.

74. *Nongcun gongzuo tongxing*, 1985, no. 7, pp. 7–8; *Nongmin ribao*, January 23, 1985, p. 2.

75. *Hebei xuekan* [Shijiazhuang], 1985, no. 1, p. 109; *Nongcun gongzuo tongxing*, 1985, no. 7, pp. 7–8.

76. *RMRB*, July 5, 1986, p. 4.

77. *Hebei xuekan*, 1985, no. 1, p. 109; *Zhongguo nongminbao*, November 23, 1984, p. 1.

78. *RMRB*, December 22, 1986, p. 4.

79. *Nongcun gongzuo tongxing*, 1985, no. 7, pp. 7, 8. In a survey conducted in three *xiang* in Jiangsu Province in 1985, there were 24,733 youths below 25 years of age, but only 0.15 percent of their age cohorts were party members. Furthermore, during 1984, the three *xiang* only recruited 42 new members, but only 3 of them were under 25 years of age. In another case in Sichuan in 1985, over 480 educated rural youths were returned to work at Qingnian *zhen*, but only 12 submitted application for party membership. *Chongqing shehui kexue*, 1986, no. 4, p. 49.

80. *Lilun xuekan*, 1986, no. 4, pp. 44–46.

81. *Nongmin ribao*, January 23, 1985, p. 2; *Chongqing shehui kexue* [Chongqing], 1986, no. 4, p. 48. For a survey of party members in four villages in Shanxi Province in 1984, see *Zhongguo nongminbao*, November 23, 1984, p. 1. In this case, those between 25 and 30 years of age constituted 2.4 percent; between 31 and 40 years, 23.5 percent; between 41 and 50 years, 36.5 percent; and between 51 and 60 years, 37.4 percent of party members.

82. *Zhongguo nongminbao*, November 23, 1984, p. 1.

83. Thus, for instance, in Nantong District in Chongqing (probably an above average rural district in the country), those with high school education or higher constituted only 4.14 percent of total party membership, but those with primary school education or illiterates and semiliterates constituted 81.52 percent. In another *xiang*, those with primary school education or illiterates or semiliterates constituted 93.39 percent of total party membership. Also, village party secretaries were predominantly primary school educated. See *Chongqing shehui kexue*, 1986, no. 4, p. 49.

84. In one *xiang* in Chongqing Municipality in Sichuan Province, 23 percent of the rural party members were listed as being too weak to do party work. *Chongqing shehui kexue*, 1986, no. 4, p. 48.

85. *Dangjian wenhui* [Shenyang], 1988, no. 1, pp. 27–29; *Dangjian* [Beijing], 1988, no. 3, pp. 28–29; *Shishi qiushi* [Urumqi], 1988, no. 2, pp. 49–51.

86. *Shishi qiushi*, 1988, no. 1, pp. 59–62.

87. For instance, a study in Inner Mongolia showed that an ordinary production brigade had only eight cadres during the collectivization period of the mid-1950s, increased to fourteen during the communization movement of the late 1950s, then to over thirty in the early 1980s. This was a quadrupling in size in less than three decades. *Neimenggu ribao*, July 8, 1983, p. 1.

88. These measures included the nearly annual "rectification of style and commune," "May revolution," "basic-line education," system of cadre participation in labor, the

four-clean movement, or management by poor, lower, and middle peasants. *Neimenggu ribao*, July 8, 1983, p. 1.

89. *RMRB*, April 18, 1987, p. 1; *Qunzhong*, 1986, no. 2, pp. 41–42; 1986, no. 6, pp. 4–5. In the case of Hebei Province, rural cadres had reportedly taken out accumulated "loans" from the public funds in excess of RMB $200 million by 1986. In addition, some RMB $40 million were dished out as stipends by various work units to their staff. *Lilun yuekan*, 1986, no. 12, pp. 2–3. In a single city in Zhejiang Province (Linhai), 2,008 cadres had "borrowed" $570,000 RMB from the public funds under their control before May 1986. *RMRB*, May 20, 1986, p. 4; August 19, 1986, p. 5.

90. Thus, for instance, the leading cadres of a single village party *zhibu* in Hebei Province squandered RMB $39,000 on feasting alone in the single year of 1985. *Lilun yuekan*, 1986, no. 12, p. 1. One party member in a Shaanxi village invited more than 200 guests in the village to a feast to celebrate his son's wedding and received gifts from everyone in the village. *Lilun xuekan*, 1987, no. 5, pp. 42–43.

91. *Lilun xuexi* [Hefei], 1986, no. 3, pp. 10–12.

92. There are a huge number of reports of rural cadre and party members' misconduct in many localities in the official press. For a summary of the key features of such misconduct, see *Qunzhong*, 1986, no. 6, pp. 4–5.

93. Ibid. Examples of such services included funeral arrangements, the settling of civil disputes, the allocation of govenment loans, chemical fertilizers, lubricants and fuels, the granting of government subsidies and relief funds, and the payment of their grain tax to the state.

94. In 1985–86, some 3,100 enterprises were illegally formed in Hebei Province by party and state agencies in the rural areas. *Lilun yuekan*, 1986, no. 12, pp. 2–3; *Qunzhong*, 1986, no. 2, pp. 41–42; 1986, no. 6, pp. 4–5; *Nongmin ribao*, June 23, 1987, p. 3; *Hongqi*, 1987, no. 2, p. 36.

95. *Lilun yuekan*, 1986, no. 12, p. 3; *Zhejiang ribao*, March 3, 1986, p. 1.

96. *Nongcun gongzuo tongxing*, 1985, no. 7, p. 8; *Lilun xuekan*, 1987, no. 5, pp. 42–43.

97. *Dangde shenghuo*, April 1986, pp. 4–6; *Dangde jianshe*, 1986, no. 10, p. 5.

98. *RMRB*, November 25, 1985, p. 1.

99. Ibid.

100. Ibid.

101. Ibid.

102. *Dangde jianshe*, 1986, no. 10, pp. 6–7; *RMRB*, May 18, 1986, p. 1; December 30, 1986, p. 1. For similar statements, see *RMRB*, November 21, 1986, p. 1; February 15, 1987, p. 4.

103. *Dangde jianshe*, 1986, no. 10, p. 5; *RMRB*, February 8, 1987, p. 1.

104. *RMRB*, November 25, 1985, p. 1; October 31, 1986, p. 4.

105. In September 1985, Shaanxi Province sent downward a total of five thousand cadres to the villages, including one thousand each from the province and the district, and three thousand from the county party and government organs. *Shaanxi ribao*, September 8, 1985, p. 1. For Hebei, see *Hongqi*, 1987, no. 2, p. 36. For Hubei, see *RMRB*, November 4, 1986, p. 4.

106. *Liaowang*, 1986, no. 41, p. 6.

107. *Hongqi*, 1987, no. 2, p. 36.

108. In Sichuan, many places were given only ten days to investigate the members' deeds and pass organizational judgment. *Dangde jianshe*, 1986, no. 9, pp. 3–5. In Gansu, the rectification on the *xiang* (*zhen*) level barely lasted two months. See *Dangde jianshe* , 1986, no. 5, pp. 5–6.

109. For instance, Sichuan reported that its rural rectification lasted from December

1985 to October 1986. During this period, 9,900 *qu-*, *xiang-*, and *zhen*-level party organs, and some 20,000 village-level party organs had undergone rectification. In the entire province, some 200,000 *qu-*, *xiang-*, and *zhen*-level party members, and some 460,000 village-level party members, participated in rectification. *RMRB*, October 3, 1986, p. 4. But Sichuan Province had 77,000 village party *zhibu* with about 1.9 million party members. Therefore, possibly more than half of the rural members never took part in rectification. *Dangde jianshe*, 1986, no. 9, p. 3. The Hebei provincial party organs admitted that some 20 percent of the village party organs did a poor job in rectification. *Lilun yuekan*, 1986, no. 12, p. 1.

110. *RMRB*, October 31, 1986, p. 4. The province of Hebei, for instance, finished the campaign before the end of 1986, at least six months ahead of schedule. *Lilun yuekan*, 1986, no. 12, p. 1.

111. For example, political training sessions were offered without paying the slightest attention to their educational effect. Many local areas did not have enough workers assigned to conduct rectification. *RMRB*, February 25, 1987, p. 4.

112. *Xuexi yu yanjiu*, 1987, no. 4, p. 3.

113. *RMRB*, December 30, 1986, p. 1. Bo Yibo issued an important statement on December 29, 1986, pointing out that while new economic concepts and techniques were important, they should not be the only or even the central point of rural party rectification. He underscored Hu Yaobang's emphasis on the "two serious offenses" and insisted that only the exposing and rectification of misconduct should be the main objectives of rural party rectification. *RMRB*, December 30, 1986, p. 1; February 8, 1987, p. 1.

114. *RMRB*, February 15, 1987, p. 4; February 25, 1987, p. 4.

115. *RMRB*, November 25, 1985, p. 1.

116. Ibid.

117. For instance, Bo Yibo, speaking in November 1986, argued that meting out harsh punishment to the perpetrators of misconduct should not be considered a "leftist" error. *RMRB*, November 21, 1986, p. 1. Also see *Dang de jianshe*, 1986, no. 9, pp. 3–5.

118. *RMRB*, April 18, 1987, p. 1. Many provinces also made their own claims of success. Sichuan, for example, claimed that its major efforts were to recover public funds embezzled by cadres, and that some 80 percent of illegally gotten funds had been recovered. See *RMRB*, October 3, 1986, p. 4.

119. *RMRB*, February 25, 1987, p. 4.

120. *RMRB*, November 21, 1986, p. 1.

121. *Minzhu yu fazhi*, 1982, no. 1, p. 24.

122. *RMRB*, August 11, 1983, p. 5.

123. *RMRB*, March 18, 1987, p. 4. For figures of Huanglong County in Shaanxi in 1987, see *Lilun xuekan*, 1987, no. 5, pp. 42–43. For figures of Yihuang County (Jiangxi) in 1985, see *Fuzhou shehui kexue* [Jiangxi], 1985, no. 1, p. 9.

124. For a case in Shaanxi, see *Lilun xuekan*, 1987, no. 5, p. 40. For a case study in Jiangxi, see *Fuzhou shehui kexue*, 1985, no. 1, p. 9.

125. For a case study in Jiangsu Province in 1985, see *Nongcun gongzuo tongxing*, 1985, no. 7, pp. 7–8.

126. In Gansu Province in 1987, for example, it was found that one out every four rural cadres customarily employed beating and cursing in their dealings with the masses. See *Lanzhou xuekan*, 1986, no. 5, p. 15.

127. *RMRB*, August 11, 1983, p. 5.

128. *Lilun xuekan*, 1987, no. 5, pp. 42–43.

129. *Hongqi*, 1983, no. 9, pp. 46–47.

130. Even in 1983, China only had 30,000 "state agricultural technique extension personnel" to serve the 50,000 communes in existence at the time. This meant that there

was only 0.6 such extension expert for every commune, or one such expert for every 50,000 mu of cultivated land. *RMRB*, June 28, 1983, p. 3.

131. These were the heads of provincial agricultural departments, district commissioners, county magistrates, and party secretaries in charge of agricultural affairs. Even when official figures are accepted at their face value, by the summer of 1982, only 4,000 provincial- and county-level agricultural cadres had been given professional training at various agricultural colleges. *RMRB*, July 16, 1982, p. 1. By the spring of 1984, only 10,000 of the leading agricultural cadres on the provincial, regional, and county levels had received any training, and only 250,000 rural technical workers had undergone short-term training programs of unknown quality. *RMRB*, February 21, 1984, p. 2.

132. Hebei had a total of 2.8 million party members in 1986, of which rural party members accounted for 1.6 million. *Gongchan dangyuan*, 1986, no. 7, p. 16.

133. *RMRB*, November 14, 1984, p. 1.

134. "Poor" peasant households constituted 10 percent of farming households in the entire province, but "poor" party members constituted 14.4 percent of rural party members in the province. *Zhibu shenghuo* [Fuzhou], August 1986, pp. 9–10.

135. A survey published in *Renmin ribao* of 210 economic enterprises in Hengji Township, Jiangsu Province, in mid-1985 indicated that party members assumed leadership positions in only one-fourth of them. *RMRB*, October 29, 1985, p. 5.

136. Ibid.

137. *Nongmin ribao*, May 21, 1985, p. 3.

Chapter 10

1. During the two decades 1958–1978, China had invested about RMB $600 billion on basic construction, yet only one-third of this sum actually resulted in improving its productivity, while the other two-thirds were mostly wasted. Even in 1976, nearly a quarter of the rural people did not have enough to eat. When this situation was brought up in a discussion among party leaders in 1980, one said the CCP would probably have been overthrown by the workers and peasants if they had known about the truth. Chen Yizi's interview in *The World Journal*, September 7, 1989, p. 31.

2. *RMRB*, overseas edition, October 10, 1989, p. 1.

3. Ibid., June 28, 1989, p. 1.

4. Jiang Zemin news conference, September 27, 1989, in ibid., September 27, 1989, p. 1. The originator of this "peaceful transformation" strategy was said to be John Foster Dulles, but the scheme has been kept alive by the entire imperialist and Western world. See "Tantan guoji daqihou" (On the international major climate), in ibid., October 18, 1989, p. 2.

5. Ibid.; and Deng Xiaoping's speech to new members of the Politburo Standing Committee, June 16, 1989, reprinted in *The World Journal*, July 15, 1989, p. 31.

6. Jiang Zemin news conference, September 27, 1989.

7. Ibid.

8. *RMRB*, overseas edition, October 12, 1989, p. 2.

9. They splashed big-character posters on campuses. Several dozen graduate students took the dramatic step of going to the People's Hall and offering to shine shoes to advertise the terrible economic conditions of intellectuals. In June 1988, a college student was killed by juvenile delinquents in Beijing, which caused a riot among students in protest against campus conditions. *RMRB*, overseas edition, September 11, 1989, p. 2.

10. Even officially sanctioned survey data corroborated this trend. For instance, two surveys of college students' political attitudes were conducted in Beijing in June 1986 and June 1988 respectively. In June 1986, 20.5 percent of the respondents believed that "it is

hopeless for China to achieve modernization under the CCP. China must adopt a multi-party system." In June 1988, this figure was 21.1 percent. Also in June 1986, 16.8 percent of the respondents favored the adoption of capitalism, but in June 1988 the figure was 34.5 percent. In another survey of Beijing college students during this time, 22.7 percent of the respondents regarded Marxism as merely another subject and not more important than other disciplines. In some schools over 50 percent of the students held such views. Both surveys are reported in ibid.

11. This was shown by the popularity of such works as "The Death of a River" (Heshang) or "The Ugly Chinese" (Choulou de Zhongguoren).

12. Hu was reported to have said that he would raise both hands in favor of the prompt retirement of Deng Xiaoping. Interview with ZZN, August 12, 1987.

13. Zhao's press conference at the Thirteenth Party Congress, *Zhongguo nianjian*, 1988, p. 62.

14. *The World Journal*, October 18, 1989, p. 31.

15. On July 23, 1989, Vice-President Wang Zhen said that Zhao's think-tank members were just like the henchmen who gravitated toward Lin Biao in the late 1960s. They were dangerous and must be eliminated. Ibid.

16. General Secretary Jiang Zemin's criticism of Zhao on August 21, 1989, at the National Conference of Directors of Party Organization Departments, reported in ibid.

17. Ibid.

18. Deng Xiaoping's speech to new members of the Politburo Standing Committee, June 16, 1989, reprinted in *The World Journal*, July 15, 1989, p. 31. It should be noted that the concept of the "third generation" should not be confused with the concept of the "third echelon." Deng's "generation" is a chronological concept counting Mao as the first generation and himself as the second. This can go on to the nth generation. But the "third echelon" is a reserve of younger leaders that should exist at any time to smooth succession. See also text of Deng Xiaoping's talk with Li Peng and Yao Yilin on May 31, 1989, reprinted in *The World Journal*, July 15, 1989, p. 31.

19. Speech by Song Ping, director of the CCP Organization Department, to the National Conference of Organization Department Directors, August 22, 1989, in *RMRB*, overseas edition, August 23, 1989, p. 1. The overwhelming majority of the twenty-some ringleaders who were included in Beijing Mayor Chen Xitong's report on the riot were party members. Many had been party members for several decades, occupied important party posts, and were people of wide popularity and influence.

20. Deng Xioping's speech to the new members of the Politburo Standing Committee, June 16, 1989.

21. They included steps to sort out the commercial companies' activities, forbid children of high cadres to engage in economic activities, terminate the special supply system to leading cadres, suspend the importation of automobiles for cadre use, forbid feasting and gifting, restrict cadres' foreign travel, and severely punish economic criminal activities. *The World Journal*, June 27, 1989, p. 1.

22. Li Peng said in late September that three things have already been completed: (1) children of national leaders have all withdrawn from commercial companies; (2) leading cadres have switched from expensive foreign automobiles to Chinese cars; (3) the special supply system for leading cadres has been abolished. *RMRB*, overseas edition, September 27, 1989, p. 4.

23. One good example is the party's handling of the Kanghua Corporation, whose irregularities were obviously serious enough to persuade the party to order its disbandment. See *The World Journal*, June 27, 1989, p. 1. Yet no further information was ever released about the details of its activities. It was widely believed that Kanghua's operations had close connections with Deng's son, Deng Pufang, yet no account was ever given

about the extent of Deng Pufang's personal involvement in Kanghua's illegal operations.

24. Thus, for example, the freshman class of Beijing University for the fall of 1989 was reduced by nearly 60 percent from its normal size, and the new students were required to spend their freshman year in a military camp to undergo political training rather than normal academic training on their own campus.

25. *RMRB*, overseas edition, editorial, October 10, 1989, p. 1.

26. *RMRB*, overseas edition, October 16, 1989, p. 1.

27. Ibid.; *The World Journal*, October 16, 1989, p. 32. By the end of September, the party claimed that about 30 million volumes and 400,000 cassettes of pornographic materials had been confiscated. Over 300 manufacturing and distributing points had been seized, and over 1,800 pornographical criminals had been prosecuted. See *RMRB*, overseas edition, October 17, 1989, p. 1.

28. Deng Xiaoping's talk with new members of the Politburo Standing Committee, June 16, 1989.

29. Ibid.

30. *RMRB*, overseas edition, October 10, 1989, p. 1.

31. This means that the central mission is to make economic progress, but this mission must be supplemented by the continuation of reforms as well as the insistence on the four cardinal principles.

32. *RMRB*, overseas edition, September 27, 1989, p. 4.

33. Deng Xiaoping's talk with Li Peng and Yao Yilin, May 31, 1989, in *The World Journal*, July 15, 1989, p. 31. Also see *RMRB*, overseas edition, editorial, October 10, 1989, p. 1.

34. "Zhengque kandai zhenggong ganbu" (Properly viewing the political work cadres), *RMRB*, January 2, 1988, p. 4.

35. Chen Yizi's interview in *The World Journal*, September 7, 1989, p. 31.

36. Using the plant manager responsibility system as an illustration, Jiang said that it would be a misconception on the part of a plant manager if he insisted on the right to make appointments of technical personnel without consulting the party secretary beforehand. Jiang Zemin's speech at the National Conference of Organization Department Directors, August 21, 1989. *RMRB*, overseas edition, October 17, 1989, p. 4.

37. For example, a long article entitled "Lingdao women shiye de hexing liliang shi zhongguo gongchandang" (The CCP is the core force to lead our endeavors), in *RMRB*, overseas edition, September 27, 1989, p. 2.

38. Speech by Song Ping, director of CCP Organization Department, to the National Conference of Organization Department Directors, August 22, 1989. Also see *RMRB*, overseas edition, October 12, 1989, p. 2; October 18, 1989, p. 2.

39. Deng Xiaoping's talk with Li Peng and Yao Yilin, May 31, 1989.

40. A provincial official from a Northeastern province informed the author that during previous student demonstrations, some student leaders had openly said that Manchuria would have developed faster if it had remained under Japanese rule. Interview with ZMC, October 31, 1989.

Selected Bibliography

Bachman, David. *Chen Yun and the Chinese Political System*. Berkeley, 1985.

Barlow, Tani E., and Donald M. Lowe. *Teaching China's Lost Generation: Foreign Experts in the People's Republic of China*. San Francisco, 1987.

Barnett, Doak A. *Cadres, Bureaucracy, and Political Power in Communist China*. New York, 1967.

Bartke, Wolfgang. *Who's Who in the People's Republic of China*. Armonk, NY, 1981.

Bartke, Wolfgang, and Peter Schier. *China's New Party Leadership*. Armonk, NY, 1985.

Bernstein, Richard. *From the Center of the Earth: The Search for the Truth about China*. Boston, 1982.

Blecher, Marc. *China: Politics, Economics, and Society*. Boulder, 1986.

Brzezinski, Zbigniew K. *The Permanent Purge: Politics in Soviet Totalitarianism*. Cambridge, MA, 1956.

Burns, John P., and Stanley Rosen, eds. *Policy Conflicts in Post-Mao China: A Documentary Survey, with Analysis*. Armonk, NY, 1986.

Butterfield, Fox. *China: Alive in the Bitter Sea*. New York, 1982.

Cady, Janet A., ed. *Economic Reform in China: Report of the American Economists Study Team to the People's Republic of China*. New York, 1984.

Chai, Joseph C. H., and Chi-Keung Leung, eds. *China's Economic Reforms*. Hong Kong, 1987.

Chan, Anita, Jonathan Unger, and Stanley Rosen, eds. *On Socialist Democracy and the Chinese Legal System: The Li Yizhe Debates*. Armonk, NY, 1985.

Chang, Ching-yu, ed. *The Emerging Teng System: Orientation, Policies, and Implications*. Taipei, 1983.

Chang, David Wen-wei. *China under Deng Xiaoping: Political and Economic Reform*. New York, 1989.

Chang, Parris H. *Power and Policy in China*. University Park, PA, 1975.

Chen Yun wenxuan (1949–1956). Beijing, 1984.

Chen Yun wenxuan (1956–1985). Beijing, 1986.

Croll, Elisabeth. *Chinese Women Since Mao*. Armonk, NY, 1983.

Dallin, Alexander, and George W. Breslauer. *Political Terror in Communist Systems*. Stanford, 1970.

Davis-Friedman, Deborah. *Occupational Mobility and the Evolving Opportunity Structure of Contemporary China*. New Haven, 1986.

Daxuesheng tan zhongguo shehuizhuyi (University students on socialism). Yanbian, Jilin, 1984.

Deng Xiaoping wenxuan: 1975–1982. Hong Kong, 1983.

Department of Planning, State Education Commission. *Achievement of Education in China*. Beijing, 1986.

Dittmer, Lowell. *China's Continuous Revolution: The Postliberation Epoch, 1949–1981*. Berkeley, 1987.

————. *Liu Shao-ch'i and the Chinese Cultural Revolution: The Politics of Mass Criticism*. Berkeley, 1974.

Domes, Jurgen. *The Government and Politics of the PRC: A Time of Transition*. Boulder, 1985.

————. *Socialism in the Chinese Countryside: Rural Societal Policies in the PRC, 1949–1979*. London, 1980.

————. *China after the Cultural Revolution: Politics between Two Party Congresses*. London, 1976.

Dorrill, W. F. *Power, Policy and Ideology in the Making of China's "Cultural Revolution."* RAND Memorandum RM-5731-PR, August 1968.

Edwards, R. Randle, Louis Henkin, and Andrew J. Nathan. *Human Rights in Contemporary China*. New York, 1986.

Falkenheim, Victor C., ed. *Citizens and Groups in Contemporary China*. Ann Arbor, 1987.

Franz, Uli. *Deng Xiaoping*. New York, 1988.

Frazer, John. *The Chinese: Portrait of a People*. New York, 1980.

Gao, Yuan. *Born Red*. Stanford, 1987.

Gardner, John. *Chinese Politics and the Succession to Mao*. London and Basingstoke, 1982.

Goldman, Merle, Timothy Cheek, and Carol Lee Hamrin, eds. *China's Intellectuals and the State: In Search of a New Relationship*. Armonk, NY, 1986.

Goodman, David S. G. *Beijing Street Voices: The Poetry and Politics of China's Democracy Movement*. London, 1981.

Guillermaz, Jacques. *The Chinese Communist Party in Power, 1949–1976*. Boulder, 1976.

Hamrin, Carol Lee, and Timothy Cheek, eds. *China's Establishment Intellectuals*. Armonk, NY, 1986.

Harding, Harry. *China's Second Revolution: Reform after Mao*. Washington, DC, 1987.

Hartford, Kathleen, and Steven M. Goldstein, eds. *Single Sparks: China's Rural Revolutions*. Armonk, NY, 1989.

Hayhoe, Ruth, and Marianne Bastid, eds. *China's Education and the Industrialized World: Studies in Cultural Transfer*. Armonk, NY, 1987.

Hinton, Harold C., ed. *The People's Republic of China, 1949–1979: A Documentary Study*. 5 vols. Wilmington, 1980.

Honig, Emily, and Gail Hershatter. *Personal Voices: Chinese Women in the 1980's*. Stanford, 1988.

Institute of the Study of Chinese Communist Problems, Taipei, ed. *Dalu dixia kanwu huibian* (Collection of mainland underground publications). Taipei, 1980.

Johnson, Kay Ann. *Women, the Family and Peasant Revolution in China*. Chicago, 1983.

Kallgren, Joyce K., and Denis Fred Simon, eds. *Educational Exchanges: Essays on the Sino-American Experience*. Research Papers and Policy Studies Paper 21. Berkeley, 1987.

Kau, Michael Y. M., and John K. Leung, eds. *The Writings of Mao Zedong, 1949–1976*. Vol. 1. Armonk, NY, 1986.

Kim, Samuel S., ed. *China and the World: New Directions in Chinese Foreign Relations*. 2d ed. Boulder, 1989.

Kirkby, R. J. R. *Urbanization in China: Town and Country in a Developing Economy, 1949–2000 A.D.* New York, 1985.

Kraus, Richard Curt. *Class Conflict in Chinese Socialism*. New York, 1981.

Ladany, Lazlo. *The Communist Party of China and Marxism: 1921–1985*. Stanford, 1988.

Lamb, Malcolm, ed. *Directory of Officials and Organizations in China, 1968–1983*. Armonk, NY, 1984.

Lampton, David M. *Paths to Power: Elite Mobility in Contemporary China*. Ann Arbor, 1986.

———. *Policy Implementation in Post-Mao China*. Berkeley, 1987.

Leng, Shao-chuan, ed. *Changes in China: Party, State, and Society*. Lanham, MD, 1989.

Lewis, John, ed. *The City in Communist China*. Stanford, 1971.

———. *Leadership in Communist China*. Ithaca, 1963.

———. *Party Leadership and Revolutionary Power in China*. Ithaca, 1970.

Lieberthal, Kenneth J., and Bruce J. Dickson. *A Research Guide to General Party and Government Meetings in China, 1949–1986*. Armonk, NY, 1989.

Lieberthal, Kenneth, and Michel Oksenberg. *Bureaucratic Politics and Chinese Energy Development*. Washington, DC, 1986.

———. *Policy Making in China: Leaders, Structures and Processes*. Princeton, 1988.

Lifton, Robert J. *Thought Reform and the Psychology of Totalism: A Study of "Brainwashing" in China*. New York, 1961.

Lin, Yitang, ed. *What They Say: A Collection of Current Chinese Underground Publications*. Taipei, 1980.

Lippit, Victor D. *The Economic Development of China*. Armonk, NY, 1986.

MacFarquhar, Roderick. *The Origins of the Cultural Revolution, 1: Contradictions Among the People 1956–1957*. New York, 1974.

Madsen, Richard. *Morality and Power in a Chinese Village*. Berkeley, 1984.

Manion, Melanie. "Cadre Retirement in the People's Republic of China, Post-Mao." Ph.D. dissertation, University of Michigan.

Mao Zedong xuanji. Beijing, 1964.

Mosher, Stephen W. *Broken Earth: The Rural Chinese*. New York, 1983.

Nathan, Andrew J. *Chinese Democracy*. Berkeley, 1985.

Parish, William L., ed. *Chinese Rural Development: The Great Transformation*. Armonk, NY, 1985.

Parish, William L., and Martin King Whyte. *Village and Family Life in Contemporary China*. Chicago, 1978.

———. *Urban Life in Contemporary China*. Chicago, 1984.

Parker, Franklin, and Betty June Parker. *Education in the People's Republic of China, Past and Present: An Annotated Bibliography*. New York, 1986.

People's Republic of China Yearbook 1986. Beijing, 1986.

Perry, Elizabeth J., and Christine Wong. *The Political Economy of Reform in Post-Mao China*. Cambridge, MA, 1985.

Radiopress, Inc. *China Directory, 1981*, 9th ed. Tokyo, 1980.

Reynolds, Bruce L., ed. *Reform in China: Challenges and Choices*. Armonk, NY, 1987.

Rosen, Stanley, and David Chu. *Survey Research in the People's Republic of China*. Washington, DC, 1987.

Rozman, Gilbert. *The Chinese Debate about Soviet Socialism, 1978–1985*. Princeton, 1987.

Scalapino, Robert A., ed. *Elites in the People's Republic of China*. Seattle, 1972.

Schein, Edgar H., Inge Schneier, and Curtis H. Barker. *Coercive Persuasion: A Sociopsychological Analysis of the "Brainwashing" of American Civilian Prisoners*. New York, 1961.

Schell, Orville. *Discos and Democracy: China in the Throes of Reform*. New York, 1988.

Schram, Stuart R. *Authority, Participation, and Cultural Change in China*. Cambridge, UK, 1973.

Seymour, James D., ed. *The Fifth Modernization: China's Human Rights Movement, 1978–1979*. Stanfordville, NY, 1980.

Shiyijie sanzhong quanhui yilai zhongyao wenxian xuandu (Major documents since the Third Plenum). Beijing, 1987.

Shue, Vivienne. *The Reach of the State: Sketches of the Chinese Body Politic*. Stanford, 1988.

Shurmann, Franz. *Ideology and Organization in Communist China*. 3d rev. ed. Berkeley, 1981.

State Statistical Bureau. *Zhonguo tonji nianjian 1988* (Chinese statistical yearbook 1988). Beijing, 1989.

State Statistical Bureau, Department of Population Statistics. *Zhongguo 1987-nian 1% renkou chouyang diaocha ciliao* (Materials from China's 1 percent sample population survey). National volume. Beijing, 1988.

Teiwes, Frederick C. *Elite Discipline in China: Coercive and Persuasive Approaches to Rectification, 1950–1953*. Canberra, 1978.

———. *Leadership, Legitimacy, and Conflict in China: From a Charismatic Mao to the Politics of Succession*. Armonk, NY, 1984.

———. *Politics and Purges in China: Rectification and the Decline of Party Norms, 1950–1965*. Armonk, NY, 1979.

———. *Provincial Leadership in China: The Cultural Revolution and Its Aftermath*. Ithaca, 1974.

———. *Provincial Party Personnel in Mainland China, 1956–1966*. New York, 1967.

Thurston, Anne F. *Enemies of the People*. New York, 1987.

Tsou, Tang. *The Cultural Revolution and Post-Mao Reforms*. Chicago, 1986.

Tudi gaige zhongyao wenxian huibian. Beijing, 1951.

Uhalley, Stephen, Jr. *A History of the Chinese Communist Party*. Stanford, 1988.

U.S. Congress, Joint Economic Committee. *China's Economy Looks Toward the Year 2000*. Vol. 1: *The Four Modernizations*. Washington, DC, 1986.

Vogel, Ezra F. *Canton Under Communism: Programs and Policies in a Provincial Capital, 1949–1968*. Cambridge, MA, 1969.

Watson, James, ed. *Class and Social Stratification in Post-Revolution China*. Cambridge, MA, 1984.

Welsh, J. Richard. *Change, Continuity and Commitment: China's Adaptive Foreign Policy*. Lanham, MD, 1988.

Wittwer, Sylvan, et al. *Feeding a Billion*. East Lansing, MI, 1987.

Womack, Brantly, ed. *Media and the Chinese Public*. Armonk, NY, 1986.

World Bank. *China: Socialist Economic Development*. 3 vols. Washington, D. C., 1983.

Wortzel, Larry M., ed. *China's Military Modernization: International Implications*. Westport, CN, 1988.

Yang, Zhongmei. *Hu Yaobang: A Chinese Biography*. Armonk, NY, 1988.

Zheng dang yinian. Beijing, 1985.

Zhongguo nianjian: 1988 (People's Republic of China yearbook: 1988). Beijing, 1989.

Zhou Enlai lun wenyi. Beijing, 1979.

Index

Hsi-sheng Ch'i is Professor of Political Science and Chairman of the East Asian Studies Curriculum at the University of North Carolina at Chapel Hill. He is also author of *The Chinese Warlord System, 1916–1928* (1969), *Warlord Politics in China, 1916–1928* (1976), and *Nationalist China at War: Military Defeats and Political Collapse, 1937–1945* (1982) as well as numerous articles on contemporary China.